CHASED by the SUN

'They knew that their best hope of safety lay in the enemy being unable to find their aircraft in the night sky. The black paint on the bomber's underside was so thick and sheenless that it increased fuel consumption. The crews flew without navigation lights and risked collisions; they did not send radio messages unless in an extreme emergency; and they worried about the glow from the exhausts of their four engines. The full moon made them vulnerable, and when they turned west towards their home stations they were chased by the sun.'

CHASED

by the SUN

The Australians in Bomber Command in World War II

HANK NELSON

ALLEN&UNWIN

Allen & Unwin
83 Alexander Street
Crows Nest NSW 2065
Australia
Phone: (61 2) 8425 0100
Fax: (61 2) 9906 2218
Email: info@allenandunwin.com
Web: www.allenandunwin.com

National Library of Australia
Cataloguing-in-Publication entry:

Nelson, Hank, 1937–
    Chased by the sun : the Australians in Bomber Command in
    World War II.
    Bibliography.
    Includes index.
    ISBN 1 74114 847 2.
    1. Great Britain. Royal Air Force. Bomber Command. 2.
    Australia. Royal Australian Air Force – History – World War,
    1939–1945. 3. World War, 1939–1945 – Personal narratives,
    Australian. 4. World War, 1939–1945 – Aerial operations,
    Australian. 5. World War, 1939–1945 – Participation,
    Australian. I. Title.

940.544994

Set in 11/14 pt Perpetua by Midland Typesetters
Printed by Griffin Press, South Australia

10 9 8 7 6 5 4 3 2 1

Front cover photo (AWM SUK14282): On 25 March 1945, the 51 Squadron Halifax heavy
bomber 'E' for Easy returned to Snaith airfield, Yorkshire, completing its 100th operation. The
crew who had flown 'E' for Easy on a daylight raid on Osnabruck were: R. Kemp, pilot, England;
A. C. Townsend, navigator, Australia; J. D. Silberberg, bomb-aimer, Australia; R. J. Williams,
wireless operator, Australia; E. S. Hawkins, flight engineer, New Zealand; R. T. Jackson, gunner,
England; and F. Thwaites, gunner, England.

Contents

Acknowledgements

Ex-aircrew of Bomber Command have been both perceptive and articulate about their experiences. The bibliography provides evidence of the quantity and diversity of their testimony, but it is also important to acknowledge the quality. Don Charlwood's writing has rightly been recognised, but others less well known provide much to advance understanding of another generation caught in extraordinary circumstances. The Western Australians, Belford, Conway and Johnson, may be taken as examples of those who have written effectively, each using a different style and perspective to illuminate his experience. And the length, density and detailed research of Nielsen's volume demonstrates the importance of the crew. I am also indebted to those surviving relatives who preserved manuscripts and those who prepared them for publication, such as Noella Lang and Denise Rope. I am grateful to Robert Hilliard who gave permission to quote from his comprehensive manuscript.

All ex-aircrew that I approached agreed to answer questions, even when the queries came in an unexpected telephone call from an unknown historian. I am particularly indebted to Arthur Doubleday, who took several calls and answered questions fully and carefully. Bob Curtis responded beyond the call of duty. Mrs Ilma Brill was both generous and hospitable, giving me access to her late husband's detailed manuscripts and papers. Other members of the Brill family, Bill's brother Vic and his sister Fay Jones, also provided information.

Sandra Griffiths allowed me to read the papers collected by her late husband for the production of his television documentary, *Wings of the Storm*. Peter and Sue Rimmer provided Joe Ford's reminiscences and enabled me to correspond with Joane Ford. Alan Fewster gave me access to the engaging letters of the brothers, Edwin and Terry Charles. Ken Inglis sent several cuttings through the Coombs mail service. Gavan Daws, Bill Gammage, Brij Lal, Jan Nelson, Lauren Nelson and Klaus Neumann read the manuscript. I am thankful for the errors they eliminated and the advice they gave to make better history. Bill also told me about relevant sources. Mignon Turpin edited the manuscript with a keen eye for clarity and consistency.

Several archives and libraries here and overseas provided efficient, professional service. I would particularly like to thank the staffs of three institutions in Canberra: the Australian War Memorial, the National Archives of Australia, and the National Library. The Australian War Memorial also provided the illustrations. My colleagues in the Division of Pacific and Asian History have tolerated this project outside the region, listened with grace to my stories, and provided information. The administrative staff of the Division has dealt with all requests about word processing with good humour and high competence. Keith Mitchell of the Cartographic Unit in the Research School of Pacific and Asian Studies, brought his skill to the maps. The talented team at ABC Books worked assiduously to produce this handsome publication.

Carl Bridge of the Menzies Centre for Australian Studies, London, invited me to give a talk in Lincoln on Australians in Bomber Command, and writing that lecture assisted with the research and form of the present book. I wrote the questionnaire and briefing notes for the Australian War Memorial's Keith Murdoch Sound Archive recordings of Bomber Command aircrew, but I am indebted to others who did the actual interviews and transcribed and indexed them.

HANK NELSON
January 2002

Introduction

Over 4,000 Australians died in Bomber Command in World War II. It is a figure disturbing in its magnitude and its obscurity. In a nation that stresses experience in war as important in determining who they think they are, Australians do not remember the men who fought in the skies over Europe, one of Australia's greatest and deadliest commitments to battle. Australians do not know who the young men were, what they did, and the demands made of them, and they have not subjected the use of those men to the scrutiny that it deserves.

This book is about the men who volunteered for aircrew, arrived as instructed with a cut lunch to sustain them through the selection process, and tried to pass the many tests of skill and aptitude: did they have the hand—eye coordination to catch a ruler before it hit the floor, were they 'nose breathers' (the oxygen mask fitted over the nose), did they have a mechanical bent, could they read three-dimensional diagrams of cogs and levers, and did they combine alertness with steadiness, and show a capacity for promptness in decision-making? This book tries to say who the men were who passed the tests, what values they brought with them to training schools, and looks at the planned and random events that channelled them through the schools, across continents and oceans, and gave them a rank and a skill – sergeant and air gunner, pilot officer and navigator. By the time they reached an operational training unit in England they were conscious that they were part of a select group, and had some idea of the demands to be made on their skill and courage. They were entitled to enter a room with bags of swank, but being in Bomber Command they didn't. The men who flew bombers did not 'shoot a line' – unless in exaggerated self-parody. Bomber Command had its own values and vocabulary, and they too helped change those Australians who entered the messes, briefing rooms and cold ablution blocks on operating stations.

The aircrew in Bomber Command fought a different war from those who served in England in Fighter Command, let alone from those who fought in the RAAF in North Africa, Burma or New Guinea. And of course it was profoundly different from that known to the men who went into battle on the *Perth* or at Tobruk, in Greece or on the Kokoda Track. The crew, the aircraft, the constant technical changes, battles with the weather, flak and fighters, oscillations between the horrific inferno over a target and the tranquillity of the English countryside (or of the Strand Palace Hotel on a 48-hour pass), the presence of women on operating stations, and again and again having to repeat the exacting physical and mental test demanded on a raid helped make the experience different from anything before or since. Yet in aftermath, Bomber aircrew have much in common with others who fought in sustained battles with high casualties.

This book tries to allow the men to speak for themselves, as well as describing and commenting on what they did. As many men spent only a few months of three or four years of service life on an operating station, much space is allocated to life outside operations. There is a brief survey of what happened to those who baled out or crash-landed on enemy territory, and of the home-coming of the men and the home-leaving of their 2,000 brides. Questions about the effectiveness, morality and legacy of the bombing campaigns are considered, and there is an investigation of the way that Australians applauded and then forgot the men of Bomber Command.

The present neglect is not because there has been no writing on Australians in Bomber Command. It is nearly 40 years since Herington's two volumes of the official history were completed, ex-aircrew have written on their experiences, other writers (such as Eric Fry) have told us about particular men, Nelmes and Jenkins in *G-for-George* have written more than a story of a Lancaster, and in general books authors have summarised the history of Australians in Bomber Command. Most of all John McCarthy has written about the Empire Air Training Scheme, and it is for this reason that much of the detail of the setting up of the Scheme and its administration has been dealt with briefly. But here, the crews and what they did are central. This is an attempt to survey the range of experiences, and to locate them in lives and national history.

The Berlin War Cemetery contains the graves of 3000 Commonwealth airmen, 215 of them Australian. On the edge of the parklands of the Grünewald, the cemetery is beautifully maintained within the city the men tried so bravely to destroy. *Janet Nelson*

1

SOMETHING WITH A BIT MORE FUTURE

At Junee the Sydney–Melbourne railway branches with the line to Hay heading west, forming a straight line alongside the loops of the bed and billabongs of the Murrumbidgee River. Just west of Junee at Marrar the country opens out and the south-west slopes become 'the sunlit plains extended'. The first towns on the Hay line – Coolamon, Ganmain, Matong and Grong Grong – squat in rich, red, gently undulating farmland. Spreading box trees and neat white cypress line the fences. Creeks with names such as Smoky, Dead Horse, Boggy and Frying Pan, names that recur across the Australian landscape, follow wandering depressions south and west towards the river.

When Arthur Doubleday was just old enough to be a useful wood-and-water joey he went with the wagon that carted wheat to Ganmain. The Doubleday's home block, named 'Anglia' after the area that Arthur's father had left as a child, was 13 miles out of Ganmain, so it took until midday before the ten-horse team brought the wagon around the football oval, through the trees along Boggy Creek and joined the queue of carters waiting to add bagged wheat to the giant stacks at the railway siding. Although there was only one tough pull for the Doubleday team on that 13 miles – a sharp rise on the Dulah road that tested the trace chains and the couplings – 13 miles was a long distance to cart, so the Doubledays camped in a paddock on the way home. There they watered, fed and rested the horses, returning home the next morning. They could not afford to exhaust the team because they had three months' carting to do, and then the team had to be fresh for the cropping.

Arthur Doubleday was born in 1912, the second son in a family of five girls and three boys. He went by horse and sulky or rode to the one-teacher school at Methul, five miles north-east of 'Anglia'. After completing his primary schooling he boarded at the new Yanco Agricultural High School. With its long drive sheltered on one side by river red gums and open on the other to lush irrigation country, Yanco Agricultural High occupied the imposing two-storey red brick homestead built by Samuel McCaughey who had once controlled over 3,000,000 acres and owned more sheep than anyone else in Australia. Those familiar with Yanco's exposed timber interiors, the 'cathedral size stained glass windows' and the artificial lake and orchard were not likely to be intimidated later when they entered the most affluent Royal Air Force (RAF) officers' mess. Arthur Doubleday spent three years at Yanco and responded well to the work in the paddocks, sheds and classrooms, and 'loved' the cricket and football. Back at 'Anglia', Arthur settled into life on the farm. He believed he was 'cut out' for country life: 'I enjoyed it and I had no intention or thought at all of doing other than living a life on the land'.

Just after Arthur Doubleday left school to work on the farm, William Brill, another boy from the red soil of the eastern Riverina, went to board at Yanco Agricultural High. 'Clearview', the Brill farm just south of the Ganmain–Matong road, was well named. From their home near the top of gentle curving slopes the Brills could see the wheat silos nearly three miles away in Matong. The seven Brill children walked downhill to the weatherboard school of Derrain, and although there were 20 years from oldest to youngest they all had the one teacher, Charles Banfield. He ruled, Fay Brill said, not with a rod of iron but with a 'switch of the pepper tree'. And when Bill's younger brother Vic went on to Wagga Wagga High, Mr Banfield had taught him so well that he learnt no new maths for the first three years. Bill left Yanco in 1930 with his Intermediate Certificate. He had failed geography and passed with honours in Agricultural Chemistry and Botany.

In February 1933 Arthur went to Sydney to see the fifth cricket test in the bodyline series. The stands were crowded, and the barrackers on the hill were in good voice, but England continued its dominance, winning its fourth test of the series. While in Sydney, Arthur went out to Mascot aerodrome, paid his ten shillings, and took a flight over the city. His second flight, seven years later, was with the Royal Australian Air Force (RAAF). By 1939 the Doubledays were farming the home block and two other properties, 'Dulah' and 'Hopewell'. The horse teams were gone, replaced by tractors, and their wheat was carted down the road in a cloud of dust – the Doubledays owned the first semitrailer in the district. The Brills too had switched to tractors in the early 1930s. Ken had married and taken up his own block at Landervale on the Grong

Grong–Ardlethan road. Bill went north to work with Ken and while there he met and courted Ilma Kitto, the head teacher (and only teacher) at Landervale.

'Anglia' was less than 20 miles from 'Clearview', and Arthur Doubleday and Bill Brill knew one another in the way that country people knew about each other. They sometimes saw each other, or heard talk about one another when they were at dances, sheep sales or waiting at the wheat silos. And the people of Coolamon and Matong were brought together by one of the few significant cultural forces that divide white Australians by place: they were on the north-east frontier of Australian rules football, the game dominant on winter Saturdays south through Victoria to Tasmania and west to the Indian Ocean. Bill played in the black and white of Matong and Arthur played in the green of Methul. Matong and Methul were in different leagues, but Arthur and Bill could read about each other in the *Coolamon–Ganmain Farmers' Review*. They would certainly read about Ken Brill, one of the stars in the strong South Western District League. By 1939 a damaged knee had ended Arthur's football days, so he no longer ran onto the clearing in the trees that served as the Methul oval. Both Arthur and Bill retained their interest in horses. Arthur rode in buck jumping shows and did some horse-breaking around the district. Bill had joined the local militia unit, the 21st Light Horse, and he was proud of his mount, Peanut.

On 3 September 1939 the Doubledays had all gathered for shearing and were sitting around a roaring fire when they heard that Australia was at war. They decided that Harry, who was the oldest and had a crook back, would stay home and run the farm and that Arthur and the youngest boy Jim would go to war. There was, Arthur said, a 'lot of the Mother Country attitude' in him and he thought he was going 'home to fight'. Early in 1940 the RAAF accepted Arthur for aircrew training and issued him with a small set of 'goldy' wings to wear to show that he had volunteered for service. Realising that he had 'cut his education level a little low' to be selected for training as a pilot, Arthur boarded in Sydney and went out to Randwick racecourse where he did the 21 lessons that the air force provided for its trainees-in-waiting. When he was called up the Methul people gave Arthur a 'send-off' in the weatherboard hall next to the oval where he had played cricket and football. The farm calendar helped Arthur remember when he left: it was just before the start of the 1940 harvest.

On 19 April 1940 Bill Brill was tested to see if he was fit for aircrew training. The men on the interviewing panel pencilled in their impressions: a 'rather slow chap but is intelligent', 'neat and respectful', and 'not striking. Quiet country chap'. They noted that he was a 'grade' footballer and was interested in cricket and swimming. They thought he would not be commissioned – they did not see him as a pilot – but decided he might make a wireless operator and air gunner and so put him in the Air Force Reserve to wait for an opening in a training school. Perhaps the panel saw what they expected to see; perhaps Bill behaved with the respectful understatement that he thought appropriate for a Matong farmer faced by well-dressed strangers; and perhaps the panel had described accurately what Bill Brill was in April 1940. Ten years after he left Yanco Agricultural High, Bill went back to his lessons – the RAAF's 21 lessons. When he solved a difficult problem he was eager to show his work to Miss Kitto, and he was ready for private tuition when the answers were elusive.

Bill and Arthur both told the air force that they were Methodists. Bill said he was a farmer and farm labourer and Arthur located himself a shade higher on the rural ladder, saying he was a 'farmer and grazier'. Bill was 24, Arthur was 28. Both were of medium height, though Bill at five feet ten inches was slightly taller than Arthur and more barrel-chested. He was, Arthur said, 'Strong as a Mallee bull'.

Brill and Doubleday were called up together. When Arthur got on the train at Coolamon, Bill was already on board. He had bloodshot eyes and Arthur was suffering from pains in the stomach. Arthur said that if the Germans could see them they'd think they didn't have much to worry about. Bill and Arthur stayed

Pilot Officer Arthur Doubleday and Pilot Officer Bill Brill, at Molesworth, Huntingdonshire (now Cambridgeshire), training with 460 Squadron in December 1941. *AWM SUK10297.*

together when they took the bus to No 2 Initial Training School, Bradfield Park, Sydney on Armistice Day, 11 November 1940. Early in 1941 both were selected for pilot training at Narrandera, just a few miles from Yanco Agricultural High, and less than 20 miles by Tiger Moth from Landervale. Arthur and Bill could check their navigation by glancing out of the cockpit and seeing how Ken and Harry (the brothers left behind) were getting on with the harvest. Arthur's other brother Jim, who was four years younger and had completed a technical course in Sydney, followed Arthur into the RAAF, and Vic Brill, five years younger than Bill and trained as a school teacher, began aircrew training in 1941 and qualified as a navigator.

In the first months of the war men were keen to join the RAAF. By March 1940, 11,550 had applied to be aircrew and less than one in five had been selected. Of those, only 184 were in training. The waiting list was already over 1,700 and the rush was on to find instructors, aircraft and training fields. Many air force volunteers came from the peacetime militia, but they did not want to go to war as soldiers. The stories of their fathers and uncles, and pictures of mud, trenches, stalemate, and slaughter, were powerful deterrents. Gus Belford's father had spent three years 'in Flanders, the Somme and other notorious places' and his 'repeated exhortations' were that any other sort of military service was better than the trenches. Bill Manifold had gone from Melbourne University Rifles to Signals, but he had a 'horror of hand-to-hand fighting' and it was the bayonet hanging from his web belt that helped persuade him to join the RAAF. John Piper, a salesman with a carpet firm, was in the Light Horse in 1939, partly because his company gave an extra ten days' leave for the training camps. But when war was declared, men with experience in the 1st AIF told him not to rush in but to wait until things settled down and then find something 'with a bit more future to it'.

The exploits of the airmen of World War I, in chivalrous combat above the mud, futile bayonet charges and pounding artillery, had been kept alive by the barnstormers, extended by the pioneer aviators such as Parer, Kingsford Smith and Hinkler, and exaggerated by writers of fiction for boys. Rockfist Rogan fought his way through daring exploits in *The Champion* and Biggles (James

Bigglesworth), ex-Royal Flying Corps, flew his first book-length mission in 1932. He, Algy and Ginger had survived 18 volumes of brisk adventure before they first went into action in the Baltic in World War II. Then the ageless Biggles defied the swastika and was on the Spitfire parade in the Battle of Britain.

Keith Ross Miller was born in 1919, just as the brothers Sir Keith and Sir Ross Smith made their epic flight from England to Australia. Keith seemed committed by name to the air force but in fact tried first to join the navy. However, when the navy rejected his friend he switched to the air force. He was a clerk with the Vacuum Oil Company and had passed his Intermediate Certificate at Melbourne Boys High. The air force despatched him to Initial Training School, Victor Harbor. The skills that had already enabled him to play football for St Kilda and represent Victoria nine times in cricket ensured that he passed out of Mallala Service Flying Training School at the end of 1942 as a pilot – Flight Sergeant Miller.

High-flying jets leave vapour trails across Canberra's clear skies. Especially in autumn the trails linger from horizon to horizon, gradually spreading, thinning, fading. Canberra is the vapour trail capital. It is strange that the clearest tracks – you can see a hundred kilometres of travel trace – are those left in thin air. But the crews in Bomber Command feared those trails. They knew that their best hope of safety lay in the enemy being unable to find their aircraft in the night sky. The black paint on the bomber's underside was so thick and sheenless that it increased fuel consumption. The crews flew without navigation lights and risked collisions; they did not send radio messages unless in an extreme emergency; and they worried about the glow from the exhausts of their four engines. The full moon made them vulnerable, and when they turned west towards their home stations they were chased by the sun. But what if they saw in the light of a half-moon that their bomber was leaving a white trail across the sky? They called it a 'contrail', a condensation trail. The forward crew might not see it because it usually formed in the wake of the point of turbulence. But it was inescapable to the tail-gunner. He sat at one end of the trail. The German night fighters could fly much faster than a bomber and they were more heavily armed. And now a night fighter could follow the contrail, and even use the contrail to hide its approach from behind and below. At times hundreds of bombers left white streams across the sky, beautiful and deadly. In 1944 Ivan Pellas, flying a Halifax out of Driffield, found himself in what seemed to be 10/10 cloud. He thought it strange because he had been briefed to expect clear skies. Perhaps he would write in his log – as he had before – 'Met PP' (meteorological report piss poor). But then he realised he was flying in bomber-made cloud, he was in the converging contrails of hundreds of aircraft. Sometimes aircrew saw where contrails came to a sudden end, and through their oxygen masks they even smelt the remnants of an exploded aircraft. Across Canberra skies the vapour trail is benign, a spectacle inviting pleasant wonder. Contrails reminded bomber crews that they were targets.

David Whishaw's father, a stretcher bearer on the Western Front, told his son how watching the air battles was a distraction from the horror of the trenches, and David himself was 'an avid reader of those books about the "aces" '. Soon after his 18th birthday David left the farm, went into the Launceston recruiting office and asked to join the RAAF.

Reg Bain said that from the time he was a 'cheeky kid' aeroplanes 'thrilled' him. When a plane came in low across Wagga Wagga, Reg knew that soon it would be landing on the paddocks on the western edge of the town. He ran as fast as his legs would take him to be one of the first kids to gather and gawk at the machine and those who flew in it. When he was a little older he rode his bike there. After finishing third year at Wagga Wagga High he went to work in Kennedy's pharmacy. When 'God, King and country' called he was determined to join the air force. By then he had friends at the Wagga Wagga Aero Club. One of the pilots at the Club thought that because he was already an experienced pilot he was likely to be called up as an instructor, but he had never taught anyone to fly. Reg was keen to learn flying and give himself an advantage when the chance came to apply to join aircrew. They made a deal: the pilot practised instructing and Reg practised flying. By the time Reg was called up he had done about eight hours but had never gone solo, partly because his instructor was nervous about letting him loose in a privately owned aircraft.

Those who enlisted late in the war, or who survived until then, could read the books about the exploits of those who had fought the early air battles. Peter O'Connor was 17 in 1939 and pestering his parents for permission to join the air force. He said that all the recruits thought they were 'going to be Biggles' and Douglas Bader. And he linked a hero of boys' fiction to a hero of the Battle of Britain. Simply called *Bomber Pilot*, Leonard Cheshire's book published in 1943 was a report of a war half fought. After the war Cheshire was to say, 'I found the dangers of battle exciting and exhilarating, so that war came easily to me'. That enthusiasm was reflected in his writing. His reaction to the order that his squadron was to make a long flight to bomb Milan was 'glorious news'. The return to action at the end of retraining on Halifaxes was 'long-overdue news, the news we had all been praying for. Operations'. Cheshire wrote of danger and death, but they were less significant than the thrills and escapes. Cheshire's war was intense and serious, but still an adventure.

Dan Conway, who first flew as a pilot in Bomber Command in 1944, sometimes found it difficult to go to sleep immediately after returning from a raid so he read in bed. One of the books that fell on the floor from his sleeping

CHASED BY THE SUN

I'd always wanted to do nothing but fly. That had been from a small boy. I was filled with the stories of Biggles and World War I exploits. All the great aces of World War I. Sopwith Camels and all that sort of stuff. SE5s. I was absolutely imbued with that.

(Ken Gray, pilot 101 Squadron, who took his first flight from the Dandenong Showgrounds with Kingsford Smith.)

hand was Richard Hillary's *The Last Enemy*. Hillary, an Australian in Oxford when the war broke out, ended his book with his finding a way to endure long rehabilitation from burns suffered when he was shot down in the Battle of Britain. For Hillary, as in the New Testament, the last enemy to be destroyed was death, and by the time Conway was reading about him Hillary had no more enemies. Hillary had returned to flying and been killed early in 1943. The beautiful and terrible acceptance of disfigurement and death in Hillary's writing had nothing in common with the writing of W.E. Johns, and little in common with that of Cheshire.

More aircrew probably saw a version of themselves on screen than on the page. Such films included: *The Lion has Wings* (1939), *Target for Tonight* (1941), *One of Our Aircraft Is Missing* (1941), *The First of the Few* (1942), *Flying Fortress* (1942), *Captains of the Clouds*, (1942), *Mrs Miniver* (1942), *Winged Victory* (1944), *Wing and a Prayer* (1944) and *The Way to the Stars* (1945). While waiting in Melbourne to be shipped overseas for further aircrew training, Vincent Winter was subjected to drill and films. He saw *London Can Take It* (about the Blitz) so often that it 'lost its impact'. The feature films that did much to establish how others saw the airmen were films about Englishmen, Canadians and Americans rather than Australians. George Hawes, lonely for reminders of Australia, crossed the mud of Bottesford aerodrome to see again *Forty Thousand Horsemen* in the station theatre, 'just to hear them singing "Waltzing Matilda" ', and he wrote home asking for a copy of Banjo Paterson's poems. Australians training at Uplands near Ottawa in 1941 paraded and flew in formation to provide the background for the film *Captains of the Clouds*. When they got to London in 1942 they could see the simulated heroics of Jimmy Cagney in the air, his winning way with the leading lady, the tribute to the Canadian bush pilots, the appeal for recruits, and little of themselves on the screen. But the nature of film and the need to entertain and to serve the interests of nations at war meant that films stressed cheerfulness in adversity, self-sacrifice for noble ends, defiance of the odds, the triumph of good over evil, and ordinary men rising to greatness, adventure and selfless cama-raderie. In film, sentiment was more common than suffering.

Those same books and movies gave families at home an impression of the air war. Rosalie Charles and her mother Beryl read *The Last Enemy* and Rosalie sent a copy to her brother Terry, then in England finishing his training to be a navigator. Terry read it and said he 'enjoyed it immensely' although Hillary had irritated him 'beyond words at times'. After Beryl Charles saw *The Memphis Belle*, a documentary about an American bomber crew of a B-17 Flying Fortress operating out of England, she told Terry that it was 'very realistic' and that she had kept thinking of him. Beryl and Rosalie learnt little from what Terry chose — and the censors allowed him — to write in his letters: the family's shared experiences came more from public descriptions than from private descriptions of war.

Those who volunteered for aircrew were, Don Charlwood said, 'children of the empire'. Nearly all had relatives in the British Isles. Most were also strongly conscious of their Australianness, but saw no contradiction in being both British and Australian. Charlwood read and responded to a letter an English family friend sent to his mother in 1940:

> The air raids are simply awful … It isn't quite so bad in the day time, but the nights are horrifying: the AA guns roaring and the explosions from the bombs …The raids have lasted from dusk to dawn and each night grows longer now … God give us courage to keep going.

Charlwood said that his swearing-in was the culmination of his upbringing, acceptance of authority and the 'Call of the Homeland'. Wade Rodgers' mother said to him before he sailed, 'Don't miss seeing Scotland for me, son'. In 1943 he picked a bunch of heather in the Highlands and posted it back to his mother in Warrnambool District Hospital. Although David Leicester's father was born in Australia, he was 'very pro-English', and David grew up in a home where 'fighting for England was really the thing to do'.

John Grey Gorton, dressed in his working clothes, left his orange orchard at Mystic Park in Victoria in 1940 and went into town to enlist. The officer was doubtful that a 29-year-old farmer should hold out hope of becoming a pilot,

> Having been born on Anzac Day 1923, with a soldier of the 1914/1918 war for a father, it was perhaps natural that I had been nourished in the Anzac tradition. An annual birthday treat was to accompany my father in Melbourne's Anzac Day march, repeated many times from about the age of five onwards.
>
> *(Robert Hilliard, bomb-aimer, applied to join air force May 1941.)*

but Gorton had an MA from Oxford, a pilot's licence and had served in the university squadron. Gorton was accepted and continued coming to the Kerang post office to learn Morse code while he waited to be called up. David Campbell was back from Cambridge and, like Gorton, working on the land when he joined the RAAF. Harold Brownlow (Micky) Martin had gone from Sydney to England on his way to Edinburgh University and a medical degree when his interest and his money were diverted. He joined the RAF in England at the start of the war. When Bill Manifold arrived in England his brother was already there. He had been at Cambridge and had joined the British army. Those Australians who by class and accomplishment had immediate personal and family contacts with Britain were likely to join the air force.

Dan Conway told his parents he was going to enlist and was surprised when they objected. His father had come to Western Australia from Ireland as an infant and his mother as a young woman, but Dan, 'brought up on English history, novels and magazines', had been unconscious of their antipathy to England. He waited and went into Initial Training School just after he turned 21. His parents accepted his and his brother's decision, and his father gave his intensely felt though casual blessing on the railway station: 'look after yourself ... see you again some time'. Later Conway was to say that 'from the beginning' he felt 'much at home in England'. English history and literature at school and his reading of *Film Fun*, *Boys Own*, *The Modern Boy*, *The Champion* and *The Triumph* had been more important than the unexpressed history known to his parents. Peter O'Connor's mother was also from Ireland and he completed his education at Sacred Heart College in Adelaide where he was reminded of a heritage different from that of the ascendant Protestants. In 1943 his first sight of the British Isles was the north-west of Ireland. He said, 'I can remember writing in my diary that I had seen the green hills of Ireland'.

Eric Silbert had gone to Christian Brothers College, Fremantle and later to Aquinas College, but he had not worn the green on St Patrick's day. The son of

Mental Attributes of Pilot

A combination of alertness with steadiness – dependability, <u>promptness in decision</u> – imagination – sense of humour – punctuality, <u>attention to detail</u> – power of observation – good education – all-round interests, with a mechanical bent – a leaning towards swift forms of locomotion and a <u>love of flying</u> – strong personality – popular type, inspiring liking and respect in his fellows, and a gift for leadership.

(Guide for selection panels, March 1941.)

Jewish parents, both born in Eastern Europe, he was conscious in the 1930s of the growing anti-Semitism in Germany. The black American Jesse Owens, who triumphed at the 1936 Berlin Olympics, was a hero to a white Jewish boy in Fremantle. Soon after he turned 18 in 1940, Silbert persuaded his parents to let him go to ANA House in St Georges Terrace and take the tests to get into aircrew training. Before he flew across the cities that his parents had passed through a generation earlier, he changed his religion on his identity disks to Church of England and his second name from Abraham to Adrian. He thought that if he survived a parachute landing, or a crash-landing, in Germany that change might give him a better chance of survival. Peter Isaacson's mother Caroline had edited *Jewish Outlook*, sponsored Jewish refugees from Hitler's Germany, provided help for them on arrival and taught them English. Isaacson, too, had no doubt about the evil of the enemy and of his obligation to fight. He chose the air force as the means because it offered 'adventure'.

Eric Silbert had lived next door to a Methodist minister and it was through that association in his multi-religioned youth that he joined the 142nd Wesley Boy Scouts. Membership of a church group was something he held in common with many of the others who joined aircrew. In September 1943 Les Knight, dambuster pilot, held his damaged Lancaster level over Holland until all his crew had baled out and then he died in a crash-landing. It was his Sunday School in Camberwell, Melbourne, his Methodist Young Men's Class and his fellow abstaining Rechabites who met to remember Les Knight, DSO, aged 22, clerk in an accountancy firm and pilot on 27 raids. Until they all went to Initial Training School, the one school experience common to many of the young men about to become aircrew was Sunday School. For many of the grandchildren of aircrew the values and style of the Sunday Schools with their emphases on faithfulness, steadfastness, duty, service, honesty, clear conscience and self-sacrifice may be the most difficult to understand.

In the early reports of battles reaching Australia, British forces were retreating before a German army that had all the tactical and technical advantages. But from 13 August 1940, the 'Day of the Eagle', when waves of German fighters and bombers began their daylight attacks on south-east England there was an apparent shift. In the Battle of Britain the British pilots had the advantage of being close to their bases and they could stay in the battle area longer. Their aircraft – especially the Spitfire – were presented as superior, and German losses were at least twice that of the British. On 20 August, Winston Churchill paid his tribute to the defending pilots: 'Never in the field of human conflict was so much owed by so many to so few'. (And never in the field of human impersonation was a sentence so repeated.) When the Luftwaffe began its frequent indiscriminate attacks on civilian targets in London, Coventry and other centres, the moral balance also swung even more strongly against Germany. In 1940, when many Australians made their decision to enlist, the airmen alone were winning battles. Airmen were on the side of the righteous, the noble few determining the fate of the Empire, and they had a technical advantage over the enemy. In August 1940, flying a Spitfire was the way to defeat evil, win praise and look good. The events of the early months of World War II had strengthened the apparent lessons of World War I: it was better in the air.

David Leicester left Unley High in 1939 and went to work in the city of Adelaide as an office boy. In his home, sympathy for England was strong and he followed the detail of the Battle of Britain and the exploits of fighter pilots such as Paddy Finucane and Bluey Truscott. If not for the fact that he could join the Air Training Corps when he was 17 and three months he might well have joined the army or the navy. By the time he turned 18 in August 1941 he was prepared and waiting. He was then called up and went to Initial Training School at Victor Harbor.

Bob Curtis did three years at North Sydney Boys High School and 'hated it'. Early in the war he worked as a clerk and office boy in a factory making cardboard boxes. When he tried to enlist in the air force he was rejected because he was under-age, but he was allowed to study the 21 lessons. On 23 September 1940, the day after he turned 18, he volunteered and was placed on the reserve list. When he learnt that the men arriving for new courses were given a final medical check at Woolloomooloo Recruiting Centre he hung around as a couple of courses arrived and then arranged for a friendly clerk to telephone him if anyone on the next group failed. One did, and Bob was there within an hour. So at 18 years and two months he was on his way to Amberley in Queensland. He said he just wanted to be 'in': 'in' the air force, 'in' distant lands, and 'in' action.

Example problem for revision:

Hostile bombers are reported off Hornsea at noon flying at 150 m.p.h. g.s. on track 010 degrees (T). Fighters from Unsworth, 100 miles from Hornsea at a bearing of 320 degrees (T), take off at 1210 and fly at 240 m.p.h. g.s. on track 086 degrees (T). What distance separates the fighters and bombers at 1230 hours? ['g.s.' is ground speed and 'T' is true north.]

(Royal Australian Air Force Standard Notebook for Initial Training School.)

After leaving Nuriootpa Higher Primary School with two years of secondary education, Syd Gooding went to work for a struggling business collecting the residue from the wineries and turning it into tartaric acid. In 1931, aged 16, he moved with his family to Ayr in north Queensland. When he was unable to find a job he reluctantly followed his father and became a Rawleigh's man. He travelled in the family's Rugby car and knocked on doors in Ayr and Home Hill selling spices and essences, creams and cosmetics, ointments and Rawleigh's famous healing salve. He was able to make the basic wage of three pounds and ten shillings a week and so was easily persuaded to dip into his tobacco tin of savings when a roving instructor from the Queensland Aero Club came north promising to teach young men to fly. Syd had long been a reader of flying magazines and had tried cadging flights around airfields. Soon all his money was being spent on flying. By the time the family shifted to Taree, Syd had nearly 60 hours in Tiger Moths. By then the economy was picking up and the government was subsidising trade training, so Syd applied. He won a place as an apprentice fitter and turner with a small Sydney engineering firm. But by the time he finished training in 1942 he was 27 and the war and the world seemed to be passing him by. When he was released from his reserved occupation he applied immediately to join the air force. Although he was older than most recruits and had less formal education he still left Bradfield Park selected for pilot training at Narrandera. Having been in the militia gave him an advantage at drill; as a fitter and turner he knew something of engines and guns – and could even make replacement parts; his studies at technical school had repaired his lack of schooling in mathematics; and he had already done some flying. The young Rawleigh's man and elderly apprentice was on his way to becoming a pilot and officer. With the fund of stories and experiences he had picked up, Syd was to be known as 'Spellbinder' to some of his later colleagues.

Ivan Pellas was born in 1923 in Harcourt, the apple centre of Victoria, and went to the Harcourt North state school on the corner block near the reservoir. In that crowded little school where the 50 or so pupils were often acutely conscious of who had the hand-me-down and home-made clothes, Ivan completed his eighth grade, obtained his Merit Certificate, and went to the Castlemaine Junior Technical School, then to the Senior Technical School. That was an eight-mile ride on the bike, morning and night on the undulating roads from the flank of Mount Alexander to the centre of the Maine. He excelled in his mechanical and engineering course, but in 1940 when he was within a year of his diploma his father Perce decided that Ivan would have to go to work. Ivan wanted to enlist in the air force when he turned 18 early the next year but his father would not sign his papers. Perce had reason to resist. He himself had volunteered soon after war was declared in 1914 and was allocated number 719. Perce had landed at Gallipoli with the 7th Battalion, was wounded on 6 May 1915 and evacuated. Suffering from illness and a severe leg injury he was lucky to survive. The Harcourt bandsmen who gathered at the railway station to welcome the first local boy to return saw his thin, frail, limping figure. They faltered in mid triumphant salute and trailed into silence. Later, two of Perce's brothers died on the Western Front. His son, Ivan Francis Pellas, carried the names of the two brothers; one whose death was recorded at Ypres and the other's at Villers Bretonneux. Ivan went to work in the State Electricity Commission testing laboratory in Melbourne and later in Yallourn.

Ivan Pellas did not build model aeroplanes and had no particular interest in the pioneer aviators. He had not been in an aeroplane and had no immediate relatives in the British Isles. But while the Battle of Britain seemed remote, sufficient of those distant events had reached him to make him want to be a fighter pilot. He was attracted by the glamour and the chance for adventure, but most of all he wanted 'to achieve something'. He had excelled in the classroom, but not in sport or in other ways in which young men might obviously distinguish themselves, and if he could learn to fly then that would be a worthy accomplishment. That desire to fly had been with him from the first time he had been close to an aeroplane, one that had landed out past the bacon factory to the north-west of Castlemaine. Ivan says he had a strong personal desire to be a pilot, though he was not particularly interested in flying in general. When Ivan turned 19 his father agreed that he might join the air force, and early in 1942 he went to Russell Street in Melbourne, did his tests and was put on reserve for aircrew training. He enlisted for 'the duration of the War and a period of twelve months thereafter' on 11 September 1942. Ivan Pellas, who would become Pelly to his crew, was largely outside the influence of Biggles, balsa wood models and Empire family, but was not outside the influence of Anzac, national obligation and personal ambition.

'I knew nothing of life outside school and university. I did not drink, was sexually innocent and hopelessly inept with girls. Just the same I had noticed they existed ... I was entirely ignorant of the things that mattered – politics, life in the social jungle and the techniques of survival ... I had never seen an aeroplane on the ground and I had no idea of how or why it flew.'

(Kenneth Marks, Lancaster pilot.)

In 1942 Vincent Winter left his job as a clerk in the Victorian Railways to join the RAAF and was soon on his way to Rhodesia. Forty years later he collected the stories of those who had followed a similar track into aircrew. One of those who preceded him was, he said, 'also … a bank officer'. Early in the war Maurice Dalton and his friend Gordon Williams were working in the Bank of New South Wales in Murgon, Queensland. Williams, the first to enlist, was killed in a flying training accident. Dalton's own application to join the air force was delayed for 'eight to ten months' because the banks, so rapidly losing staff to the services, persuaded the government to delay calling up any more until the banks could train replacements. When Dalton eventually arrived at Narrandera to take his first flight in a Tiger Moth he was relieved to see that his instructor was Flying Officer Peter Smith who had recently been working in the Commonwealth Bank in Murgon.

It was no accident that Dalton and Winter encountered bankers in the RAAF. In September 1939 the Commonwealth Bank had 3,860 male clerks, and of these 2,750 joined the military forces – 46 per cent into the air force, 46 per cent into the army, and 8 per cent into the navy. But the RAAF was less than one-third the size of the army, and as the bankers were not being recruited as mechanics, armourers or other ground crew this was a significant flow from the ledgers and the heavy wooden counters to aircrews. By the end of the war, 309 Commonwealth Bank officers had been killed, 232 in the RAAF and 72 in the AIF.

In the foyer of Canberra High School there is a standard dark stained wooden shield on which are painted the names of 43 ex-students who died in World War II. One name appears twice in the foyer: Robert Kennard is listed as school captain in 1940, and in 1945 he was killed over Germany while flying a medium bomber in the Second Tactical Air Force. Of the 43 named on the honour roll, 22 died while serving in the Australian or British air forces. Donald Easton completed his Leaving Certificate, entered the public service, joined the RAAF, qualified as a wireless operator and air gunner, and was killed in March 1945 when part of a raid by 235 aircraft on a synthetic oil plant at Bohlen in eastern Germany. Easton was 20 years old and was on his 25th operation. Robert Baker went from school to the public service, to the RAAF, to England and to his death in a flying battle over Stuttgart in March 1944. Baker was 23 when he died. That was the pattern of so many of the Canberra High boys on the honour roll. Having done well at school, they won a place in the Commonwealth public service. Their school and work records then gave them an advantage when they applied to train as aircrew. Eight of the Canberra High boys died in Bomber Command.

More members of the Melbourne Cricket Club died in the RAAF (73) than in the army (59). Coincidence of class, education and sporting ability got them into aircrew.

Assheton ('Ash') Taylor and Ron Chambers went to Sydney Boys High, and by 1940 both were part-time economics students at Sydney University. They served in the Sydney University Regiment and worked as junior clerks – Ron with the Shell Company and Ash with the Sydney City Council. In September 1941 they left Central Station in Sydney for Initial Training School at Somers. There they would meet many others like themselves. When John Herington came to write the official history of the RAAF in Europe, at times he must have thought he was writing of flying clerks. In his account of a raid by Halifaxes on an oil plant at Bottrop in the Ruhr on 20 July 1944, he referred to aircraft piloted by H.R. Hagstrom (clerk), T.W. Anthony (junior clerk), J.T. Rogers (clerk), B.P. Cosgriff (clerk), H.A. Jowett (clerk), P.D. Wilson (clerk) and J.D. Murtha (farmer).

Robert Honan matriculated in maths and sciences and had taken the prescribed preliminary classes before he entered the corrugated iron-sided classrooms at No 4 Initial Training School at Victor Harbor, South Australia. The standard was, he said, 'very high' and the competition strong, as many of his fellow recruits had come straight from classrooms where they had been the teachers.

The average age of an Australian soldier in a 6th Division infantry battalion in December 1940 was 27. Some battalions in the 8th Division that were recruited later were younger, with an average age of just over 25. Australian airmen were around 24 years old when they died, and those recruited late in the war were more likely to be 22 or 23. On these figures airmen were three years younger than the average Australian in an infantry battalion. In some courses for pilots the average age was around 20 or 21 – navigators were sometimes a little older. Bill Brill was older than average, and at 28 Arthur Doubleday was among those seen to have exceptional qualities to compensate for their age. That preference for the young was confirmed by performance: 18-year-olds had a better pass rate at flying schools than 23-year-olds, and a much better rate than 27-year-olds, in spite of the fact that fewer of the older men were selected to begin pilot training. Late in the war most of the men in bombers over Germany were at school when the war started. Kurt Vonnegut's 'jumbled and jangled' novel *Slaughterhouse–Five* has the alternative title, *The Children's Crusade*. It refers equally to Vonnegut and his fellow American prisoners and to the men in the bombers who brought Operation Thunderclap to Dresden on 13 and 14 February 1945.

Peter Knox, educated at a private school then an arts student at the University of Melbourne, later reflected on his decision to apply to join aircrew. He wrote: 'There was I suppose a certain middle-class appeal about it'. After eight years of attending a one-teacher primary school, followed by manual labour and looking for more manual labour, Stanley Hawken said that when he went to Initial Training School at Somers he realised 'even at that early stage' that this was his chance to join those who had education and did not have to take whatever job was on offer – fruit-picking, fencing, timber cutting or sewerage-tunnelling.

In the late 1930s the young schoolteachers, bankers, civil servants, tertiary students, journalists, draftsmen, and clerks in insurance offices, wool-broking firms and customs houses were all clearly part of an elite. The basic qualification for many of the white-collar jobs was four years of secondary school. In the first year of recruiting for the Empire Air Training Scheme 92 per cent of graduating aircrew had four years or more of secondary education. For pilots the figure was 96 per cent and for navigators it was 99 per cent. But in 1935 only 2,866 Victorians qualified for the Intermediate (fourth year) Certificate. (By 1968 more Victorians were qualifying for university degrees than were being presented with their Intermediate Certificate in 1935.)

In the 1930s, anxious parents in an economy slowly pulling out of the

> I am in a crew – and am Grandpapa. They are a happy bunch but the Nav. is the exception – a quiet type.
>
> *(Willliam Hooper, after crewing-up, Lichfield, 7 June 1944.*
> *A schoolteacher turned bomb-aimer, Hooper was 25.)*

Depression had pushed their children towards jobs that were thought to offer prestige, opportunity and security, and the children then had to compete against crowds of contenders. By the time the successful sons applied for selection for aircrew training, they had an obvious advantage when it came to stating their level of education and their current employment. This was also the case in the practical tasks of filling out forms and doing the written tests on literacy, general knowledge, maths and sciences. Also, they were more likely to be living in large towns and therefore could join the Air Training Corps and find tutors to help them with the preliminary studies while they were waiting to be called up. And they were likely to see the air force as an escape from employment that gave them an excess of security, restraint and slow promotion. The clerk who had a good school record, played football at the weekend, and looked like he might have the presence to skipper an aircrew was likely to impress the selection panel.

By contrast, few pastry cooks, fencing contractors, share farmers and factory hands won selection for training as pilots and navigators. Many of the farmers who were selected for aircrew training (Gorton, Manifold, Rowling, Whishaw, Williams) had been away to private schools. Rawdon (Ron) Middleton will always stand out because he has VC after his name, but his background also distinguishes him among the pilots of Bomber Command – jackaroo of Yarrabandai near Bogan Gate, New South Wales. But Middleton had gone to Dubbo High until part way through his fifth year, and in 1938 he went to Sydney for a few weeks and took flying lessons at Mascot. Middleton entered Bradfield Park with a record as a sportsman, a higher level of education than most Australians and demonstrated commitment to and knowledge of flying. Brill and Doubleday were unusual, and men such as Wade Rodgers whose highest qualification was grade eight at a Victorian primary school were exceptional. The grade eight Merit Certificate might have been the BA of the bush, but few other pilots had so little schooling. Rodgers was rightly proud of his achievement.

Many of the men who trained as aircrew enjoyed motorbikes and cars – they wanted to talk about them, own them, ride and drive them, and pull them apart and put them together. It was likely that many of those same men read aero magazines and aspired to fly. Some were licensed to fly before they had a licence to drive. That coming together of an interest in machines of the road and machines of the sky was reinforced by questions on the 'Application for Air Crew' asking about 'experiences' with internal combustion engines, and officers on selection boards were asked to look for a 'leaning towards swift forms of locomotion'. Applicants were also questioned about any crimes they had committed. The young men had to say too whether they were 'of pure European descent'; but the number of men deterred by this question, or rejected because of it, is unknown. Applicants had to give the nationality of both their parents as well as their own. Aircrew were more likely than most Australians to know about Buicks, Baby Austins and BSAs, more likely to have fiddled with carburettors, and more likely to be law-abiding, white and British. They were also more likely to have completed senior years in high school, lived in cities and have had an income above that of the battlers.

Australia trained over 10,000 pilots under the Empire Air Training Scheme. Leonard Waters, from Nindigully west of Goondiwindi in Queensland, was Aboriginal, had little education, and had worked as a ring-barker and then as a shearer. Having joined the air force as a member of the ground staff, Waters trained as a mechanic, continued his education, was accepted for aircrew and qualified as a pilot. Warrant Officer Waters was posted to 78 Squadron, flying fighters out of Dutch New Guinea against the Japanese. He said he was 'pretty proud': he was one in 10,000.

This is a Man's job!

Join the

R·A·A·F

2

THIS IS A MAN'S JOB

Utilitarian combat aircraft had few adjustments for the comfort and particular physical attributes of airmen: they were one size fits all. The very tall or short or fat were excluded. They could not reach controls or fit through escape hatches or sit with their knees jammed against hard metal for ten hours or more. Bobby Gibbes, at 5 feet 4^1/$_4$ inches, knew that he was likely to have trouble. When the doctor told him to sit with his backside jammed against the wall and his legs stretched out, he inched his buttocks forward. Wing Commander Bobby Gibbes, DSO, DFC and Bar only just passed the leg reach test; he could have full rudder control without undoing his safety harness and sliding off the pilot's seat. Just how G.J. 'Piddley' (because of his piddling size) Oakeshott kept passing the successive tests for pilots was a mystery to his colleagues. At Binbrook in Lincolnshire the ground crew fitted blocks and cushions so that he could reach the controls and see over the curve of the instrument panel. The modifications to the Lancaster must have worked, as Piddley Oakeshott, DFM, completed a tour with 460 Squadron. By 1943, pilots of heavy bombers had to be at least 5 feet 7 inches and have an inside leg measurement of 41 inches. Wireless operators and gunners had to be at least 5 feet 2 inches, no taller than 6 feet and not over 175 pounds. Selecting officers were told the 'small stocky man is desirable. He should be a keen sportsman (team player and marksman) possessed of energy and stamina … [Have qualities of] imagination (but not over developed) – sense of humour – punctuality'.

Ted Park, an American who flew in New Guinea, noted the uniformity of his fellow fighter pilots in the United States Fifth Air Force: 'we were all five feet ten or less and all 160 pounds or less'. The Americans did not impose the same limits on bomber crews and that was why Jimmy Stewart DFC was seen winding and unwinding his long limbs in and out of Flying Fortress cockpits before and after missions over Europe. Flight Lieutenant Gough Whitlam was one of a four-man Ventura crew flying out of northern Australia in 1943 and 1945, and he was able to press his equally tall frame around the navigator's bench. Joe Wesley, an Englishman and navigator, wrote of his pilot, Dan Conway: 'A big fellow 6'3" – 13 stone. A real solid Australian'. The multi-engine planes had the space, and sometimes required a strong pilot. When on a parade at Bournemouth in England, Tom Simpson learnt that all the gunners were going to be drafted to Defiant aircraft except for those over 5 feet 11 inches who could not fit in the Defiant's cramped gunner's cockpit. Warned that the Defiant, a new English night fighter, gave gunners a short life, Simpson stood on his toes and just escaped Defiants. Bomber crews varied in height, but when photographed before taking off, the bulky flying clothes emphasised their uniformity.

Once provisionally accepted, volunteers were called up for medical and other tests. The candidates were told to bring their lunch with them and they waited, queued and were examined through the day. Some prepared for the physical tests. Len Williams, timing himself with an alarm clock, tested how long he could stay immersed in the bath water. This, and running miles around the local oval, ensured he could force mercury a long way up a glass column, so it was assumed he had the lungs to perform at altitude in aircraft. Men were tested for general fitness, hand and eye coordination, colour blindness, and ocular muscle balance. Unless the applicants were able to use both eyes effectively they had no hope of judging distance, and that was obviously important for air gunnery and landing a plane. The most elaborate piece of equipment, devised by Professor R.D. (Pansy) Wright, required the candidate to keep two lights close together by using foot and hand controls. But at Preston Motors showrooms in Russell Street, Melbourne, Robert Hilliard remembered a more expedient apparatus: he was

Australian officials were careless with the tape measure because by 1944 over 100 under-sized pilots were in England. The 'bantams' could have been sent to Mosquito and light bomber squadrons, but other men had stronger claims to those postings. Some were sent to Transport Command as map-reading spare pilots, a few were employed as staff pilots, and three or four volunteered to re-train as glider pilots. With still about eighty bantams waiting at Brighton or doing courses, it was decided to send them home. Most did not leave England until after the end of the war in Europe.

(RAAF Narrative of Flying Training, 8/2/A AWM 173.)

spun on a revolving chair, a primitive test of his capacity to tolerate violent aerobatics in combat. The air force also tried to test whether the young men in the queues would be able to withstand the accumulating stress of war in the air, and they eliminated those who confessed to effeminacy and mental deficiencies. However, experienced pilots knew that it was impossible to recreate the reality of combat. Many recruits who failed a test were dismissed immediately. It was already a select group who remained to swear that they would serve Our Sovereign Lord the King as a member of the Air Force Reserve. Those men were then sent home to wait until called up. They were given a badge they could choose to wear that testified they had volunteered to serve in the air.

The appeal to fly, to be a knight of the air and accept the risks of combat in the air, was strong, but even more men applied to join the ground crews. In the same time that 11,550 applied to fly, 56,777 applied for the more numerous jobs on the ground. That more young men chose service with safety is not surprising. As expected, the initial rush of applicants faded and the educational standard required, especially for air gunners, was lowered. But what is hard to explain is that even after the high death rate of pilots became known there were still more young men trying to get into aircrew than could be trained or found a seat in an aeroplane. Keith Dunstan was only 14 when the war started. His scrapbook of war cuttings was dominated by stories of airman Cobber Kane (the British ace) and Battle of Britain incidents. He kept the totals of aircraft shot down like 'the football results'. While still a schoolboy, Dunstan had served in the Air Training Corps and as soon as he turned 18 he joined the RAAF. He was determined to be a pilot. When he was directed to begin training as a wireless air gunner, his father (a VC winner, member of clubs and wielder of influence) intervened to keep him on course to become a pilot. Keith got his wings and sewed them on his winter and summer rig. 'What a pity' he wrote, 'they could not also be worn

I applied to join the air force. But I had difficulty because, according to them, I was underweight for my height. But I was playing football, did a bit of boxing ... I had so much energy I couldn't walk, I had to run everywhere, so I thought that was a bit ridiculous ... I had to try to put on weight, and I waged a campaign against the doctor. I'd go down and see him every month, until finally he says, 'Right! I'm sick and bloody tired of the sight of you. I'll mark you B1. And don't blame me if anything happens!' [Then] I waged a campaign against poor old dad for two or three months, and finally he signed the papers – because I was under twenty-one – and as he did so the tears were rolling down his eyes ... he honestly believed he'd signed my death warrant.

(Harold Wright, navigator.)

on pyjamas'. But by the time he was posted to Sale in 1944 there was an obvious excess of pilots crowded into the mess: 'Pilots had to manoeuvre, connive and plead just to get their hands on an aeroplane'. The RAAF sent pilots to exacting re-tests of their skills – the 'scrubbing courses'. Dunstan, with the majority of those tested, was 'scrubbed' and re-mustered to ground staff. He felt humiliated. He wrote: 'I could visualise no future'. But he would live.

Men waiting to be called up could study the 21 lessons (or its modified successor course) or practise Morse code, and a few went to special tutors to bring their maths and physics up to standard. Studying was especially relevant for those who had left school early or who, like Brill and Doubleday, had been away from study for a few years. Don Charlwood (eight years out of Frankston High) and two others drove into Coleraine in western Victoria three nights a week where the telegraphists at the post office taught them Morse code. Wade Rodgers, with a lot of catching up to do, went to night classes at Warrnambool Technical College. Murray Maxton, who had gone barefoot to the Kalgan River school until he was 14, went into Albany where Mr Paul taught him maths at Albany High and Mrs Edwards taught him Morse code. Reg Bain went back to Wagga Wagga High at night for his instruction. There were about 30 in the class and they worked hard. However, unlike the last time he was at the High School, after these classes they went to one of the local hotels where the publican locked them in a room to give them privacy – and protection from the licensing law. Even at the pub, Reg says, much of the talk was serious discussion about flying and the lessons to be mastered.

The *Manual for Air Crew Reservists* issued in 1940 was a broad introduction to navigation, meteorology, aerodynamics, flying and aircraft engines. Much of it was based on RAF training manuals and many of the examples were drawn from England. It increased the trainees' expectation that they were to fly in Europe. The example weather map of 15 January 1938 was centred on the Greenwich meridian and showed a depression off the Scottish coast and many 'cpr' scattered about. The abbreviations 'c' for cloud, 'p' for showers and 'r' for rain were to become only too familiar. Much of the *Manual* gave basic practical information

90. A crown and two stars denote a: GENERAL COLONEL MAJOR BRIGADIER
91. salient: OUTSTANDING SALTY SIMPLE SAFE
92. stupid-foolish: clever-IDIOT CLOWN WISE CLEAN
93. Alfred Noyes is famous as a: PAINTER POET MUSICIAN SCULPTOR
94. incarcerate: INUNDATE EXHUME IMPRISON BEND

(Questions from general knowledge section of aptitude test for aircrew applicants.)

I'm sure that everybody who was at Bradfield Park would remember the iron wardrobes down the centre with these wire beds and palliasses on them; and they used to wake you up by running down the centre of the hut belting these wardrobes with a truncheon.

(Bruce Pitt, Bradfield Park 1942 WOP.)

on the advantages and disadvantages of air cooled and liquid cooled engines; on the functions of carburettors, spark plugs and magnetos; on how to recognise and name different cloud formations; and on applying the Beaufort scale to measure wind strengths. There was instruction about flying: if the pilot of an aircraft in level flight increased engine speed the plane would climb, so to increase speed and remain at the same height the pilot had to push the column forward. All of this was grasped enthusiastically by young men eager to step into an aircraft and give a casual thumbs-up and chocks away to the ground crew. But the *Manual* was also an intimidating document for those who had left school soon after they had turned 14. Even what was called elementary navigation had references to the 'the parallelogram and the triangle of velocities', and the discussion on the variable pitch airscrew told the aircrew reservists that:

> The ratio of the thrust to the torque of a coarse pitch airscrew is very much lower than that of an airscrew of fine pitch, and therefore for a given torque, provided by the engine during take-off, a considerable gain in thrust can be obtained by reducing the airscrew pitch.

And the *Manual* made flying an aeroplane far more cerebral than it seemed in the pages of W.E. Johns:

> When once an aeroplane has begun to spin, the difference of the incidence of the wings is considerable, since the inner wing is descending vertically and so has an incidence almost equal to the angle between the longitudinal and the spinning axis, whereas the outer wing is descending in a spiral round the spinning axis ...

The extent to which a grasp of the language and detail of the theory of flight helped a pilot to react quickly and come out of a spin was uncertain, but the *Manual* reinforced the belief that those men aspiring to be members of aircrew were going to be tested in the classroom, as well as in the cockpit.

At the start of the war the few pilot trainees (then called 'air cadets') went into the peacetime training institutions trying to meet the demands of war. At Mascot most recruits were housed in the Brighton-Le-Sands and ate at the Aero Club, with the costs being deducted from their pay. Civilian instructors were employed at Mascot, Essendon and Archerfield, some still on their old hourly rates. But from early 1940, as the Empire Air Training Scheme got under way, the hopeful aircrew trainees began moving through a sequence of training schools, most lasting two or three months. By December 1940 there were five Initial Training Schools: Somers on Western Port in Victoria, Bradfield Park in Sydney, Sandgate on the north of Brisbane, Victor Harbor south of Adelaide, and Pearce north-east of Perth. At Initial Training School the Aircraftsmen Second Class (AC2s) were issued with their 'Best Blue' (their formal air force tunic and trousers) and their goonskin, the overalls that they wore throughout the day. One recruit, when asked to rush around and fill a bag with straw to make a mattress, decided that the air force was not adequately prepared to receive trainees. He thought it helpful to offer to go home and come back when the air force was ready. The officers of the Royal Australian Air Force did not think this advice either helpful or appropriate. Instruction at Initial Training School ranged from basic drill and aptitude tests to classes on first aid, maths and air force law. Recruits ran between classes, and entered no aeroplanes. Each course was numbered and normally a new course began each month; as 10 course marched out, 11 course finished its second month, 12 finished its first, and 13 stuffed straw into hessian bags to make mattresses, swapped clothes to find something corresponding to body sizes, and wondered who among them would survive the course – and survive the war. Leave between schools was – inevitably – known as 'inter-course leave'.

By January 1942 some 30 new aircrew training schools had been opened. Many of the flying schools had staffs of over 500 and were equipped with 50 or

> On other weekends Peter [Isaacson] and three other trainees, Geoff Reeve, 'Tilly' McCracken and Brefney Littlejohn, grandson of Dr Littlejohn, long-time headmaster of Scotch College, used to make a dash for Melbourne in a Morris 8/40 owned by Reeve. As soon as training ended at four o'clock on Friday at Bradfield Park they would set out for Melbourne, driving all night. They would have Saturday and Saturday night in Melbourne with their girl friends and then leave for Bradfield Park early on Sunday afternoon, breaking their journey both ways to eat steak and eggs and toast at the Niagara cafe in Gundagai.
>
> *(Warner, Pathfinder, p.42.)*

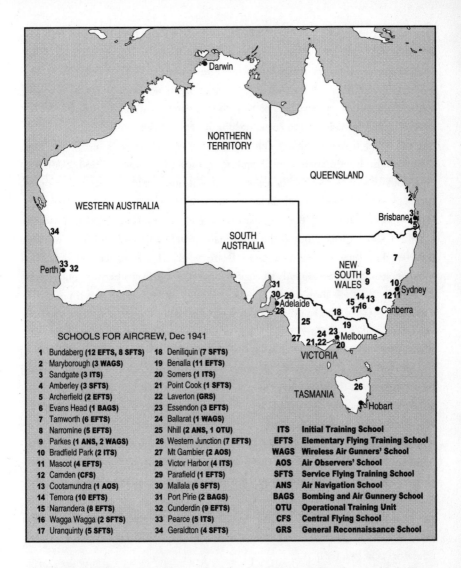

SCHOOLS FOR AIRCREW, Dec 1941

1	Bundaberg (12 EFTS, 8 SFTS)	18	Deniliquin (7 SFTS)
2	Maryborough (3 WAGS)	19	Benalla (11 EFTS)
3	Sandgate (3 ITS)	20	Somers (1 ITS)
4	Amberley (3 SFTS)	21	Point Cook (1 SFTS)
5	Archerfield (2 EFTS)	22	Laverton (GRS)
6	Evans Head (1 BAGS)	23	Essendon (3 EFTS)
7	Tamworth (6 EFTS)	24	Ballarat (1 WAGS)
8	Narromine (5 EFTS)	25	Nhill (2 ANS, 1 OTU)
9	Parkes (1 ANS, 2 WAGS)	26	Western Junction (7 EFTS)
10	Bradfield Park (2 ITS)	27	Mt Gambier (2 AOS)
11	Mascot (4 EFTS)	28	Victor Harbor (4 ITS)
12	Camden (CFS)	29	Parafield (1 EFTS)
13	Cootamundra (1 AOS)	30	Mallala (6 SFTS)
14	Temora (10 EFTS)	31	Port Pirie (2 BAGS)
15	Narrandera (8 EFTS)	32	Cunderdin (9 EFTS)
16	Wagga Wagga (2 SFTS)	33	Pearce (5 ITS)
17	Uranquinty (5 SFTS)	34	Geraldton (4 SFTS)

ITS	Initial Training School
EFTS	Elementary Flying Training School
WAGS	Wireless Air Gunners' School
AOS	Air Observers' School
SFTS	Service Flying Training School
ANS	Air Navigation School
BAGS	Bombing and Air Gunnery School
OTU	Operational Training Unit
CFS	Central Flying School
GRS	General Reconnaissance School

more aircraft. Over 90 yellow ('just on the buttery side of pumpkin') Tiger Moths were parked at No 10 Elementary Flying Training School on the north-west of Temora. With 700 men and women on the station, separate satellite and emergency landing fields and designated low flying areas, the School had a significant impact in, around and above Temora throughout the six years of its life. Some of the schools, such as Narrandera, were developed on prewar town airstrips. Others, such as Uranquinty, needed the resumption of farmland, the filling of dams, grubbing of trees, the destruction of fences and sheds, and the grading and rolling of crop and grazing land. When the first staff and trainees arrived, the contractors were still building a dozen or so vast hangars and workshops, a shooting range, a distant thick-walled concrete bomb store, 40 rectangular huts where staff and trainees slept, ate and learnt, and a hall where they went to assemblies, picture shows, dances and physical training. The central parade grounds were trim, and the sports grounds rough.

No 10 Elementary Flying Training School was close to Temora, and the town's eight hotels with their standard names (Terminus, Grand, Railway, Shamrock, Royal, Federal), the cafes and the Strand picture theatre were open to the airmen. Other schools such as Uranquinty (Quinty) were more isolated. Quinty was often called 'Bar 20', named after Hopalong Cassidy's ranch. At Mt Gambier Terry Charles noted the long main street, 13 hotels and two picture theatres, but they were seven miles from No 2 Air Observers School. The schools, so rapidly developed, were a vast investment in preparing young men for war. By the time they were being closed down, most schools had trained and examined 2,000–3,000 airmen: nearly 3,500 had been trained at 2 Bombing and Air Gunnery School, Port Pirie; 2,850 at 5 Elementary Flying Training School, Narromine; and over 2,100 at Service Flying School, Mallala.

All the flying schools in Western Australia and South Australia were established on land that baked in the summer sun. This was also the case for those schools north of the Great Dividing Range in Victoria and New South Wales: Nhill, Benalla, Deniliquin, Narrandera, Uranquinty, Wagga Wagga, Cootamundra, Temora and Parkes. Flying conditions were often ideal in the still early morning air, but later in the day thermal currents and massive drifts of cumulous clouds and threatening thunderstorms could bounce a plane around the sky. Queasy aircrew looked with envy at the wedge-tailed eagles that rode the currents with arrogant grace. The turbulent air was a tough test of aircrew's capacity to keep the mess food in their stomachs, especially for navigators, radio operators and gunners.

At Elementary Flying School those selected to be pilots were issued with their log – the record that would run for the duration or end suddenly, the last entry written in another hand and closing with the word 'Missing'. On the inside cover the trainee read, 'This book is an official document and is the property of his Majesty's Government'. But the brief formal entries, often just one line to a flight, became for many airmen – or their families – their most important personal record of war. At Elementary Flying School the trainees climbed into a Tiger Moth, sat behind the instructor and listened to his shouted advice that

For Deniliquin, hit by the Depression and men leaving to join the forces, the opening of 7 Service Flying Training School was the town's 'Commercial War-Time Blessing'. Soon over 1,000 airmen and 130 aircraft were stationed on the airfield on the edge of the town. The apparently endless plains stretching away from the trees on the Edward River provided emergency runways of unlimited length, but in the drought years of 1943 and 1944 dust storms came out of the plains in swirling clouds as black as any of the storms that aircrew were later to see lowering across the North Sea. Dust settled in huts and classrooms and the wind threatened the aircraft on the tarmac.

With 200 trainees learning to fly Wirraways on what had once been their civilian aerodrome, the citizens of Deniliquin were soon accustomed to seeing many aircraft flying cautiously and flamboyantly in their skies. They were less accepting of night flights, and disturbed by the accidents. On 1 December 1942 two trainees were incinerated: LAC A.B. Kirkwood and LAC W.J. Woodbury, both 19. On 24 December three more men were killed. Another two were killed on 29 December, and one on 31 January 1943. More accidents followed, with another concentration at the end of 1943 and early 1944.

There are now 29 war graves beyond Wirraway Road, the airfield, and the western edge of the town cemetery. Nearly all the headstones are for trainees and their instructors, one for each month that 7SFTS operated. Close to 1 per cent of the 2,200 pilots who trained at Deniliquin were buried there – below red brick pavement, white headstones, flowers and hardy shrubs, and surrounded by the scent of pepper trees and lemon scented gums.

came down the primitive speaking tube. For many it was their first flight. That first flight and their first solo some ten flying hours later were remembered with a clarity reserved for few other firsts in their lives.

Compared to what they had known, flying was so different and so sensually intense that they were, as one said, like interlopers in someone else's dream. Bill Manifold had his 21st birthday on 19 August 1941 and his first flight two days later. He remembers the flight but not the birthday. On his first solo, Ivan Pellas remembers singing from take-off to touch-down. From Tiger Moths of the Elementary Flying School they went to Service Flying Training School where they flew aircraft such as Wirraways or Avro Ansons, planes that were too slow

Just as you were due to take off from the down-wind end of the airport, the instructor – he's seated in front of you – he suddenly undid his straps, hopped out of the aircraft and said, 'Okay, off you go.' And you just went round ... the birds were singing and you got up there and you sang to yourself as you went round the circuit – still terrified – back over the windsock to make sure you were right down the right path, and in you came ... Just the one circuit and landing. You'd gone solo.

(Ken Gray, 28 Elementary Training School, Rhodesia.)

and cumbersome for battle, but at least they were twice as fast as a Tiger Moth, had an enclosed cockpit, a retractable undercarriage and looked more like machines of 1940 than of 1914.

'Boards' had power at each school. Aircrew Selection Boards and Medical Boards determined lives. At the end of each school (and sometimes during schools) there was a posting of names or a reading of lists. After Initial Training School, the 85 per cent still accepted for aircrew were divided into wireless air gunners, navigators (earlier called observers) and pilots. The chance – the threat – of being scrubbed and re-mustered because of a failure in a course, or because of a mental or physical condition, continued through the schools. Those instructors who were thought to impose harsh standards at the training schools became notorious, for example 'Scrubber' Scott at Deniliquin and the 'Screaming Skull' of Quinty. At Temora the trainees faced the 'scrub ride'. That was the day when the Chief Flying Instructor arrived and told a trainee to take him for a flight, adding the unnecessary warning: 'If you give me a rough ride I'll scrub you'. In 1941 Peter O'Connor went to Initial Training School at Victor Harbor in South Australia and went on to fly 'the lovely little Tiger Moth' at Cunderdin in Western Australia. But after repeated failures to judge height when landing he was given the brutal judgment: 'Well, that's the bloody end of you'. He found it difficult to tell his parents and fiancee that he was to be trained as a navigator: 'I still do a little weep over that, to think I didn't make the grade'. He had failed the 'realisation of a boy's dream'.

Terry Charles left his job in the Commonwealth Bank and served in the 41st militia battalion guarding the east coast of NSW from attacks that never came. By late 1942 he had been promoted to lieutenant, but was sick of all 'this war and no fight racket'. After being accepted for aircrew training, he said:

> Goodbye to my old felt hat, my tin hat & respirator, my revolver & binoculars, my gaiters & short puttees etc – all those things which seem to have grown on me. Goodbye young Dave, who has been bringing me tea & toast at 6 am … All that is over.

Early in 1943 he joined the 'new show': he gave away all privileges of rank and seniority and went into Bradfield Park as a lowly trainee. He was selected for pilot training and went to Temora, but in May he became one of the 'scrubs'.

In Mount Gambier, Charles began learning to be a navigator. But the fact of missing out, he told his mother, 'still hurts'. The rumours that at other schools the instructors were more generous and gave second chances were no comfort: he had to admit that his one hope was lost. He wrote that now it would be 'hard work, damned hard long work ... in front, with the regret of piloting behind'. His regret was all the greater because he left just when the newspapers were full of 617 Squadron's raid to bust the dams in the Ruhr, and when his twin brother Edwin, who passed through pilot training schools at Narromine and Uranquinty, was sending back his first reports of flying Hurricanes at an Operational Training Unit in Scotland.

Failure and disappointment were common. About 30 per cent of those who flew solo on the Tiger Moths failed when asked to apply their skills to service aircraft. Trainees in one course often heard talk about the failure rate — always said to be high — in the course just ahead of them. And rumours circulated; a friend of a mate had wandered into the orderly room and seen the directive demanding that five be scrubbed immediately because the instructors were required for active service, or because the Canadians had complained about the quality of the last course, or because fuel had to be conserved. As demand for pilots decreased late in the war, the scrub rate increased. Only half of the 76 men who entered Course 44 at Uranquinty in February 1944 were presented with their wings. But generally there was no fixed failure rate, and even in 1944 another course had a pass rate of over 80 per cent. For that diminishing group who kept on making the grade as pilots, other determining decisions were being made. Were they going to fly single engine aeroplanes (fighters) or multi-engines? Which theatre were they going to? The RAAF was flying from stations in England, North Africa and elsewhere on the Mediterranean, Asia, Australia and the Pacific islands, so the conditions — and chances to excel and to die — varied greatly. If destined to fly in multi-engine aircraft then aircrew might end up in bombers, long range ocean reconnaissance and fleet protection or transport. There were obviously vast differences between flying bombers over Germany, Catalina flying boats on 20-hour flights over the Pacific, Liberators in Burma or Dakota C47 transports from short hillside strips in New Guinea.

Some men, such as Don Charlwood, chose to be navigators. But nearly all wanted to be pilots. The instructors assumed that they aimed to be pilots.

Whishaw, conscious of his lack of schooling, had at first said that he wanted to be an air gunner, but on classification day at the end of his Initial Training School he was asked, 'You don't really want to be an air gunner do you?' He was allowed to change to pilot training with the assurance, 'I expect you'll soon be flying Spitfires'. But he was not: he was on his way to Coastal Command. John Beede in *They Hosed Them Out*, the novel that he made of his time as a rear gunner, said that he was on parade at Initial Training School when the Commanding Officer took the microphone and called for volunteers to become air gunners:

> The 400-strong course stood lined up in their blue dungarees, felt hats pulled down over their eyes against the glare of the sun and the dust whipped up by a squally southerly: a hush fell over the parade ground after his appeal. No one volunteered for, even in those early days, rumours of the unhealthiness of this particular calling had filtered in from 12,000 miles away. To a man they stood fast.

The CO simply named 40 men, and soon they were on a ship and intensely conscious of the 'class distinction' that divided them from pilots and navigators. Tom Simpson was drafted to be a wireless operator and air gunner because when he left Initial Training School at Somers there were no places in flying schools. The possibility of transferring to pilot training was held out to him, but once he was grouped with gunners he stayed with them. Eighteen-year-old Bob Curtis, who had stepped forward to take the place of a man rejected at Woolloomooloo Reception Depot, found that he and 40 others were on their way to Initial Training School Sandgate (in fact then at Amberley) and all were destined to be wireless air gunners – 10-Course WAGS. They and the 40 Queenslanders who entered the gates at Amberley on 6 January 1941 had simply arrived when wireless air gunners were scarce. Having been trained as a signaller in the militia, John Worely was sent to be a wireless operator and air gunner – and to his death over Berlin. Whether they chose not to be pilots, were drafted to meet a shortage or were randomly selected, the gunners, wireless operators, bomb-aimers and, to a lesser extent, the navigators, all knew that some people would brand them 'scrubbed' pilots.

Aircrew trainees met instructors who had joined the air force to see the world and had got no further than 2WAGS, three miles out of Parkes on the road to distant Orange. Or they went eagerly to class only to encounter an instructor who was suffering the depression that sometimes followed the elation of battle and survival, and who had doubts about training innocent young men to do what had given himself so much anguish. But most trainees remember being well taught by gifted and dedicated teachers. Many courses were short and concentrated, for example courses in air force law and physics. For the wireless operators, mastery of Morse code demanded complete immersion so that the 'tooting of cars and the chirping of birds came to register as Morse signals'. When Terry Charles shifted on from Mt Gambier to 2 Air Navigation School at Nhill he wrote, 'Hell, I have never worked so constantly'. He said the trainees were often up till 1.30 a.m., and 'all the boys' had 'puffed up eyes'. Having completed his navigation course at Mt Gambier, Ash Taylor went to No 3 BAGS (Bombing and Gunnery School) just west of Sale. Before Taylor climbed into the open rear cockpit with its mounted machine gun, the pilot told him to save a few rounds for the kangaroos on the way back. He gave no further instruction, but the city-boy Ash saved a few rounds and when they plunged below tree-top height on the way home he blasted away, but to his relief – and the disappointment of the pilot – he hit no 'roos.

On their way through the schools the airmen were shifted around their own and other continents. Gus Belford went from his parents' farm at Ballidu in the Western Australian wheat belt to study engineering at the University of Western Australia, then to Initial Training School at nearby Pearce, to Elementary Flying Training School at Parafield near Adelaide, and finally to Service Flying School at Deniliquin in New South Wales. His fellow Western Australian, Dan Conway, did his first three air schools in Western Australia: Pearce, Cunderdin and then into emu country at Geraldton. Charlie Williams applied to join the air force in Townsville, and was sent south to Bradfield Park in Sydney, west to Parkes, and north to Evans Head. Dalton, the Queensland banker, went to Initial Training School at Kingaroy and then did Elementary Flying at Narrandera. John Holden did the short trip from his home in Melbourne to Somers, then to Parkes and Port Pirie, before coming back to the Melbourne Showgrounds to wait for a place on an American ship crossing the Pacific.

When trainees completed the last school, and before they began operational training, many of the courses had a formal passing out dinner. For its dinner on 23 June 1943, course 32 at Deniliquin had a printed menu, and it included the names and nicknames of both flights. 'Sparks' Pellas was one of those listed – he had used his skills from Castlemaine Tech to fix the radiators that protected his

I was told to fly straight to Coolangatta and then to return along the coast as far as Southport, to fly no higher than 2 or 3 thousand feet so it would not be too cold for my instructor to sleep, and to disturb him as little as possible.

(Evan Webb, Archerfield, 1941.)

course mates from Riverina frosts. At the end of an Air Observers School at Cootamundra, Gough Whitlam proposed the toast of the graduating navigators to their instructors – in verse. The lists of those going to the passing out dinner, retained as a souvenir, was used to keep track of fellow students through the war and later through peace. Aircrew were fixed as members of numbered courses, and it was against their classmates that they measured their success and their luck.

Graduating aircrew were divided by rank. By early 1942 fixed percentages were commissioned as officers at the end of courses: one-third of pilots and navigators, 10 per cent of wireless operators and 5 per cent of air gunners became pilot officers. The rest were sergeants. Syd Johnson, who had already graduated in law from the University of Western Australia, went before a Categorisation Board at the end of Initial Training School and, in spite of his plea to be a pilot, was sent to be trained as a navigator. He accepted that judgment, but he was not prepared to be passive when he learnt that seven out of the 70 on his course were to emerge as officers: 'This time when interviewed in threes by the people who would decide whether you were officer material I didn't shut up when they asked if anyone had played any sport, but held the floor for five minutes, and walked out of Nhill as a Pilot Officer'. Perhaps his age (27), education and performance in the training schools had more impact than his eloquence, but the system granting a fixed percentage of commissions to each course clearly made some trainees eager competitors. George Hawes was not impressed by his interview by 'big bugs' to select officers:

> They ask all kinds of stupid questions making one feel like a slave up for auction ... it makes me nice and mad to see the extremes some of the chaps go to impress the officers. We don't forget to remind them either!

Later in an answer to a question from his family he assured them he would 'far rather be a plain sergeant. I could see myself getting stuck into some of these "old school tie" chappies if I was in the Officers' Mess'. But later Hawes thought it 'hardly a fair go' when the Canadians and others gave commissions more readily, and when he was out-ranked by newly arrived officers who had never seen the inside of a combat aircraft let alone demonstrated competence in operations.

David Leicester was just 18 when he left Service Flying School as a sergeant. In mid 1943 he was serving in 158 Squadron, a British squadron, and soon all its senior officers were killed. Although he was still under 20 years old, Leicester

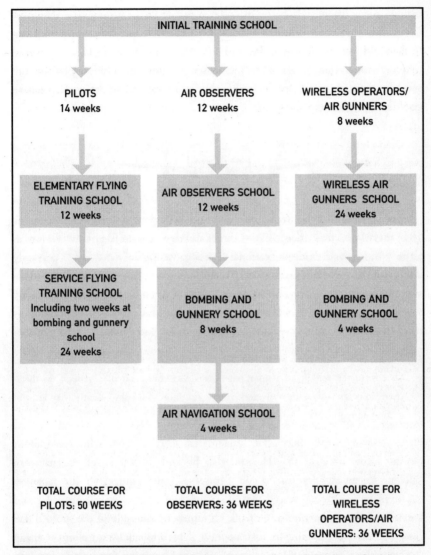

INITIAL TRAINING SCHOOL

PILOTS	AIR OBSERVERS	WIRELESS OPERATORS/
14 weeks	12 weeks	AIR GUNNERS
		8 weeks

| ELEMENTARY FLYING TRAINING SCHOOL 12 weeks | AIR OBSERVERS SCHOOL 12 weeks | WIRELESS AIR GUNNERS SCHOOL 24 weeks |

| SERVICE FLYING TRAINING SCHOOL Including two weeks at bombing and gunnery school 24 weeks | BOMBING AND GUNNERY SCHOOL 8 weeks | BOMBING AND GUNNERY SCHOOL 4 weeks |

AIR NAVIGATION SCHOOL
4 weeks

| TOTAL COURSE FOR PILOTS: 50 WEEKS | TOTAL COURSE FOR OBSERVERS: 36 WEEKS | TOTAL COURSE FOR WIRELESS OPERATORS/AIR GUNNERS: 36 WEEKS |

The training paths followed by the various aircrew. The system varied at times. 'Straight Gunners' did not complete Wireless Operator training.

had then flown 25 operations, far more than any of the commissioned pilots on the squadron: Leicester went from sergeant pilot to acting squadron leader in about six weeks. Circumstance and ability had enabled him to overcome the fact that his assessors had probably believed it unwise to commission a teenager; but other Australians thought they were handicapped by the early division between officers and sergeants. Had promotion been decided after aircrew flew their first operations, then the accents, grooming, academic skills and feats on the sporting field would have receded and the qualities of more immediate relevance would have become dominant. As Frank Dixon saw it, the system did not favour 'the son of a labouring man from the bush ... but again later in the war we might have confounded them on that one'.

The early aircrew trainees expected to go to England; but from 8 December 1941 there was a new enemy, a new threat and new reasons to go to war. Hawes, already in England doing operational training, wrote the next day: 'I certainly don't want to be over here if good old Aussie is to be anywhere near this darn war, so if you see a Manchester over Coota [Cootamundra] it's me!'. Paddy Rowling was also in England when he learnt that 'things [were] not looking so hot in the Pacific'. After the fall of Singapore in February 1942 he wrote home:

> All the Australians over here want to get somewhere where there's a war on ...
> Of course the middle of winter here gives the boys a bit of a grouch, as flying
> conditions are bad, with snow and icing conditions, and consequently they are not
> getting enough work.

Hawes told his family they could imagine his 'surprise' when he heard about bombs falling on Australia. He said that he and the other Australians were 'kicking up an awful stink' to get themselves sent home. After the Japanese captured Java, Rowling feared that 'it's a crack at Darwin next'. Again he said that all the 'boys' wanted 'to be back scrapping on our side of the globe', and 'putting Australian training to Australian use'. But while he wrote about wanting 'to get stuck into those Yellow buggers', Rowling accepted that he was acting in Australia's interests by flying in Europe, that Americans were landing in Australia to make up for the men in England and that he would be more value when he did get home if he was an experienced airman.

Those Australians who had almost completed their training were most anxious to fight the Japanese. Men newly arrived at the reception centre in Bournemouth, England, petitioned to be sent back. In Canada Don Charlwood said that his and other courses were lectured by visiting RAAF officers to tell them that they were still on their way to England and to persuade them that this was the best way to win the war and protect Australia. Harold Wright said that he would not call the Australian reaction a 'rebellion or anything like that, but there was a tremendous amount of bad feeling' before the men agreed to cross the Atlantic rather than the Pacific. A lone Don Smith, who had just qualified as a pilot in Rhodesia, did not accept official assurances. So determined was he to get back to Australia that he deliberately failed the next course. He was then offered further training as a navigator but said he wanted to go home. By the time he reached Australia the threat of invasion had declined, and he asked to be allowed to complete his pilot training. The RAAF decided it had invested enough in his training and accepted him as an air gunner. Posted to England, Smith wore his pilot's wings on one breast and his air gunner's single wing on the other.

But even as Japan began its surge south, men completing their training in Australia still chose to fight in Europe. Robert Honan was at Mallala Service Flying School in December 1941 when the trainees were told to adopt 'Brown-out' conditions, dig slit trenches and divert training flights over the sea to increase surveillance on shipping routes. Yet in March 1942, as the Japanese were pushing further south into New Guinea, he put bombers as his first preference because he thought that gave him a better chance of getting to England. He was sent to Catalinas and stayed in the Pacific. Those who joined up after the immediate threat of invasion to Australia had passed were certainly keen to fly in Europe. Syd Johnson had trained his way across the continent, through initial training in Western Australia and then schools in Mount Gambier, Port Pirie and Nhill. In 1943 he was waiting for embarkation orders in Melbourne: 'There was', he remembered, 'a roar of approval for those destined for the European Theatre'. Johnson was one of those told to board the *Queen Elizabeth*, but he did not join the cheering. While he wanted to see Britain, he thought it unwise to draw the attention of the fates to the track he was about to follow. Ivan Pellas was another at the Melbourne showgrounds waiting to be sent closer to the war.

The expected has happened at last. Japan is taking aggressive action in the Pacific. It appears she will cause quite a lot of trouble before she is through. Although I have expected it for this past six months, it comes as a shock. But I still feel that I am doing the right thing in arriving over here to fight the Hun. After all, they are the cause of all this. If I am fortunate to get through all this, I will be more than a match for the Jap. I am sure the rest of the fellows feel the same.

(Ralph Wilson, at sea on way to England, 24 December 1942, diary.)

He said he did not care which enemy, but he did not want the 'backend of somewhere', living in a tent with no grog and no girls, and he did want to see the other side of the world. He got his wish. He went on board a 'little tub', was directed to a hammock in the hold, and was on his way to Britain. When Dan Conway looked back on the chance that shifted him to a course whose members ended up flying out of England, he thought he was fortunate because he got more 'interesting aircraft and flying'.

When the *Westernland*, its holds full of swinging hammocks where there had once been refrigerated beef, sailed with over 1,000 aircrew from Fremantle in September 1942, one Sergeant air gunner was making his second trip across the Indian Ocean to war. It was, Roberts ('Bob') Dunstan said, a strange feeling, but he was a 'very different person to the youth' who had previously sailed with the 2/8 Field Company of engineers. Having enlisted when under-age, Sapper Dunstan trained in Palestine and followed the Australians in their rapid advance across North Africa. Just before the assault on Tobruk in 1941 he was with a group mapping mine fields, tank traps and trenches. As he checked the primus they were using to boil their billy, a shell exploded and a splinter sliced into his knee. In hospital in Alexandria his leg became infected and the doctors decided to amputate above the knee. Dunstan awoke to the realisation that he had lied to get into the army, was now 18, had scarcely had the great adventure, and had lost a leg.

Having learnt to walk on his aluminium leg and recovered his health on the beaches near his home at Mount Eliza, Dunstan went back to Geelong Grammar, the school he had left to join the AIF, but he was 'wanting like hell to be in it again'. Attracted by the RAAF poster that shouted: 'This is a man's job', he applied to join the air force. If Douglas Bader, injured in a prewar car accident, could fly a fighter in the Battle of Britain and become an Empire hero with two tin legs, then surely the air force would accept a one-legged gunner. At first he was rejected, but Dunstan persisted and persuaded the air force to give him a trial. Not required to do recruit training, he went straight to No 2 BAGS (Bombing and Gunnery School) at Port Pirie. He found that when flying he could work most effectively without his artificial leg, so used his crutches to reach the aircraft, stacked them in the fuselage, and hopped, levered and crawled his way around. In cramped turrets he had more room than other gunners. When other trainees were on the windswept parade ground doing physical jerks, Dunstan gained exercise by walking around the snooker table. Leaving for overseas on his 'second great adventure', Dunstan was indeed different from the person who had first sailed to war in 1940. With his reduced training and his artificial leg, Dunstan was also different from other aircrew, but at 19 and coming from a city, a privileged private school and considering studying law, he was like many of the others who 'lounged on the sunny decks' and looked forward to leave in South Africa.

The crew of 'D' for Donald, 460 Squadron, under the nose of their Lancaster, at Binbrook, September 1943. Flight Sergeant Roberts Dunstan, the one-legged gunner, is on the left. The others are: Flight Sergeant V.J. Hegarty, Flight Lieutenant J.H. Clark, Sergeant I.V. Murray, Flight Sergeant L.H. Richards, RAF; Flight Sergeant C.S. Francis, Sergeant E.F. Clemens RAF.
AWM UK0543.

Ralph Warner, Australian war artist,
After a Blizzard, Saskatchewan.
No 5 Bombing and Gunnery School,
Dafoe, Saskatchewan, Canada, 1944.
AWM ART23088.

3

MANY WAYS TO WAR

In December 1939, Great Britain, Australia, Canada and New Zealand formally agreed to the Empire Air Training Scheme. South Africa and Rhodesia made separate agreements with Britain. The white settlers of the Empire affirmed their fealty: they gave their sons, and Britain gave the machines. Australia committed itself to send Britain 10,400 pilots and 15,600 navigators and wireless air gunners, a total of 26,000 men, by March 1943. Under the Empire Scheme many Australians were to do part of their training in Canada and a few were to go to Rhodesia. In July 1941 Bob Nielsen, one of 41 selected for training as navigators, went on board a Dutch ship at Pyrmont, sailed from Sydney Harbour, changed ships in Auckland and crossed the Pacific. Once through the locks of the Panama Canal, the navigators – keeping their own check on where they were on the globe – sailed into the Caribbean, and then north to anchor in rain and fog at Halifax, Nova Scotia. On the train to Malton navigation school in Ontario they saw:

> The land of the birch bark canoe, deerskin moccasins, crystal clear streams, quick flowing rapids, high fir trees, beaver and squirrels, French trappers and Indian braves, the blazing stars above the mountains, and the beauty of the Northern Lights.

And it 'wasn't hard to take' the breakfast of cereal, scrambled eggs, coffee, toast and marmalade that was served on the train. For Nielsen, Canada was hard work, high quality instruction, confirmation of romantic preconceptions of the landscape, and generous hospitality. On a 48-hour leave the Australians were entertained at Oakville, on the shores of Lake Ontario, by hosts who provided a butler, maids and the use of three cars. Over 40 years later Nielsen wrote that the days at Malton were 'among the happiest in his life'. He recorded his debt to the Canadian bush pilots – the men idealised by Jimmy Cagney in *Captains of the Clouds* – who did the flying for the novice navigators.

In 1941 Don Charlwood, another trainee navigator, went across the Pacific in the United States liner, the *Monterey*. As the Americans had not yet entered the war, he travelled in the civilian graciousness of a stateroom with private toilet, two portholes, full-length mirrors and the services of a splendidly dressed steward. On the train from San Francisco other uniformed black men called them to dinner. All this was exotic and familiar – exotic to Depression Australians coming from air force tents and temporary huts, and familiar from numerous talkies at the Royal, Rex, Star, Odeon and Princess. In Canada Charlwood trained at Edmonton and Lethbridge in Alberta, Rivers in Manitoba, and then he too went to Halifax to wait for a cross-Atlantic convoy. Harold Wright, in the same group as Charlwood, said it was so cold at Edmonton that blizzards confined them to classrooms and the icicles on the hut eaves reached the ground. But inside the buildings the Australians sweltered; they thought the Canadians had the central heating set too high and that 'caused fights and blues'. When an Australian broke the thermostat, the Canadians replaced it and put a guard on it. A stroppy Australian, asserting his right to fresh air, responded by breaking a window.

George Hawes landed on the west coast of Canada, gained his pilot's wings and sergeant's stripes in Saskatoon, and on pre-embarkation leave saw Niagara Falls. Bob Murphy, a navigator, was another of many Australians who made the diversion to Niagara. Earlier he had made another unscheduled stop when an engine 'packed up' on a training flight north of Edmonton and the pilot made a forced landing on a frozen lake. Because of the extreme cold, the three aircrew stayed in the plane until a man 'looking like Davy Crockett' in his fur hat arrived in a horse-drawn sleigh and drove them into the local town. Canada, Murphy says, was 'a fantastic experience'.

Ilma Kitto left her school in the Riverina to make a rushed trip to Sydney to see Bill Brill, to whom she was now engaged. She was too late. Brill and Doubleday had continued their partnership and sailed together for Canada on

> When we saw our quarters we could scarcely believe our eyes. There were kapok mattresses on our double-decker bunks, and sheets and pillow-cases. The floor was covered with lino, and toilet room attached. It seemed like a dream – a veritable home away from home.
>
> *(Errol Crapp, navigator trainee, arrived Edmonton, August 1941.)*

21 March 1941. For Arthur Doubleday, who arrived at No 3 Service Flying Training School at Calgary in the spring of 1941, the 'whole experience in Canada was memorable and pleasurable'. Arthur and Bill both marched in the parade for the 1941 Calgary Stampede and both graduated with almost identical total marks. After Brill completed 54 hours as pilot in multi-engine aircraft, his Canadian instructor looked at the section of the report headed 'Any points in flying or airmanship that should be watched' and wrote 'Nil'. Both Brill and Doubleday were commissioned at the end of Service Flying School. In the language of the time they were 'commissioned off course'. In Canada, the Australians did well in the air and the classroom, but were less tolerant of petty regulation than their dominion brothers, and a few Canadian base commanders were pleased to see them leave.

Len Williams enlisted in Sydney, did his initial training at Somers in Victoria, crossed the continent in a hot railway carriage and sailed from Fremantle. In Durban in May 1941 he photographed zebras and was photographed in a rickshaw. After another long train trip he went into camp at Bulawayo, then transferred to Salisbury for his first flying lessons. He was one of three co-owners of a Graham Six sedan so he toured Southern Rhodesia in style before hitting a bridge on the way to Victoria Falls. At the end of a succession of flying schools Len was posted to Coastal Command and went to George, Cape Province, to learn further navigation. He sailed from Cape Town for Britain in January 1942.

The last three drafts for Rhodesia (in June, September and November 1941) all joined ships crowded with AIF troops on their way to the Middle East. In the midst of thousands of soldiers spoiling for a fight, the airmen found it 'wise to be inconspicuous and polite'. When they were off-loaded at Suez ports, some of the airmen had the chance to visit Cairo and the area notorious to two generations of Australian troops. They went, of course, just to look and not to 'jig-a-jig'. Back on the transports, now staffed by Italian prisoners of war, they

The rumour started: a bunch of Australian airmen had lost the kangaroo which they brought with them to Canada. It was vital that this mascot be recovered immediately; the alarm was sounded. Authorities were advised, the Royal Canadian Mounted Police lent their assistance ... householders reported that a large queer 'animal' had hopped right over their houses during the night. Old farmers claimed that 'it went that way'. The fun was furious while it lasted, but strangely enough the kangaroo was never captured.

(Australiana, 1943.)

sailed down the east coast of Africa to Durban and then joined the train for the three-day journey north to the schools near Salisbury, Gwelo and Bulawayo. In Rhodesia the Australians faced technical and social adjustments: the high altitude reduced the performance of aircraft and, granted the rank 'acting sergeant unpaid', the lowly trainees could use the sergeants' mess and hire black servants to wash and clean for them – and to chase and return balls on the tennis court. The Australians demonstrated their own cultural peculiarities when they played Australian Rules football on a crowded rugby field. Ken Gray's 'abiding' memory of the grass airfield outside Salisbury was of nervous pilots coming in to land. All were so conscious of the need to head into the wind that they flew over the top of the windsock. This resulted in up to ten Tiger Moths in line astern coming in to make their slow, unsteady novice landings. Many of those who trained in Rhodesia did their first operational flying in North Africa but some, like Len Williams and Ken Gray, were sent to England and the war over the Atlantic or Europe.

From September 1940 when the first 154 Australians left for Vancouver there was a constant traffic of aircrew trainees across the Pacific, and from November 1940 to November 1941 a lesser traffic across the Indian Ocean. In all, about 10,000 Australians did part of their training in Canada and 674 went to Rhodesia before they arrived at the war. Snow so thick they had to follow guide ropes to reach lecture huts, landing strips made into canyons by snow ploughs, ice hockey games when they spent more time on their backsides than on skates, the mistaken belief that Canadian beer was as weak as Sunday School cordial, and advice on lighting fires to protect downed airmen from prowling lions became memories of Australian trainee aircrew. But most of the 27,000 Australian airmen who went to Britain did so after finishing training courses and earning a double or single wing in Australia.

Although Clarrie Herbert trained at Somers, Mascot and Wagga Wagga he was a Western Australian, an ex-student of Fremantle Boys High, and so took his final leave in Fremantle. No friends or relatives were supposed to be on the wharf to see the Australians sail in March 1941. But his dad was there. Clarrie wrote in his diary:

I could see his reflection greatly exaggerated in the water as he was standing below a light. Could still see every move he made long after we had passed the boom. I felt pretty blue & found a quiet spot & let go. Sat in the dark until all lights ashore & Rottnest Lighthouse had disappeared.

Herbert 'rubbernecked' in Durban, Cape Town and Lagos, 'went over big' with some girls in Cape Town, got a 'couple of niggers' to catch him some fish at Sierra Leone, and on board he gambled. He lost 30 shillings at crown and anchor, but picked up seven pounds at poker, about a fortnight's pay for Flight Sergeant Herbert.

Others also gambled their way across oceans to face worse odds in the air. Another sergeant pilot, Warren Wilson, was said to have won so much he was known as 'the filthy plutocrat'. It was as 'Pluto' Wilson that he flew with 467 Squadron, and held his luck. But 19-year-old Doc (Archibald) Page played 'endless rounds of bridge' for low stakes on his long sea voyage from Newcastle, New South Wales to Glasgow via South Africa. Unlike the Americans, he says, aircrew felt it 'unfair' to take a lot of money from colleagues. The choice of game said something about social origins (Page had been to Hutchins School, Hobart) and the stakes reflected something of national ethics.

Unlike Clarrie Herbert, most Australians who already had their wings joined those on their way to Canada and went by ship across the Pacific (sometimes picking up New Zealanders on the way) and by train across America. When they crossed the International Date Line and repeated a day, the airmen debated whether they would be paid for both days. Perhaps the bastards in the pay office, the cynics said, would leave it to even up on the way home – when there might be a lot fewer men to miss a day. Those making the voyage after the Americans began their build-up of men and materiel in the south-west Pacific were often back-loaded on American ships. They were often travelling with men wounded on Guadalcanal, going on leave or being sent home because they were more trouble to their fellow Americans than to the Japanese. In March 1943 the peace of 700 Australian airmen on the *Nieuw Amsterdam* was disturbed by a burly

On the aft well deck, a non-stop two-up school operated throughout the daylight hours, and in the main lounge roulette and crown and anchor held sway. The chief promoters of the two-up ring were twin brothers, both sergeant pilots, who took turns as ring master and were obviously no novices to the game. They were reputed to have enriched themselves to a substantial extent during the course of the voyage.

(Robert Hilliard, navigator-bomb-aimer, 466 and 35 Squadrons.)

war-shocked American who armed himself with a knife and a revolver and prowled the recesses of the ship. With the demand for shipping high, the quality of accommodation and service became a matter of chance. Maurice Dalton went on board the *President Grant* in Brisbane and he and the other Leading Aircraftmen were directed to three-tiered bunks on the deck. Sheets of canvas lashed across the top gave the only protection against the weather, and they washed on the forward deck with salt water. They saw no land until San Francisco and its new Golden Gate Bridge. Terry Charles was eager to tell his mother about slipping past Alcatraz Island, half concealed in fog, before docking at San Francisco, but the censor thought it unwise for her to have other details and snipped out so many words and clauses the page was close to disintegration.

Tom Fitzgerald says that as soon as he set foot on San Francisco's pavement in 1943 motorists stopped to pick him up, they 'insisted on that'. In bars Australian airmen did not pay for drinks. When Wade Rodgers went to wander the streets, he found no British restraint. Puzzled by the strange uniforms, Americans 'ran alongside us and waved to us and asked all the damfool questions'. Those men crossing the United States on the southern lines were in country recently recreated for another Australian – in 1940 Errol Flynn had starred in *Santa Fe Trail,* 'A thousand miles of danger with a thousand thrills a mile'. J. Boormann, on his way to being a bomb-aimer in 467 Squadron, noted in his diary the oil wells, the beads bought from an Indian lady, and the women of Dodge City who had handed out coffee, cigarettes, matches and packs of cards. It was February and the train was ploughing through snow before they reached Boston. The streams were 'slabs of ice & look[ed] pretty cold'. In Boston they were invited to homes (two-storeyed and air-conditioned) where chaperoned young women joined them in songs and games. At a local school the Australians sang 'Waltzing Matilda' '& boy did they sing'. The icy roads and the streets were strange to most of the men and Boormann feared he would break his neck, but it was Jones who 'fell ass over head on his back on the ice'. Equally strange were toilet bowls with the water turned to ice. In his month on the east coast, Boormann went to several dances ('girls not bad'), took a bus to Providence, tried bowling, and used the hospitality of the Union Jack Club.

Being an officer, Terry Charles was in a train compartment with bunks and a black steward at his call, but when he went down to see the sergeants they were adapting equally well to life in the 'States': they were all playing cards and smoking large cigars. Uncertain what to do when confronted with black porters and tipping, the Australians were often awkward and less generous than expected. Wade Rodgers says that the 'raw Aussies ignored the palms and silver salvers and went on [their] way'. On the northern line the airmen travelled through Salt Lake City, the Rocky Mountains and into Chicago. Taking advantage of the brief stop, Charles 'Grabbed a cab & ... dashed down town, ablaze with lights & crowded with people, live joints with bands playing, & the usual majority of women to menfolk'. Terry drew the short straw on the first night in New York and had to stay in camp as orderly officer. His companions consoled him by ringing him up from exotic locations to tell him what a great time he was missing. But he made up for it. He wrote to his sister of his impressions and experiences: 'beaut ice cream sodas', kids with muffs over their ears roller-skating down the streets, grapefruit and iced water served at meals, groceries packed in strange paper bags, Sonja Henie skating at Madison Square Garden, cabarets where the band leader came down and spoke to the Australians, and an invitation to the President's Ball at the Waldorf-Astoria. He enclosed a candy wrapper and a serviette from an officers' club as souvenirs and evidence. Letters and cards from a Long Island woman followed Terry through the war and into the postwar when she asked him to remember how 'we danced on 58th Street in the wee hours of the morning to the strains of the car radio'. Keith Ross Miller did not forget the woman he met while waiting for transport across the Atlantic: he married Margaret Wagner of Boston in 1946.

Coming north from the Panama Canal in August 1943, the 97 Australians on the *Umtali* slipped by a 'ghostly' convoy strung out line astern on its way east across the Atlantic, passed the Statue of Liberty, watched the dream-like skyscrapers of Manhattan appear through smoky mist and docked in New Jersey. Exploiting contacts made through the Anzac Club (on 106E 56th Street), the Services Club and the Boomerang Club, the *Umtali* men made the best of their

Scranton, Pennsylvania, was just another town on the map to the Australian navigators or at least until their bus arrived there. Then they found their progress blocked by the local police chief ... [He] told the Australians that they would stay in the Jermyn Hotel as guests of the city. Further, they would be guests of the Chamber of Commerce at dinner, and then he would conduct them on a tour of the city ... The hotel rooms were extremely comfortable. The steak dinners were first rate. But the personalized tour was something totally unexpected. The police chief insisted on taking them on a tour of 23 of the 26 licensed brothels in the city ... The Australians never did find out what the police chief had in mind, but the group stayed together and none of them wandered off with any of the girls.

(Nielsen 1984, p.183.)

five days in New York. They accepted invitations to private homes, went out with selected escorts who paid their own way (or picked up their own companions who were expensive) and saw the sights, shows and clubs. Some even caught the train at Pennsylvania station for a trip to Washington. Ken Moss and Bob Lange, both sergeant pilots, tried to sell one of their songs to a publisher, but had no luck. Always attracted to the radio and film studios, some of the Australians went to see the new-fangled 'television', and saw themselves on it.

Geoff Berglund, a sergeant air gunner, found it hard to accept all of the differences he met in New York: 'What pubs! Women line up & drink like men – more like glorified brotherals [sic]. Yanks call them dives'. But elsewhere he picked up an attractive 'mannequin' and had a good night. Before Berglund's group went on board the *Queen Mary*, they were called to a 'short arm parade', and, Berglund wrote in his diary, 'Quite a few of the blokes look worried'.

Many of the men waiting at northern ports in New England and Canada for a trans-Atlantic crossing also went south to New York where they had a formal meeting place at the Anzac Club and an informal one at Jack Dempsey's. Boormann got leave in New York ('Boy Oh Boy') where he took the subway, walked down Broadway, saw a newsreel, had ham and eggs for 45 cents and went to the theatre where he met the stars. Like many other visiting Australians, Maurice Dalton took a lift to the top of the Empire State Building and climbed the metal stairway inside the Statue of Liberty to look out the hole under the arm that held the torch. Demure companions escorted Australians wanting to go to Billy Rose's Diamond Horseshoe nightclub or to dance to Victor Sylvester's famous band. Before leaving the United States the Australians stocked up with those items that wartime rationing had made scarce in England – chocolates, soap, cigarettes, nylon stockings (for an opportunist exchange) and the 'ultimate item', a Ronson cigarette lighter.

Some men sailed from Boston and New York, but many left from bleak Halifax in Nova Scotia. It was the one place in Canada the Australians disliked. Rear gunner Joe Grose wrote in his diary, 'Halifax is a dump'. It was cold, grey and dominated by sailors. The liquor laws that restricted sales and consumption to few places frustrated the Australians. Even the founding of an Anzac Club in February

1942 did little to appease those waiting to escape. Wade Rodgers had one and a half days to fill in, but found the town so 'drab and dreary' he made just one brief venture into the streets. Australians held in barracks resented getting out of bed at six o'clock in the morning in the freezing cold to salute the Canadian flag – or any flag. They got some respite when one airman, a timberman prewar and known in the air force as 'Dorrigo', took a fire-escape axe, went out into the night and felled the flagpole with a few clean blows. When given a chance to escape Canada, Bill Lees was sent on board a ship that had just brought Italian prisoners of war to the Canadian east coast. The Italians had left a welcome for the dominion troops by defecating on decks, in passageways and cabins. Lees expressed his objection by jumping from the moving ship to the wharf, but his protest cost him a broken ankle. Determined to get into action quickly, Lees had forced instructors to send him to the short air gunners course – but he was not prepared to travel in shit. Lees got to the war, volunteered for a second tour, was killed on 18 March 1944 in a raid on Frankfurt and is buried in Durnbach, Germany.

In mid 1941 Australian ground crew also refused to enter a hold just left by Italian prisoners of war. In addition to the refuse strewn about by the Italians, bags of rotting potatoes on the deck oozed a stinking black liquid into the hold. The Australians elected a spokesman, demanded change, then walked off. Don Delaney, later a flight engineer with Pathfinders, said that 'really did it'. For a fortnight they were treated as criminals with route marches, extra duties and 'no pay – no leave – nothing'. Without a guarantee of better conditions on board and threats of worse on shore, the Australians went on board the next available ship and sailed via Iceland to a sunny Clyde.

Airmen were always joining and leaving groups: initial training schools, the schools that gave them their specialist training, and the schools that prepared them for operations. It was against these cohorts that men measured their progress – and their luck. Those who travelled for long periods in small groups formed another cohort. On 22 June 1943 at Bradfield Park Embarkation Depot, 97 airmen received their first pay in English pounds and went on board the SS *Umtali* at Dalgety's Wharf, Sydney. The men, from five states, and one from both the ACT and Fiji, had gained their wings at Mallala (South Australia), Geraldton (Western Australia), Point Cook (Victoria), Sale (Victoria), Deniliquin (NSW), Uranquinty (NSW), and Bundaberg (Queensland). For 74 days, as they crossed the Pacific and Atlantic, they went ashore together, played cards, entertained and bored each other and formed another cohort. From the seafront hotels at Brighton they dispersed again, into the schools that prepared them for operations, and then most went into Bomber Command, but not with more than three or four in any one squadron. Now when they looked down names in the visitor's book at Codgers Inn, or lists of casualties, promotions and decorations they had many groups to measure themselves against.

Like other Australians, Tom Simpson was glad to escape Halifax. Crowded on the *Aurenia,* the airmen slept on mattresses and used their kitbags for pillows. The convoy steamed slowly in dense fog and still waters, accompanied by the constant wailing of many different ships' sirens. On 14 July 1941 Tom was lying on his mattress, his 'arse up against the side of the ship' when there was a bang, the ship lurched and Tom thought they had been hit by a torpedo. He grabbed a life jacket and his flask full of Canadian rye and raced on deck. The ship had ploughed bow first into an iceberg and tons of ice had crashed on the deck. The *Aurenia* pulled out of the convoy and limped back to Halifax. Tom Simpson had another four or five days in Halifax before he went on board the *Strathnaver*, a prewar passenger liner, to have another try to cross the Atlantic.

Given a few days before they had to report to Sunnyside, an embarkation base on Prince Edward Island, Tom Fitzgerald and others caught rides from Minneapolis to Chicago on the 'huge food trucks that hurtled through the night'. From there they went 'down to New York'. At Sunnyside the waiting aircrew were told that if they agreed to go to an Operational Training Unit at Nassau in the Bahamas they could then go to Coastal Command and be in operations earlier. Fitzgerald chose to go to the Bahamas, completed the course and began flying out of Cornwall, patrolling the Channel just before D-Day. But most of the men at Sunnyside decided that they wanted to wait for passage on an Atlantic convoy and go straight to England. Those crossing the Atlantic in the build-up of troops before D-Day were on transports so crowded they were served just two meals a day. And the queues were so long that they finished the first meal and lined up for the second.

For many of the minority of Australians who went through the Panama Canal their encounter with the Americas was brief. Ivan Pellas escaped the 'little tub' that he had boarded in Melbourne, spending a few hours in a nightclub at the western end of the canal, but returned to the same ship for the journey through the locks and across the Atlantic. The airmen took their turn on watch, looking at the endless waves and wondering just how, in all that turbulent water, they would recognise a U-Boat periscope. Conway, who also sailed on the same boat from Melbourne to Britain, was not allowed ashore at the western entrance to the Canal because a previous group of Australian sergeant airmen had disturbed the peace and ended up in court. But at Colon at the eastern end his group drank rum in the bars before finding 'excellent beer' at a hotel. The Dutch ship *Boisevain* came through the Panama Canal and then steamed up the Mississippi and gave its 16 Australian airmen three weeks in New Orleans. Syd Gooding, one of a small group of aircrew who boarded the *Umgeni*, a South African freighter-passenger ship, had a leisurely trip broken by a month in New Zealand as she wandered from port to port loading mutton and coal. After crossing the Pacific the Australians then had another six days in Colon, waking at sea on the seventh day to find themselves in a 120-ship trans-Atlantic convoy. Although a sergeant, Gooding was treated as a first-class passenger. And while he appreciated the fact that the canvas swimming pool was filled with heated water, he thought the civilian steward was taking service too far for fighting men when he offered the Australians breakfast in bed.

To avoid the German U-boats some Atlantic convoys pushed north where other hazards made shipboard life less comfortable and marginally less dangerous. Both Don Delaney (on his second attempt to get to England) and Rawdon Middleton changed ship at Reykjavik. In mid 1941 one group of Australians on a convoy that had already been harried by submarines spent three weeks in Iceland waiting for another ship and less voracious wolf packs.

Keen to have a souvenir of their voyage, many Australians went ashore in England with more than menus and ashtrays. One group had been such aggressive scroungers, Ralph Wilson said, they were forced to undergo a kit

Born in England, Geoff Coombes came to Australia as an infant in 1921 when the family took up a closer-settlement block at Tongala in Victoria. He was keen to enlist: 'probably a little too British', he says. After earning his pilot's wings in Rhodesia, in September 1942 he sailed from Cape Town on his way back to England. Relying on its speed, the transport ran alone into the Atlantic. With the temperature rising as they went north, Coombes suggested to his cabin-mate that they sleep on the deck. At daybreak two torpedoes slammed into the transport, and many of those below decks went down with the ship. Rowing by night and sailing by day, Coombes and about 18 others in a lifeboat set out for the distant African coast. They were soon down to just a few ounces of water a day: 'barely enough to wash the fur off your tongue'. On the eighth day a Sunderland flying boat saw their smoke pots and dropped a note saying a destroyer was on its way. In the night they saw lights shine then fade, each light rising higher than the one before. As a destroyer, HMS *Brilliant*, came over the horizon they saw that it was firing star shells, each one appearing to climb higher as the destroyer came closer. The men in the lifeboat scrambled up the nets, sailors grabbed them, threw them through the blackout curtains, the destroyer took off for Freetown, and the survivors settled to mugs of tea and tinned sausages and tomatoes: 'It was good tucker, really good tucker'. In Freetown Coombes joined a 'bloody awful old ship', and continued his voyage to England and 466 Squadron.

(Coombes transcript.)

inspection. Ralph Wilson said the captain had been left with little more than his personal belongings and an anchor.

Ron (Tubby) Fuller left the farm at Booleroo Centre in South Australia in 1939 to begin flying training as a civilian at Port Pirie. Admitted to the first course at Initial Training School in Sydney, he went on to train as a wireless operator in Ballarat and an air gunner at Evans Head in New South Wales. He sailed for the Middle East on the same ship as men from the 6th Division, then had a 'Cook's tour' around South Africa and to Nova Scotia before landing in Britain. He flew first in Defiants and then Beaufighters, guarding the Liverpool–Manchester area, but 'didn't do much'. Transferred to 458 Squadron, he went on one operation in a Wellington bomber over Brest before the squadron shifted to the Middle East early in 1942. In 50 operations, many to Tobruk, Fuller showed 'zest and pugnacity'. Rested from operations, he was instructing at Lichfield in 1943 when he volunteered to fly again in the war over Europe.

After ten weeks of slow voyaging around Africa, Clarrie Herbert took his poker winnings ashore at Greenoch, and wasn't sorry to go:

> My last act before leaving the ship was to get revenge on the chief purser who had done his best to make our lives miserable. Hoppy and I went into his cabin while he was busy on deck and set off a big fire extinguisher which sprayed his cabin and clothes & wireless.

Clarrie kept a straight face as he passed the purser, and walked into a cold, Scottish, May evening. Like Fuller, he flew briefly from England before being posted to the war in the Mediterranean. After flying eight or nine operations from Malta, being on the receiving end of over 400 air raids, and escaping punishment for punching a military policeman, Herbert was sent back to England. For the second time he sailed in a convoy from Lagos on his way to Bomber Command.

After finishing his training as a navigator at Mt Gambier and Parkes, Reg Bain hoped for a posting to flying boats – their long flights over ocean were the ultimate test for a navigator. The air force decided he was to go to England, but the threat from Japan increased and the air force held him in Australia and then sent him to Port Moresby. It was late in 1943 before he sailed for Canada for further training to prepare him to navigate Sunderland flying boats operating out of the Bahamas. At first the Australians in Toronto behaved like the Canadians who quietly played crib in the evenings. But soon they took over the piano and livened the place up with singing and drinking. In the basketball games the Australians played 'Rafferty's rules' making the non-contact sport 'pretty bloody rough'. The one accepted rule was to attack the only officer who was willing to play. Some Canadians joined the Australians in rowdy relaxation but others complained that they could no longer hear each other talk let alone play crib. When the Australians' shift to the Bahamas was delayed the Canadians diverted them to England. Reg Bain thinks that it was the boisterous pugnacity of his colleagues that sent him to Bomber Command.

Aircrew went east or west around the globe. They went ashore in Fiji, New Zealand, Hawaii, Iceland, and in many points in the Americas and Africa. They left Australia after Initial Training School or with their wings, they travelled in comfort and squalor. Most had no experience of operations before going to Bomber Command and only a few had been in many air battles. They left Australia when war was still far away and when much transport was still run by civilians and they also left Australia when war was close and pervasive. They went according to plan and suffered diversion, delay, accident and administrative stuff-ups. There were many ways to get to the air war over Europe. In their letters and diaries aircrew wrote much about their travels to war. The sea voyages gave them time to write and the censor allowed them to say more about their travels than about the details of training or later operations. Accounts of things and people seen were less disturbing for writers and readers than what lay ahead, and the journeys were significant in their lives. The journeys, protracted and boring but with flashes of the extraordinary – Hollywood, Niagara Falls, the Empire State Building, Table Mountain and Lagos – helped the clerks, farmers and the Rawleigh's rep change how they saw themselves. The journeys were always full of intense anticipation and many airmen would spend as much time travelling and waiting as they did on operations.

> Today seems to have started a new era for me by suddenly clicking me from a spirit of holiday to a known nearness of war.
>
> *(Kemble Wood, Lancaster pilot, diary, 13 August 1942, on first seeing the Irish coast.)*

Australian airmen on the Brighton waterfront. *AWM UK 3131*.

4

ALL THE GRASS LOOKS
JUST LIKE VELVET

Australian airmen arriving in Britain came ashore on the west coast at Avonmouth and Liverpool and many arrived at the Clyde port of Greenock. They saw what they expected. Before he stepped on the gangplank George Loder wrote: 'The colours of the landscape are beautifully soft and moist, the green of the fields and the trees the gentlest I ever remember'. Don Charlwood, looking at those same banks of the Clyde, said:

> It is like a garden. The hills that fade down to the harbour are vivid green and patterned with hedges. Among the clumps of trees are church towers and steeples and along the waterfront stand rows of straight-fronted houses … very Presbyterian-looking.

George Hawes wrote home:

> By gosh Mum you would like Scotland. I have never seen anything like it. Flowers and grass and trees and little creeks, old castles and those silly little thatch houses where the grass grows out the top. All the grass looks just like velvet and everything seems so unnatural that one would think it was all artificial.

When walking through Dorset villages near Lyme Regis, Terry Charles knew that he was in a landscape that conformed to his mother's ideal of prettiness: there were 'little streets & stone fences, mills & small creeks & ponds & everything with thatched roofs'. And he told her, 'You would have loved it, Mum'.

Australian sons wrote to mothers of postcard England, although more Australian fathers and uncles had been there. Of more than 330,000 Australians who sailed for overseas in the Australian Imperial Force in World War I, less than 2,200 were in the Australian Army Nursing Service. WAG John Ansell of Yanco in New South Wales was one of the few who followed the track of a mother to war. As Sister Cecil Gordon, Mrs Ansell had nursed in Heliopolis in Egypt before reporting for duty at Australian hospitals in the south of England. Aircrew flying over the hills west of Salisbury were reminded of that other generation of Australians when they looked down on a rising sun badge, 60 yards across, cut into the white chalk below the green turf by men of the 1st AIF.

On their way from port of arrival to southern England, the Empire airmen had a long introductory tour. 'There was something about the trains, the food and the green countryside that seemed to welcome us', Eric Silbert said. In the diary that he began as he left Sydney Harbour David Scholes wrote:

> I look out the window trying to take it all in. I see tiny cottages and little fields, hedges and rock-fences, long rows of brick homes, men and women, children too, poorly clad wave to us with the Victory and Thumbs Up. Everything seems so small, dingy and pokey – and damp.

Scholes fell asleep on the train and awoke on the outskirts of London:

> At once I notice the shabbiness of it all. Everything needs a coat of paint. Here and there I see evidence of bombing …

> Past London we get into a little country which I like the look of. It is very like Tasmania … It is all green – a wandering greenness.

It was a country so familiar from pictures and descriptions that memories and eyes combined to turn the landscape into another book illustration, another picture on a biscuit tin. Many of the words used in letters and diaries came readily to the Australians – they too lay in memories. When they first began flying that sense of looking on a familiar but artificial Britain was strengthened. Tom Fitzgerald, a navigator stationed at Leuchars on the east coast of Scotland, wondered why he was so 'deeply attracted' to the Scottish landscape, and decided it was the influence of Robert Louis Stevenson's *Kidnapped*. He was recognising but not entering the land that Balfour and Breck had travelled in their journey across Scotland. The view from the air made the Australians more conscious of the compressed neatness of England. Within a few minutes of taking off from Lichfield they could look down on five counties. England was beautiful, William Murphy wrote to his mother, 'but there's so little of it'.

One popular illusion was shattered as we rolled through the English countryside. Australians in general and Melburnians in particular learn from the cradle that the whole world pauses during the running of the Melbourne Cup. In the twelve weeks since we left home, we had been almost entirely cut-off from Australian news, and as the Cup is traditionally run on the first Tuesday in November, it was naturally assumed this famous horse-race had been decided two weeks earlier. As our train stopped or slowed down within earshot of locals, a chorus of voices called out, 'Who won the Melbourne Cup?' The only reactions were puzzled looks. We were to learn later that as a gesture to the gravity of the times, Melbourne's singular public holiday had been abandoned and the race meeting switched to Saturday, in this case 21st November [1943], still three days in the future at the time we arrived in England.

(Robert Hilliard, navigator-bomb-aimer, 466 and 35 Squadrons.)

The airmen saw the British people as they had been described recently in newspapers, on radio and in newsreels. The salt of the earth were enduring all that 'old Hit' could throw at them with quiet determination and humour. Scholes imposed those qualities on people he could not see:

[in] these long lines of little brick homes in which I feel sure just by looking at them live hard-working people, men, women and children who in a time of awful tragedy can fall back, not on tears – but laughter.

Later he was to be more critical of the class distinctions, his treatment as a colonial, and of his preconception of England as the 'battle-scarred island of heroes'.

One term that annoyed Australians was 'colonial'. When it implied they were inferior it cut into their notion of themselves as British and Australian, and equal to those in the home islands. At Penrhos Advanced Flying Unit, Errol Crapp wrote in his diary:

For being late on parade owing to very late serving of breakfast at the mess, we N.Z., Canadian and Australian pilot-officers were severely reprimanded by an R.A.F 'wingless wonder' Flight Lieut who said that so far he has had <u>decent</u> officers under him. I mention this here as this R.A.F. attitude of being a step above the 'Colonials' is apparent wherever you go.

Bill Pearce was more tolerant of his English commanding officer at 156 Squadron who would announce on days of stand down: 'We will play the "black troops" a game of rugby'. 'We' were from the British Isles and the 'black troops' were the Australians and New Zealanders.

On arrival in England most Australian airmen went to Personnel Dispatch and Reception Centres on the south coast at Bournemouth, later Brighton, and briefly Padgate. Apart from having to take commands from English RAF NCOs, march on cobblestones and get lost in fog, the Australians had a gentle introduction to England. 'God it's pretty as the devil', Boormann scribbled in his pocketbook. Installed in a Bournemouth waterfront flat with a view to white cliffs on the Isle of Wight, John Beede has one of his rear gunner mob say, 'This place will do me'. Hawes wrote of his 'posh' hotel. But some of the men were worried about having seats in the dress circle if the enemy tried a landing or wanted to flatten a close target and destroy a few airmen. For aircrew who went on the cliff walks, the beaches (wired, mined, spiked with rusted steel and overlooked by gun sites) and the gap in the pier (to stop the Germans marching ashore) provided the few material signs of war. But occasionally on a clear day the Luftwaffe did come in low across the Channel, drop small bombs and try to disappear before the British fighters retaliated.

Then on a Sunday afternoon in May 1943 the Germans made a sudden heavier raid on Bournemouth. Wade Rodgers was sipping coffee in the Royal Bath when 'all hell was let loose'. It all happened 'in a flash, a sudden crash and rumble ... and the snarl of flat-out engines and cannon fire ... the chandelier swung, jerked and crashed to the floor'. Direct hits destroyed 'Bobby's Restaurant, two hotels and Beale's Emporium', killed 140 people, including six Australians in the RAAF, and left much smoking wreckage. In 1944 with the build-up towards D-Day, German nuisance raids on the coast increased and the Australians in holiday Brighton had a grandstand view of German bombers pursued by Spitfires and Mosquitoes, the tight curling contrails of dogfights and of men dying in air battles. The Australians saw the brief battles as warnings of what was to come and as justification for their training and their presence, and some were even exhilarated by them. Scholes, caught in a raid with the sight and sound of battle above him, wrote: 'This is wonderful fun'. Rodgers, who helped pull dead from the rubble of a hotel, said the Australians 'now had a hate feeling that was to carry us to the end of the war'.

Returning to Bournemouth in 1943 as two-tour men from Bomber Command, Bob Nielsen and Bill Copley shared a room in the Royal Bath Hotel. Nielsen wrote in his diary:

There seem to be thousands of aircrew from everywhere – Australia, New Zealand, Canada, England, India, South Africa and even Jamaica. They all look so new and so innocent. Bill Copley said, 'Would you look at all of those poor bloody sproggs – I wonder how many of the bastards are going to get the chop?'

Flight Sergeant Ronald McCauley, armed for a snow fight. Wireless
Operator/Air Gunnner McCauley of 12 Squadron, aged 27, was
killed in a flying battle over Germany on 9 September, 1942.
AWM SUK10449.

The novice airmen were keen to talk to the experienced men, and while Nielsen and Copley could give them advice they could not tell them what they most wanted to know: what it was really like to fly a bomber over Berlin.

The numbers of men in Bournemouth and the time they spent there fluctuated with demand and supply. When Bomber Command decided to replace second pilots with flight engineers there was an excess of pilots and a scarcity of engineers. Times of high losses, maximum effort and expansion in Bomber Command all had an obvious impact, but supply varied more widely. Over 2,500 Australians arrived at Bournemouth in the second half of 1941, and just over 1,000 in the first half of 1942. By late 1942 arrivals were higher than ever. Month by month arrivals could fluctuate widely: in 1942, 83 arrived in September, 134 in October, 1,123 in November and 597 in December. Gunners were still in short supply at the end of 1942 and so might have just a few days in Bournemouth, but pilots and navigators were more likely to be there for two or three months. Clarrie Herbert, arriving in May 1941, took just ten days from the time he fire-extinguished the purser's cabin until he went to an Operational Training Unit (OTU). It was two months after his arrival in England in August 1941 before Bill Brill was flying at Lichfield OTU. Ash Taylor, who arrived at Bournemouth with the mass of men in November 1942, waited five months before being sent to an advanced flying school and six months before he got to Lichfield. By the time Taylor was at Bournemouth, men were being sent to refresher, leadership, escape and naval liaison courses – some of which seemed to be just ways to prevent men from becoming bored or dissolute.

On 1 October there were 200 pilots who had been in Brighton for six months and eight who had been there for over nine months. Too many men were qualifying for the 'Bournemouth Long Service Medal', even with bar, for meritorious service in teashops and hotels and on dance floors. Ralph Wilson said that after a parade in Bournemouth 200 air gunners were marched to a lecture, but only 50 made it all the way. Out of 50 pilots, just four arrived. It was, Wilson wrote, 'a poor show', but the lectures were 'all bull anyway'. It was soon part of aircrew lore that there were 600 pubs in the Brighton area, and airmen were welcome in 598: 'almost one each'. Those Australians wanting a quieter immersion into the old country could go to the Sunday concerts at the Bournemouth Pavilion where 'Gentlemen [were] respectfully requested to refrain from smoking pipes during the performances'. They could respond to the blandishments of Hope Brothers, Military and RAF Tailors and Outfitters of London, who had opened a shop on the Square in Bournemouth.

At tea I went along to the Pavilion with Bastian for a few drinks. Here one sees one of the harmful aspects of war. Men and women collect at the bar here and drink, and do things that they would not do under the steadying influence of home life.

(Ralph Wilson, diary, 3 January 1942.
Wilson joined the RAAF when he turned 18 and while still at school.)

Australians at Brighton were housed in two of the best prewar hotels, the Grand and the Metropole, but both had been stripped of furniture and floor coverings. The rooms were filled with army beds (with sheets, some surprised Australians found), and men tramped the stairs because the lifts were not operating. Like others held in Brighton, Eric Silbert, Bung Barrett-Lennard, Flip Burrows and Steve Clarke took a flat within walking distance of the parade ground.

On Bournemouth and Brighton's many dance floors the Australians had their first chance to lay hands on English women. Geoff Berglund went to Sherry's dance in Brighton and was unimpressed: 'They were the biggest mob of trolls that you could find anywhere. I didn't dance once'. Two days later he took a girl home from the Dome, and then at the Regent he 'got confiscated by pretty brunette' and arranged to see her again the next day. On his third day in England Doubleday went to a Bournemouth dance and met Phyllis Buckle, and then saw her again and again. In Brighton Terry Charles met 'Frankie', and she gave Terry all she had given her husband, and he came back for more. In an air raid shelter Helen stripped and offered herself to a surprised David Scholes. She was compensated for his rejection – she had helped herself to his wallet. On their voyages to England, whether they went via the Americas or Africa, many young Australians from suburbs, country towns and farms had encountered women who took the initiative to invite visitors in uniform to have a good time. They had seen queues outside brothels, and they had watched (or heard graphic accounts of) shows at nightclubs where women stripped, or played beauty to the beast, or were lovers to Frankenstein. Within days of arriving in England, Australians learnt that women were available for a range of fleeting or sustained, distant or intimate relationships. The Australia that most of the airmen had left was yet to go through the changes already obvious in England. So many women were for the first time earning wages, so many were living away from home or coming from homes with fathers, husbands and brothers absent, and all were so conscious that these were extraordinary times.

After attending an early morning parade many Australians went walking or took bus rides on short trips along the coast. Len Williams wandered along the cliffs in the spring of 1942, then walked 'a good four miles inland':

> I came across a church's canteen so I went in and had some supper and here met a Mr Orchard who invited me to come along to the Methodist church and also to his home to tea on Sunday. So Sunday morning I attended the service and later in the afternoon went to Mr Orchard's home where I met his wife, daughter Barbara and son Douglas who is going to Oxford for the RAF university short course next week.

> I enjoyed that evening very much as it is the first time I have been to a private home down here in the south of England.

Coming from a family strongly committed to the Salvation Army, Williams had used the church to meet civilians in Rhodesia – and was pleased to tell 'Mom' about it. Len returned to the Orchards' home and 'again had a pleasant evening'.

Groups arriving at reception centres were met by women of the Lady Frances Ryder and Miss MacDonald of the Isles Dominion Hospitality Scheme and the women tried to match the likes and dislikes of dominion young men with those English families who volunteered to take them for a weekend or leave. Arthur Doubleday asked to go to a farm in Yorkshire with a dairy and he 'got exactly that'. Lady Ryder and Miss MacDonald had looked after Rhodes Scholars and then Empire soldiers in World War I so they were experienced in meeting the needs of young British men far from home. Their card announced that 'during the war' they were 'at home' between 10.00 a.m. and 10.00 p.m. (including Saturday and Sunday), and invited telephone and telegram requests. Flying Officers Les Kingsmill of Renmark and Eric Cathcart of Mackay were asked to call on the ladies at their flat in London's Sloane Square where Miss MacDonald 'poured' at afternoon tea. After discussion of the two men's likes and dislikes, Lady Ryder suggested 'the Dales' who 'for Australians keep beer in the refrigerator', and Miss MacDonald plucked the Dales' card from the file. Cathcart and Kingsmill stayed a fortnight at the Dales, and supplemented the beer in the fridge with visits to the local pub, but even there the beer was 'on the house'.

The Lake District was favoured by Lady Ryder and the Australians. Boormann summed up his stay with Mrs Dalthwaite: 'Rowing & cycling, marvellous scenery & wonderful leave'. Sam Weller, a butcher, farmer and horseman from Gympie in Queensland before he became a pilot, admitted an interest in horses and Lady Ryder matched him with Lord Somerville from near Kendal on the east of the Lakes. Sam treated the infected hoof of Lord Somerville's Arab stallion, yarned with Lord Somerville and was invited back for another visit. Later when Sam was in Stalag IVb (where he gave lectures on catching and breaking brumbies) he received a food parcel from Lord Somerville.

The dominion men taking English hospitality often entered middle-class and upper middle-class homes that, like so much else, was familiar, although certainly different from those they had left. These had a maid and a breakfast gong and 'wow! – nobody is more than 20 seconds late'. In case the dominion boys were uncertain of what was expected of them, Lady Ryder and Miss MacDonald gave them written instructions. These gave them directions about which train to catch and where to alight, and warned them that names had been removed from stations and that therefore they would have to ask advice. The instructions also told them to be certain to telephone their hosts in advance and reminded them to take their ration cards. The young men were advised too that in houses with more than one servant it was appropriate to tip just one servant 2/6d for a weekend or 3/6d for a week, and that hostesses appreciated a letter of thanks. Often the young airmen entered homes offering privacy and independence. They were allowed to sleep in, walk through surrounding streets and fields, and just join the family for meals and at other times when it suited them. Most of the men were delighted by the manners and generosity of their often elderly hosts. David Scholes left his hosts waving at their gate, and he promised himself that he would write to them and keep them informed of what he was doing on the squadron.

Other dominion boys also developed closeness with families they had entered as strangers. Bob Nielsen, a navigator from Wollongong, regarded going back to Bournemouth after operations as 'another homecoming'. He spent all of his recreation leaves with the Goad family:

> From the first time he came to stay, Nielsen was treated like one of the family. More correctly, he was treated like a very special member of the family. Mrs. Goad lavished on him love and concern; she saved ration coupons for his visits so that she could prepare healthy and attractive meals. Mr. Goad made a point of talking to him about many topics.

As a sad consequence of that intimacy some English hosts wrote their first letter to the airman's Australian family after their guest was reported dead or missing.

They tried to share the anguish: 'My heart goes out to you in your trouble, and believe me when I say he is very often in our thoughts … He was often singing, especially when he helped me to wash up'. 'It was our great misfortune and sorrow that we had so short a time in which to share and enjoy his friendship … His name is always cropping up in our conversations.' Just before leaving England, Tom Scotland visited a family that had befriended him on his arrival in England. He was the sole survivor of four airmen who had stayed with the family, and the mother of the household wept at the reminder of the other three young men. The next day Tom and the family went into New Forest and boiled the billy – as they had done before.

Paddy Rowling and Gus Rowcroft, two Flying Officers recently arrived at Bournemouth, accepted a Lady Ryder invitation to go to a house in Shropshire. It was a double-storey stone manor house set in 1,000 acres. Paddy, when farming around Quambatook and Charlton in Victoria, had often been shooting and was pleased to watch an English shoot. He was surprised to find the six shooters were served by loaders carrying spare guns and by 30 beaters who set the startled pheasants flying towards the shooters. Paddy thought they should never have missed. At lunch the two Australians ate in the same room as the six shooters and were offered beer while the shooters drank port. But at least they were a step higher in the social order than the beaters who were outside. Paddy came away 'sadly disillusioned' with the English upper class. They were, he decided, nice, condescending and useless. Later he formed close relationships with families at Newark near his airfield, sometimes staying overnight and getting poached eggs for breakfast in bed. And out of the parcels from home he contributed his mother's cakes and his sister's 'nutties' to the household larder.

Thank you – Lady Frances Ryder!

During 1942, more than ten thousand visits to different parts of Great Britain were arranged, and this figure was exceeded in the first eight months of 1943 … It is common practice for a family to keep a 'Visitor's Book' recording the names and addresses of all the men who come to their home – many Aussies while signing their own names, have discovered the names of friends who stayed there before them. A large number of women desire to write to relatives of their guests, saying that a son or husband is well, giving news of him and assurance of his welfare. And in every house there is that vital link of discussion which has greatly assisted understanding – English peoples are now far less perturbed about aborigines, and quite a number of Aussies are less critical of 'Punch' and 'plus-fours'.

(Australiana 1943.)

He also arranged to add to his repayments; he said that if he went 'for a burton' (was killed) the adjutant was to give his Hercules bicycle to Len Nettleborough 'for the many kindnesses he and his wife have shown me'.

English members of crews and English girlfriends also gave Australians entry into English households. Frank Dixon, a pilot, was the only Australian in his Lancaster crew and he often went either to his navigator's home or to the navigator's aunt's 'little country pub' in Oxfordshire where they could 'kick up [their heels]'. He was, he says, 'a member of the family'. And so many Australians had actual family to visit. At the 1933 census more than one in ten Australians were born in the British Isles. Len Williams, whose mother had come to Australia in 1919 as the bride of Private Stanley Williams, AIF, went to Kent and met for the first time grandad and grandma, and numerous aunts, uncles, and cousins. Maurie Dalton's father had met the woman who became his war bride in Brighton, and on his first night there Maurie went to see Uncle Les and Auntie Kate. Given seven days' leave, Clarrie Herbert did his duty and went to Manchester to see 'Mum's relatives', and after spending a 'day meeting dozens of distant relatives … Was very bored'. Dan Conway had to borrow a suit so that he could see his relatives in Killarney – Ireland demanded that the servicemen go in civvies. He stayed with his mother's sister, went to the Gaelic football and a dance, and became accustomed to people introducing themselves to him, 'all of whom seemed to be my cousins'. Tom Fitzgerald also went to Ireland to see 'the land of [his] mother and [his] grandparents which was Tralee'.

Don Charlwood searched for more distant relatives. He says 'hundreds' of dominion men were looking for evidence of their forebears. Perhaps, he says, it was their own impermanence that attracted them to the permanence of the past. The past was now fixed. At St. Martins-in-the-Fields in London he found the baptismal entry of his grandmother; and in Surrey, in 'loveliness beyond expectation', he found the village of Charlwood and the gravestones of James and Phoebe Charlwood, the parents of his great-grandfather who had settled in Melbourne. The Charlwood rectory became 'another home' to the Australian navigator who was four generations from the giant elms, the silent river Mole, and the church of St Nicholas. When Tom Simpson went to the bank in Greenlaw to enquire about his father's origins, the lone banker looked up old ledgers, then closed the bank to take him to meet some elderly Greenlaw citizens. Few Australian airmen had thoughts similar to those that disturbed Tom Scotland. On 13 June 1944 he piloted a Halifax bomber dropping markers to guide two bomber streams converging on Munich, and was suddenly aware that he was over his mother's 'home country'.

In the early years of the war some Australians posted to stations were billeted with nearby English families who were paid sixpence a day. While at Coningsby, Tom Simpson stayed with the Browns in their cottage at Woodall Spa. He had an attic room without electricity, but no matter what time he arrived home Olive Brown was waiting for him in the little downstairs kitchen. On some evenings he went with Arthur Brown to the Railway Hotel for a game of darts or dominoes, and he went with both Olive and Arthur to dance among the potted palms at the Woodall Spa winter garden. Simpson tried to return the hospitality of these 'good folk' with butter or jam from the mess or fish and chips that he bought. He continued to return to the Browns when he was flying from other fields.

From Driffield airfield in East Yorkshire, Ivan Pellas crossed the wolds to York where he could catch a train to Edinburgh. Often he walked alone through the streets of the old town, and came to appreciate its beauty. Another Australian with 466 Squadron preferred to learn about Edinburgh from the comfort of the King George and Queen Elizabeth Dominion Officers Club. There he could 'look through the large window up at the castle, across Princes St & the huge gardens, [while] sipping a beer & munching a roll with tomatoes & lettuce & mayonnaise'. Australian aircrew watched Shakespearean plays at Stratford-on-Avon, wandered around Stonehenge and visited miners' villages in Wales. Bob Murphy and a

> Out of doors the ground is frozen hard, brittley hard. At least there is no mud or dust to dirty one's feet. All day long a white icelike frost covers everything – grass, roof tops, aircraft. Underfoot the grass crunches attractively. How on earth it remains alive goodness only knows. Puddles, ponds & lakes are frozen over. To-day one of our company braver (or more foolhardy) than the rest, walked over a frozen pond in safety. All lakes in the vicinity are cluttered by innumerable bricks & stones – thrown you may be sure by Australians. Stones skidding over the frozen surface make a delicious sound, not unlike the swish of a whipbird before the crack of his whip.
>
> (*Evan Webb, pilot, Lichfield, 9 January 1942.*
> *He died in a flying accident on 17 January 1942.*)

Canadian friend saw the village of Beer on a map, and thought they would like a few days in Beer. And they went down to the south coast, found one small pub in the village and spent their time in Beer. At Moreton-in-Marsh airfield, Gloucestershire, a map recorded pub intelligence: different coloured pins indicated whether meals, music and other services were available. But for all aircrew, London was the main attraction and few were content with just one visit.

From kindergarten rhymes ('Oranges and Lemons says the bells of St Clements'), songs ('Goodbye Piccadilly, Farewell Leicester Square'), films (*Waterloo Bridge*, *Pygmalion*), the novels of Dickens and Arthur Conan Doyle, and sport (Lord's Cricket Ground, Wimbledon, and Wembley) to the dominant sites of King, Church and Empire, London was familiar. For the Australians, Fleet Street was as well known as most of the streets in their home towns, and Fleet Street was invested with a significance unattached to Murphy Street, Wangaratta, or Pitt Street, Sydney. And there was another source of familiarity. After he took a bus from Euston station Herbert wrote, 'Allee same Monopoly'. But Londoners stared at the unfamiliar when Clarrie Herbert of Fremantle walked through Trafalgar Square in his RAAF shorts.

The Australians made The Strand their own. They operated out of the area bounded by Charing Cross and Trafalgar Square on the west, Fleet Street and St Paul's Cathedral on the east, Waterloo Bridge, the Thames and the Embankment on the south and Covent Garden on the north. The Strand Palace Hotel, 372 The Strand, London WC, 'an art deco showpiece', was not the swankiest prewar London hotel but it pretended to some class, and it was better than most of the guest houses and pubs known to the Australians in their civilian days. Don Charlwood wrote that it gave him a 'comfortable & beautifully clean room'. On the high ceiling of the impressive entrance the Australians registered their passing. To the cheers of patrons, they built a rickety pyramid of furniture, one of them made 'the ascent of Everest', dangled precariously at the top, and planted his blackened feet on the ceiling. Often just one Australian booked a room in The Strand, and others who knew him or knew someone who knew him dossed in any vacant bed or on the floor.

The Strand was central to many of the places the Australians had to or wanted to visit. In December 1941 the Overseas Headquarters of the RAAF opened in Kodak House. At 63 Kingsway just off The Strand, Kodak House was the first address of many airmen in England. The address consisted of a number, rank and name C/-AUSPO, Kodak House, Kingsway, London, WC2. Australians entered the bank-like entrance of the six-storey austere Kodak House to sort out postings, pay, promotions and mail. Kodak House was seen (justly and unjustly) as the haven of shiny bums, mindless bureaucrats, and those too ready to kowtow to the British. Rollo Kingsford-Smith, believing that Australian reinforcements were going to English squadrons while the Australians were starved of men, took the train to London where he 'Went to Kodak House. Then came straight back … Did not achieve much'. His diary, Kingsford-Smith says, disguised the fact that he was 'bitterly disappointed'.

Australia House, also just north of The Strand on the Aldwych curve leading into Kingsway, housed the Boomerang Club, which opened early in 1942. The Club took up two floors of Australia House and served all Australian services and ranks. Men registered at the reception centre (entrance off Melbourne Place), scanned the Club for friends and consulted the noticeboards – one for men to attach notes for mates and the other listing entertainment. The Club helped men find accommodation, sold drinks, snacks and meals, and provided a place to write letters, read Australian newspapers, gather around the piano, have a haircut, play billiards and yarn. The Boomerang Club attracted and disturbed aircrew. They wanted to catch up with news and comrades, but so often they learnt of the deaths of another three or four of their old course from Narrandera or Parkes or Calgary. On his way to join an operating squadron, Don Charlwood wrote in his diary that Kodak and Australia House were frequented by 'squadron lads' with tales of deaths: 'I confess that I felt depressed. London life lay so appealingly about me and London people seemed so free of war worries, that our own dark future made a far from happy contrast'.

Along and beyond The Strand and down towards Fleet Street where wig and pen mixed were the less formal meeting places of Australians: Ye Old Cheshire Cheese Inn where Dr Samuel Johnson had talked and talked and drunk; Dirty Mick's café where a 'lean hawk-nosed character' served a reasonable imitation of steak for those who had not tasted steak for a long time; and Codgers Inn. Just off Fleet Street, and said to have been patronised by Dickens, Goldsmith and Macaulay, Codgers was the Australians' bar. The BBC even went there to record a session of 'Anzacs Calling Australia', so from Codgers Australians spoke to mum and dad, their wife and their friends. By 1944, when air gunner Cliff Halsall was reporting on London for his home town *Euroa Gazette*, at least 7,400 Australians had recorded their names and comments in Codgers' visitors' book: 'Next best to Fosters', 'We of the Never Never', 'Just a banana bender having a few over the New Year'. Doc Page went into Codgers in 1942 and immediately found four fellow Tasmanians.

From The Strand it was only a short walk into the theatre area and many of the other sites of world, Empire, Australian and male-wartime interest. Quickly and relentlessly they saw, heard and tried all that London offered and all that their time, tastes and morals allowed. It was just as well major museums and galleries were sandbagged and their treasures stored against blast and fire. On 7 July 1942 George Hawes met his fellow crew member and Londoner, Bill Smith, and went to Australia House where he 'had a good talk to the chaps there'. He checked on promotion and then saw 'Big Ben, Waterloo Bridge, Parliament House, 10 Downing Street, Marble Arch, Buckingham Palace and dozens of other places'. He went to a 'show' in the evening and the next day returned to Buckingham Palace to see the changing of the guard: 'spectacular' but 'a lot of "bull"'. Cliff Halsall had a look at the Thames, went to Australia House, saw 'plenty of 460 [Squadron] bods', had a 'good meal' and later listed a reminder of where he had been and what he had seen: 'St Paul's – free publications … St Clement Danes – Trafalgar Square – Wimpole St – the Discovery – Covent Garden – Temple – Strand – Saville Row – Fleet Street – The Embankment – the cabbies – the police – V2 damage etc'.

Clarrie Herbert, 'rubbernecking in London', went to the Windmill Theatre 'which puts on a glorified carcase show. Very good and the women are certainly the tops. Went to the Studio Club and met Sally'. A fortnight later he returned to London and saw Stanley Holloway's show. The next night he went to see Flanagan and Allen at the Palladium and again kicked on at the Windmill. And he went back to the Studio Club. Terry Charles regretted the gloom of the blackout, the queues and the congestion of bodies in the underground, but liked London – even if a few details were hard to recall:

> Somehow, sometime, I can't remember when, I went to a Russian lass's place for a cocktail party out at Queensway near Kensington Gdns, & also took a lass drinking at the Dorchester on Park Lane. I guess a lot of little things will come back in time.

> Met some jolly nice WRENS and took them to their duty posts at Lambeth bridge. Was highly amused by the newspaper men. In deep stentorian voices, 'Evening Standard' followed by in an undertone, 'Any rubbers tonight pal?'
>
> *(Geoff Maddern, pilot, diary, 16 January 1943.)*

Charles wrote to his mother of another night in London when he went to the Regent for a beer, took in a newsreel, and went to the New Theatre which 'of course' started the evening show at 6-30:

> It was my first ballet, we had excellent front stalls, & I really enjoyed it. It was the Sadlers' Wells Company, an English ballet, & it turned on Promenade, La Spectre de la Rose & The Rake's Progress. The usual alert on when we came out, but we had a snack down near the station, & then went home to bacon and eggs.

At the New Theatre, patrons were told that 'if an Air Raid Warning is received during the performance, those desiring to leave the Theatre may do so, but the performance will continue'.

In the richness of the wartime London theatre, Charles had a choice of Shaw's *Doctor's Dilemma* with Vivien Leigh, *Watch on the Rhine* with Lillian Hellman, *Flare Path* by Terence Rattigan, *Blithe Spirit* by Noel Coward, *The Importance of Being Ernest* with John Gielguid, Edith Evans and Cyril Richard, and the London Philharmonic at the Royal Albert Hall. Often the Australian airmen

> Tuesday we booked into the Strand Palace ... Bob [Rees] and I sharing a room, and he and I had lunch with a Boomerang Club Hostess, a Mrs Tennant ... and did the rounds that night ...
>
> Wednesday I went out to Barratts at Twickenham, saw a show with Sandra and stayed the night. Thursday we ran into Charlie Walker who was on 48 hours leave from his gunnery course, so we went along to see [comedian] Lupino Lane in '20 to 1', which was really good. Charlie knew Lupino, so we had a chat with him back stage afterwards, and he's really nice, and funny as a circus. Have an open invitation to make use of his theatre anytime if we want to see a show, which was very good of him. We went from there to Victoria and met two more of Charlie's friends – Aussies who had stayed over after the last war, and had dinner with them, Bob Minear and Bill Munday, at the R.A.C. which is one of the most palatial clubs in the world. The roast duckling was alright too! On Friday Bob and I took Sandra to see 'Dancing Years' with Ivor Novello, which was excellent.
>
> *(Paddy Rowling, diary. Six weeks later, on 17 December 1942, Rowling and Walker died together in a raid on Soltau, Hanover.)*

were invited backstage to meet the performers – whether international stars or scantily clad Windmill girls.

Women for conversation, dancing and sex were readily available. They could be bought at Piccadilly Circus but, as Beede said, there was no need to pay in hard cash. In wartime London, four gins were worth, he said, four months' acquaintance at other times, in other places. There were thousands of women in and out of uniform and liberated from many constraints, a post-blitz city in social and material turmoil, and thousands and thousands of young men from all over the world in urgent need of a good time. London on a 'forty-eight' (a 48-hour leave) could be an extraordinary experience – even when the fog was so thick 'People a few feet away looked like shadows silhouetted in the yellow mist'.

Stella Bowen, *Bomber Crew*, London, 1944. The preliminary sketches and photographs of the 460 Squadron Lancaster crew were made in April 1944 at Binbrook. The crew was shot down on a raid on Friederichshafen on 26 and 27 April, 1944. Lynch, badly wounded and the only survivor, became a prisoner of war. Back row, left to right: Sergeant D.G. Champkin, flight engineer (England); Pilot Officer Thomas Lynch, rear gunner (Toowoomba); Flying Officer Hector Harrison, wireless operator (Lismore); Flying Officer Ronald Neal, mid-upper gunner (Grenfell). Front: Flying Officer Marmion Carroll, navigator (Ferntree Gully); Squadron Leader Eric Jarman, pilot (Yeppoon); and Flying Officer Francis Jackson, bomb aimer (Lismore). *AWM ART26265*.

JUST WHAT I NEED:
A WIRELESS OP WHO DRINKS

Most pilots wanted to fly fighters, but by the time they reached England many had trained on multi-engine aircraft and they knew that increased their chances of being posted to Bomber Command. Just a few had chosen bombers from the start. Arthur Doubleday kept saying in Australia and Canada, 'I want bombers, the bigger the better'. As he said when he started training early in 1941, the bomber was the only weapon then available to hit back at the enemy. Perhaps his familiarity with tractors and the semitrailer on the red soils gave him confidence in his capacity to handle the world's largest and most modern aircraft, and confidence in the effectiveness of the machines to do the job. Bill Manifold, too, chose bombers while in Australia. Mick Martin was as unorthodox in the way he came to a bomber squadron as he was when he got there. After joining the RAF in England, Martin trained as a fighter pilot, but was posted to the north and missed the fighting in the skies over the south-east during the Battle of Britain. Determined to get into the war, he applied for a transfer to bombers. He may also have wanted to join other Australians because early in 1942 he put together one of the first all-Australian crews to bomb Germany.

But most men found little agreement between desire and disposal. Although in their apartments and hotel rooms of Bournemouth and Brighton many aircrew could say what they wanted to do, they were in fact told what they would do. Asked to rank the aircraft he wanted to fly, Gus Belford wrote Spitfire, Mosquito and Lancaster. Others in his group wrote 'Spit, Spit, Spit'. The cards were collected, and all were told that for the present they were to train on twin-engine aeroplanes in preparation for Bomber Command. Of the 52 pilots who filled in their cards on that day early in 1944, 46 eventually flew with Bomber

Command. David Scholes had arrived in Brighton on 8 July 1943 and learnt on 12 September that he was on his way to bombers. He said, 'now I realize what this means – simply I am one of many mugs'. On his second day flying the twin-engine Oxford he complained of the 'wallowing, slow, clumsy, toy-like, flimsy guts-breakers'. The dashing of hopes to join the pin-up boys of the air war in high performance Spitfires was frequent and intensely felt.

The reason why so many Australians went to Bomber Command was simple: it had the vacancies. Bomber Command was expanding. From 1942 most of its aircraft required a crew of seven, and its losses were the greatest. Even when it was obvious that the death rate was high in Bomber Command, a few men still chose to go into the less glamorous and more deadly bombers. Dan Conway was one who put down bombers – and got his choice. Later his brother John also volunteered for bombers, although he could have gone to Coastal Command. Those who went to bombers were also likely to be in action more quickly than those who went into other sections of the air force, another result of high casualties. And some men chose bombers because it was a fast way to battle. Some changed muster from navigator to bomb-aimer to get into action quicker, and there was little doubt about which section of the service was most likely to want bomb-aimers. Others had themselves reclassified as 'straight gunners', dropping the need to continue training as wireless operators. A sense of obligation seems to have motivated a few young dominion men to choose extreme danger, and many men to accept it. Conway says when he made his choice he knew that his chances of survival were slight. Death might have been the last enemy, but among those forces applied to young men who were gathered together, instructed, pushed about the world, and given exciting, prestigious, brutal and terrifying tasks, it was not always the strongest.

On arrival in England the airmen were a long way from being prepared for battle. Pilots and navigators in particular found much that was new. They were posted to Advanced Flying Units and had to learn English methods of contacting

I am feeling terribly old. In one month I will be twenty. I have done nothing important yet. I feel so much as if I have wasted a hell of a lot of time. And yet, my plans for the post war period are growing clearer every day. But there is so much time wasted in this air force. For the past six months I have done practically nothing. True, I have travelled from Australia to England. But as yet, I have not done anything useful. Not that the spirit is unwilling. It is most anxious to do something. Something big.

(Ralph Wilson, diary, 1 March 1942.
He was killed on 25 July 1942 in a raid on Duisburg.)

Good lecture on aircraft recognition followed by a couple of hours of morse. Went for a march on a slippery road and what a joke – quite a number falling over. Organized games in afternoon and had a couple of hours of football. The WO (new one) had a lot of trouble drilling the boys ... says he 'I'll send you back to Bournemouth.' 'Hurrah,' cried the the boys, which doesn't improve his temper, then he adds, 'I'll take off your stripes' and the reply, 'a lot of difference that will make.' So he gives over his job to the Sgt and returns a sadly broken man.

(Geoff Blacket, on wireless operators' course, Hastings, diary, 3 December 1941.)

and directing aircraft in flight, the way English air fields operated in conditions where traffic was dense and enemy attack possible, how to exploit various navigational aids not used in Australia, and the peculiarities of the weather in northern Europe. Stan Hawken, who passed out of the wireless operators' school at Ballarat with 'top marks', spent two hours on his first flight over England but in the turbulence and competing radio traffic did not send or receive one message. The Australians had to recover skills lost over several months on board ship and on the Bournemouth seafront, and they had to become familiar with aircraft that were much larger, more powerful and more sophisticated than they had previously flown – or seen. At special schools pilots learnt how to use instruments to land in fog. Radio controlled signals told them when they were on the 'beam' and how far they were from the end of the runway.

The Advanced Flying Units were often in the west, centre and north of the UK: Ash Taylor went to Dumfries in Scotland 'in pouring rain', Peter Knox went to Penrhos in north Wales and Maurice Dalton went to South Cerney in Gloucestershire. It was deliberate British policy to spread the dominion men widely through different Advanced Flying Units. But as they trained, the crews tended to move east towards the operating fields close to the wolds, downs and fens.

The Australians were scattered again through Operational Training Units (OTUs) where they began to fly bombers that had recently been in battle. Even in October 1944 when the system was most organised and demand for crews slackening, Australians were training in 20 different OTUs. But there was one OTU – 27 OTU Lichfield in Staffordshire – that the Australians tried, with modest success against British indifference and obstruction, to make their own. In 1941, 160 Australians went through Lichfield and by 1943 and 1944 up to 700 Australians might have been training at the one time in any of the four ten-week courses.

At Lichfield the Australians were more likely to encounter Australian senior officers, more likely to be instructed by Australian 'screens' (men who had

On their way to or from Lichfield many of the Australians on the Derby road went through Burton, crossed the Trent bridge – and smelt the breweries. 'Gone for a Burton', adopted from the prewar advertising slogan for Burton ale, was the common air force slang for killed. It was at OTU, uncomfortably close for many Australians to Burton, that the trainees began to use air force language – technical, comic and evasive – that helped bind them together. So they began to talk of a 'shaky do', 'piece of cake', 'kite', 'bags of', 'gen', 'stooge', 'chop', 'prang' and 'line shoot'. A 'prang' was broadened in meaning, and became a transitive verb, as in we 'pranged' Hamburg. To 'get the chop' was to be killed, but it too was extended as in 'chop flight' and 'chop kite'. Things that were poor were 'duff', if they were numerous, there were 'bags' of them. To 'shoot a line' was to exaggerate, and the best 'line shoot' was done with apparent understatement. To use air force slang before OTU was pretentious; to use it later was to demonstrate graduation.

completed a tour and been 'screened' and posted to a training unit) and more likely to be sent to an Australian squadron at the end of training. The main Lichfield airfield was next to Fradley village on the north-east of the town: 'The windows of the sergeants' mess', Don Charlwood wrote, 'looked across gently-descending fields and woods to the triple spires of Lichfield cathedral'. Church Broughton, a satellite field, was further to the north, across the county border in Derbyshire. The many Australians passing through Lichfield on their way to war, and the few returning, wandered Lichfield's cobbled streets opening off market square. They used the dark brick cathedral rising above Stowe Pool to check navigation when walking, bike riding and flying. On rare hot days they swam in the canal that curved around two sides of the airfield and on at least one occasion some did a literal crawl from one pub to another – they swam from one canal-side pub to the next.

Australians at some OTUs found few 'screens' who could tell them about operating over Europe. Those brash enough to ask why this was so were told that there were not enough men completing tours in Bomber Command, so many instructors came from the Mediterranean. 'Screens' sometimes behaved at the extremes of what new crews thought ordinary – they were either morose and cynical or they were excessively exuberant. The 'screens', by their absence and presence, could present unspoken warnings.

At OTU most aircrew flew their first modern bomber, the Wellington, which required the gathering of a crew of six: pilot, navigator, wireless operator, two gunners, and a bomb-aimer. When compared with all the controlled, formal and tested training given to aircrew, crewing-up was strangely informal, personal and unsupervised. And the airmen were making what may have been the most important choices of their flying careers. A failure by any crew member could mean the death of all of them, and as they were going to be in a confined space and under extreme stress for hours they had to be compatible. Gus Belford thought that if men had survived this far in their training then they knew their trades, and compatible personalities were more important than skills. Bill Manifold said that finding a navigator was 'as important' as getting a wife. Rather than trying to find out who was the best navigator on the course, he proposed to Tom Moppett because of his 'cheerful disposition'. From the time of their arrival at an OTU the men knew they were about to form crews. Some men, usually just pairs, decided early that they would fly together, but at the end of a few weeks of theory and practical details about fuel consumption and conservation most men were still uncommitted. Assembled in a hangar or an operations room, the airmen milled around, gradually forming the groups that would live, and perhaps die, together. In the summer of 1943, 18 crews would form themselves every four weeks at Lichfield, and when winter cut flying time 11 crews would be formed. Often a pilot took the initiative, as it was he who would command the plane in flight, and pilot and navigator came together as the first combination, a duo who were so obviously going to be mutually dependent. They then chose, or were chosen by, the rest of the crew. However, there was much variation in who took the initiative and the bases on which choices were made.

Nationality was important. Don Collumbell said that 'being a good Australian I looked around for an Australian and I found one, a fellow called Bill Coolsby from Glenelg in South Australia'. When they could not find Australians they looked for New Zealanders and, according to Don, New Zealanders who could not find other New Zealanders looked for Australians. Don was 21 and Coolsby was 20, so it may have been age that brought them together. Age may also have been a factor when they selected a 30-year-old New Zealand bomb-aimer. Loyalties to Australian states could also have an influence. Arriving at Stanraer for a wireless operators' school, John Holden heard a 'good Australian voice' say 'There's a bunk here mate!' He teamed up with the bomb-aimer who gave the welcoming advice, and the two of them decided that they would try to remain together on operations. At Lichfield they were approached by an

Australian pilot and an air gunner. The pilot already had a navigator so needed just a wireless operator and a bomb-aimer to complete a Wellington crew. John 'was a bit dubious' because the others were from New South Wales and he was going to be a lone Victorian, but he decided the Murray River was not sufficient barrier and crewed up with the New South Welshmen. Later when John was wireless operator on a Lancaster especially equipped to take movie film, an Indian cameraman from the Royal Indian Air Force flew with the crew.

In spite of the fact that Canadians might have looked first for Canadians and Australians for Australians, the numbers milling around meant that it was often impossible to form an all-Australian crew. There might only be ten Australians in the room and none of them navigators or wireless operators. Peter Knox was one of ten bomb-aimers crewing-up at Silverstone in 1943. The bomb-aimers were the only Australians there and so knew they were going to be lone Australians in their crews. When Knox's crew finally came together they found they were uniform in rank and age – they were all sergeants aged between 18 and 21 – and, with the exception of their Brylcreemed wireless operator, they 'tended towards the quieter side of life in the mess'. Even at Lichfield most men crewing-up were not Australians. With Australia sending few gunners to England and the bomber requiring two gunners, Australian pilots and navigators often had to look for foreign gunners. But those Australians who, by choice or chance, ended up in crews of mixed nationality were generally satisfied with their lot. They point to two advantages. In an all-Australian crew the men were within the one system and therefore competing with each other for promotion, positions and awards, whereas when the men were from different air forces they were being measured simply as a crew, not against each other. Also, an Australian crew found it difficult to escape being judged as representative of Australia, and upholding the national reputation brought additional pressure on the crew as a whole, and on particular men within Australian crews. David Leicester, who flew over 60 operations without ever having a fellow Australian in his crew, says simply, 'there was no back-biting'. Bob Nielsen extends the advantage of the mixed crew to the multinational squadrons in which the success of one crew was shared by all crews, but when

the squadron was composed primarily of one nationality – English, Canadian or Australian – local jealousies often took over and what should have been a smooth-running, happy operation was sometimes quite the reverse. The envy shown by some crew members against their own countrymen was something that was hard to understand.

Those in all-Australian, or predominantly Australian, crews usually deny internal competition or any sense of increased pressure to perform, but at times familiar accents and uniforms that drew men together when crewing-up could come at a price.

Random factors were always important in forming crews. Frank Dixon said that on parade he stepped forward when he thought he heard his name called, but it was another man with the same surname and different spelling. That meant that Dixon and Dickson 'had a good look at each other'. They later introduced themselves and Dixon the Australian pilot and Dickson the English navigator became the basis of a crew. Ivan Pellas, fresh-faced, fair-haired and 21 years old, was sitting on his bunk when he was approached by an older Queensland navigator and his gunner mate. They had decided that they would look for a married man to be their pilot – they wanted a man with the added incentive of getting home to a loving wife. Ivan was surprised by their assumption and told them he was single, but they decided to stick with him. Ivan says that some 'instinct' quickly told them they had made the right decision. Don Charlwood watched other navigators teaming up with pilots but he waited, partly because he was hoping for a transfer to Coastal Command and also because he was uncertain how to choose a 'good' pilot. He fell into conversation with a pilot who was equally uncertain about how to judge his fellow men. That was how Geoff Maddern and Charlwood joined forces. Maddern was one of seven Western Australian pilots who were crewing-up that day, and before the end of 1943 he was the only one still flying. Five were dead and one was a prisoner of war.

At a break in a dance at Lichfield, Bill Manifold was attracted to a crowd giving all attention to a dark energetic speaker. The centre of attention was George Currie. He was talking to just one person – and the rest of the crowd had been engaged by George's energy and eloquence. He had his sleeve rolled up displaying an intriguing scar, a brutal tattoo that circled his arm. He was explaining how he was helping his mate run a fence across a flooded creek. Holding the barbed wire in a pair of pliers he had waded in, his mate playing out the coiled barbs. But the water rose, George stumbled, let go the barbed wire, it snapped around his arm and he went under. His mate, thinking he could haul him to the bank, pulled on the wire. With the wire digging deeper, George yelled every time his head emerged, but his mate thought he was being urged to greater effort, and – one thing leading to another – George's arm was a mess by the time his helpful mate landed him on the bank. It was only when the crowd gave him a burst of applause that George became conscious of the fact that he had more than one listener. Bill Manifold then became determined to have George as rear gunner. At crewing-up, George arrived just at the right time and Bill was able to recruit him.

Gunners had a reputation for wildness. It was based on the belief that many gunners had been scrubbed from pilot and navigator training because they had excelled in bars, brawls, parties and sport when they should have been studying. Armed with this doubtful knowledge, Bruce Otton and his wireless operator Bill Brett went into the gunners' hut and selected one man who was ironing a tie and another who was reading a book. The gunners asked to see Bruce and Bill's logbooks. A quick scan of a log, pausing on any green and red ink endorsements of high competence and incompetence, was an act of sensible caution, but not often applied. Picking crew was often like selecting a horse in a yard or a girl at a dance. You made your choice then the test of performance came later.

Nev Morrison entered a lasting partnership in the air from an encounter that was a result of luck, misdirected passion and the ridiculous. On New Year's Eve, 1943 he was at Silverstone, Northamptonshire:

> It was an extremely cold night, big log fires in the Pub, hundreds of RAAF types and one enormous WAAF who was the centre of attraction. I barely noticed her as I entered the den of iniquity, but it is amazing what a few ales can do – the more I drank the better she looked, and by 10 o'clock closing time she was only half the size and twice as beautiful! Naturally the boys were like 'bees round a honey pot', all arguing who was going to take her to the dance, and by some quirk of fate she came over to me, lifted me bodily off a stool and said, 'I'm going with you'. I vaguely remember trudging through the fields, falling over several times only to be lifted bodily to my feet by this massive female. Eventually we reached the Sgts' Mess and here I made a conspicuous entrance – I grabbed the lass's arm and dashed into the

A medley of pilots, bomb-aimers and gunners were assembled in a large room ... Suddenly, a voice said that we were to pick our crews ... I was riveted to the spot without the slightest idea of who to pick or why. I did not know who was there, but the others seemed to know exactly what they were doing. In a matter of minutes the boys in the room had re-formed into little relevant groups. I remained motionless as if shipwrecked. Then I noticed that there were five or six in a similar state and this is how I 'picked' my crew.

(Kenneth Marks)

dance, but alas the floor was heavily coated with French Chalk, and I shot halfway across the room on my back with this great WAAF on top of me!

The next thing I knew, a big hand grabbed me and pulled me up from the floor. Then an incoherent voice said, 'Ah, just what I need, a Wireless Op who drinks, what's your name, son?' We wrote each other's names down – it took us three days to decipher the writing and find one another.

That was how Nev Morrison met Ted Vidall. Soon they were on their way to 467 Squadron and 38 shared operations.

There was also the question of rank. A sergeant pilot might not want to fly with an officer navigator or gunner. There was no doubt that the pilot was in command in the air – he was captain of the ship – but around the station the differences in rank would be apparent. For a start the officer would eat and drink in the officers' mess, and the extent to which he might assert any other privilege of rank varied from person to person. Maddern, a sergeant pilot, wanted and got an all-NCO crew. Dan Conway, a pilot and an officer, was diffident about pressing others to gamble on his skills. But he was approached by an English

Soon after turning 21, Murray Maxton left the family farm at Kalgan, east of Albany, and entered Pearce Initial Training School just as the Japanese bombed Pearl Harbor. Having gained his pilot's wings at Geraldton, he completed further training in Victoria before sailing for England. At 18, his only brother, Eric, followed him into the air force and qualified as a wireless operator air gunner at Ballarat and Sale. At the Grand Hotel in Brighton waiting for a posting, Murray caught the mumps and suffered. While he recovered, his course mates moved on. Having completed advanced flying training, Murray was in London early in 1944 on his way to 27 OTU Lichfield. He stopped to have a cup of coffee, and there was his brother. Murray knew that Eric had got to England, and the last he had heard of him was that he was in Dumfries in Scotland. Eric explained that he too was on his way to Lichfield. Murray's illness and Eric's shorter course had brought them together. The brothers celebrated the coincidence with a few beers, and so arrived late at Lichfield. As other crews were already formed, Murray and Eric picked up four other uncommitted Australians, and began flying together. With the addition of an English engineer the crew converted to heavy bombers and then went to Lancaster Finishing School. At Binbrook they had a meeting with the station commander, Hughie Edwards, who said that, although it was against policy to allow brothers to fly together, as the crew worked efficiently it could stay together. But the brothers were not to tell their parents that they were in the same crew. Edwards flew with them on their first operation, bombing German army positions at Caen. Murray and Eric flew every operation together, and completed their tours with 460 Squadron late in 1944.

sergeant navigator who knew a wireless operator who knew a gunner, and the crew grew through a chain of associations. To get to know each other they visited local pubs where the bars made no distinction between officers and other ranks. Later, when he needed a flight engineer, he asked the 'spruce RAF sergeant' who came forward, 'Do you drink?' The sergeant hesitated, but confessed that he did. Conway immediately said, 'You'll do'. Conway had decided that the camaraderie of the pubs was important to the crew and was not to be jeopardised.

Crews could change during operational training, but that could mean disturbing two crews, and it was difficult to arrange without criticism and grievance. It was better to get the crew finalised at OTU. At Lichfield in 1943 Peter O'Connor first teamed up with a stocky, fair-haired pilot from Sydney. They remained 'pals' on the ground, but did not cooperate efficiently in the air. The pilot wanted course settings more quickly and O'Connor wanted the pilot to fly the given course more accurately. An instructor decided it was in everyone's interest to split them, but that meant O'Connor had to join a crew that was not so far advanced in training and had to repeat part of the OTU course. With the new pilot, another Australian, 'It was a perfect marriage from the word go'. The crew that O'Connor left did not survive.

Bill Brill's crew on his first tour was not unusual for its time and place. Brill and Doubleday had gone to Breighton with the first nine crews of the recently formed 460 (Australian) Squadron, and began flying operations in March 1942 before the one-pilot policy was introduced. In Brill's Wellington he usually had Les Shepard as second pilot. Brill had met Les, a bank clerk from Wagga Wagga, on the day they joined the air force. At Lichfield they had agreed to fly together, and they did so until Les took over a crew of his own. Hugh Thompson, MA BSc, the 'cool, calm navigator' from Surrey, was a biologist concerned with brain research. Dave Wilkinson the wireless operator, sometimes called Dracula, was a professional golfer and at Breighton he was in his home county of Yorkshire. The rear gunner, Kevin Light, was an aeronautical engineer from Sydney and, Brill said, 'one of the driest sticks I ever met'. Fred Lofts, front gunner and bomb-aimer, was a London salesman. When members of the regular crew were unavailable because they were sick or on courses, Peter Gome, an art student from Birmingham, flew four operations and Tom O'Donohue, a clerk from Brisbane and 'born humourist', also flew four. The accents on the Wellington intercom were from Australia city and bush, England north and south, educated and uneducated.

In the Lancaster navigated by Don Charlwood, Don was a Victorian,

Maddern was a Western Australian, Doug Richards (flight engineer) was Welsh, Frank Holmes (mid-upper gunner) was from Lincolnshire, Arthur Browett (rear gunner) was from Nottingham and Ted Batten (bomb-aimer) was from London. Batten, the oldest, was 30 and Frank Holmes (who transferred his poaching habits to the estates around the airfield) was 19. The Wellington crew that flew – and baled out – with Ted Coates was made up of two Canadians, three Australians and an Englishman. Ron Wall, a wireless operator, baled out of a Halifax over Denmark with four Britons, a New Zealander and a Rhodesian. Frank Dixon was the only Australian in his RAF crew when his plane was shot down over north Germany. David Scholes had three Victorians, a Queenslander, a Tasmanian and one Englishman in his crew and they made safe landings on return from operations 35 times. An increase in Australians in a crew was more likely late in the war when there was an attempt to place Australians in the nominally Australian squadrons. But even in those squadrons the greatest concentration of Australians was around 60 per cent. On 1 January 1945 the 2,621 men in the RAAF flying out of the British Isles were scattered through 214 RAF squadrons, and 110 of those squadrons had fewer than ten Australians on them. In Bomber Command all combinations of dominion, colony and county were possible, and Australians were often in crews that looked like the result of an Empire lottery.

Some men, especially those arriving early in England, could be sent to fill gaps in crews in operating squadrons. Then there were few choices and brief training. Tom Simpson, a lone Australian allocated to 97 Squadron at Coningsby late in 1941, was simply told that he was to fly as a gunner in a crew on a Manchester. The plane, turret and Browning machine gun were all strange to him, and he had the armourers give him a quick course on the Browning before he flew over enemy lands the next night. Bob Murphy, another who arrived at Coningsby when it was still a grass strip, says he was simply selected by a pilot and put in his crew. In his first two years in the air force Syd Johnson was always in a group being shifted to new places and tested with new experiences, but when he went to his first operating squadron, 156 Squadron, at Warboys in Huntingdonshire he was alone and different – other men were in crews and had been to war. The adjutant allocated him to a crew, but this was a crew of sergeants and he was an officer. He wanted the chance to get to know the rest of the crew other than when they 'were working for the government'. He was offered another crew.

Airmen feared being a squadron spare, the bomb-aimer called up to fly with the crew whose bomb-aimer was injured, sick or for other reasons relieved of flying duties. That meant flying with strangers, no reassuring voices in the earphones, no confidence in mutual competence, a high chance of filling-in again and again with inexperienced crews, and no friends to share the easing of post-flight tension and the generous breakfast prepared for returning crews. R.J. Cantillon, a wireless operator, was told at the last moment to replace a sick crewman in a Halifax. He found himself flying as mid-upper gunner with two Englishmen, a Scot, an Irishman, a Canadian and an American on their first operation deep into Germany. They were without teamwork and they survived long enough to bale out over Holland on the return flight.

Men who came as a replacement to an experienced crew could not hope to complete a tour in one crew. When the original crew finished its 30 operations the replacement had to shift to another crew and that might mean joining a sprog crew and again going through the hazards of those first four or five raids. Even where a crew began operations together, and all demonstrated the capacity to do their job when reality replaced practice, they were unlikely to do all their flying together. Men became ill, were wounded or involved in minor accidents. Cliff O'Riordan went to 'Quite a bright party' that started in the mess, tapered off in the early hours of the morning, then resumed at ten the next morning. It was some time later that O'Riordan tried to ride a horse, fell off and broke a bone in his arm. He missed operations.

Experienced men could be asked to fly with new crews, and some volunteered. Bob Murphy went with several crews on their first trip over enemy territory 'to point out the difference between light flak and heavy flak and what the different searchlights were and so on'. And to boost their confidence. After his first tour Arthur Doubleday sometimes flew with a scratch crew. Given that it was both his duty and his inclination to ensure that the bombs fell in the right

This whole crew was together about six months and we were all the very best of friends and the life of a crew of this kind makes the strongest friends that anyone could ever have.

(W/O Johnson, Canadian gunner and only survivor of a
Lancaster piloted by Kemble Wood of Sydney.)

place, this would have been both exhilarating and terrifying. Doubleday also learnt the danger of flying with unknown men. Over the target he heard the unfamiliar voice of the bomb-aimer say in a matter-of-fact voice, 'Flak on the port, skipper'. Normally, says Doubleday, a flat statement like that implied the flak was some distance away. But he had no idea that his scratch crew bomb-aimer was not given to excitement or exaggeration. This bomb-aimer meant exactly what he said. The flak was in fact on the port wing, and within a few feet of the bomb-aimer's nose.

Bob Kellow, who flew as wireless operator in Les Knight's dambuster crew, said that their crew was together through 27 successful raids: 'We had the utmost confidence in each other and were like a little band of brothers'. That crew of two Australians (Knight and Kellow), three Englishmen and two Canadians was unusually stable. But even in that group which was bound together by extraordinary training, operations and publicity, the flight engineer Ray Grayson, an Englishman, had joined late and was going to have to complete his tour with another crew, having done seven less operations than the rest of the crew. In fact they did not return from their 28th operation. Knight was killed, Kellow evaded capture and Grayson was one of those taken prisoner. Most crews, having selected themselves, were welded together by experience and tried to stay together. Often four or five stuck together, but very few crews flew a tour unchanged.

By the time most dominion men were being fed into Bomber Command, the slow, low-flying, under-powered and under-armed early bombers were being replaced by Wellingtons, Stirlings and Halifaxes. Stirlings and Wellingtons were then phased out of major operations in October and November 1943, and from 1944 the superior Mark III Halifax replaced less efficient models. From early 1942 the two most efficient and admired aircraft in Bomber Command, the Mosquito and Lancaster, were being delivered to operating squadrons. The sleek two-engine Mosquitoes, relying on their superior speed to keep out of trouble, marauded widely. Carrying a light bomb load, the Mosquitoes guided the main bomber stream by dropping marker flares at turning points and over the target; flew independent raids (sometimes on distant and specific targets); confused

German defences about the direction of the main force raid; gathered weather information; checked the damage done to targets; and fought the German night fighters. The Mosquito was much less likely than any of the main aircraft in Bomber Command to be destroyed by the enemy, and equalled the Lancaster in its low accident rate. But the Lancaster transformed the destructive capacity of the bomber.

In some of the major final raids of the war, there might be about 500 Lancasters, 250 Halifaxes and six Mosquitoes, and sometimes the Lancaster was the only heavy bomber. But the Halifax had its supporters. David Leicester, who flew 30 missions in a Halifax and more in a Lancaster, thought the later Halifaxes were easy to fly and could be manoeuvred quickly at height and when fully loaded, and that was essential to keep out of trouble. Ivan Pellas said 'We loved our Halibags'. The Halifax Mark III was, he claims, mild in manner, stable in flight, and while they could be flown with one finger, they could also be thrown around the sky. One Halifax of 158 Squadron, known as Friday the 13th, flew 128 missions. Grateful and astonished crews gave it an unofficial VC. It was also more difficult to bale out of a Lancaster. Aircrew in terminally damaged bombers had more chance of getting to and through the escape hatches on a Halifax than they did on a Lancaster. By the end of the war, however, the Lancaster was dominant. Although not used on a raid until 3 March 1942, Lancasters went to war nearly twice as often as any other heavy bomber: 156,192 times compared with the Halifaxes' 82,773.

When the crews of 103 Squadron at Elsham Wolds heard late in 1942 that they were changing from Halifaxes to Lancasters 'Pandemonium broke out … The dark days were over'. In September 1942, 460 Squadron was running out of operational aircraft; its Wellingtons were not being replaced because the

Before we were posted to our Squadron we enjoyed one of those experiences which enriched our lives. One day towards the end of April the day dawned without a cloud in the sky – a perfect day for flying. With that wonderful perversity of the nameless authorities on high, some commander with a soul decreed that our station should be closed for the day so that we could all enjoy the sunshine. Porky Bowering and I went for a memorable walk along the Trent to Newark. It was a pleasantly warm, still, clear day which lingered on late into the evening. He was to die within two months along with many others on the course. I have always thought that the officer who freed us from duties so that we could breathe in some true English country air in pure peace had true humanity.

(Peter Knox, bomb-aimer, 619 Squadron. Bowering was an 18-year-old Canadian gunner.)

squadron was about to convert to Halifaxes. When it had just five aircraft left, the squadron was taken off operations to learn to fly the four-engine Halifaxes, but on 20 October the squadron was suddenly switched to Lancasters, a 'very popular' decision. Lancaster crews cheered when they learnt that other bombers, such as Stirlings, were on the same raid. The Stirlings, lower and slower, were likely to draw the German night fighters.

Air Officer Commander-in-Chief Harris had no doubt that the Lancaster was the 'finest bomber of the war':

> Not only could it take heavier bomb loads, not only was it easier to handle, and not only were there fewer accidents with this than with other types; throughout the war the casualty rate of Lancasters was also consistently below that of other types. It is true that in 1944 the wastage of Lancasters from casualties became equal to, and at times even greater than, the wastage of Halifaxes, but this was the exception that proved the rule; at that time I invariably used Lancasters alone for those attacks which involved the deepest penetration into Germany and were consequently the most dangerous.

Harris so admired the Lancaster that he wanted to lose a year's production of Halifaxes while the factories were converted to Lancaster production. His superiors thought the cost too high and did not agree. Because Harris pressed as many Lancasters as possible into front-line service, few were available for training, and the crews began their heavy bomber flying on Wellingtons, Stirlings and Halifaxes. Often these aircraft were worn, battered, early models, and some of the enthusiasm for crews for the Lancaster was simply a result of encountering for the first time an aircraft that was new, the most advanced available, and carefully maintained.

Harris was right in his claim about the performance and reliability of the Lancaster. The number of Lancasters on operations that crashed in England was significantly less than that of Halifaxes, half that of Stirlings and one-quarter that of Wellingtons. In its capacity to avoid flak and fighters, the Lancaster's superiority was not so marked, but the Lancaster's loss rate was still marginally less than that of the Halifax, clearly less than that of the Wellington and markedly better than that of the Stirling. The enthusiasm of squadrons when they learnt they were converting to Lancasters might have been tempered had they known that their commander was now going to ask more of them and their machines, but on the figures – then yet to be recorded – their celebration was justified.

The Lancaster gave pilots hope, and they returned admiration, even affection. George Hawes encountered the Lancaster soon after it was used in operations. He told his family in April 1942, 'They certainly are wizard kites'. After his first solo flight in a Lancaster Geoff Maddern wrote in his diary: 'They are the most beautiful kites imaginable to fly – they climb like a bat out of hell, very light and responsive to the controls. The main trouble is trying to keep the speed down ... Quite easy to land – you feel them down like a Tiger Moth'. A few days later he tested it further by 'shooting up' Scunthorpe and then: 'Coming back feathered an engine and flew hands and feet off on three. Cut another engine and flew on two. It maintains height easily ... They're wizard'. At the other end of the aircraft Tom Simpson, a rear gunner, liked the stability of the Lancaster: 'To me every time that you climbed into the Lanc it seemed to say "Pleased to have you aboard. I'll try to make the flight comfortable" '. The Lancaster could climb on three engines; bent and battered it would get the crew home. Fifty years after he flew K for Kitty, Dan Conway wrote: 'Just to sit in the cockpit and admire its layout was a great pleasure'.

Arnold Easton flew 20 times as a navigator in a Lancaster 'F' for Freddie and 50 years later he stood beside its nose and cockpit resting wheel-less on the first floor of the Imperial War Museum in London. He asked himself whether his intense feeling for part of a machine was a 'type of love', or 'admiration', or 'just deep respect'. When he wrote about the war he chose not to write his memories, but to write a biography of his Lancaster, 'Old Fred – the Fox'. Old Fred had joined 467 Squadron in November 1943, and by the time it was carrying Easton over occupied Europe in 1944 it had been bruised, holed and patched many times. As a result, drag was great and Easton had to set a track out to the Welsh border to give Old Fred a chance to gain height before turning east and joining the bomber stream on its way to occupied Europe.

Brill and Doubleday left 27 OTU at Lichfield in December 1941 and flew together as first and second pilots on a training flight with 460 Squadron in

Soon after arriving in England Wade Rodgers, having grown up on a farm in western Victoria, asked Lady Francis Ryder and Miss MacDonald to find him a place in the country with 'home cooking'. They sent him to Kilpin Lodge on the River Ouse in East Yorkshire. There the Pilling family treated Wade and other Australians with casual generosity. Wade was to call Dick Pilling, 'Uncle Dick', and make several return visits. Kilpin Lodge was just south of Breighton where the Australians in 460 Squadron were flying their new Lancasters. Rodgers recalled, 'I said, "That's for me", as I watched the graceful brutes coming and going'. (Wade Rodgers, *There's no future in it.*)

January 1942. They had flown Wellingtons at OTU, 460 was equipped with Wellingtons, and Brill and Doubleday both flew their first operations as second pilots in Wellingtons on 12 March 1942. But the crews arriving in England soon

Stella Bowen, pencil sketch of Hector Harrison, for the painting, *Bomber Crew*. Bowen was 50 and Harrison 23 (the same age as Stella's daughter) when they met at Binbrook. The sketch catches an innocent, vulnerable, youthfulness. *AWM ART26252*.

after them were on their way to squadrons equipped with the true heavies, the Halifaxes and Lancasters. The OTUs kept using Wellingtons so that meant the crews had to go to other schools to learn to fly four-engine aircraft, and they now had to become familiar with more complicated navigational aids, bomb-aiming devices and target indicators, and follow more precise instructions on speed, route and concentration in the bomber stream. Gunner Cliff Halsall went from Lichfield to a gunnery school, a heavy conversion unit where the crew flew Halifaxes, and then to Lancaster Finishing School. By the time Brill (a pilot) went to 460 Squadron he had flown 33 hours at night; when Halsall (a gunner) reached 460 Squadron over two years later he had 53 hours night-flying in his log. The sequence – OTU, a heavy conversion unit equipped with lumbering Stirlings or outmoded Halifaxes, and then a brief introduction to the new Halifaxes and Lancasters – became standard.

Changes in aircraft and decisions about crew functions early in 1942 had their impact on crew composition. By deciding that the co-pilot should be replaced by a flight engineer and that the specialist bomb-aimer had to have the basic training of a navigator, Bomber Command effectively halved the demand for pilots (and recognised that the factories produced new planes faster than the schools trained new pilots), increased demand for navigators and created a new crew member – the flight engineer. As the Australians at home were not set up to recruit and train flight engineers, no Australian flight engineers were arriving at Bournemouth. The men with the sorts of skills most easily trained to be flight engineers were motor mechanics, particularly members of the ground crews already responsible for maintaining and repairing the Lancaster's Rolls Royce Merlin engines. But there were only about 1,800 Australian ground crew in England and the Middle East, less than half that required to service the aircraft in Australian squadrons. Also, the Australians were already dependent on British ground crew; some Australian ground crew were due for home leave because they had been overseas for a long time; demand for skilled tradesmen within Australia was high; and the British were not sympathetic to Australian aspirations to form all-Australian crews. As a result, few Australians trained as flight engineers to serve in Bomber Command. In April 1943, 460 and 467 Australian Squadrons had positions for 68 flight engineers. Just ten of them were filled by Australians.

Don Delaney was one of the scarce Australian flight engineers. Having left his inner-Sydney school at 13, Delaney took different jobs then qualified as a motor mechanic and worked in country New South Wales. By 1939 he was a Royal

Automobile Club patrolman. After training as a fitter in the RAAF, he sailed for England in 1941 and while working as ground crew with 460 Squadron applied and was accepted for training as a flight engineer. Before the end of 1942 Delaney was back at 460 Squadron wearing a sergeant's stripes and an aircrew wing. When Delaney went with Peter Isaacson to 156 Squadron in early 1943, Isaacson wrote home to Melbourne saying that he then had the first all-Australian crew in Pathfinders. Delaney had repaired flak and cannon-torn aircraft; he had spent many hours talking to crews; and he knew about the men and machines that left Breighton and did not return. The British and Australian ground crew who chose to retrain as aircrew did so with an immediate and detailed knowledge not available to other airmen – or to most other men who went into battle.

The crews formed at OTU spent about ten weeks flying together before going to a heavy conversion unit and being allocated a flight engineer. The flight engineer then joined a crew that had selected itself and come to know one another. The engineers, by trade and by the way they got to aircrew, were different. That difference was all the greater when the engineer was the only Englishman among a group of Australians. On leave, when the Australians made a dash for the Strand Palace, the English flight engineer went home – perhaps to Birmingham or Newcastle where he had recently finished his apprenticeship.

After Lancaster Finishing School the crews went to operating squadrons and war, but they did not, and could not, know if they were ready.

Bombing up long-serving 'S' for Sugar,
a Lancaster of 467 Squadron,
Waddington, Lincolnshire, 1944.
AWM SUK12154.

6

VICTORY, SPEEDY AND COMPLETE

The Royal Air Force had learnt a lot about bombing in a modern war, much of it gathered from lessons disastrous to men and machines, before most of the Australians in the Empire Air Training Scheme reached Bomber Command. At first the senior officers of Bomber Command were using new aircraft and new crews in new ways, and they had few lessons from theoretical or training exercises to guide them. Often they simply had to send crews on missions, assess the results, then decide whether a better result could have been obtained by more resolute or skilled crews, or whether other machines or techniques might have been more effective. They had to decide, too, whether circumstantial factors such as the wind, cloud or moonlight could have been decisive, and whether the outcome was sufficiently obvious to force agreement on their superiors in the air force and on army and navy commanders. Some lessons that seemed to show that costs outweighed benefits had to be repeated and repeated because there were always many variables, and senior officers did not readily abandon their self-interest and fixed positions.

> We can wreck Berlin from end to end if the U.S.A.A.F. will come in on it. It will cost us 400–500 aircraft. It will cost Germany the war.
>
> *(Sir Arthur Harris to Prime Minister, Winston Churchill, 3 November 1943.)*

GERMAN CITIES FACING DEATH-BLOW
One More R.A.F. Attack
London December 9 – One more full-scale R.A.F. attack on each of six big German cities would completely dispose of them, Air Vice-Marshal R.H.M. Saundby, Senior Air Staff Officer, Bomber Command, said in a speech yesterday.

The cities, which were terribly knocked about, were awaiting their death-blow, he added.

(Sydney Morning Herald, 10 December 1943.)

On 26 April 1937 German airmen bombed Guernica in Spain. Guernica, a Basque town, was known to be loyal to the Popular Front government and to oppose General Franco, but it was not a military target. It was well behind the front line and no troops were then retreating through the town and valley. Monday 26 April was market day, and the single peal of the church bell that warned of an air raid was heard by peasants in smocks as well as the town dwellers and the two Basque battalions quartered on the north of the town. The aerial attack went on for over three hours. High explosives shattered the town, incendiaries fell in the splintered wood, and low-flying aircraft machine-gunned fleeing people. Pablo Picasso's painting, *Guernica*, with its severed horse and animal and human heads with mouths open as though shrieking in startled anguish, became one of the most widely known and powerful images of the century. From 1939 it hung in the Museum of Modern Art in New York.

The bombing of Guernica, recorded so quickly and eloquently by the eye-witness journalist George Steer, and so aggressively by Picasso, made the world well aware of the danger of random assaults from the skies prior to September 1939. The world saw the brutality of the bombing, with civilians being punished for their sentiments and not their actions.

But the Royal Air Force drew its lessons more from its own history than from the immediate demonstrations of air power in the rest of the world. In 1915 Major-General Hugh Trenchard became commander of the Royal Flying Corps, and in each of the four years of his wartime command German Zeppelin airships and aeroplanes bombed England. In the most serious raid of 13 June 1917, German 'monster aircraft of the Gotha type' crossed the coasts of Essex and Kent and bombed London, leaving 162 killed and 432 injured. In Poplar, on the edge of London, bombs fell on a school and 'forty-six small children in the kindergarten stage of life were blown to pieces'. On the Western Front Allied aircraft crossed the trenches and penetrated over 100 miles into German territory to bomb ammunition and store dumps, railways, and soldiers' camps. They reached centres of iron and chemical production where their small bomb loads threatened disruption rather than disaster. On the eastern front and in the Middle East British bombers were more effective, particularly against the Turks in Palestine.

Arthur Harris, born and educated in England, went to Rhodesia when he was 16. He returned to England to fight in World War I, joined the Royal Flying Corps and led a squadron trying to intercept German bombers. He stayed in the Royal Air Force, and in the immediate postwar period served on the North-West

Frontier. There, he said, the airmen 'always' gave the tribesmen 'fair warning before their villages were destroyed, and casualties were extremely few'. He said the army could then walk in and 'take the credit and the K.C.B'. Harris again used his squadron as police and strike force in Iraq. When 'a tribe started open revolt', he sent an aircraft over the defiant villages and warned them by loud speaker and leaflet that if the rebellion continued the villages would be destroyed. If that was not enough to re-impose British order, the bombers destroyed the villages and kept the people from their homes until they gave up. This, Harris was convinced, cost less in time, money and lives than an army pursuing the tribesmen through their homelands. Other nations apparently agreed that the bomber was an effective way of controlling unruly frontiers: the French, Spanish and Italians bombed civilians in North Africa, and the United States bombed Nicaraguans. Early in 1939 Harris was in Palestine demonstrating to the British army the utility of the aeroplane in modern warfare. By September 1939 Harris was convinced that the bomber would be the 'predominant weapon' of the next war, and control of the air would be 'the predominant factor in other operations either on sea or land'.

In 1928 Air Marshal Sir Hugh Trenchard, in his tenth year as Chief of the Air Staff, prepared a memorandum for his fellow Chiefs of Staff to 'lay down explicitly … the object to be pursued by an Air Force in war'. The aim, he said, would be to destroy the factories that made the guns and aeroplanes and all the other equipment needed by a country at war, attack the store houses that held them, the railways and roads on which they were carried and the docks where they were loaded. There would be 'incidental destruction of civilian life and property' when factories were bombed but that was inevitable. The forcing of munition workers to flee from their tasks or wharf labourers to abandon loading ships, and the general lowering of worker efficiency and morale were, Trenchard said, all legitimate aims. While no ratified international law controlled bombing, what was illegitimate in draft codes was 'the indiscriminate bombing of a city for the sole purpose of terrorising the civilian population'. Trenchard and others, hoping to appear to conform with what was internationally acceptable in war, tried to make a sharp distinction between an attack on a centre of population and a factory making aeroplanes, although that factory might employ civilians and be alongside civilian housing. But Trenchard came close to arguing that the greatest impact of the bomber as a weapon of war would come from the apparently incidental killing and terrorising of civilians.

In the next war, Trenchard said, the bombing of the enemy's means to make war was inevitable. All sides had taken steps towards this in the last war, and in the next they would send out their waves of bombers without scruple. Constant bombing and the inescapable false alarms and panic that would follow would quickly destroy the will and capacity of a nation to wage war. The bombers could, and perhaps would, decide a war.

If the bomber had such terrible potential, then it followed that the air force in the next war would be the service best able to mount a great strategic offensive; it would not just be providing tactical weapons assisting the army to defeat the enemy on the field of battle. And if the air force was the decisive weapon then that gave it an importance in planning and a priority in funding that other services did not like. Using rational argument, prejudice and smug indifference they would oppose the elevated position of what they saw as a new and minor component of His Majesty's forces.

Over the next decade senior military officers gained some idea of what bombers might do, but were uncertain how, or even if, they could be opposed. It was likely that bomber forces would be on their way within hours of the start of a 'war of the first magnitude with civilised nations'. Britain could expect more than a thousand casualties on the first day, and a high rate of casualties would continue. The bombers could come by day or night, and within weeks they might have delivered the 'knockout blow'. The government could give some protection to its citizens by providing air raid warnings and shelters, special fire-fighting services, and enforcing blackouts, but that, Britain's senior military officers conceded, might merely prolong the devastation. The extent to which fighter planes could intercept and shoot down the bombers, or anti-aircraft fire could

> The aim of the Air Force is to break down the enemy's means of resistance by attacks on objectives selected as most likely to achieve this end ... Such objectives may be situated in centres of population in which their destruction from the air will result in casualties also to the neighbouring civilian population. What is illegitimate, as being contrary to the dictates of humanity, is the indiscriminate bombing of a city for the sole purpose of terrorising the civilian population. It is an entirely different matter to terrorise munition workers (men and women) into absenting themselves from work or stevedores into abandoning the loading of a ship with munitions through fear of air attack upon the factory or dock concerned. Moral effect is created by the bombing in such circumstances but it is the inevitable result of a lawful operation of war – the bombing of a military operation.
>
> *(Sir Hugh Trenchard, 1928.)*

destroy them, was uncertain. Some experts thought the bombers would always get through. If that were so, then the only defence for a nation, and the only policy for a government, was to have a bomber force equal to that of any enemy and therefore able to threaten the same or greater damage.

In a war to be decided by marauding bombers the British thought they would be at a disadvantage. If the Germans had bases on the French or Dutch coasts their bombers could make short flights, check their navigation as they crossed the English coast and easily locate a centre with high population density and factories supplying the armed services. By contrast, British aircraft would have to make long flights over enemy territory, taking them beyond the range of escorting British fighters and giving the Germans a longer time to put their own defences into action. German people and industries were more dispersed, and that increased problems for pilots trying to find and annihilate them. And German cities in the east were at the limit or beyond the range of the existing British bombers.

Throughout the 1930s, scientists were changing balances between offence and defence in a future aerial war, and adding new unknowns. One of the most important of these was radar – radio detection and ranging. By bouncing radio wave pulses against a distant object the scientists could find out its shape, how far away it was and the direction in which it was travelling. In 1935 the first British radar station began operating and by 1939 the Chain Home system covered much of the coast. Enemy bombers would no longer have surprise on their side, but whether the forewarned defences could do much about them was still not certain. The evidence from the rest of the world seemed to strengthen the arguments of those who predicted slaughter from the skies. The Japanese in China, the Italians in Libya and Abyssinia, and the Spanish in Morocco had certainly demonstrated that the aeroplane was a formidable weapon, and – as in Spain – it caused havoc among civilians.

At the end of 1938, Londoners taking a quick read of a paperback on the tube or lingering over a pint in the Old Bell Tavern in Fleet Street were warned that they were in danger. A new orange Penguin Special, *The Air Defence of Britain*, told them that there was no defence against the bombers of Germany. The world, the Penguin experts said, had 'gone savage'. And in a coming war there was no doubt civilians would be targets; if the Germans did not drop gas then that would simply be because they thought that blast and fire would do greater damage; and German bomber crews would machine gun roads crowded with refugees. London, with 9,000,000 people within 15 miles of Charing Cross, would 'receive the first and heaviest air blows'. The bombers sweeping in from the sea, their pilots guided by the Thames, would be over London within ten minutes of crossing the coast, and the city's defences would have no chance to react. Not even heavy cloud could protect a target so large from the bombers. Londoners learnt that at Barcelona the Italian bombers came in high from the sea, cut off their engines before crossing the coast and only opened their throttles after they had dropped their bombs. The bombers were leaving before the anti-aircraft gunners responded. The numbers, power and persistence of the bombers in Spain and in China, Londoners were warned, would be just a 'tithe' of what could be expected in a war between major powers. But one lesson from Spain and China was clear: 'the bomber can get through'. The Penguin readers were told that by taking war into another dimension, avoiding a clash between enemy ground forces, making fortresses and natural land barriers irrelevant, and securing victory by destroying the capacity and will of the civilian population to support an army, the bombers were not just bringing a new and terrible weapon to war, they were changing the very nature of war. Just in case those readers on the underground were not sufficiently alarmed, G.T. Garratt asked them to consider the impact of concentrated bombing of Euston and King's Cross railway stations, and of the panic that might follow the dropping of both gas and high explosives on a foggy, still London.

On the eve of war in Europe, the sorts of readers who read the Penguin Specials and the current affairs journals could share the fears of their military planners. The civilian readers knew almost nothing of the radar warning system being put in place, but even those senior officers who were fully informed were uncertain about how effective it would be. The writers, 'specially qualified' to enlighten the British public on their vulnerability, did not even offer a sense of moral superiority over an enemy that was about to bomb them into quick submission. Air Commodore L.E.O. Charlton told them that the thing that decided World War I was that the British naval blockade eroded the German people's will to make war. By forcing food shortages so severe that people died of malnutrition, the British themselves had been 'baby killers'. The British had not then doubted that they were right to impose the blockade that made no discrimination between soldier and civilian, young and old, men and women, and they could not now expect the enemy to leave idle a weapon that was equally indiscriminate, but more terrible and more immediate in its impact.

In the years immediately before the war the British made critical decisions. To counter the threat of enemy bombers, they would have their own; they would develop four-engine heavy bombers. That prewar decision enabled Britain to have better long-range bombers than Germany before the war was half over. And although many still believed that the only counter to bombers was the threat of an equal or greater force of bombers, Britain also invested in fighters and early warning systems, especially radar. By 1940 Britain would have the means to defend British skies. Strangely, the British thought little about protecting their own bombers from high performance fighters and the gadgets of the enemy boffins that could warn of the coming of bombers and find them in the night sky.

When Britain declared war on Germany on 3 September 1939 no German bombers attempted to deliver the knockout blow on Britain, and the British did not attempt a pre-emptive strike. The German forces were engaged on their east, and the Luftwaffe were attacking points of Polish resistance, striking communications and factories and bombing civilians in Warsaw. In their air force the Germans had a fearsome weapon, but they were using it in conjunction with their land forces. The bombers were not, perhaps not yet, single-handedly destroying the will and capacity of peoples to make war.

Guy Gibson was a young Englishman who joined the RAF in 1936, not to be in the military but to fly. He thought of himself as 'no serviceman'. On 31 August 1939 he was sailing off Monkstone Beach with Ann ('blonde and pretty') asleep on cushions at the back of the boat, when a young boy swam out to him with a telegram in his mouth. The telegram told Gibson to return to his unit immediately. Freddy Bilby, just down from Oxford, picked up Gibson in his 1928 Alvis, and they passed everything on the road. Beyond St. Edward's, Guy's old school, they stopped at a pub for a convivial meeting with Freddy's friends, including some in the Oxford University Squadron. After a dozen cans and a 1928 burgundy, Gibson caught the train to Lincoln and reported to 83 Squadron at Scampton. Nothing much happened for the next two days with the crews 'standing by'. There was Jack Kynoch, 'a swimming champion', Pitcairn-Hill who had played 'rugger' for the RAF, and Allen Mulligan and Ellis Ross, two Australians who had joined the RAF in 1937. The airmen talked of girls and parties, played cricket on the tarmac, and listened to gramophone records in the mess. Each morning Gibson's batman woke him with the words, 'Here's your cup of tea, Sir ... Shall I run you a bath, Sir?' On 4 September 1939, the second day of the war, the novice crews were ordered to attack the German ships at the entrance to the Kiel Canal. As they had never flown their Hampdens with a bomb load, they were given advice on what effect the extra weight would make to their aircraft. The station intelligence officer read from a pamphlet that it was best to attack from 3,000 feet, above the height of machine-gun fire and below the heavy flak. They were warned more than once that on no account were they to bomb civilian targets, including the dockyards. They took a technical innocence and a purity of intent to war.

Recalling the beginnings of war after nearly five years of battle, Gibson revealed much of the style of the RAF in 1939, and of how airmen wanted others to see them. They were not career army officers, but the sorts of chaps who drove fast cars, casually mentioned that they played a bit of rugger when in fact they had tried out for England, went to a lot of parties, knew how to drink and dine well, had friends at Oxford and Cambridge and always had attractive women waiting for a telephone call – and a weekend. Leonard Cheshire, the other English Bomber Command pilot who was to be as famous as Guy Gibson, was later represented as having all those qualities. From being a boarder at Stowe school where he had worked hard and excelled at tennis, Cheshire went to Merton College Oxford to do law. Elegantly dressed, with his super-charged Alfa Romeo hidden in a back street, Cheshire indulged in rags, pranks, parties, serial girlfriends and forays to a London dog track to gamble and mix with riff-raff. In the Oxford University Squadron he learnt to fly, but for all of his last minute cramming through the night he missed first-class honours in law. Not attracted to practising as a solicitor, Cheshire applied for a commission in the air force a few months before the outbreak of the war, and was posted to

Two Australians, Allen Mulligan and Ellis Ross – 'Mull' and 'Rossy' as they were known to Guy Gibson – had both joined the RAAF as air cadets in 1936, transferred to the RAF on short-service commissions in 1937, became Flying Officers in 1939, served with 83 Squadron, won DFCs, and flew their last mission on 13 August 1940 against the Dortmund-Ems Canal. In a low-level attack against the waterway connecting the Ruhr with the North Sea, Ross was shot down in flames and killed, but Mulligan managed to crash-land his damaged Hampden, an airscrew coming through the side of the cockpit and pinning him in the bomber. The Germans took over four hours to release him, 'but' Mull said, 'there was no hurry, they could have taken 4 years'. Mulligan was on his 24th operation; and while a prisoner of war he learnt that he had been awarded a DFC for 'utmost skill, determination, courage and devotion to duty'.

102 Squadron, which was then equipped with Whitley bombers. He carried with him the suggestion of flannels, boating, common room conversation, periodic excess, an attraction to the excitement of speed and gambling, a dedication to superior performance, and an apparent indifference to his own excellence when it was conspicuously displayed. Gibson and Cheshire were not alone in values and background; at the start of the war the Oxford University Squadron supplied some 700 pilots to the RAF. In spite of the early deaths of so many in Bomber Command, there was still a lingering hint of the 1939 air force in the officers' messes when most of the Australians began arriving in 1942.

At the end of the war, Flying Officer A.T. ('Ack') Loveless was asked to write something of his background. He said that he had been to Melbourne Boys High where he 'had indulged in the odd drop of sport – football, rowing, hockey'. There had also been the 'occasional spot of trouble (a court case for breaking a fire alarm)', and once or twice he had 'incurred the wrath' of his father when he 'pranged his car'. Describing his initiation as a pilot, he said: 'on my first solo flight in a Tiger I put down a respectable landing, but suddenly ground looped and nicely dug my port wing into the turf'. Loveless had taken over the style of the prewar RAF – 'the odd drop of sport', the 'spot of trouble', the careful omission of any suggestion of competence as a scholar or sportsman, and the understated and humorous account of his first flight. The style survived even though aircrews were transformed in their expertise, and in their realisation of the terrible tasks they faced.

From September 1939 the RAF learnt much about a bombing war. In February 1941 Hughie Edwards flew his first operation in a Blenheim. It had a crew of three: himself as pilot, a navigator (wearing an 'O' on his badge because he was known by the World War I term of 'Observer') and a wireless operator. The navigator and wireless operator also manned the guns. The Blenheim was not an old aeroplane – it had first been flown in 1935 – and early in 1939 the RAF was still trying to speed up production to get this new bomber to the squadrons.

Edwards was born in Fremantle in 1914 and left Fremantle Boys High at the age of 14. He was underemployed and unemployed until he joined the coastal artillery in 1932. A well known sportsman with South Fremantle, Edwards won a place in a course for pilot officer cadets at Point Cook. Having transferred from the RAAF to the RAF in 1936, he flew slower and older twin-engine planes before being allowed to fly the faster, valuable Blenheim in 1937. His crew were ground staff who volunteered to fly – for the thrill and the extra shilling a day in flight pay.

Of the other main bombers used in the early months of the war, the Hampden had a crew of four, the Whitley five and the Wellington six. Only the Wellington – durable in spite of its fabric covered frame that creaked and groaned under stress – continued to be an effective operating aircraft. In the Wellington there was a pilot, a second pilot, a navigator who left his maps and tables to act as bomb-aimer, a wireless air gunner, and a gunner. Soon the air gunners were given specialist training, but it was two years before the first of the seven-crew bombers (the Stirlings and Halifaxes) were delivered to the squadrons. It took three years of war before the second pilots became flight engineers and the navigators, no longer called observers, were given more specialist training in navigation than pilots. Navigators then graduated from training with rank equal to that of pilots and had no other function other than to navigate. The bomb-aimer became an assistant navigator in flight as well as ensuring that the aircraft was in the right place when he released the bombs.

Given that crew functions and numbers were changing over the first three years of the war, and equipment and tactics were always changing, there was little that was fixed or 'traditional'. The men who sent crews on operations were learning how to do their job by looking at what happened to those crews. The Americans could offer little advice. The 8th US Army Air Force did little bombing in Europe until late in 1942, and in any case the B-17 Flying Fortress had a crew of ten and flew in daylight. Even the enemy, from its experience of bombing England in the blitz of 1940–1941, could have revealed little: its Junkers 88 had four crewmen and they sat together in the nose of the aircraft. Australian senior officers and airmen could learn something about modern multi-engine bombers after the arrival of the twin-engine Hudson in 1940 and from flying boats, particularly after the Catalinas were ferried across the Pacific early in 1941. But the Hudson, with a crew of four, and the Catalinas, with a crew of eight to ten, were vastly different in purpose and performance from the Halifaxes and Lancasters. To be one of a crew of seven in a night bomber was to be dependent on and subjected to the world's most advanced technology, and it was to undergo a new and extreme experience again and again.

The changes in the performance of aircraft were more easily measured. The Blenheim could carry a 1,000 pound bombload, the Lancaster up to 14,000 pounds. So when, after nearly two years of war, Bomber Command sent Hughie Edwards to lead 12 Blenheims on a raid on Bremen on 4 July 1941, they carried less weight in bombs than one Lancaster could carry. On 14 January 1944, 496 Lancasters bombed Brunswick, on 20 January, 495 bombed Berlin, and on 21 January, 421 bombed Magdeburg. Just by the weight of bombs dropped, those Lancasters were 500 times more destructive than the Blenheims that attacked Bremen at such cost and to slight effect. And the Lancasters were only part of the attacking force. This was a change in a weapon comparable to the change from a single shot rifle to a machine gun – from one bullet to a stream of 500 bullets. What bombers could do had been transformed. They could now do what prewar lay and military experts had said they would do. Throughout the war the way bombers were used was determined more by what bombers could do than by what commanders wanted to do or what was morally

This bomber shows a kangaroo with a bomb in a joey's pouch. The usual bomb symbol marking each raid has been replaced with a foaming beer mug. On a Lancaster, 467 Squadron, Waddington, 1943. *AWM UK0466.*

desirable. And what bombers could do had to be learnt in practice; it was constantly changing and was always at the limits of the men and machines.

After the Germans attacked Poland on 1 September, the American President, Franklin Roosevelt, appealed to those already at war and those about to go to war not to bomb 'civilian populations or unfortified cities'. Britain agreed immediately, and after some delay Germany welcomed the appeal and said it would conduct the war 'in a chivalrous and human manner'. But by then the Germans had bombed Polish cities. Hitler made a gesture of compliance with the Roosevelt appeal by calling Warsaw a 'fortified' city.

Immediately after Britain declared war on 3 September 1939, Bomber Command sent its aircraft on missions, but they dropped no bombs. The bombers searched the North Sea for German warships and at night flew over German cities in the west, from Hamburg to the Ruhr, dropping leaflets. They found no ships and all aircraft returned safely. The influence of over five million leaflets on the Germans as they ventured out in the autumn morning is unknown. The British senior commanders had decided in 1938 that propaganda leaflets would have a 'most useful effect'. They even thought that in the Ruhr they might 'cause great panic and seriously disorganize the industrial life'. In spite of the scepticism of the crews who tossed them into the night, Bomber Command persisted in scattering leaflets across Germany and occupied Europe. 'Bumphleteering' or 'bumph chucking' became a common introductory operation for new crews.

On 4 September, 15 Blenheims and 14 Wellingtons took off in mid-afternoon to attack German ships off Wilhelmshaven. Ten returned without having found the ships, and of the 19 that tried to bomb the German fleet seven were shot down by anti-aircraft fire, over one-third of the attacking force. Bomber Command had suffered its first casualties. On 14 December, 12 Wellingtons tried to find a way to attack German shipping through cloud, flak and fighters, and five were shot down. On 18 December the Wellingtons tried again. This time, to protect themselves from flak, they were to bomb from above 10,000 feet. The 21 Wellingtons, flying in close formations of six mutually protective aircraft, bombed in daylight in clear visibility. As they cleared the flak, German fighters attacked and shot down 12 of them. In those two raids in December half of the 36 Wellington bombers that left England had been destroyed, and they had been flying just to the close north-west German ports, not across enemy territory. The German fighters and anti-aircraft gunners had both shown that they could shoot down Wellingtons. Obviously the British bombers were not always going to get through. But senior RAF officers were not sure why. Perhaps more determined pilots could have kept tighter formation, more skilful gunners could have protected the bombers, and better armed and more durable Wellingtons might have defied flak and fighters. Although the arguments and losses continued, by April 1940 Bomber Command decided that the heavy bombers would have to have the protection of night. The light bombers, such as the Blenheims, were left to try to attack brazenly in daylight.

Changes in the war on land and sea constantly influenced the tasks set the bombers. When the Germans attacked Norway in April 1940 the bombers flew long missions against enemy aerodromes and shipping on the south-western Norwegian coast. (They did not have the range to reach the distant Norwegian ports.) When the blitzkrieg rolled across Belgium, Holland and France and forced the British back against the sea at Dunkirk, the bombers attacked German troop concentrations, railway junctions and airfields. As the Germans threatened to invade England, the bombers destroyed barges assembled to transport the invading force across the Channel. When the German submarines and aircraft threatened to cut Britain from Lend Lease and aid flowing across the Atlantic from countries within the Empire, Bomber Command was instructed to attack the ports used by the U-boats, the factories that built their diesel engines, the shipyards where they were launched, and the factories and aerodromes of the Focke-Wulf Condors that also preyed on British merchant shipping. As well, the bombers were 'gardening' – mining the shipping lanes, the waters where the U-boats were trialled, and the ports and waterways used by German ships.

What was said to be a military target widened as the Germans swept across northern Europe. The British night bombers dropped incendiaries into the Black

It seems probable that a very serious shortage of food may be felt in Europe this winter. The time to attack crops in Germany is within the next two or three weeks, and the new 'pellet' incendiary will be available in quantity early in July. You should be prepared to distribute these 'pellets' over selected areas of Germany immediately after the current moon phase.

(Directive to Commander-in-Chief, Bomber Command, 20 June 1940.)

Forest and the ripening autumn crops, but that did little to diminish German supplies or divert German resources to fire-fighting. On 14 May 1940 the Germans bombed Rotterdam, destroying the old city centre and killing civilians. They aimed not at a military target, but at the will of the Dutch to keep fighting – it had taken nearly nine months of war before the terror of the bomber was unleashed on the Western Front. The British War Cabinet responded by allowing Bomber Command to attack targets beyond the Rhine. On the night of 15 May nearly 100 aircraft were sent to bomb factories and railways in the Ruhr. Although it was more a matter of self-interest than morality, British leaders were still arguing for restraint. The British knew that whatever they could do then, the German bombers could return fourfold. The French, with less capacity to reply with bombs, were even more worried about provoking a bombing war.

At the start of its intense aerial assault in the Battle of Britain, the Luftwaffe attacked military targets, especially the RAF in the air and on the ground. But accidentally and deliberately, German bombs fell on British cities. On 24 August the Germans bombed Birmingham, Bristol and other towns, and for the first time bombs fell in central London. The next night British aircraft dropped their first bombs on Berlin. As German hopes for immediate invasion faded, Hitler ordered the Luftwaffe to attack 'by day and night', destroy the British capacity to wage war, and punish the British people for their resistance. On 7 September, 180 bombers left over 400 Londoners dead, 1,600 injured, and destruction through the city and suburbs. Through September and October the industrial towns and ports suffered: Birmingham, Coventry, Nottingham, Clydeside, Merseyside, Plymouth, Portsmouth, Southampton, Bristol, Hull, Newcastle, Belfast, Cardiff, Swansea and Bristol. On 21 September 1940 the British Air Ministry and the Chief of the Air Staff directed the commander of Bomber Command to cause the 'greatest possible dislocation both to the industrial activities and to the civil population [of Berlin] generally'. To do this he was to strike at the city's power sources. On 30 October 1940 he was told to attack German oil plants, but when weather or other factors made this impossible he was to strike cities with as 'many heavy bombers as possible'. The bombers were to carry 'high explosive, incendiary, delay-action bombs with perhaps an occasional mine' – the weapons of maximum dislocation in time and space. On 9 July 1941 he was informed that a review of the enemy had disclosed that one of Germany's 'weakest points' was the 'morale of the civilian population', and that the most satisfactory results would be obtained by 'heavy, concentrated and continuous attacks of large working-class and industrial areas'. Three significant steps had then been taken: an 'area', not a specific target such as a railway yard or a particular factory or a dockland, was to be bombed; civilians at home, and not just the places where they worked, were to be attacked; and the intent now was to destroy the morale of the German population. It followed that if civilian morale was the target then burning and blast should be combined because of their greater impact, and harassing raids and delayed action bombs should be used to prolong the terror and impede fire services and repair. 'Area' bombing of civilians was never the only aim of Bomber Command, and in the directives it appeared secondary, but policy had gradually come to allow, even demand, the relentless destruction of civilians.

Attempting to carry out the new policy on 16 December 1940, Bomber Command sent 134 aircraft to destroy Mannheim, a river port on the junction of the Neckar and Rhine rivers. Mannheim was a commercial and manufacturing centre and had been the home of Mozart and Schiller. It was not primarily a military centre, and the bombs were not concentrated on those factories or the transport system that served the armed services. The first wave of Wellingtons aimed their incendiaries at the centre of Mannheim, and the following planes tried to feed the fires. This was Bomber Command's first deliberate area attack, and this was the largest number of bombers that it had sent to destroy a single target. The crews said that they had left Mannheim in flames. Later photographs showed that there had been some damage but it was scattered, with many bombs falling outside the centre of the city. Of the 34 citizens of Mannheim killed, just one was a soldier. The French army had been more effective when it burnt Mannheim in 1689. The first 100-bomber raid had neither confirmed nor denied that a concentration of British bombers could destroy a German city.

In February 1942 Arthur Harris moved into Springfield, 'a pleasant old-fashioned house', and each morning he drove the five miles to Bomber Command headquarters situated in wooded country at High Wycombe in Buckinghamshire, and there he assumed office as Commander-in-Chief. Confident, opinionated and aggressive, Harris took with him his conviction that the bomber was the 'only hope of getting at Germany, and I determined to see to it, as far as I could, that the offensive got there, and got where it hurt'. Harris, who had commanded 5 Group in Bomber Command and been Deputy Chief of the Air Staff, thought that events had so far confirmed his belief that bombers could destroy the capacity of Germany to wage war – but he was the sort of man who normally found his opinion strengthened by events.

Victory, speedy and complete awaits the side which first employs air power as it should be employed. [Germany had missed its chance by a 'hair's breadth', and now Britain had the opportunity.] We are free, if we will, to employ our rapidly increasing air strength in the proper manner. In such a manner as would avail to knock Germany out of the War in a matter of months, if we decide upon the right course.

(Sir Arthur Harris to Winston Churchill, 17 June 1942.)

Lübeck was a Baltic port of 120,000 people with medieval buildings, canals and modern factories, including one that made the oxygen equipment for U-boats. On the night of Palm Sunday, 28 March 1942, over 200 British aircraft dropped 400 tons of incendiaries followed by high explosives on the narrow streets and congested half-wooden buildings of the old city. Lübeck had been chosen because it looked like its crowded wooden buildings would burn, and they did. Half the city was soon shattered or reduced to ashes, over 300 people were killed and many injured. At Lübeck the bombers demonstrated that they could get through, and they could destroy German cities.

Through 1941 many factors had been pushing British political and military leaders to send massed bombers over concentrations of civilians. Within Bomber Command and the War Cabinet no one had been sure just how many bombers were finding their targets. In August David Butt, from the British war cabinet secretariat, studied over 600 photographs taken by night bombers who thought they had bombed their designated target. He decided that just one-third of the bombs had fallen within five miles of the centre of the target. But in his survey he had included raids on French ports, and they were easy to find. When he looked just at flights over the Ruhr, where the bombers were nearly one hundred miles inland and the valleys lay under a haze of industrial smog, he found that few crews dropped bombs anywhere near the target. With the help of a full moon only two-fifths got within five miles, and on other nights just one-fifteenth got within five miles.. Had Butt taken into account those aircraft that took off but did not bomb because of equipment failure, accident, enemy fire, weather or simply getting lost, then his figures would have been even worse. One-third of the crews despatched did not claim to have bombed the target. That meant that on a moonless night one plane in 20 might get within five miles of a target in the Ruhr – five bombers in a hundred hitting an area of 75 square miles. The chance of a particular factory being hit was remote.

From the photographs of bombing raids the British also learnt that their bombs were not as potent as they thought they were. The German raids on

Britain were more destructive than the British raids on Germany, and that seemed to be because the Germans used more incendiaries. Fire did much of the damage. To get the maximum destruction from the few aircraft flying over the target, the British needed to use bigger and better bombs and more incendiaries. But incendiary bombs – light and numerous as they showered from the bomb bays – were not designed for precision bombing. After two years of war the War Cabinet was at last finding out what the bombers were doing and could do.

By mid 1941 British commanders had few strategic options. The army, defeated in western Europe, defeated in Greece and Crete and fighting desperately in North Africa, would be in no position to attack in Europe for years. In any case, nobody wanted a repeat of the fighting on the Western Front of World War I. The navy, if it failed to protect the convoys crossing the Atlantic, or if it was defeated in the Mediterranean, or if it failed to intimidate enemy movement on the west coast of Europe, could lose the war. It could not win it. Fighter Command had demonstrated its defensive significance in the Battle of Britain. But the fighters with their short range could not attack the enemy much beyond the French coast. Only the bombers, it seemed, could carry the fight to the enemy, and perhaps, just perhaps, deliver the fatal blows.

The German bombing of British cities was already declining when Germany began shifting much of its air power east. On 22 June 1941 Germany invaded Russia and the Luftwaffe was committed to supporting an army that was advancing on a front stretching from the Baltic to the Black Sea. For the British, the threat of the fourfold retaliation by German bombers was fading. It was in Britain's interest to keep Russia in the war, and that meant Britain had to keep German resources at home or in the west.

Put starkly, after two years of war the bombers were Britain's only weapon of attack, the only means of taking the war to Germany itself, the only force that

The Prime Minister [Churchill] then described the bombing activity over Germany and his hopes for substantial increase with American participation. Here came the first agreement between the two men. Stalin took over the argument and said that homes as well as factories should be destroyed. The Prime Minister agreed that civil morale was a military objective, but the bombing of working men's houses came as a by-product of near-misses on factories. The tension began to ease and a certain understanding of common purpose began to grow. Between the two of them, they soon destroyed most of the important industrial cities of Europe.

(Averell Harriman, present at the Churchill–Stalin meeting of 12 August 1942.)

could relieve pressure on the Russians and the only chance to win the war. The new Commander-in-Chief, Arthur Harris, was the bombers' aggressive advocate and he offered Churchill, 'Victory, speedy and complete'. Bomber Command had learnt that its aircraft could not fly by day without excessive losses, and at night most could not drop their bombs within five miles of the centre of a target. But the bombers had shown that if 200 or more of them attacked a densely populated area they could, sometimes, wreak havoc. They might just be able to do what their fervent supporters said they could do. The pragmatic and easy conclusion was to do what was almost the only thing that Britain and the bombers could do – bomb cities.

The Americans entered the war in December 1941 and they were determined to fly by day in their more heavily armed Super Fortresses. At the end of 1942 heavy losses were forcing them to admit that they might have to fly with the protection of darkness, like the British. But regardless of whether or not they had to make that change they had reached agreement with the British on general policy:

> The aim of the bomber offensive is the progressive destruction and dislocation of the
> enemy's war industrial and economic system, and the undermining of his morale to
> a point where his capacity for armed resistance is fatally weakened.

It was no longer claimed that the bombers would 'at once shatter the enemy's morale'. This was to be a long process, and most success was likely to come when the bombers were so dense in the sky the German defences were 'saturated'. And it was no longer thought that the bomber alone could bring victory; the armies would have to fight a land war against an enemy weakened by the bombers. Roosevelt and Churchill confirmed the policy on the

What shouts of victory would arise if a Commando wrecked the entire Renault factory in a night, with a loss of seven men! What credible assumptions of an early end to the war would follow upon the destruction of a third of Cologne in an hour and a half by some swift moving mechanised force which, with but 200 casualties, withdrew and was ready to repeat the operation 24 hours later! What acclaim would greet the virtual destruction of Rostock and the Heinkel main and subsidiary factories by a Naval bombardment! All this, and far more, has been achieved by Bomber Command: yet there are many who still avert their gaze, pass by on the other side, and question whether the 30 Squadrons of night bombers make any worth-while contribution to the war.

(Sir Arthur Harris to Winston Churchill and the War Cabinet, 28 June 1942.)

destruction of German cities when they met at Casablanca in January 1943. A 'Bomber's Baedeker', the guide to the economic importance of German towns, was prepared.

Bomber Command was finding out what it could do at the time Australians began arriving in numbers, and by the time most Australians were being posted to its squadrons it was committed to the area bombing of cities.

The crew of *Whoa Bessie*, a Lancaster of 463 Squadron, Waddington, 18 April, 1944, before take-off. Left to right, Flying Officer R.W. Board, Flight Sergeant L.J. Manning, Flying Officer B.A. Buckham, Flight Sergeant E.J. Holden, Flying Officer E.H. Giersch, Flying Officer J.W. Muddle and Sergeant W. Sinclair. This was the crew's sixth raid. Bruce Buckham, the pilot, was to fly another 42 operations. *AWM UK1212.*

7

THE SUPREME NONCHALANCE
OF THE YOUNG

A few Australians were in Bomber Command from the start – through the years of gallant amateurism, poor equipment, and little understanding of what bombers might reasonably be asked to do. In September 1939 about 450 Australians were in the RAF. Most were pilots and they were spread through the Commands. Some had been in England as students (as Richard Hillary was) or because they were supposed to be students (as Micky Martin was) or for other reasons, but most had trained in Australia and then transferred to the RAF (as Hughie Edwards did). Another smaller group had responded to RAF calls for recruits in Australia and done all their training in England. Under a 1923 agreement, each year ten cadets who had completed flying training were selected to go to Britain for further training with the chance of being given a short-service commission of four years in the RAF. In practice the number varied, generally increasing, so that in some years over 20 went from the RAAF to the RAF. Donald Bennett, who came from 'deep in the rich mud of the Darling Downs' of Queensland, shifted with the family to Brisbane where he went to high school and then worked in his father's business until he was old enough to apply to join the air force. Having trained at Point Cook in 1930, Bennett sailed for England with all but two of his class of 15. He left the RAF in 1935, joined Imperial Airways and returned to the RAF after the start of war. Hughie Edwards was one of six who, at the end of their training at Point Cook, decided there were more opportunities in a bigger and better equipped RAF. In 1936 he left his home town of Fremantle and sailed for Plymouth.

On the eve of war the RAF made a direct appeal to 'Gentlemen of the Dominions, Colonies and Territories under the Crown' of 'pure European descent' aged between 17¹/₂ and 28 years to train as pilots. The men selected were offered a free second-class passage to England, a return ticket if they failed to qualify, and were advised to pack a 'Dinner suit or full evening dress (both if possible)' and study the 'Manual of Flying Training' on the voyage. From many applicants in all states, the RAF was able to select a few who had already done some flying, including Philip ('Micky') Moore, a farmer from Pyramid Hill in Victoria, who had just obtained his commercial licence. In August 1939, 22 Australian 'gentlemen' sailed from peacetime Australia, landing in wartime England in October. After courses at Jesus College Cambridge, Ansty and Cranwell, 19 graduated (one was failed for punching an instructor) and went to squadrons from mid 1940. Eight were dead before the end of the year. Six of the 12 who served in Bomber Command died over the course of the war. Micky Moore was Squadron Leader Moore, DFC and had started flying his second tour before Paddy Rowling and other early graduates of the Empire Air Training Scheme joined him at 50 Squadron, Skellingthorpe. Moore survived 55 operations and added a bar to his DFC.

Hughie Edwards, badly injured in an air crash in 1938, did not fly his first operation until early 1941. At that time the Blenheims were still being used in daylight raids on shipping and coastal targets and in 'circuses' when they flew with fighters who were supposed to destroy the German aircraft attracted by the bait of the Blenheims. At 139 and 105 Squadron Edwards normally flew in tight formations of six or so aircraft, with much of the detailed planning of the raid being done at squadron level. After two aborted raids, Edwards led an attack by 12 Blenheims on Bremen. Taking off at dawn, the Blenheims crossed the German coast and, as the citation for his VC said, Edwards:

> brought his formation 50 miles overland to the target, flying at the height of little more than 50 feet, passing under high-tension cables, carrying away telegraph wires,

In the high-ceilinged spacious dining room at the Royal Air Force College Cranwell there is a portrait of a cheerful Air Chief Marshall Sir Wallace Kyle GCB, KCVO, CBE, DSO, DFC. Born in Kalgoorlie, 'Digger' Kyle went to Guildford Grammar School, and in 1929 won a scholarship to Cranwell. Having served in various sections of the RAF, Kyle was appointed commander of 139 Squadron in 1940. He remained in Bomber Command, often flying operations while station commander. He supervised the development of the Mosquito as a low-level bomber and as a target marker in the Pathfinder Force. He retired from the RAF in 1968 and from 1975–1980 was Governor of Western Australia. Digger Kyle died in England in 1988.

and finally passing through a formidable balloon barrage. In reaching Bremen he was met with a hail of fire, all his aircraft being hit and four of them destroyed. Nevertheless he made a successful attack, and then with the greatest skill and coolness withdrew.

Edwards, who had previously been awarded an immediate DFC, epitomised the spirit of 'pressing on'. But in 1941 that spirit demanded an excess of gallantry for little return. The cost of one-quarter of the attacking force and damaged aircraft and injuries among the survivors was unsustainable. Those crews who did get through had little chance of hitting the designated target of the docks, and the weight and explosive impact of the bombs they carried was low.

On 15 October 1942 Don Charlwood paraded with 103 Squadron aircrew. It was, he said, 'two and a quarter years' since he started his 21 lessons. A couple of months later he flew on a raid on Frankfurt, 18 months after being issued with a uniform on his first day at Initial Training School at Somers. Arthur Doubleday and Bill Brill took just 14 months from going solo at Narrandera until both flew their first missions from muddy Breighton on 12 March 1942. That 14 months included waiting in transit camps and travelling across the Pacific and Atlantic Oceans. Brill had just ten hours and 20 minutes as first pilot at night on a Wellington when he arrived at 460 Squadron. Most of those who trained later took longer before their first operational flight. Dan Conway caught the bus to Pearce RAAF station on 11 October 1941 and he joined 467 Squadron at Waddington in December 1943. He flew his first bombing raid with his own crew on 14 January 1944, two years and three months after starting training. By 1944 the training was more thorough, the aircraft and its equipment more complex, and the demand for aircrew less urgent. But gunners, given short training and in high demand, were often sent into action more quickly. John Beede has his fictitious rear gunner complain that he 'and thousands of other young gunners … had been sent out to face a … ruthless foe with hardly a clue'. His gunner was given an effective training course after he had completed over 60 operations. Joe Grose – and Joe was real – arrived at Breighton on 25 August 1942, met most of his crew at the White Swan in Bubwith and told his

incredulous companions he had never flown at night. On the 26th August he spent time in a Wellington on the ground, at midday on the 27th he completed his first flight – of 30 minutes – in the rear turret of a Wellington, and just after 10 p.m. that night he began his first night flight. He was then rear gunner in Peter Isaacson's crew in a raid on Kassel. On that flight Grose shot down a fighter and Isaacson brought a holed Wellington back to Breighton. Grose was adaptive, brave and competent, and he and the crew were lucky.

Aircrew sometimes thought cynically that their commanders acted as though an aeroplane was more valuable than those who flew it. In terms of cash, that was probably not true. The investment of time alone in a novice crew totalled around ten years, and investment in an experienced crew much longer. The problem was that there was more likely to be a shortage of efficient aircraft ready to fly than of sufficiently trained men to crew them. Men waited at Brighton and Bournemouth; there were no paddocks full of new Lancasters waiting for crews. But in times of high loss, there were shortages of some categories of aircrew, and sustained high losses would have meant that soon nearly all crews would have flown fewer than five operations. The result would have been declining morale and efficiency. Both accountants and commanders valued trained crews.

Most airmen had already witnessed disaster and encountered death before they flew their first operation. In November 1940 the Air Observers School at Cootamundra was still in its first year when a flying classroom – an aircraft with pilot and five trainees – took off, climbed, faltered and crashed at the edge of the town. All six men on board were killed. It was a terrible accident in a small town that was just beginning to think of the airmen as theirs. Nearly all the training airfields were to have their own war cemeteries: 22 white headstones at Port Pirie, 11 at Benalla and 13 at Temora (out of the 18 who were killed there). At Western Junction in Tasmania, David Whishaw, aged 18, had just taken his first tentative flights in a Tiger Moth when two aircraft, each carrying an instructor

> **split-arse** This adjective denotes 'daring' or 'addicted to stunting', hence 'reckless – dashingly reckless.' Deriving from *full-split* (at full speed), it occurs in numerous combinations e.g.
> *split-arse cap.* The field-service, as opposed to the peaked dress-service, cap
> *split-arse landing.* A daring or very chancy landing.
> *split-arse merchant; split-arse pilot;* a test pilot; a stunt pilot.
> *split-arse turn.* A particularly hazardous manoeuvre.
>
> *(Eric Partridge, R.A.F. Slang.)*

and pupil, collided above the airstrip. One pupil parachuted to safety, one instructor, probably killed on impact, was thrown out and plummeted to earth, and the other instructor and pupil crashed with their aircraft. Whishaw and other trainees guarded the Tiger Moths until investigators arrived. Fragile particles of humanity still lay on the ground near the planes. Both aircraft had their tails pointing upwards, 'the rest just a tangled mess'. Later, on Vancouver Island in Canada, Whishaw's classmate Ted Watson recorded on 14 March 1943 that four men were killed when their plane 'dived into sea just off drome'. And five days later another crew disappeared into the same sea.

On Friday 13 February 1942 at Mallala in South Australia, two aircraft collided killing four trainees. Later that same evening an instructor and four trainees took off to carry out a night flying exercise. All trainees took their turn at calculating drift caused by wind. When they had finished, the instructor and pilot said, 'OK let's go in. Where are we?' But they had flown a dozen different headings and no one then knew where they were. Normally this would not have been a problem; they would have picked up the lights of towns and quickly decided where they were. But because the Japanese had just landed in New Guinea and were about to bomb Darwin, Australians had pulled their blinds down and switched off their outside lights. Without radio and unable to pick up landmarks in the brownout, the instructor and trainees eventually thought that they had found the distinctive point at the top of St Vincent's Gulf. But by then they did not have enough fuel to get back to Mallala. One trainee volunteered to parachute down, and ask someone in Port Augusta to turn on the airfield lights. He jumped into the darkness. Deciding that it was unwise to put all their chances of survival in just one hazardous leap, another trainee also baled out. But the pilot saw a salt lake and fearing he would run out of fuel before he saw a lighted runway decided to put down on the white surface. He landed safely, and the two men who baled out were astonished to meet each other in the gloomy main street of Port Augusta.

While doing introductory classes, Bill Manifold and his group at Calgary were often called upon to form burial parties for crash victims, a disturbing introduction to flying in Canada. On a later course at the Services Flying Training School at Calgary, Maurice Dalton and others contrived to fly navigational exercises into the neighbouring province of Saskatchewan where they bought as much liquor as they could before making the return flight. Having bypassed Alberta's restrictive liquor laws, they had the stocks for a 'slap-up-do with all the trimmings' to follow their 'wings' passing-out parade. They sure had a great celebration, but on the printed list of graduates alongside the banquet menu were two names encased in black, an Australian instructor and a trainee killed in a mid-air collision. By the end of the war, 114 Australian airmen were buried in Canada, half of them in the central prairie states, a long way from home and any battleground.

The Atlantic was always dangerous, and many airmen crossed it in the 14 months from February 1942 to April 1943 when the German U-boats were at their most lethal. Clarrie Herbert was in a 30-ship convoy out of Lagos. They had sailed a long way west but suddenly a Focke-Wulf dived out of cloud, bombed and sank a meat-carrying cargo ship and machine-gunned the deck of Herbert's transport. In July 1941 navigator Robert Mitchell was on a transport that was torpedoed. Mitchell was interned by the French after being in a group that sailed a lifeboat 1,000 kilometres to Africa. He then escaped across several African borders and finally got himself to England and Coastal Command.

At air schools in England the weather, the need to make training realistic and the use of repaired and strained aircraft retired from battle sustained the accident rate. At an Advanced Flying Unit in Scotland in 1942 Max Bryant was 'surrounded by the Reaper' – there were 'three prangs resulting in the deaths of fourteen blokes'. One aircraft was destroyed in a mid-air collision, one crashed in poor visibility, and an 'Aussie sergeant' pilot 'bounced off a hill on the Isle of Arran'. At Lichfield in July 1942 Errol Crapp wrote in his diary that 16 men died in crashes in four days. These deaths included two crews disappearing into the sea. Just before he went on his first operation, David Scholes heard the engines of a Lancaster change, and 'unfortunately' he had time to see it dive vertically and explode 'with vivid flames'. Next day he learnt that there was to be no funeral as there was nothing to bury. The rear gunner alone had got out, and survived, but he was badly burnt. Three crews that were training alongside Ken Marks were shot down by German fighters over England before they had a

Left Station about midday for Humboldt [Saskatchewan], a town 65 miles from camp, where two Australian boys who had been killed were to be buried. It was cold, and the trip out in an open truck was far from enjoyable. The funeral was a military one, and very impressive – about 100 airmen attending. It was spoilt by the morbid interest of the Humboldt residents, for whom it was a great spectacle and a form of social entertainment.

(Errol Crapp, navigator trainee, 4 December 1941.)

chance to go on their first operation. On one of his last night exercises, Merv Fettell was told to fly a triangular course from Lichfield to Norfolk and Bristol. In a violent mid-air jolt his Wellington lost all power, one engine being almost knocked from its mountings. The crew baled out, but Fettell, who had no parachute, tried to guide the Wellington to an airfield. He was killed attempting to land on a short strip. What had happened to the parachute is uncertain – it may have fallen through the open escape hatch. The crew did not know what had hit their Wellington at the time, but they later learnt that it had collided with a Lancaster which crashed killing all seven on board. One of Fettell's crew, Robert Hilliard, says that he and the four other survivors were required to fly again before being given seven days' leave. Crewed-up with another pilot, Hilliard went to 466 Squadron, already entitled to wear the caterpillar badge of those who had been saved by silk.

High losses in Bomber Command late in 1941 put pressure on the training units. One Sunday at Lichfield Arthur Doubleday had already flown when he was called to fly again that night, and the 'weather was really lousy'. Arthur and an instructor took off in one Wellington and a New Zealander in another Wellington followed them down the runway. Before they reached 250 feet, Arthur said, they had disappeared into cloud and rain. Circling to try to find their way under the cloud to get back to the runway, they saw the New Zealander's aircraft hit the ground and explode. Having climbed quickly out of danger Doubleday and the instructor contacted the Lichfield tower and were given permission to set the plane to fly east while they baled out. But Arthur said he opened the small window on the Wellington, peered into the black murk, and said it was 'pretty damn cold' out there. They had another try to land, coming down gradually, and as they broke through the cloud just above ground level there was a flare-lit runway. They landed at Tatenhil – in the right county but ten miles from Lichfield. It was one of Arthur Doubleday's narrowest escapes. Later he would say that in Europe they had faced two deadly enemies, and the first encountered was the weather.

The weather was so important in determining if they flew, or how dangerous or pleasant it would be, that for the rest of their lives ex-members of Bomber Command would, on awakening and going outside, consider the weather and think about what it once might have meant to so many lives at Binbrook, Waddington, Driffield and Elsham Wolds.

It is not surprising that aircrew saw death before battle. The RAAF suffered at least 2,800 casualties in training units and flying schools. In the training units

Heard the sad news that Bob Chapman had been killed at 10.15 am on Sunday in an air raid. The hospital at Torquay where he went to have his tonsils out was hit by a HE bomb dropped by a Jerry tip and run raider. We couldn't believe our ears when we heard it. Fancy going through raids on Dusseldorf, Bremen and Essen and then being killed in an air raid. It only shows how uncertain the future can be and to disappear (I think) my £2 pair of grey trousers, also 7/- cash, which Bob had borrowed from me.

(Errol Crapp, diary, 26 October 1942.)

serving all commands in Europe, 834 Australians died – more than those who died in Fighter and Coastal Command combined. Of the 23 Canberra High boys on the school honour roll who went into the air force, six were killed in flying accidents. And that was not exceptional. Total casualties in training units were one-third of those in operational squadrons. For airmen who went into the less dangerous forms of operational flying, practice was more dangerous than operations.

The impact of deaths in training and in operations was intensified when they were marked by public ceremony. In February 1943, 36 Australians who had recently arrived in England were suddenly told that they would be the escort and firing party at the funeral of Rawdon Middleton VC. After two days of intense drill under a 'savage' RAF instructor they slow-marched in the rain to the graveyard of St John's Church, Beck Row, Suffolk, and with rifles at the prescribed angle fired into the wet Suffolk air. As in Australia, the training airfields in England generated their own graveyards. In Fradley, the village next to 27 OTC Lichfield, there are 23 Australian graves in St Stephen's churchyard, close to the towpaths that the men walked and the canals where the adventurous had swum.

Although Australian airmen faced a hazardous journey to England, death in occasional air raids and, from June 1944, random danger from flying bombs, the most lethal enemies of Australian aircrew were the limited time they had to master complex skills, the emotional and physical demands of the tasks they were set and re-set, their own and their machines' fallibility, the weather and the Germans who attacked them while they were flying.

Some men flew within range of enemy guns while still at an Operational Training Unit or a Heavy Conversion Unit. More than anyone else, the Australians at Lichfield were likely to go to war while still at OTU. Many partly trained crews joined dummy runs to the French coast to confuse German radar and German fighters, then returned while the main raid continued on another route, or they did some 'gardening' or a 'nickel'. To 'garden' (drop mines near occupied ports) and 'nickel' (shower leaflets on French citizens) had started as code words and became standard RAF language. John Beede's rear gunner flew with one of five OTU crews selected to do a nickel, but the wireless operator chucked the pamphlets down the flare chute, all still roped in bundles. That was, he later told the rest of the crew, easier for him, the plane was less time over enemy territory, and anyway a bundle on the head was going to leave a greater impression than a single pamphlet. When Peter O'Connor was making his initiating flight from Lichfield to drop leaflets over Paris, the aircraft was hit by flak and one crew member was injured. O'Connor could not count that as an operation, but if it was practice then it was difficult to distinguish from the real thing.

When there was 'a flap on' or a long-planned maximum effort, the crews at training units were called into service. In May 1942, OTU Lichfield was told to have 21 aircraft ready for an operation. Three of them were to be manned by crews-in-training and the others by instructors and 'screens'. Because of bad weather they were on stand-by for three days. On 30 May they were told that they were to take-off just after 10 p.m. that night and bomb Cologne – they were to take part in the first 1,000 bomber raid. In fact to get the 1,000 bombers, nearly one-third of the aircraft came from training units. The Lichfield crews, with an hour's flying before their heavily laden Wellingtons reached the east coast of England, had to leave early, and they got home late – but all got home. Bob Nielsen, navigator in one of the Lichfield Wellingtons, said that at the time of the Cologne raid the crew (three Australians, one Scotsman and one Canadian) had been given just three weeks to know each other and the Wellington. Lichfield crews flew again to Essen in June and to Düsseldorf in July. Two Lichfield crews were lost on the Düsseldorf raid. Errol Crapp, at Lichfield in September 1942, just a month after first flying in a Wellington, went on a raid to Bremen and then three days later flew to Essen. He left his navigator's table to help his English pilot control their battered Wellington back across the English coast where they baled out. He too went to his operating squadron qualified to wear the caterpillar badge.

Later in 1942 the training crews were again in demand as Harris tried to keep the raids going while he built up the main force and converted to Lancasters. Harold Wright, a navigator, flew two operations from Lichfield 'in old D-rated Wellingtons that had been thrown off squadrons because they were clapped out'. A member of Sydney Cook's crew, Wright says that they came back from the first raid on Düsseldorf in a Wellington riddled with about 50 flak holes. They scarcely spoke, but they later found out that all of them were thinking, 'If that's ops, how the hell can you live?' Three nights later they were selected to fly again to Germany. Over the centre of Bremen the electrical system failed and they could not release their bombs. On the same Bremen raid the first of the men that had trained with Wright in Canada died on operations – before reaching an operating squadron. Cook and his crew had their two OTU raids logged as operations before they went to 103 Squadron at Elsham Wolds in north Lincolnshire. Cook, DFC, DFM, did not survive the war, but he flew over 50 operations before he was killed in a raid on Frankfurt on 3 October 1943. Bomber Command lost a total of 133 aircraft on operations flown from training units. Nearly all of them were old Wellingtons, Whitleys and Hampdens.

Crews had little choice of squadron. Like their Australian political and air force superiors they might have wanted Australians to be posted to Australian squadrons, but Bomber Command retained the right to dispose of them as it thought fit. Having trained at Church Broughton, a satellite field for Lichfield, and with an all-Australians crew except for his north-England flight engineer, Syd Gooding assumed that he was on his way to an Australian squadron. When he applied to go to an Australian squadron he was assured that his request was unnecessary. At Lancaster Finishing School, Hemswell, he stepped forward to receive his posting and said, '460?' And he was told, 'No, 101 Squadron, Ludford Magna'. Syd was on his way to an older English squadron that had started the war with Blenheims, changed to Wellingtons and was then flying Lancasters. While an Australian soldier could not enter a British regiment without being conscious of

> We are posted to 61 Squadron, Skellingthorpe. I am of course furious about it all, because I was almost certain that we would go to either 463 or 467 at Waddington. However all the bitching that I can do cannot change the situation, and off we go in the bus ... The Squadron Commander is W/C Doubleday DSO, DFC and Spam. He is an Australian, coming from somewhere near Wagga – farm people I believe. He is a wizard fellow and I like him very much straight away, when he has a little yarn with us in his office.
>
> *(Scholes 1997.)*

unit history, the Australian airmen joined small number (and therefore old) squadrons and had little idea whether the squadron had fought on the Western Front, the North West Frontier, the Middle East or France before Dunkirk.

The Canadians were more successful than the Australians in keeping their citizens together in crews and squadrons, even having most Canadian squadrons in a Canadian group, Group 6. However, Canadians also flew in other squadrons. Kemble Wood, a Sydneysider who began his training at Mascot, was posted to 405 (Vancouver) Squadron. After arriving at Bournemouth, Wood had been diverted to non-operational flying. At the time he could not understand why he had been sent 'all those thousands of miles from Australia to go on to staff work', and it took him six months to get a posting to Pathfinders. At Heavy Conversion Unit, he picked up a 'headless crew' (one that had lost its pilot) which included three Canadians. As a result, Wood and his crew went to 405 Squadron, the first-formed of the Royal Canadian Air Force Squadrons in Bomber Command and the only one in Pathfinders. But in Pathfinders Donald Bennett ensured that all squadrons were composite. He seemed to take pride in his rejection of Australian hopes of bringing their countrymen into one squadron. 'I refused point-blank, much to their surprise', he said. He made sure that 405 Squadron was never more than half Canadian.

At 29 OTU Bruntingthorpe, Maurice Dalton formed a crew 'out of the conglomeration'. When they all came together to fly four-engine bombers, there were two Australians (Dalton and Arthur McInnes), two Englishmen, a Scot,

Article 15 of the Empire Air Training Scheme Agreement said:

> The United Kingdom Government undertakes that pupils of Canada, Australia and New Zealand shall, after training is completed, be identified with their respective Dominions, either by the method of organising Dominion units or in some other way, such methods to be agreed upon with the respective Dominion Governments concerned. The United Kingdom Government will initiate inter-Governmental discussions to this end.

The Australian Prime Minister (Robert Menzies), cabled the Australian High Commissioner in London (Stanley Bruce) on 4 July 1941 saying that he thought he had agreement for Australian squadrons to be '100 per cent Australian personnel', and that those Australians would come from new trainees and 'Australian personnel available within the R.A.F. on posting, attachment, or otherwise'. Neither the Menzies nor Curtin governments came close to achieving that aim. Article 15 allowed the dominion men to be identified 'in some other way', required two governments to reach agreement, and seemed to leave the initiative to the United Kingdom.

a Welshman and a Canadian. One of the Englishmen, Norman Glover, was a servant of Empire. At the start of the war he had been a policeman in Rhodesia, and he then joined the air force and started his training there. At Lancaster Finishing School, Dalton was told he was on his way to 44 Squadron at Spilsby, the one nominally Rhodesian squadron in the RAF. The crew blamed Glover for their posting – and they were probably right. At Spilsby Dalton found there were 'probably more Australians' than Rhodesians, and anyway, he said, airmen learnt to accept what they could not control. Early in 1944 Hugh Coventry learnt with 'dismay' that he was posted to 149 Squadron. Having teamed up with one fellow Australian (Dave Skewes), two Canadians, two Englishmen and a Scot, he was uncommitted by nationality, but 149 Squadron was still flying Stirlings. In 1944 aircrew knew that Stirlings meant a greater chance of disaster. Men volunteered for aircrew, but then had few choices about category, theatre, aircraft, command or squadron. The selection of fellow crew members – within the constraint of who was on the same OTU course – was the one exception.

Most of the airfields of Bomber Command were on the east coast. A few lonely stations were near Kinloss and Elgin in northern Scotland. In England they were clustered around York, with the greatest concentration in Lincolnshire and Nottinghamshire. Then there was a gap to the fields in Norfolk, and the stations of the flat lands east of the Wash almost joined those that curved north of London from Cambridgeshire to Oxfordshire, Gloucestershire and Warwickshire. There were over 100 fields in England – from the Tees to the Avon. The names of many of the stations – Little Snoring, Skipton-on-Swale and Honeybourne – were difficult to associate with the destructive bombers. The fields that were best known to the Australians were Lichfield (where so many of them did their operational training, and where a few returned as 'screens'), Bottesford, Driffield, Leconfield, Breighton, Binbrook and Waddington ('Waddo').

Established before World War I, 'Waddo' had more permanent buildings, fewer curved Nissen huts and less mud and slush than the fields built quickly after 1939. When flights left, the rear gunner could watch the light on the central tower of Lincoln Cathedral just to the north, and it was a welcome sight for crews returning. It not only told them that they had survived, but also that they did not have to worry about a final hazard. When the Cathedral light was sharp

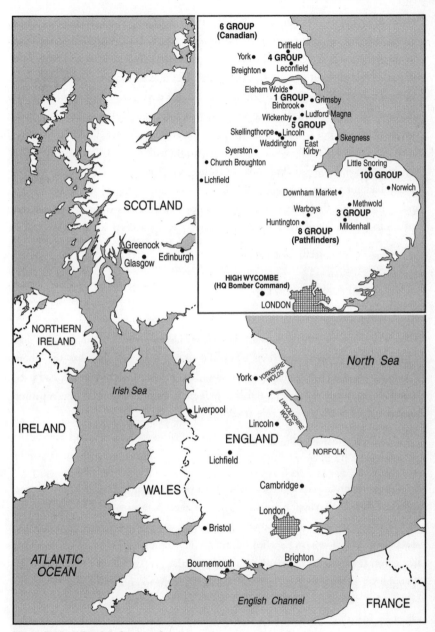

The airfields of Bomber Command.

the weather on the flat lands of Lincolnshire was usually clear. Taylor described one of the new airfields as simply a 'vastness of runways and Nissen huts, fens and turnip fields, where Lincolnshire ended and the North Sea began'. Ludford Magna, although built on one of the highest stretches of the Lincolnshire Wolds, was still marshy. It was, Syd Gooding said, 'Mudford Magma'. Binbrook, strongly associated with the Australians after it became home to 460 Squadron in 1943, was another new field on the windswept wolds. (The 'wolds', Cliff Halsall wrote, were not really hills, but what Australians would call 'rises'.) On the east there was no barrier between Binbrook and the grey North Sea. But to the west a stream had cut a gully through gentle hills. Near Tilby village it gurgled over falls and in the spring flush ran close against houses. Australians went to look at this stream that so many of them had heard about – it was Alfred Tennyson's brook:

> I come from haunts of coot and hern,
> I make a sudden sally,
> And sparkle out among the fern,
> To bicker down a valley.

The *Fifth Book* of the Victorian Education Department's readers even had sketches of it winding between trees and under bridges. This was the poem schoolboys and girls had chorused because, the teachers said, the poet had used sound to reinforce sense. But did the airmen, a decade on, recall the repeated lines that told them they were transitory?

> For men may come and men may go,
> But I go on for ever.

One compensation for those sent to the raw new stations was that the obvious speed of their construction told airmen that these were places without history: they belonged to whoever was there. And while some dominion men regretted the absence of an officers' mess with the furnishings of a gentlemen's club, they felt less constrained by the formalities of rank and the precedents of the old stations. By contrast, at Waddington they had to assert a right to equality in the 'beautiful, large and comfortable officers' mess'. Finding all the prime places around the fire taken by British officers in nine-to-five staff positions, an Australian displayed a handful of live .303 shells and then tossed them into the fire. After the 'mad scramble' the staff officers returned to find all the best chairs taken by aircrew who had been quicker on the rebound. (In fact, bullets that explode in a fire throw ash around, but do not send lead whizzing as if it came out of a rifle barrel.)

A bomber airfield might have 20 operating Lancasters, more if a squadron had three flights (and 460 at Binbrook did), and 40 if two squadrons were operating off the one field (as when both 463 and 467 were at Waddington). The need to maintain, repair, fuel and arm the bombers, support the crews and be ready to carry out demanding tasks at short notice turned each airfield into a single purpose temporary factory town. At Binbrook, 2,500 people were on the payroll. Trucks constantly arrived with food, bombs, fuel, engine and airframe parts and other necessary supplies. Each Lancaster could consume 2,000 gallons of fuel and drop 12,000 pounds worth of bombs, so just equipping one night's operations required prior movement of up to 300 tons of dangerous materials to airfield storage, and then to the dispersed aircraft on the day it was to be used. And this was a factory constantly replacing its most valuable machines and workers.

Many crews arrived at new stations with little ceremony, sometimes having to find their own way from railway stations, and then ask preoccupied officers where to leave their kit and find the mess. Hundreds of yards of wet windswept space often separated quarters, ablutions, administration and mess, and that increased the discomfort of men uncertain of directions and forced to backtrack. Many newcomers were saved by meeting men known from schools and training units, and sometimes other Australians already on the station would come looking for new arrivals to pick up news of mates and home. Reception was also

The Bomber Command operating fields were divided into Groups. By March 1943 the groups from the north were: 6 (Royal Canadian Air Force) Group in the Tyne valley and north Yorkshire, 4 Group in north and east Yorkshire, 1 Group south of the Humber in north Lincolnshire, 5 Group from Scampton in central Lincolnshire to Woodall Spa in the south, 2 (later 100) Group in north Norfolk, 3 Group in Suffolk, Cambridgeshire and Bedfordshire, and 8 (Path Finder Force) Group further west in Cambridgeshire centred on its headquarters in Huntingdon. Of the main Australian squadrons, 460 was in 1 Group (Lancasters), 462 was in 4 Group and then 100 Group (Halifaxes), and 466 was in 4 Group (Halifaxes), 463 and 467 in 5 Group (Lancasters). Other Australian squadrons that operated in Bomber Command were 455 (1941–42 then transferred to Coastal Command), 458 (1941 then transferred to the Middle East) and 464 (1942–43 then transferred to Second Tactical Air Force).

determined by immediate events. At the end of March 1944 Peter O'Connor and his crewmates went to 44 Squadron. They were ushered into a Nissen hut, but personal belongings indicated that all space was taken. They asked the guard what the story was. He said, 'They went off ... last night, they won't be back. They're your beds'. The new crew had arrived just after the disastrous Nuremburg raid. Later as they walked around the airfield they found people 'stunned and dazed' and 'WAAFs crying all over the place'. O'Connor said they were like 'strangers at a funeral'. But once accepted, aircrew could find operating stations infectiously exciting. Arriving at Binbrook in May 1944, Cliff Halsall drove up the rise to the main gate and saw the dispersed Lancasters outlined against the sky. He wrote in his diary, 'Set up in the married quarters – it is going to be great here – the atmosphere is fine'. The next day he confirmed that he was 'going to like this place very much'.

Arriving together, often the only new crew joining the squadron on the day, and conscious of being untested outsiders, crews were pushed closer together. However, rank divided nearly all crews. Officers and sergeants slept in different quarters (officers' beds had sheets), ate in separate messes (officers had better meals), and in the evening sat and smoked in different sorts of chairs and played snooker on different tables. Officers had higher rates of pay, a share of a batman (or batwoman) to clean shoes, bring shaving water and look after their quarters, and they drank on credit in the bar. Rank also divided men doing exactly the same task. Navigators, and the bomb-aimers who were back-up navigators, often went early to a pre-flight meal as they needed greater preparation time; and that meant the smaller group of commissioned navigators and bomb-aimers went to one mess and the non-commissioned (who may have been more experienced) went to another. Where it was standard practice in army units to transfer men promoted from the ranks, on squadrons men were routinely promoted and stayed in the same squadron, flight and crew. David Scholes arrived at 61 Squadron with a crew of sergeants. After four operations he was commissioned. Having been outfitted in London, he came back to the squadron 'a different uniform, a different mess, but

> I still believe that the only place for snow is on Christmas cards. When snow covered the runways, we could not use them ... The snow ploughs would go over them first, but they did not scrape right down to the runway surface ... I did not like it at all, getting out of my nice warm bunk at midnight, to do a four hour shift of snow shovelling, usually with more snow falling all around me.
>
> *(William (Bill) Pearce, wireless operator, 100 and 156 Squadrons.)*

not a different fellow'. Soon his navigator was also commissioned. That was two of the seven then separated by rank. Gus Belford, an officer, said that the separate quarters for the commissioned and non-commissioned was:

> a cardinal dictate of the British caste system, [and] had no place with operational aircrews. Men who flew together and depended absolutely on the expertise of each other, and often died together, should have been housed together in their off duty hours.

The division in rank was all the more strange because it had little to do with the giving and receiving of orders in an emergency. Jack Currie, an English sergeant pilot, was out-ranked by his wiry, puritanical Australian navigator, Pilot Officer Jim Cassidy. Currie said that although it was sometimes a nuisance having Cassidy eating and sleeping separately, within the crew he was 'Jim' or 'Jimmy', not 'Sir'. In the air the pilot as captain was in charge irrespective of his rank, and the common use of 'Skipper' or 'Skip' on the intercom recognised his position, but the specialised knowledge and equipment of the rest of the crew meant that each could claim authority at particular times. At least sergeant pilots had chances to even the score. George Hawes, about to take some 'high class Army officers' on a flight to test English searchlights heard one of the officers express surprise that sergeants were allowed to fly bombers. Hawes passed the word along and 'the boys ... let them see if we flew them or not ... with the good result that all the brass hats were beautifully sick'.

Most crews joining an operating squadron had not 'nickelled', 'gardened' or joined a major raid. Pilots might be given the chance to fly once or twice as 'second dickey' – sitting in the pull-down dickey seat alongside the pilot. Occasionally a navigator might also have a chance to fly as second navigator to an experienced crew. Other crew members were given a guided tour to war less often. Peter Knox, posted to 619 Squadron at Dunholme Lodge just north of Lincoln, found it was squadron policy to send only the bomb-aimer on a raid with another crew, probably recognising the importance of a calm bomb-aimer over the target. Taken as second bomb-aimer to destroy a railway junction in Belgium in May 1944, Knox saw a lot of cloud, no flak, no searchlights, and no fighters, and dropped the bombs in the Channel, but he had been closer to action than any member of his crew.

Established crews were not keen to carry a stranger. He disturbed the tribal closeness of the crew, and crews avoided disturbing their routine, as though any change was likely to break their run of luck. And a second dickey was not normally carried on an easy stooge, so once a crew knew they had a sprog passenger they expected a tough target. Dan Conway flew as second dickey to Berlin on 16 December 1943 and four days later to Frankfurt, two tough introductory flights. Maurice Dalton said, 'I went as a second pilot to gain experience, well I surely got that in large measure'. The route took the bombers across southern France to Italy, then north over the Alps to Munich. As 44 Squadron was target-marking, Dalton was early over Munich, carried back into the bomber stream, taken across the target a second time to bomb, and over ten hours later and suffering from a splitting headache, was again on the ground at Spilsby. Frank Dixon went 'purely and simply as an observer' all the way to Stettin on the Baltic. It did not increase his confidence:

> And I just thought that there was no way you could possibly fly an aeroplane through all that stuff that you could see bursting out there, and there was no way in all that darkness that the best navigator in the world was ever going to find the target.

With time to look around, worried about whether they would be able to perform when in command and with the experience intensified by its novelty, the second dickey flight was fixed as deeply in memories as the first solo in Tiger Moths.

In those first days on an operating station the new aircrews confronted the reality of the 'chop rate'. The losses were irregular but persistent, and – for some – disturbing. When Geoff Maddern's crew arrived at 103 Squadron in September 1942 one of them asked:

> 'How long does it take here to do a tour?' We knew, of course, that many failed to reach thirty, or even twenty; but what we wanted was some estimate of time taken by the successful. We all *hoped* to be successful. The men were communicative on everything else – but not on this. Only in quiet asides did we learn that no one had reached thirty for some time; how long, no one seemed to know – before July anyhow.

Men whom new crews had just met and men with whom new crews shared quarters left on an operation, and the next morning the Committee of Adjustment packed their gear and quickly all trace of them was gone. Eric Silbert said that each morning at 622 Squadron, the first of the aircrew into the room where the operating crews were listed went up to the blackboard and rubbed out the names of any who had not returned the previous night: 'This was done to save embarrassment to those who followed and it became quite an automatic act'.

The danger of operations was inescapable for those crews who lost men on familiarisation flights. In June 1942 when pilots were initiated by flying several times as second pilot, navigator Paddy Rowling's pilot, 'an ace chap and wizard pilot', was shot down flying with another crew. Three days later he had teamed up with an Australian pilot, Jasper Peters, but Peters too was killed with another crew. Rowling then teamed up with a third and experienced pilot whose navigator had been injured, and in July he flew his first operations. Wing Commander R.A. Norman, Commanding Officer of 460 Squadron, flew in a raid on Hanover on 8 October 1943 and took with him Flight Sergeant E.J. (Blue) Ellery, a pilot of a crew that had arrived that day. Norman was shot down, Ellery, who had not even unpacked his gear at Binbrook, became a prisoner, and his crew lost its pilot within 24 hours of arriving. Wireless Operator Bruce Pitt went to Waddington and his pilot and flight engineer both flew with other crews to the Ruhr. The plane in which the flight engineer was flying was shot down, and so Jock Smith, who had recently joined the crew, had to be replaced. The statistics that the new crews had been hearing about were now specific: particular planes and particular men went 'missing'. Rowling wrote to his mother that aircrew were conscious of the 'odds against' them, prepared her for the worst, and said 'there must be no regrets. I would have it that way'. Pitt – and others – were more able to push aside the immediate and accumulating evidence. Over 40 years later he thought he had been protected by 'the supreme nonchalance of the young: it was always going to happen to somebody else'.

Crews liked their own aircraft. They were uneasy when a regular aircraft had to be replaced, even when the replacement aeroplane was superior. Paddy Rowling wrote in his diary on 26 August 1942 that their normal Lancaster, 'K' for King was 'u.s.' (unserviceable):

so N.F.T.'d [night flying tested] 'G' for George and [we] were taking it. Quite a good kite too, better in some respects than K, but it's marvellous how attached you become to your own aircraft. I've done all my ops in 'K', and would rather fly in it than any other, although she's done a lot more hours.

Weather still holding us up – played few games billiards and snooker. Went to pictures in Stranraer ... and saw 'Beyond the Blue Horizon' with Dorothy Lamour. Had bath on returning to camp and just as I was to leave the Mess, a corporal came with a message for me ... saying that a TELEGRAM had arrived from Australia saying DAUGHTER BORN BOTH WELL ... Although expecting it, I must say it 'rocked' me for a bit – didn't know what to do so continued on to bed and this diary! Wrote to Ethel also.

(Kemble Wood, diary, 17 December 1942, on news his wife, Ethel, had given birth to their first child. Wood wrote his 99th letter to Ethel on 16 October, and was killed in a raid on Leipzig on 20 October 1943.)

Crews made slight modifications to aircraft to suit themselves – perhaps altering a gun turret to give the gunner better vision – and learnt to operate equipment that another might find faulty. Even aircraft that should have been identical varied in the extent of the vibration that jiggled the navigator's equipment on to the floor, in the way they had to be wrestled and nudged to maintain even flight, and in the speeds and heights they could reach. Crews taking over a new aircraft had a say in painting an insignia on the left side of the nose. For 'K' for Kitty, Dan Conway chose a lion's head similar to the one that roared to introduce the Metro Goldwyn-Mayer films, and Bill Manifold had a kookaburra with a snake in its beak painted on 'V' for Victory. Cliff Halsall noted the consciously Australian names on the Lancasters at Binbrook: Anzac, Jumbuk, Kanga, Advance Australia, Jackass, and Billabong Battler. But many of the Lancasters had just the austere identifying code letter. Each operation was recorded with an appropriate painted symbol so 'G' for George, which ended up in the Australian War Memorial, had evidence of 90 raids on the panel immediately below the pilot's port window. Crews sometimes changed the word that gave their aircraft so much of its identity. Right from the start Micky Martin turned 'P' for Peter into 'P' for Popsie. That change might not have been so apt or even accepted had any other pilot tried it, but Martin's skill and daring at strip poker and at the controls of a bomber won him privileges.

Crews were photographed against the nose of their plane, showing its identity and evidence of their shared operations. Like the reluctance to break an established crew, the desire to keep one aircraft was both rational and irrational. A pilot pushing an aircraft's capabilities to its maximum needed to know its limits and eccentricities, and when anticipating or under duress crews wanted the familiar – right down to the smells and scratches. And, like Rowling, they thought that if 'K' for King had brought them home 11 times, it was foolish to change to another plane for the 12th flight. (In fact 'K' for King survived the 12th but went down in flames over the target on its 13th; but it was then flown by a different pilot on his first operation.)

In October 1943 Ash Taylor had just six days on an operating station before he went on his first operation. Already most of the crew had flown in a raid on the Ruhr with an experienced pilot and navigator. David Scholes arrived at 61 Squadron, Skellingthorpe, on 22 July 1944. On 23 July he was listed to fly as second dickey, but the raid was scrubbed. On 24 July he flew as second dickey, and on 25 July, his fourth day on the station, he was 'Off to war', flying as skipper on a daylight raid on France. After his first favourable impression of Binbrook,

Cliff Halsall and the rest of Doc Davey's crew took seven days' leave. They were back at Binbrook on 26 May 1944, and Halsall was 'teed up' to fly second dickey four days later, but the raid was cancelled. The crew was 'teed up' again on 1 June and again the raid was scrubbed. They flew their first operation on 2 June – after nine days on the station. When he arrived at Binbrook, Halsall had just three hours and 35 minutes of night flying in a Lancaster, all carefully recorded in his log. The speed of the men through the final schools and their brief time on a station before they were in battle, was in strange contrast to the leisurely months many had spent at sea and then Bournemouth and Brighton.

Brill and Doubleday, having flown no raids while at Lichfield, arrived at 460 Squadron before it began operations. The squadron was formed in November 1941 at Molesworth in Huntingdonshire (now Cambridgeshire) and was the third Australian squadron to fly in Bomber Command. However, with 455 Squadron transferring to Coastal Command in April 1942 and 458 Squadron shifted to the Middle East in February, 460 Squadron was soon to be the only squadron carrying the Australian name in Bomber Command. In January 1942, when the squadron went north to Breighton, just south of York, the crews found the newly opened station as raw as they were. Snow lay everywhere and the Australians prayed for frost so that they could walk on top of the crisp surface rather than plough knee-deep in snow and mud. They were so short of equipment, Brill said, that they did not even have a plug spanner, and each Wellington with its 18-cylinder twin-row Wasp engines had 72 spark plugs. The men spent a lot of time shovelling snow and trying to start the Wellingtons in the cold. But there were compensations. Once started, the reliable Wellingtons kept going. Brill said he could not remember one case of engine failure while he was on the squadron. And the village of Bubwith was so close against the airfield perimeter that some of the Wellingtons in the dispersal bays were almost parked in the village. It was just a mile's bike ride through the gates to the Bubwith pubs, the Black Swan (soon known as the 'Dirty Duck') and the Seven Sisters (the 'Fourteen Tits', or more decorously, the 'Fourteen Titties'). Both Doubleday and Brill left their names in the Black Swan visitors' book, Brill commenting: 'The nectar of the gods flows here'. The squadron had nearly two months' flying before being called for its first operation. When it was, Brill wrote, 'the whole station was quite excited'. Both Doubleday and Brill were selected to fly, and they were briefed and the operation scrubbed at least twice before they finally took off into the night on 12 March 1942.

Briefing for the operation against railway yards at Juvisy, France, 463 Squadron, 18 April, 1944, Waddington, Lincoln. Wing Commander Rollo Kingsford-Smith, commanding officer of 463 Squadron, is standing at the left. *AWM UK1224.*

THE GUT-GRIPPING THEATRE

There was little saluting and few formal parades on an operating station. At about 9 o'clock airmen who had not flown the night before reported at a casual assembly. The conscientious called 'Present' for the few who were still in bed or not yet back from a night of indulgence. By mid-morning the crews on the battle order for that night were listed on the blackboard. Most men learnt informally that there was 'a war on', and that they were to be in it. Fellow crew or musterings told them in corridors, billets and cold ablution blocks. Some who had flown the night before, or come back late from the pictures in Grimsby, a dance in York or a late session at the Marquis of Granby or the Saracen's Head, had to be shaken awake with the 'magic word "Ops"' or 'We're on again tonight'. Once a squadron knew it was operating, it was closed: people could not leave, the public telephone was disconnected and the outward mail held. For the crews, the timetable for the day was set with specific times laid down for briefing and the pre-flight meal. Experienced crews fell into a routine, new crews hoped that their rawness would not be obvious, and all were conscious of increasing tension. Roland Winfield, an English medical officer and pilot who flew with several bomber crews, said he always had a 'queasy feeling' before operations. He thought he disguised his anxiety until a Wing Commander told him he looked like an undertaker with 'obsequious gloom' breaking through his 'brittle' grin.

All crews attended their aircraft to check that everything was working satisfactorily. If they were worried about some part that had recently been repaired or something that could only be tested in flight they might do a night-flying test. Before a raid on Maintz on 12 August 1942, Paddy Rowling wrote in his diary, 'Did an N.F.T. this afternoon, and the boys tested their guns in the Wash by shooting up some sea lions'. Crews not needing to dress in flying gear and draw parachutes for a night-flying test checked their aircraft at the dispersed perimeter parking station. They systematically ran up each engine, and tested controls, electrical circuits, communication systems, bomb sights and guns. The ground crew sergeant reported about equipment that had given trouble in the past and anything that had been repaired or checked. The ground and aircrew, already drawn together by their common concern for the aircraft, came closer because they met in the uncertainty before operations and the release afterwards. Emphasis on detailed pre-flight checks was good sense when the aircraft were then the most technically advanced machines flying and had recently made long flights through man-made and natural storms. But air force commanders were also determined that any crew turning for home short of the target because of a mechanical fault in an aircraft would have to show that the fault developed in flight and could not have been found by systematic testing before take-off. A 'boomerang' had to be a result of weakness in the aircraft, not in the crew.

The crews that so conscientiously carried out their night-flying tests were unwittingly telling the Germans that they were preparing for a raid, and provided an idea of how many aircraft they would be using. The German monitoring devices could pick up the increased traffic when radios and the H2S radar sets (introduced in 1943) were switched on and checked.

The weather, the moon and the season gave aircrews an indication of what they might be doing. They had heard one forecast by the time they were testing their aircraft and their own senses were constantly monitoring the weather about them. Already they had an idea about what it would be like at take-off, the amount of cloud that might protect them and obscure the target, fronts that they would have to pass through and the chances of the raid being scrubbed because of duff weather. Normally they did not fly at all when there was a full moon; it simply gave too much advantage to the night fighters. At the height of the northern summer the nights were so short that the bombers could not attack distant targets without being in dangerous airspace in daylight. And there was always likely to be more of what they had just been doing. If they had recently been bombing the Ruhr, Hamburg, Berlin, railways, flying bomb launch-sites or supporting the D-Day troops then they knew there was every chance that they would soon be back there again.

The German defences were equally conscious of the weather, moon, season and precedent, and making their own guesses.

As the ground staff needed several hours to fuel and arm a bomber for combat, the crews left their parked aircraft and then had time to themselves until they went to briefing. Some wrote letters home, knowing that these might be their last, and that if they were, then their words would arrive perhaps two or three months after the telegram announcing that they were missing. Cliff Halsall wrote a careful entry in his diary while around him men were 'writing, reading or dozing'. Halsall was concerned with both the spiritual and the material:

> My thoughts always wander homewards and linger there when 'ops' are on – I say a prayer (more than once) asking God to protect them all at home and keep them well and that should I be killed, that he will comfort them and lighten the sorrow.

> I hope, should I be killed, that Joy receives a good pension. I often worry about my life insurance not covering war risk. I should have insured before I did. My darlings – Joy and Billie.

Halsall's diary entry was intended for his wife and child, and other airmen wrote instructions on the inside covers of diaries to make sure that they were delivered. One of the last things that Don Charlwood did before going on a raid was to hand his diary to the padre. He always returned to claim it – and later it was the basis for a novel and an autobiography. In the event of his death, George Hawes arranged for his Canadian friend Bob Weatherell to look after his possessions. When Hawes was killed, Weatherell arranged for Hawes' things to be sent to Cootamundra, but he held Hawes' diary so that he could post it from Canada and avoid the censors. But then Weatherell himself was killed and it was an English woman who had hosted the dominion boys who waited for peace and the lifting of censorship to post the diary. Conforming to instructions about the disposal of his assets, Paddy Rowling wrote a letter to the adjutant saying that his camera, gold eversharp pencil, Swan fountain pen and diary were to be posted to his father in Horsham. When Paddy was killed in 1943 the diary was withheld, but after the war his father asked about it and it was then sent to him.

Peter O'Connor says that before operations he went 'down to the priest' who heard his confession, and 'many chaps used to see the padre'. But those who

> Now I realise there is not much between life and death in this racket, and we have to face the fact that Jerry might get us any minute on these excursions. So without being morbid, I want to say that if he does get us please don't grieve. Our troubles are over; and don't feel bitter because hundreds of families have made bigger sacrifices.
>
> *(Errol Crapp to 'Dad & Family', 16 September 1942.)*

prayed may be over-represented in the records because station church services were often not well attended. The Sunday School boys who had continued in church groups may have been those most likely to keep reflective diaries and write letters of comfort home. A heavy hangover on Sunday morning encouraged neither diary keeping nor church attendance.

Men tried to sleep or play billiards or cards, but most could not stop glancing at a clock or watch. In mid-afternoon they went for the 'last supper', the pre-op meal with its generous inclusion in rationed England of bacon and an 'operational egg'. There were vitamin pills for those who thought they needed them and occasionally fresh oranges. Robert Hilliard says that sometimes there were even bowls of strawberries and cream. Some squadrons had thought it better to serve the most generous meal on return, when the crews were hungry and winding down from operations. But the irreverent took the chance to bargain for the right to consume the meal of those who might not come back. Or they claimed that the post-op meal was a deliberate ploy by the air force to save on the ration bill. Because the bombers were not pressurised, aircrew suffered if they ate gas-generating food before flying. As the aircraft gained height and the air pressure fell, gases within the crews' digestive tracts expanded giving them intense pains in the gut and a prodigious capacity to fart. Crew putting on their oxygen masks early in the flight were making a comment on the quality, not the thinness, of the air. The serving of the best food to the crews looked like a reward for those on the station doing the most dangerous work. That was true, but the meals also recognised that the crews faced a physically demanding task. To act efficiently and make quick and appropriate decisions aircrew needed sustaining food. Most crews carried with them little more than a thermos or a bottle of drink and some chocolate and nuts, and often did not eat anything until nearly home. 'Wakey wakey' pills were available for those who feared falling asleep, but most aircrew avoided them. They thought that stimulants were unnecessary, and if the raid was called off they were left wide-eyed and restless through the night, and would have greater difficulty staying awake on the rescheduled raid the next night.

[Before a raid] the dawdling hours passed slowly ... but with ... a relentlessness not to be denied by doing the customary small things of pretended normality – a quiet smoke, a letter to be written, a stroll in the sharp Yorkshire air, a restless nap, a shave, a book chapter to be finished ... waiting, wondering or, if your faith was still firm, a hasty and apologetic prayer for good luck.

(Geoff Taylor 1979, p.43.)

The bomb and fuel loads provided the first firm evidence about the task ahead. The more fuel, the greater the distance, and that usually meant more hazards. The number of packets of 'window', the strips of aluminium to confuse German radar (and also tossed on the bridal couple at air force weddings), indicated how long the aircraft would be over enemy territory. When Gus Belford learnt that his plane was being loaded with a 4,000 pound bomb (a 'cookie') and 14 armour piercing bombs he guessed that they would have to attack a railway yard or an oil refinery. A cookie and incendiaries might have meant a town. News of what was being loaded soon drifted back to aircrew.

The crews sat together for the 'gut-gripping theatre' of the general briefing. The navigator, pilot and bomb-aimer, those most in need of space for maps, sat at the centre of the table. Where crews met in a Nissen hut, the length of the building and the curve of the roof concentrated attention on the map on the end wall. At Elsham Wolds Charlwood remembers a windowless room, fluorescent lights and 80 or 90 men waiting for the five or six officers to commit, inform and encourage them. The curtains were parted revealing a map of western Europe and the ribbons that marked the outward and return routes. The station commander announced, 'Gentlemen your target for tonight is …'. Often the men were given a reason why the target was important, and experienced aircrew greeted the justification with cynicism. It was always going to be the final destruction of reserve oil storages, German aircraft production, railway communications, ball bearing factories, Nazi headquarters, but the men doubted their capacity to hit precise targets and they often suspected that they were being diverted from thinking about the many bombs that would fall in suburbs and on worker dormitories. The details of the flight legs, times, bombing heights and the night's colours of guiding and identifying flares were given. Specialist officers then told them about the weather, where anti-aircraft batteries were located and what was known about enemy fighter strength along the route. The intelligence officer gave advice for those who might find themselves alive and mobile on enemy land. The aim was to get the men travelling in the right direction and in contact with the underground but without giving any information that could compromise the underground. Much of the briefing was delivered to silent

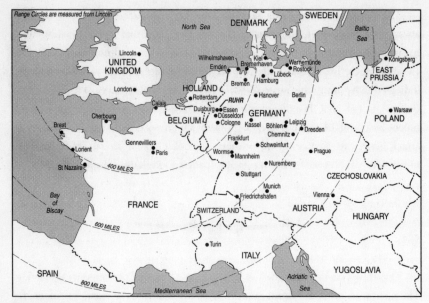

Targets and range

crews, but experienced airmen might make sardonic comments. Ivan Pellas remembers the met officer saying that conditions at take-off would be fine, then his next words were drowned out as a rain storm lashed the iron roof. He recovered, quickly shouting 'with occasional showers'. The crews roared approval. Navigators with most to do, either went early to briefings or stayed behind.

Once they knew the target the men could make more precise calculations about their chances. For a few men the tension eased once the target was announced – irrespective of what it was. A particular task was preferable to an uncertain one, and now they had work to do. But for many, apprehension increased when certain targets were named. And they could look around the room and speculate about who was for the chop. Some men thought they could tell by small signs those who were most under strain and therefore most at risk. And men nominated themselves. Joyce Brotherton, intelligence officer at 207 Squadron, Spilsby, looking at the seated crews, could not avoid selecting those least likely to return. She thought that in new crews over-confidence, rather than nervousness, was an indicator of disaster.

Crews, already dressed in flying gear, picked up Mae Wests, parachutes and escape kits (including silk maps, German-English phrase guides and foreign currency) in the locker room. With packs, helmets and harness, they now assumed the bulky look familiar in crew photographs. Their layers of clothes were not just for comfort but also for survival. The heating in the Lancaster was effective close to the navigator, less effective in the nose of the aircraft and did not reach the rear gunner at all. He had a plug-in suit, like an electric blanket, to wear. But failure of aircraft heating was always possible, and flak holes might expose the crews to sub-zero winds. Men could suffer frostbite or die of exposure, especially the lonely rear gunner whose freezing might be unknown to his mates.

Lucky charms hung about the bodies of most aircrew, including those who prayed – although the distinction between faith and superstition could be slight. Dalton had with him the Bible his grandfather had given his father. It was dated 12/9/1915, and stained with the mud of the trenches. Halsall's fellow gunner also carried his father's World War I Bible, and Halsall himself always wore an old jumper with a hole in it – and when he needed a 'line-shoot' he said it was a flak-hole. Charlwood, after a 'dash' to his room, spent a 'few quiet moments beside his bed' and then gathered a pack of family photographs. He flew with the conscious support of his family. Ivan Pellas, having started operations with dirty flying boots, had to leave them unpolished – the crew decided the skipper's dirty boots were part of the crew's success. The St. Christopher medals, lucky coins, charms carried by crews completing tours and handed to sprogs, WAAF lingerie and desiccated sprigs of wattle that men stowed in pockets, around necks or next to hearts were all overshadowed by the flamboyant Flying Officer Goulevitch's top hat.

John (Jan) Goulevitch's parents came from Poland and he was born in Siberia in 1919. His family moved to China and then to Australia, arriving when he was six years old. John became a carpenter and cabinet-maker, working in Ayr, Queensland. In 1941 he joined the RAAF and flew five operations with 100 Squadron before transferring to 460. He picked up the black top hat in a pub where it was thought to have been left by an absent-minded undertaker. Goulevitch wore the top hat on operations, dipping it as he passed the control tower on his way to take-off. When it disappeared at 100 Squadron, he stood up

It got pretty cold at 20,000 ft so it was essential that I wrapped myself up well. Woollen 'long johns', two pairs of long flying socks, shirt, long woollen crew necked jersey, battle-dress, leather flying jacket and over this lot a Mae West and parachute harness. The finishing touch, flying boots and four pairs of gloves – silk, woollen, chamois leather and leather gauntlets. I felt enormous.

(Dan London, mid-upper gunner, before flight to Berlin, 27 March 1943.)

at the end of briefing and said he refused to fly because 'some pommy bastard' had taken his lucky charm. It was returned. Goulevitch was known to throw the Lancaster around the sky in violent evasive action, but the stories of him doing this with one hand on the controls and the other on his hat are probably exaggerations. The hat rode to combat on a shelf behind him.

A WAAF drove the crews to the distant dispersal bays. Here too crews wanted the comfort of repeating what had led to their return last time. They wanted the same WAAF, the same navigator calling false directions, the same clashing of gears between second and third, and the same bomb-aimer asking if he could help the driver put more force on the clutch pedal by putting his hand on her thigh. They climbed aboard their waiting bomber, ran up the engines, again did their checks, and the pilot signed that the aircraft was serviceable. Back on the ground the crew had a last smoke, a cup of tea and a biscuit, kicked the tyres or had a last pee on the rear wheel, and climbed back up the metal steps.

Bill Brill, outwardly calm to his colleagues, wrote of his response to his first raid as sole pilot against a German city:

> I learned what the target was about midday, and for the whole afternoon I wandered around with a feeling of having half a pound of cold lead in the pit of my stomach. I have yet to analyse what that feeling was. Perhaps it was fear – who knows – fear of reaction. How can I get back from this, when others who are better than I'll ever be, have fallen on such targets? Will I funk if I'm in a tight spot? Will I let the rest of the boys down? Who am I to hold the lives of five other men in my hands?

By contrast, the seemingly more introspective Arthur Doubleday said that before an operation:

> I never felt any different, other than for waiting to go into bat at cricket. You know, the fast bowler looked a lot faster from the fence, but when you get in there it's not so bad.

I had the boomerang that my mother had given to me, and I also had a small kangaroo, made from a piece of kangaroo hide, which was sewn to the inside front of my battledress jacket. I never got airborne without these two lucky charms. The boomerang must have worked, because it eventually returned to Brisbane, with me closely attached to it. There was also the superstition that, if the last nervous 'pee' before boarding the aircraft for an 'op' were done on the tail wheel, it would maintain good luck.

(William (Bill) Pearce, wireless operator, 100 and 156 Squadrons.)

Before his first raid Syd Johnson, who played interstate hockey, used a similar sporting comparison: 'I'm not frightened. It's just the feeling in the solar plexus as before a hockey final. Or more like my first try out in "A" Grade'. The operation was scrubbed and Johnson had to go through the same pre-match tension before the raid on Stuttgart the next night. Posted to 21 Squadron at Watton, Clarrie Herbert was 'pinched' for being drunk and disorderly and spent 10 October 1941 in the guardhouse. On 12 October he flew his first operation, a raid on the port of Boulogne. He wrote, 'I was surprised I wasn't more excited than I was. I have been more excited in a bike race'. Young men recorded their feelings for themselves and for others by referring to sport because of the pervasive and misleading metaphor that connected sport to war and because, for many, sport was one place where their capacity to perform at their best under stress had been tested.

Syd Gooding said he was calm before an operation because his mind decided that all this was happening to someone else and he could watch Lancaster pilot Gooding prepare to fly 'R' for Roger to Gelsenkirchen. From the middle of his first tour Bob Murphy's mind created a voice that seemed to come from outside him, and it said, 'Murphy, this is your last trip. You're going to be shot down tonight'. The voice stopped after the aircraft left the ground, but sometimes came back over the target in 'some pretty hairy situation'. This 'same guy' started talking to him on his second tour, then, to his relief, it stopped. It was not, he said, a dialogue that he wished to continue. It was many years after the war before he told others in the crew about the part of himself that had given such clear, false predictions.

In some men the tension was expressed in false jocularity as they shouted or laughed more loudly than they would at other times. Others become more silent or more short-tempered. And some, as Doubleday said, were physically sick before operations. Beede has his rear gunner confess, 'I never got over my fear of death or mutilation and sweated just as freely on my last as on my first op and every other flier that I spoke to privately admitted fear in the face of real danger'.

At any time the raid could be scrubbed. Even as they sat with engines warming the flare could be fired to call it all off, and after take-off the wireless operator listened for a recall. On 27 November 1942, 32 Lancasters and Stirlings had set course for Stettin when they were recalled. They dropped their bombs in the North Sea. Unless the target or the conditions were thought to push the odds too much in favour of disaster most airmen did not want operations scrubbed at the last moment. George Hawes wrote in his diary for 13 July 1942 that, at Bottesford:

> All the boys were out in their machines ready for takeoff tonight when a storm hit the place and it simply pelted down. Of course this delayed takeoff and messed up all the times, so they were all scrubbed, much to everyone's annoyance.

In case there was any doubt he added the underlined statement, 'We hate ops to be scrubbed!' All that waiting, all that exhausting tension, had been wasted, and they would still have the same number of operations to complete. On 15 November 1942, Paddy Rowling was briefed to go to Genoa, but a leaking radiator meant they did not take off. Of the 78 aircraft that made the attack on Genoa none were lost. On 17, 18 and 19 November he was briefed for raids and all were scrubbed. He wrote to his mother on 15 December saying that he had only two more trips to complete his tour, and how he regretted missing raids, especially ones to Italian targets that were 'marvellously lit up, and it [was] just a shame to take old Musso's money'. He flew to Germany the next day and was posted missing.

But crews were pragmatic, and the early scrubbing of a tough flight was likely to be greeted with boisterous and rapid redirection of all the tension and energy preserved for the raid. In the dismal winter of early 1944 when 463 Squadron at Waddington had taken heavy losses, Rollo Kingsford-Smith said:

> when we were strapped in to our places and ready to start our engines to taxi out for take off on another raid on Berlin, the operation was cancelled. Everyone felt the same and there was a wild party in the mess and some keen types, determined we would have some action, exploded thunder flashes and put signal cartridges in the fire. The whole building was rocked with the explosions, green and red smoke poured out of the doors. The alcohol seemed to prevent suffocation.

Cliff Halsall, too, was sitting in an aircraft waiting to taxi out when a long raid was scrubbed. He wrote in his diary, 'Boys pleased – truck load blew whistles at watch tower'.

Yet with all the apprehension there were compensations. A young pilot sitting 20 feet above the tarmac in a bomber, goggles pushed up, oxygen mask flapping, could look out his port window and acknowledge the waves of the WAAFs and ground staff who gathered in all weather to see the crews away. At the end of all that training and selection, in command of that machine, about to undertake a daunting task that would be world news the next day, he could feel satisfied at the transformation of the bank teller or office boy.

Getting a heavy propeller-driven aircraft carrying a maximum load of aviation fuel and explosives clear of the runway was always dangerous. A tyre blow-out or a loss of power made the chances of surviving slight. Dan Conway says that the four or five minutes of take-off and holding the aircraft close to the ground to build up air speed were equal in tension to the bombing run over the target. As 'Z' for Zebra raced down the rapidly shortening runway Geoff Taylor recalls himself urging it into flight, 'Get up, you old bitch. Get up'. It was distressing for other crews waiting in the queue to see an aircraft crash just beyond the end of the airstrip – it was one of their own. Many of them knew immediately which particular plane it was and who was on board, and they had to fly over the burning wreck, the crew that was being incinerated, and the five tons of bombs that were about to explode.

Two disasters at take-off, both meetings of farce and disaster, involved Australians. Ack Loveless, taking off from Spilsby in a Lancaster on his first operation as sole pilot, took a violent swing to port, raced across the grass, and destroyed an unmanned Halifax and a Nissen hut before stopping. Most of the crew leapt out as the plane burst into flames. Seeing the bomb-aimer was trapped, Loveless and a station officer freed him just before the Lancaster exploded. The waiting ten aircraft were called to take-off, and as the fourth was halfway down the runway another and greater explosion threw flaming debris far and wide. Apparently the first explosion was the fuel load and the second the bomb load. The aircraft on the runway was travelling too fast to stop, and it charged through tangled scraps of Lancaster and smoke, and took off as though nothing had happened. Other operations were cancelled. But burning fragments had landed on another Halifax, set it on fire, and destroyed it. A briefing room and crew rooms were 'a pitiful sight. Not only were the windows and most of the window frames gone, but the roof was damaged, and sheets of corrugated iron were hanging down …The squadron offices were in the same plight …' Three aircraft and much of an aerodrome were destroyed, but no one suffered more than superficial injuries. Loveless soon returned for a second start to operations – and a successful record.

At Binbrook on the evening of 3 July 1943, ground staff accidentally released the bomb load in a Lancaster. They tried to roll the bombs away but incendiaries took fire and they fled. The bombs exploded and debris landing on the Lancaster in the next dispersal bay set it alight, and it too exploded. Scattered incendiaries threatened other aircraft and buildings. In the chaos of explosions and threats of explosions ground and aircrew entered burning aircraft to fight fires and disconnect electrical systems. In half an hour two Lancasters were destroyed and seven made unserviceable. While on the ground 'G' for George had suffered its greatest damage in its long career. In the dash for safety before the second Lancaster exploded, Hughie Edwards claimed he was driving at 50 miles an hour when he was passed by one of the ground crew on foot. Some airmen claimed they were passed by Roberts Dunstan, the one-legged gunner. The runways were cleared and 17 of the 460 Squadron bombers flew to Cologne that night. One crew died on the raid, but no one was injured in the destruction of Binbrook on 3 July.

On major raids the crews were conscious that on another 40 or 50 airfields other airmen were running up engines, queuing, and urging other aircraft into the air:

> For the next hours, at dispersal after dispersal, squadron after squadron, throughout all the groups that were Bomber Command, this would be the scene. The bomber country on England's east coast was alive.

During the major assault on German cities in the winter of 1943–1944, between 200 and 1,000 bombers were taking off night after night. East Lincolnshire throbbed to the sound of Lancaster engines.

Each bomber crew was alone in the sky and conscious of all the other crews on the same course, suffering the same conditions and with the same hopes and fears.

When Brill and Doubleday and two other crews took off from Breighton on 12 March 1942 on 460 Squadron's first operation, they were instructed to bomb Emden, one of the closest of the German North Sea ports. Brill, flying as second pilot to Squadron Leader Frank, said that they soon ran into cloud and bombed through cloud when they thought they were over Emden. 'Even at the worst', Brill wrote, 'we should have frightened a cow or two'. He thought perhaps they might have put them off their milk and cut the supply to the German war machine. The next night Brill flew to Dunkirk, but when it was obscured by haze

> Just as we reached Goole [East Yorkshire] and nearing the top of our climb, there was a great burst of light immediately beneath us. The light changed to a huge chandelier-like object, dripping burning masses and falling rapidly towards the ground below, there to form a glowing blob of fire. It could only be a mid-air collision, but it was not until we returned more than five hours later that we learnt that both aircraft were from 466 Squadron.
>
> *(Robert Hilliard on first raid to Germany with 466 Squadron.)*

they dropped their bombs in the sea — French citizens (and cows) were protected from indiscriminate bombing. On his third operation Brill dropped leaflets on Lille, and it was not until then that he saw — in the distance — flak for the first time. His fourth operation was his first as captain, and again he was nickelling but had a 'torrid time' in flak. Although he could not remember chewing the gum he held in his mouth, when he landed he found he could not open his exhausted and aching jaws. It was not until his seventh operation that he flew against an inland and strongly defended Germany city, and then it was because he was needed to add one more Wellington to the 263 bomber raid on Cologne. Doubleday had an equally gentle introduction with coast and nickel operations until he too flew to Cologne on his seventh raid. For Doubleday it was then Hamburg, Essen, Dortmund, Hamburg, Rostock, a submarine search, and Kiel — all in April 1942. Later Doubleday flew four mining operations and one raid on factories in Paris.

Just when the great bulk of Australians began going to operating squadrons at the end of 1943 and early 1944, Bomber Command was beginning its assault on Berlin and other German cities. From late autumn, when they had the protection of the long nights, the bombers flew as often as the weather allowed. In three months, beginning on 22 November 1943, bomb-aimer Ronald Lawton of 460 Squadron flew 12 raids on Berlin and one each on Frankfurt, Stettin, Magdeburg and Leipzig. Dan Conway, arriving at Waddington in December 1943, flew as second dickey to Berlin and Frankfurt, and then took his own crew on 12 successive raids into Germany, five of them to Berlin. By then Brill and Doubleday were coming back for a second tour.

After serving as instructors at Lichfield, both Brill and Doubleday returned to operations in December 1943. Having flown Wellingtons on their first tour and at Lichfield, they had to go to a heavy conversion unit to learn to fly Halifaxes and then Lancasters. On 8 November 1943 Brill and Doubleday shared control of a Lancaster. Both were now Squadron Leaders, both had been awarded DFCs on their first tour and both were now appointed to Waddington – Brill to 463 Squadron and Doubleday to 467 Squadron. It was 15 months since they had last been to war. To ease their way back to operations both flew as second dickey. Doubleday flew to Berlin in December and Brill flew to Stettin on 5 January 1944. Doubleday then flew eight times to German cities in his next ten operations. Brill began his second tour with three successive operations to Berlin, and then went to Leipzig, Stuttgart and Augsburg, all long flights into eastern Germany. Neither Brill nor Doubleday had gone to Berlin – 'the big city' – on their first tour, but on their second tour Bomber Command had the bombers with the range and carrying capacity and a commander with a belief that he could destroy the German cities.

In April and May, as part of the build-up to D-Day, both Brill and Doubleday began flying against targets in France and the ports used by the submarines that could threaten the invasion fleet. Doubleday flew 12 successive times to France. On 6 June, D-Day. Doubleday flew twice – once to attack gun sites and once to destroy the rail and road communications in Argentan. Halsall, who began operations from Binbrook on 2 June, took part in a raid on a radar jamming station at Berneval in France and then flew consistently against targets in France. On the eve of D-Day, when Bomber Command put over 1,000 bombers in the air, Halsall said: 'The scene above the clouds was a marvellous one with hundreds of kites milling around prior to setting course'. On 6 June on the way to bomb bridges behind the German forces he flew over 'bags of shipping' in the Channel. His fifth operation on 10 June, to attack a railway junction on the edge of Paris, was then his longest, at five and a half hours, whereas it was eight hours to Berlin. On 16 June Halsall was diverted to attack V-1 flying bomb sites and on his way south he flew over the lower incoming V-1s and the furious flak barrage that was being put against them. But the V-1s were being launched from the Pas de Calais, and it was still a short flight. It was not until Halsall's 15th operation, when he flew to Revigny in eastern France to attack railway yards, that he was in the air for over eight hours.

From 14 June 1944 Bomber Command returned to daylight raids. On 15 June Halsall flew to Boulogne with 13,000 pounds of bombs, and after a three-hour flight was back in bed early in the afternoon. On 29 June he did a 'daylight "doodlebug" bash' on Siracourt and from his rear turret it was a 'beautiful sight' as the bomber stream went out over the white cliffs of Dover. Those beginning operations in August and September 1944 as the Allied armies broke out of Normandy continued to fly in support of the Allied armies' advance across France and Belgium, but now Bomber Command also returned to Germany to destroy oil supplies, communications and cities. Gooding, starting operations in October, went to a succession of German targets: Saarbrücken, Emmerich, Duisburg, Stuttgart, Essen (twice), Wanne-Eickel (oil plant) and Dortmund. He said Duisburg on 14 October 1944 was the most worrying, not because of the intensity of the opposition, but simply because it was a 1,000 bomber raid in daylight and all that was dangerous was obvious, particularly the boxed flak that left the sky dense with black and blue explosions. Pellas, who completed 37 operations between August 1944 and March 1945, flew 15 times in daylight. Nearly all his final operations in February and March were to Germany: Chemnitz (east Germany), Worms, Essen, Mainz, Cologne, Kamen (oil plant) and Hamburg. William Hooper, a bomb-aimer, left Brisbane in July 1943, continued training in Canada, went to 463 Squadron and flew his first operation in November 1944. He had been on 25 operations when the war ended. Although he joined the air force in 1942, he had not quite finished a tour.

On 25 April 1945, Anzac Day, 460 Squadron flew its last operation. In a daylight raid the crews crossed France, flew over the northern edge of the Swiss Alps and attacked the Berchtesgarden, Hitler's eagle nest, and the chalets of his henchmen and the SS barracks, further down the slopes. Mist and snow obscured the target so the lesser buildings, rather than the eagle's nest itself, were destroyed. On the night of 25 April Lancasters from 463 and 467 joined the last major heavy bomber raid of the war when they attacked the oil refinery in Tonsberg in Norway. Germany surrendered on 7 May 1945.

Except for those who flew only in the winter of 1943/1944, most crews included a variety of trips in a tour. Paddy Rowling could not suppress the exhilaration of the raid on the Schneider factory at Le Creusot in France. Ninety-four Lancasters took off in the afternoon of 17 October 1942, assembled over Heyford in Oxfordshire and set off to the south-west, flying low so they were below German radar. Almost immediately they ran into 'low cloud right down to the deck'. Planes loomed out of the clag forcing quick evasions, but all emerged into clear air still in close formation. They roared south and then west across the Bay of Biscay 'at nought feet', sweeping across the coast of France near La Rochelle still 'packed like sardines'. German gunners raced for their gun pits but did not open fire. The bombers dashed east across France almost to the Swiss border:

I've never seen so many bolting horses, oxen etc ... Everything stampeded as we crossed France on the deck, some of the people stood and waved, others just stood, and others, like one farmer, dived for cover or lay flat ... This particular farmer had the quietest of horses and he was playing ostriches under his drag, head down and arse up, with the arse very much in sight.

'K' for King collected a bird in one engine over England, later three French partridges came bouncing through the bomb-aimer's perspex and another bird lodged in the camera, but no ground fire or fighters came near them. The Lancasters climbed to bomb, and in the dusk the crew could see the factories, warehouses and workshops. Explosions, fires and rising clouds of thick smoke seemed to confirm the power and success of the raid. The ten-hour flight was, Rowling wrote in his diary, 'a wizard trip and the whole world is talking about it today'. The *Daily Express* claimed the Lancasters had done a '"Grand National" over hedges to blast French Krupps'.

Halsall, too, responded enthusiastically to the bombers coming in low to attack oil storages at Pauillac on the French coast: 'It was a great sight to see the stream of bombers stooging along near the calm water – many of them were actually leaving a wake'. It was, of course, also dangerous: one 'kite', was 'caught in another Lanc's slipstream and dipped, hit the water, bounced and exploded'.

The long flights across the Alps to bomb targets in Italy also had their rewards. In April 1943, en route to bomb La Spezia, Bill Manifold flew close to Mont Blanc 'with its jagged ridges knifing up through the snow'. His navigator, Tom Moppett, left his table and maps:

Rubbing his hands together, his eyes wide in the delighted expression we had come to know so well when his face was not covered by the oxygen mask ... Back home his great pleasure had been hiking and skiing, even camping out in the snow of the Bogong High Plain.

Paddy Rowling, after a flight passing close to Geneva and on to Genoa tried to express his response:

The Alps in the moonlight were really wonderful, but gave one the impression of great groping fingers reaching up to drag you down amongst them. They are the most precipitous mountains I have seen with sheer drops of a couple of thousand feet or more, in some cases, some of them even seemed to be leaning out.

The next night some aircraft from 50 Squadron were again briefed to bomb Italy. Rowling and the rest of the crew just back from Genoa were not listed to fly. Rowling wrote that he was 'very envious of the boys ... It should be a wizard trip'.

On the long flights to distant targets in eastern Germany and beyond, the pilots sometimes crossed southern Sweden before turning south across the Baltic. Looking down on lighted towns and car headlights sparkling on roads, one airman remembers repeating to himself, 'Please let the engines fail now, please let the engines fail now'. The Swedish gunners opened up, but usually made sure their shells were exploding below the bombers. Alan Stutter, on the long haul to Königsberg, said that the Swedes fired pairs of guns aimed away from them, and they were able to fly over the centre of the Vs of tracer. It was, he says, with a 'great sense of loneliness' that they 'passed from Sweden to the blackness and hostility of the Baltic'. As commanding officer of 463 Squadron, Brill chose to fly to Königsberg. He said he had twice been briefed but both raids had been scrubbed and now he took the chance to fly the longest standard raid for Lancasters. Flying as leisurely and economically as possible at just 9,500 feet in a half moon and clear weather, Brill found the operation 'uncommonly pleasant'. The peculiar red flak of the Swedes seemed to be fired at where they had been. The whole trip took over ten hours, and he refuelled at a northern airfield being used by the Canadians before returning to Waddington. The bombers also crossed the borders into Switzerland when it suited them. Bill Manifold began his bombing run on Friedrichshafen from over Switzerland, but the Swiss gunners did not open up until he was over Lake Constance. That meant the flak and unexploded shells fell outside Swiss borders, and in any case he did not think the gunners tried very hard.

Hugh Coventry, disappointed that he had been sent to fly old Stirlings at 149 Squadron, found that he had to drop supplies to the French resistance. On the long trips to southern France he chose to fly at around 500 feet so that he was gone before any anti-aircraft gunners could get him in their sights:

> Dropping supplies to the Maquis I thought was great; we had to start the run over flares in a triangle and would run over once and then round again at 500 feet and drop the supplies to the people below. We were dropping guns, clothing, ammunition, boots, you name it.

Although demanding on the navigator, the flights in support of the maquis avoided the moral problems about bombing civilians, and the maquis – praised

for their daring raids against a ruthless invader and for hiding downed aircrew —
were the deserving allies. Coventry said successful drops were 'always a great
satisfaction'.

The Dam Busters raid of 16 May 1943, the best known of the extraordinary
operations carried out by Bomber Command, brought many of the skilled crews
together to form 617 Squadron at Scampton. To fly at low level over Holland and
Germany, arrive at the dams and drop into the valleys, especially into the steep-
sided Eder, called for skilled and precise flying. The pilot then had to hold the
aircraft at exactly 60 feet above water at 220 miles an hour and release the
bombs at the right distance from the wall. At the Möhne Dam, in particular, all
this had to be done under intense enemy fire. The dams raid called for all those
skills that selection boards tried to see in the recruits: the hand-eye
coordination, the capacity to anticipate the position of objects moving rapidly in
space, the intelligence to solve complex problems quickly, and the ability to
think and act when in extreme danger. Four of the 18 aircraft to cross the Dutch
coast on 16 May 1943 were piloted by Australians: Micky Martin, Dave
Shannon, Les Knight and Robert Barlow. And Guy Gibson, the English Wing
Commander on the raid, recorded a peculiarly Australian conversation while
flying over the Eder dam. Dave Shannon made five attempts but failed to come
down the steep slopes and hold the Lancaster steady at the right height and
distance from the wall. A second pilot, the Englishman Henry Maudslay tried,
bombed too close to the wall and the blast destroyed his aircraft. The quiet Les
Knight then started to drop his Lancaster down the steep sides of the valley, and
he too found it difficult. Dave Shannon guided him on the radio telephone with
Knight replying:

'O.K., Digger. It's pretty difficult.'

'Not that way, Dig. This way.'

'Too right it's difficult. I'm climbing up to have another crack.'

On his last run, Knight released the bomb and it shook, then shattered the wall.
Shannon called:

'Good show, Dig.'

Two dams were destroyed releasing a flood that killed over 1,200 people, one-
third of whom were foreign workers in Germany. The damage and the diversion
of German resources were significant, and the demonstration of what could be
achieved by special bombs dropped with precision was important to Allied ideas
of what was possible. But the cost was high. Of the 19 aircraft that had set out,
eight were shot down or crashed, and only three of their 56 crewmen survived

as prisoners of war. Thirteen Australians had flown on the dams raid; one became a prisoner, two were killed, and ten returned to become, as the official history said, 'Homeric figures'. To the applause of home newspapers, eight Australian dam busters were decorated. Guy Gibson was awarded the VC.

The bomber crew was tightly knit and mutually dependent. Through the intercom the members could talk to each other, and the pilot called up each man regularly to make sure all were well and alert. No crew wanted to fly with a gunner frozen or unconscious from lack of oxygen. But the crews rarely contacted base or any other plane: radio simply told too many people where they were. Crews, and particularly pilots, made basic decisions about their own welfare, when they should vary from the plan given at the briefing and, ultimately, whether they might abandon the raid altogether. They often made decisions that were rarely made in armies by such a small group. But the crew was also part of this larger force of bombers assembling in the air over England, setting course to the north-east across the North Sea to a given point, turning south-east across the German coast as though heading towards Hamburg and then changing course again to bomb Berlin. In that bomber stream they were both protected and endangered by other bombers. They were something like a flock of penguins forced to go into the water to catch fish for food but knowing that once in the water they would be preyed upon by leopard seals and killer whales. Those that strayed outside the flock, those who were early and those who were slower or late were the most vulnerable, and while they were being attacked the rest were more secure. Other aircraft were a danger simply because of the chances of collision. Night bombers did not fly in formation. Each pilot was not trying to maintain a fixed position relative to the wing of another plane: the bombers flew 'column of mob'. Each plane had particular height, time and route instructions, but error, wind, avoiding storms, enemy action, equipment failures and crew decisions pushed aircraft off course. At every turning point and over the target the chances of another bomber slicing through a wing or tail was at its greatest. With greater efficiency of planning, more uniform and higher performance machines, better navigational aids and more flying experience, the bomber pilots could in the end get 800 aircraft across a target in less than

30 minutes. In such density of aircraft, buffeting from slipstreams was inevitable and mid-upper gunners and pilots often reported the startled expressions of a rear gunner who momentarily appeared just a few feet in front of them. But collisions were rare, partly because the volume of sky relative to the specks of bombers was vast.

As the crews set course they began taking whatever action they could to ensure their own survival. When they were among the first to take off, Gus Belford and his navigator Doug Wheeler ignored the flight plan requiring them to keep to a delaying route before setting course at a specific time. They immediately left for the first marker, but at a slower speed. By the time the main force caught up with them they had saved fuel, a factor they thought might well be critical. They were defying orders and Wheeler carefully disguised the record of their flight, but as the enemy radar could not track them so early in the raid they believed they were doing nothing to assist the enemy or endanger other crews.

As they approached those skies where German fighters preyed on bombers, most pilots chose to fly a weaving course. The frequent changes of direction to port and starboard were thought to confuse German radar, make a less predictable target, and as the plane banked on the turns the mid-upper gunner could see below him – and the lethal night fighters struck from below. Weaving was not often officially recommended in the flying schools and some senior officers told pilots not to weave. Dan Conway was introduced to weaving on his two trips as second dickey and later he was grateful to those two experienced pilots.

The coast of occupied Europe was defended by anti-aircraft batteries: 'flak ships' and islands that provided platforms for an early welcome of concentrated fire. The interdependence of the crew on their individual skills and responsibilities now became apparent. The navigator, assisted by the bomb-aimer, had to keep them on course. John Beede has his rear gunner on a flight to Cologne record that 'the flak arose in its deadly splendour on all sides as sprog pilots blundered off course to run into the dangerous areas'. The gunners had to monitor systematically the sky that was visible to them. When a rear gunner saw a night fighter he instantly warned the pilot but did not open fire. The fighter might not have seen them and it was better to let him pass than to alert him to their presence. If the fighter was obviously attacking then the gunner waited until the fighter was committed and called 'dive port' or 'dive starboard'. The pilot then responded as rapidly and aggressively as he and the machine could tolerate. The timing of the gunner's call was crucial: if he called too early then the fighter could follow the bomber; if he called late then the fighter's opening burst was at an easy target; but if the gunner got the timing right then the fighter's greater speed caused it to sweep past outside the bomber's turn. The pilot pulled out of the dive, climbed and rolled, going into the standard corkscrew evasive move. The gunners might get in a burst at the fighter, but their machine guns were of light calibre and not as destructive as those of the fighters – or of the American bombers. The gunners' greatest value was their vigilance and their ability to estimate distance, remain calm and direct the pilot as a fighter came at him at well over 100 miles an hour faster than the bomber was travelling. Experienced gunners did not want to fly with novice crews, and experienced crews did not want sprog gunners.

If and when a bomber emerged from a contest with a night fighter, then it was the navigator who had to tell them where they were in the sky – after ten minutes of spiralling – and set a course avoiding flak and 'candles'. After throwing the 'poor old kite' around in the raid on Dortmund, Brill said that 'old Hugh [Thompson, the navigator,] led us out to the coast as surely as if we were walking down a main road'. As hard flying consumed fuel, increased responsibility then fell on the flight engineer to ensure that he got the greatest distance from the least fuel. While monitoring the engines and gauges, he had to keep calculating just how long the fuel would last. After the Dortmund raid, Brill put down at Swanton Morely in Norfolk, contemplated the flak holes, refuelled, and flew home to Breighton. The radio operator received and told the crew of all communication with the outside – about changes in the weather forecast, diversions or, most importantly, recalls. On a raid on Essen, Brill noted that 17 aircraft turned back when one had been recalled – but it was worse to fly on alone after missing a recall.

The approach to the target, the release of the bombs and the flight away from the target was the most dangerous time and the most demanding on the crew. The lethal exchange that took place between ground and air through 25,000 feet created a scene of intense brilliance and horror. Those who looked upon it, passed through it and became part of it knew that they had been selected – selected to be a witness, to function in that deadly, colourful maelstrom, and to be among those who would pay with their lives. To ease the tension in new crews, Dan Conway sometimes told them, 'you can count yourself lucky, you're going to see a most spectacular fireworks display you would pay a fiver to see in peacetime and here you're getting free transport and even being paid to go'. On his first raid over enemy territory David Scholes flew as second dickey:

Searchlights come from nowhere. We are at 9,000 feet. We weave violently towards the markings. Flak is coming up more now. I see a PFF A/C [Pathfinder Force aircraft] coned below and to port and they are giving him merry hell, however he escapes – good show! Now we are almost there. Never have I ever experienced such a feeling of tense excitement as this. The whole sky is lit up with weird lights – just like a ten times glorified Henley Night. Bombs burst with vivid white flashes. Flak is all around, and light flak, like snakes, comes up to meet us in long red streams. We steady up for the bombing run. It seems ages. One feels like a sitting pigeon, so exposed or like a man walking across Piccadilly with no trousers on would feel. At length the bombs go, and the crate shudders as they leave the carriers. Away we go weaving violently with much power on.

A fortnight later he wrote in his diary: 'my notes about my ops are somewhat brief and inconcise, however all my life I shall remember every minute of every one of them'.

Scholes's attempt to describe the scene over the target followed a 24 July raid on the oil depot at Donges. But Donges, close to the west coast of France, was not a major target, and even on the 24 July the main effort of Bomber Command was directed at Stuttgart. On that night 21 bombers were lost over Stuttgart and three were lost on the Donges raid. Scholes was also to know the longer raids and the vast furnace of flak over Germany only too well: he went to Stuttgart, Darmstadt, Königsberg, Nuremburg and other targets where the Germans concentrated their defences.

The hundreds and hundreds of search lights in the Ruhr ('Happy Valley') could be seen from miles away, and the anti-aircraft guns and lights covered an area enclosing several cities – Essen (home of Krupps armaments), Düsseldorf, Dortmund and Wuppertal – and extended north into the Rhineland and south

All the time we were flying over France the countryside below was a-twinkle with an incredible variety of lights – something like a fantastic pin-table with the little bulbs going off and on. Most of these fleeting pin-points were flak guns aimed at us and other R.A.F kites. Bombs bursting in a lazy, sullen glow under clusters of vivid flares showed us where some of these other bombers were doing their work. We could see, too, the flickering glow of large fires, the flashing of beacon lights, the steady glare of R.A.F. target indicators, pyramids of search-lights, photo-flashes dropped from our planes, fighter flares and an odd bomber going down in flames. There were flares over the Channel indicating Jerry was probably having a look at our invasion fleet below.

(*Cliff Halsall, bombing in support of the troops on Normandy, diary, 14 June 1944.*)

to Cologne. To attack the heart of the Ruhr was not a sudden dash into and out of the flak, but was sustained flying through flares and explosions. That meant the crew had to work hard and deliberately. Some pilots said that was their saving: the demand on their skill and concentration was so great that they had little time to watch, calculate the odds and be terrified.

Apart from gardening operations, Bob Murphy made his first flight as navigator over Rostock on the Baltic coast. At that early stage of the war the navigator was also the bomb-aimer. As the aircraft approached the target at about 6,000 feet Murphy turned off his light, left his work bench, pulled aside the black curtain, climbed down past the pilot into the nose of the plane and continued directing the pilot over the target. He had already calculated the air speed, wind speed and direction and set them on the bomb sight:

> You are lying on your stomach looking through clear perspex … And that was my first sight of flak. … the tracer shells … used to curve up in an arc and you would swear that they were going to hit you right between the eyes and [were] only two or three feet in front of you. They either whiz over the top of your head or whiz to the left or right.

> You just had to do it … We had to guide the pilot over the target, telling him to turn port or starboard … release the bombs and then climb back.

Later the navigator could remain protected from the sight of the fury outside, but he could hear the exchanges of the others on the intercom and feel the responses of the aircraft. Don Collumbell mentioned to the pilot that he had not seen the target, and one night over Berlin when they did not have to alter course for ten or 12 minutes the pilot said, '"Well you better come up and have a look …" I went up and had a look and I couldn't get back quick enough. Lights flashing, flak going off, search lights and oh my goodness'.

The light flak that could be seen streaming upward and bending – 'hosepiping' as aircrew often said – did not rise above 12,000 feet, and on most raids it was just adding to the theatre below the bombers. The heavy flak often gave no notice of its coming but suddenly exploded with a shower of metal fragments and left a jagged dark patch floating in the air. With radar the anti-aircraft gunners could calculate the height and speed of an aircraft and the first flak burst could be accurate. Flying across a black world an airman would sometimes see the flash of a gun muzzle, and shout a warning so the pilot could alter course violently in the 15 seconds the flak took to reach a high-flying bomber. Or with distress or relief a crew might see an explosion alongside them, and realise that the gun crews four miles below them had been tracking another bomber. But in the confusion of a raid, and with radar and radio being jammed, the gunners were often simply directing concentrated fire into what they thought was the path of the bombers.

Airmen looked at a 'layer' of bursting flak, and wondered how any plane could find a gap. Understandably, a few crews were known to be 'flak happy'; sheering away and dropping bombs wide of the target. Even crews that were determined to bomb as accurately as they could tended to release early so that the area being bombed advanced in the direction of approach. In the raid on Hamburg on 25 July 1943 the 'creep back' was some seven miles. But Bomber Command thought that the losses from flak were never over 2 per cent of the aircraft that left the airfields, and the number of enemy anti-aircraft guns did not influence the selection of targets. Experienced pilots learnt that there was a lot more sky without flak than with flak: they had a 98 per cent chance of surviving the flak on each raid. But they were also right to take every action they could to evade the shell bursts and confuse the gunners. Even so, a 1 or 2 per cent loss was significant when that risk had to be taken many times.

On 24 June 1943 Gordon Stooke could see the target, Wuppertal in the Ruhr, burning about ten miles ahead of him. Suddenly, 'night was turned into day' as his Lancaster was held at the meeting point of searchlight beams. Having been coned before, he reacted quickly, stopped weaving and dived. Still carrying bombs, the Lancaster quickly dropped 5,000 feet and built up speed to 400 miles an hour. Stooke was following one of the standard ways of evading searchlights: dive to gain speed, throw the aircraft into a violent turn, and escape into darkness – or keep on making unpredictable movements. It did not work. Just before the Lancaster cleared the light, two shells exploded on its nose and destroyed two engines. The crew baled out at less than 3,000 feet over Belgium. Airmen knew that to be coned over the Ruhr could be deadly. There were so many searchlights that more than 50 could seize on one black silhouette of a bomber and they operated over such a wide area. The master blue beam was particularly feared. Guided by radar, it did not have to wave about the sky in hope but could be switched on and instantly bathe an aircraft in its intense blue-tinged light. Other beams then fastened on the aircraft. The coned bomber might be attacked by night fighters, but over a target where the flak was thick and other hazards numerous the night fighters left the bomber to the gunners. They filled the cone with shells.

Most pilots who survived a tour often flew through beams and were coned several times. Sent on his first flight as pilot over enemy territory to drop pamphlets, Doubleday was suddenly 'grabbed' by one searchlight and 20 or 30 others joined in. New beams caught him as he moved out of range of others. The Lancashire tail gunner yelled unnecessary warnings as the guns gave them a hammering. Doubleday remembered being told that one way to escape was to get under the flak, and as he was near the coast he went down to the waves and raced clear. Later he was coned 'plenty of times'. Bill Brill was over Essen when Ned Watch, flying as second dickey, went to close the flare chute. A flak burst gave the 'plane such a kick' that Ned was knocked over: 'From then on, what with flak bursts and evasive action, Ned was rolled around the fuselage like a pea in a whistle'. As Deputy Controller on a raid on a seaplane base at Brest on the French coast in May 1944, Dan Conway had to arrive early and leave late. In his time over and around the target he was coned three times. The first time he tried violent jinking – unpredictable changes of course – but could not escape the lights. As the bombing was at 6,000 feet he was within the range of the light flak that was streaming upwards. Remembering that there was a hill to the south he dived, using the hill to shield him from the lights and guns. He got the location and altitude right, and escaped into darkness, but it had been a gamble. The next time he jinked his way to safety, and the third time was at the end of the raid so he took off out to sea and kept going across the Channel. The one experienced crew that was lost on that raid on Brest was caught in the searchlights, hit while it still carried its bomb load and flares, and it exploded in brilliant colours.

Escape from the searchlights over the vast flak belts meant diving, turning, climbing and turning, and keeping on doing that 'thirty or forty times'. It was physically exhausting and as death was doing the chasing it was even more exhausting for the mind and emotions.

On his 11th operation Brill said he was 'getting a little accustomed to being scared'. By coming in over Dortmund at 15,000 feet and dropping to bomb at 13,000 he hoped to use the drop in altitude to pick up speed and sweep through the 'cauldron'. But coming in from the north he ran into a forest of searchlights and dense flak:

> Never have I worked so hard, or have I done so much evasive action. The poor old kite stood first on one wing, and then on the other, on its tail, and on its nose. The sweat poured off me, half from exertion and half from fright. And still those beams played across us, until I prayed for them to shoot us down and finish it all. Sometimes I wonder if I was a bit mad during part of that show. Can remember looking up at

times and seeing a big blue beam cutting a track in the sky a few feet above. I screamed laughing ... and cried – 'Ha! Ha! Missed again'.

Brill had flown, he said, through 30 miles of 'candles'.

On his second tour Brill was in even greater danger over the target. Brill and his new crew had flown their first operation together when they went to Berlin on 20 January and on 27 January they went to the 'big city' again. As flight commander he thought he ought to fly 'R' for Robert: it was said to be a jinxed aircraft, a 'chop kite'. On its last flight it had come back with a dead rear gunner. He had died when the oxygen failed. At other times its crew had claimed an engine had lost power, but no faults had shown up when the ground staff tested it. The take-off for the long flight to Berlin was in daylight and Brill flew north-east out over the North Sea and then came south with a tail wind. But one engine did indeed give trouble and Brill was lower and slower than normal. Over Berlin the bomb-aimer, Bill McMahon, had just released the bombs when the Lancaster was hit in several places. Brill had been watching gun flashes from below and counting the seconds from the flash, ready to exploit the time that he had to take action if he became the target. Brill thought they had been hit by flak, but in fact another bomber above them had released its incendiaries on them. One had gone straight through the perspex in the nose of the plane, but McMahon had the presence of mind to pick it up and throw it straight back out again. Other incendiaries hit the navigator's table, severed the rudder controls, jammed the rear gunner's escape hatch and destroyed most of the aircraft's electrical system. As Brill was struggling to regain control Tubby Fuller, the mid-upper gunner, said there was a plume of flame coming from the port wing, so long that it was streaming way past the tail. Brill told the crew to stand by to bale out and he put the Lancaster into a dive, a standard way to try and blow a fire out. But he could still see the flames and told the crew to jump. McMahon jettisoned the front hatch and sat with his legs dangling and the navigator Bluey Freeman was next in line to jump, but neither was eager to plunge into the inferno of Berlin. Fuller, unable to open the rear door, kicked a hole in it, put his hand through and opened it from the outside, but before he jumped he pulled the emergency hatch in the roof to release the dinghy so that he could have a last look outside. He too decided to stick with the plane, but the wind gripped him and almost sucked him out. Bill McDonald, the rear gunner, said he could not open the rear turret, so he had no choice: if the plane went down he went with it. Brill said that McDonald, on only his third operation, did not change 'the tempo of his voice'. Brill said he would stay with the plane until McDonald was free. Then Bob Curtis, who had gone up into the astro dome, saw that the fire was nearly out and yelled to everyone to wait. As Brill had levelled off and almost had the plane under control he told Len Smith, the flight engineer, to go around and tell the crew not to jump. On his way back to his turret Tubby Fuller pressed past Curtis whose parachute released and yards of silk 'spewed out'. Knowing that at any moment his life might depend on his parachute, Curtis tried to stuff silk and cords back into its pack. By this time 'R' for Robert was down to 14,000 feet and no one was sure where they were or where they were heading. Holding a torch in his teeth, Freeman worked out their position and gave Brill a course. With limited control, freezing wind streaming in hatches and bomb holes, and bits of aeroplane threatening to tear in the wind, they set off for home. Brill climbed in spite of the cold, and in spite of the fact that Smith passed out because of a lack of oxygen and Curtis was vomiting. Curtis kept working on the electrical system and had some of it repaired before they got back to Waddington. They landed after a nine-hour flight, the second last home. Thirty-three other Lancasters did not get back from the raid – 231 airmen. In Berlin about 700 people were killed and 20,000 had their homes destroyed. When Brill's crew inspected their plane on the ground they found that seven or eight incendiary bombs had hit them, and the fire in the wing, which just missed the fuel tanks, had been caused by a bomb penetrating the wing, burning its way through and falling out.

In a letter home written on the day that they got back to Waddington, Curtis began:

'Dear Dad,

Phew! Have I got some news for you ...'

And he ended: 'Every time I tell this story in the mess or nearby pubs I get a couple of free drinks'. Brill wrote: 'it was not my idea of an evening's entertainment'. They flew again to Berlin three nights later. The Waddington squadrons lost six Lancasters that night, three from each squadron.

Brill said, 'I am always getting into tight spots'. And Doubleday said of Brill, 'He always caused me some anxiety'. When the 460 Squadron aircraft circled before landing, the formal calls between tower and pilots would be broken by, 'How are yer mate?' And all 460 would know that Brill and Doubleday were checking on each other.

A WAAF mess officer chats with Halifax crews of 466 Squadron, Leconfield. The WAAF Aircraftwoman serves the post-op breakfast. The airmen are just back from Frankfurt, December 1943, when over 6 per cent of the force was lost. *AWM SUK11668.*

CANOODLING ON A
LITTLE STONE BRIDGE

Soon after he arrived in England in 1941 Paddy Rowling wrote, 'Everywhere you go you see women in uniform, and it appears that they are certainly doing their bit to keep things going'. At Bottesford in 1942 George Hawes said that there were 'a hundred WAAFs on the camp and I think they must have been hand picked. Most of them look like ex-bullock drivers or heavyweight champs'. On his first morning at Lichfield Errol Crapp noted, 'I was awakened at 6.50 by a WAAF batwoman!'

The men arriving early had left Australia before there were many women in uniform – or in trousers – and they were surprised by the WAAFs on training and operating stations. Those arriving later were still surprised by the numbers of women and the amount and variety of work that they did. In December 1944 at Downham Market, a Pathfinder airfield, there were over 300 WAAFs housed in more than 20 Nissen huts.

Women cooked and cleaned, typed and did much of the office work – ordering, keeping accounts and filing – and they nursed in the station hospital. Bill Pearce says the women who served in the mess were 'tough' and they had to be, as the men gave them 'plenty to go on with', and they gave plenty back. But, inevitably he says, the men and women got to know one another, and when crews failed to return after a raid the WAAF staff would be serving and clearing away 'crying their eyes out'. The batwomen, often old in the eyes of young officers, knocked on the door in the morning, waited, entered, opened the curtain and offered a cup of tea or brought hot water for a shave. But the batwomen knew as well as anyone on a station that they served fleeting lives, for there was always a 'Sir' failing to return and another quickly taking his place.

When I joined I wanted to be something with electrics but ... I was to be a Bat-woman at the Officers' Mess, Driffield, and whilst there we had 466 and 462 Squadrons, mostly Aussies ... we were taken by lorry at 6.00 am to the Mess. Here we had to prepare huge jugs of tea which we used to wake the officers at 7.00 am ... After calling them with tea, we would wait until they went out and then make their beds, clean their rooms, press uniforms and take laundry. After a while you got used to seeing an empty bed – someone not returned from ops.

(Peggy Mills, joined WAAFs at 18, posted to Driffield 1944.)

While the presence of women who did women's work made a bomber airfield different from the militia camps that many Australian aircrew had known, it was other women who transformed operating stations.

Women could volunteer to join the WAAFs at 17½ years of age, so some women went straight from school to initial training. After being examined to see that they were 'FFI' (Free From Infection) and their hair was clear of nits, they were issued with clothing that some found as embarrassing as the inspections: 'two different types of knickers, one light blue wool pair and one dark blue pair. Known as "blackouts" and "twilights" they came down to our knees'. The 'pink cotton brassieres looked like jelly bags'. On those first nights away from home many remember the suppressed snuffles and sobs as young women regretted leaving familiar comfort for the strange, disturbing world of a military camp. Different in accents, backgrounds and knowledge of the world, the women went to training schools in the Blackpool area where they were billeted in boarding houses and marched to the public baths for weekly ablutions. Once equipped with specialist skills, and with the most privileged women discarding the issued uniform for one tailored in London, they went to station 'Waaferies'.

Although few had driven a car before the war, WAAFs were drivers. They drove the Hillmans, Vauxhalls and other cars to chauffeur officers. When going to the satellite station at Sleap near Shrewsbury, they always had to put up with the joke from the guards who asked, 'Are you going to Sleap with an officer?'. They drove vans, buses, small trucks and heavy trucks. They drove the petrol 'bowsers' (the refuelling tankers); they delivered the meagre coal ration; they drove the bomb trains – the Fordson and David Brown tractors that pulled the trailer loads of bombs; and they concealed themselves in the cabin of the lorry that collected the lavatory cans (Italians prisoners of war riding on the back). As well, they drove the 'follow-me' van that guided 'foreign' aircraft around the field – controlling the backward facing illuminated sign that said either 'STOP' or 'FOLLOW ME'; they carried the flares to the runway, replacing them when the wind changed; and they drove the truck convoys – at set distances between each vehicle, straining to see with the limited slit of light allowed in the blackouts. They drove the buses that picked up airmen at railway stations, the ambulances that raced to crashed aircraft and to meet planes bringing back injured, and the lorries that carried the flag-draped coffins to the cemetery where they were met by the padre and the German prisoners waiting to fill in the grave. But driving the crews to their parked aircraft and then picking them up when they returned was the 'glamour job'.

WAAFs were pilots who delivered aircraft, including the heavy bombers, to operating fields where their brief appearance provoked comment – usually in their favour – from non-pilot aircrew. WAAF technicians repaired the reported faults in the instruments of operating aircraft. The Map Queen controlled the station's store of maps and produced those relevant for raids. Even the most extravagant charm was unlikely to make her say which maps she had been told to prepare for briefing. WAAFs worked in the Met Office, the parachute section, radio and engine maintenance, and in the Watch (or Control) Tower – the square block building with windows that survives on many old bomber fields. They loaded rounds into the belts used by the bombers' guns.

At Waddington the women R/T (radio telephone) operators were at first not welcomed, but according to Pip Beck they were soon in a majority and they transformed their work place. In the slack hours after the flights left and before the aircrew returned one woman set out her embroidery silks and others knitted, read and wrote letters. The station commander, surprised that the R/T operators ran a women's work and craft centre, ordered an immediate clean out. But gradually the women returned to a productive use of the waiting hours. In fact, Beck says, she often worked for male officers: 'I sewed on buttons, changed sleeve-braid after a promotion, turned shirt-cuffs – even darned socks in an emergency'. But it was on the return of the bombers that the women did the

---

When I was seventeen and a half, I had a tremendous fight with my mother when I volunteered to join the WAAF: she thought I would be doomed for ever, and my sister, ten years older, told me not to come home with a baby! Educated by nuns and completely naive, I was almost paranoid about even kissing and I can only speak for myself and friends in MT [Military Transport] that we were all unsophisticated.

(Rosemary Hayes. Hayes married an English airman
after her Canadian boyfriend was killed.)

work that won the affection and admiration of the crews. Wearing earphones and speaking into a microphone strapped to her chest, a WAAF responded as each pilot called in, giving him a place in the landing order. And with 40 aircraft from two squadrons – one to follow another in less than a minute – and crews who were tired and eager to be on the ground, she faced a demanding task. When damaged aircraft or wounded crew demanded priority, or weather made landing difficult, her capacity to remain clear and calm was critical. Beck wrote of her distress at failing to make contact with a 'scared boy's voice' unable to find an airfield in fog.

WAAFs served as intelligence officers. At Spilsby, Joyce Brotherton said she took the morning phone call that told the squadron whether it would be operating. If it was, she simply put the phone down and said 'War'. As intelligence officer responsible for collecting information to help crews who might be shot down over enemy territory, she attended briefings and debriefed crews on their return. No crews wanted to be held long at briefings. Those that had been in torrid action, had seen other crews go down, and were physically exhausted, demonstrated what they had been through by their behaviour as much as by their words. Some had hands shaking so much they were unable to sign their reports.

Women were sometimes among the experts who visited operating stations and gave advice on meteorology, photo-interpretation, nutrition and other topics. Dorothy Robson, an English scientist, was a leader of research on bomb sights and she checked with crews to see that the sights were fitted and operated effectively. In November 1943 she was in a 76 Squadron Halifax on a test flight when it crashed in Yorkshire. As she had requested, her ashes were scattered in the air. Dorothy Robson was 23 years old when she died. Jimmy Steele, English pilot, Roy Brawn, Australian gunner, and Harry Welch, a Canadian, died in the same crash. On that night 76 Squadron lost another two aircraft in a raid on Düsseldorf.

WAAF officers out-ranked many aircrew, and they were often longer on stations than aircrew. In fact Joyce Brotherton became the longest serving officer in the Spilsby officers' mess. Rank, familiarity with a station and known competence could give a woman officer standing, but in informal situations aircrew often had a cavalier attitude to WAAF officers. Seeing a WAAF officer approaching, sergeants might not salute or they might give an exaggerated parade ground salute. Or they might wait until the last moment and then snap a salute so that the WAAF had little chance to return the compliment. Brotherton, who was nearly 20 years older than the youngest pilots, was not immune from having a pilot swing a taxiing Lancaster so that the full blast of the wind from the propellers nearly bowled her over.

Women on airfields were caught in the deliberate and incidental violence of war. In May 1941, before the Australians arrived at Waddington, the Germans bombed the airfield and village. Among those killed were seven women working in the station canteen. At Sleap, a Whitley slewed off-course, crashed into the watchtower and killed the two WAAF drivers on duty. In Bomber Command a total of ten WAAFs were killed and 49 wounded. With women engaged in so many tasks on a station, in such frequent contact with aircrew and sharing experiences with them, it was inevitable that the women should feel that the successes and failures of a squadron were also theirs, as did the ground staff. And it was inevitable also that the men and women became personally involved with each other. Brotherton thought of one crew in 207 Squadron as 'hers'. Skippered by Albert Hollings, all were Australians except for the English mid-upper gunner and flight engineer, and most were on their second tour. She talked to them off-duty and she went out with them to nearby Boston and Skegness. She usually knew before they did when and where they would be flying, and she always debriefed them. When a difficult raid on a factory in Toulouse was scheduled in August 1944 and Hollings, as deputy leader, was going to be a long time over the target, she postponed going on leave, waited through the night, and went out to meet them. 'It was only then', she wrote, 'that I really grasped the fact that I'd got them back again'. She says she was sparing of her emotional attachments to new crews for they might be transitory – and one of the squadron's new crews was lost on the Toulouse raid.

Rollo Kingsford-Smith began flying operations with 467 Squadron at Bottesford. There he met Jane:

> She was a vivacious petite WAAF sergeant in our Operations Room. She was fun to be with and I really enjoyed her company. But my marriage vows were not challenged. It seems that war was better than sex or should I say war was stronger than sex. The fear before combat, then the excitement followed by the exhilaration of striking the enemy and surviving and the long periods in intense stress over enemy territory plus flying fatigue put sex right out of my mind and possibly my ability.

When Kingsford-Smith, aged 24, went to Waddington to command 463 Squadron Jane went with him. But, he says, with long hours, responsibilities of command and writing letters of condolence he was in no mood for relaxation.

Before a raid on Hamburg, Don Charlwood wrote in his diary:

> I am writing by a fire in the stores in Janne's company. She is quite pleasant in these tense hours. We are not talking much; but she is somehow good to have around.

Janne was married to someone else and Charlwood was committed to Nell, a girl he had met in Canada, but both Janne and Don were clearly important to each other. Charlwood had friendships with other women on the station, including one which he had difficulty keeping on a 'pals only' basis. While Charlwood retained his commitment to Nell through letters, Wade Rodgers with 630 Squadron decided that he was different from the person who had left western Victoria, and he did not want a telegram of his death being sent to his distant fiancee. But there were women on the station who 'spoke the same slang and language as we did'. He thought of 'Silksheen' who called them on the radio, and Joyce who 'knew all their cares and woes', and Pegs and others, and he wrote and called off his engagement.

It was inevitable, too, that many aircrew would begin romantic and/or sexual relationships with women that they met on airfields and elsewhere. Mary Giddings of Wiltshire joined the WAAFs at 19, trained as a nurse and was posted to Mildenhall. There she met Rawdon (Ron) Middleton. They decided to go to Tilley's pantry in the small town of Mildenhall for afternoon tea and 'that's how it all started'. Middleton's 149 Squadron then moved to Lakenheath just a few miles north of Mildenhall. Both Giddings and Middleton had bicycles, and when Ron had a break he would ring and, if possible, they would meet and talk – not of flying or the war but of their contrasting homes and what they might do when the war was over. Sometimes they rode their bikes together through the flat Suffolk country or went to the pictures, but many of their meetings were brief. If he was likely to be on operations he told her, and either he rang immediately he returned or a telephonist friend of Mary's let her know that all the 149 Squadron Stirlings were back. Middleton and Giddings agreed to announce their engagement at the end of 1942.

Enticed by the excitement and duty of service (and the 'great escape' from her mother), Joane Gargate of Durham joined the WAAFs. Trained in high speed Morse, she served on stations in England and Ireland before being posted to the Overseas Signals Section in Whitehall. On a tour of Kew Gardens organised by the Services Club she met Joe Ford, a bomb-aimer with 576 Squadron operating from Elsham Wolds. Ford was from Shepparton in Victoria and had crewed-up with a New Zealand pilot, a Kenyan, an Englishman and three other Australians. After their ramble through Kew Gardens, Joe and Joane continued to see each other. Joane said:

> Joe was not a dancer but we went to the theatre or cinemas often or went sight-seeing around London. London was very generous to service people – theatre ticket prices greatly reduced and sometimes free – so we saw productions such as Margot Fonteyn and Helpmann in ballet, Noel Coward plays, musicals with celebrities such as Tauber, Irving Berlin's 'This is the Army' with Irving Berlin sitting beside us in the audience.

With Joe on operations, the meetings in London were often rushed. Much of their communication between visits was by letter, and so Joane says she did not know when Joe was flying, but seeing bombers leaving on major raids she wondered whether Joe was with them. When they were together they did not talk about the risks he faced, although Joane concedes she may now have eliminated such memories from those 'happy and precious' days in London.

Hughie Edwards' friend, the English fighter pilot Hugh Beresford, was killed in September 1940. Earlier that year Beresford had married Pat Kemp. Two years later Hughie and Pat married in London. Pat was still only 21 and Hughie was 27. By the time Edwards was appointed station commander at Binbrook early in 1943, he and Pat were parents. As Binbrook was an old peacetime station it had a commander's residence, and Hughie, Pat and their young son moved in. By July 1943 Edwards thought he had sufficient experience on Lancasters to return to operations, so he borrowed a crew and flew to Hamburg. On the 11 occasions that Edwards went to war from Binbrook he left behind a wife and

Baby layettes for the wives of the R.A.A.F. men in England are now furnished by Australian Red Cross. Some are being despatched from Australia, from the stores of the Civilian Relief Depots, and some purchased for immediate distribution by the [Australian Red Cross] London Committee.

(Australian Red Cross Society, Notes on Activities, July 1943.)

child. When he flew to Freiburg on 19 November he left behind two children, for his daughter had been born just eight days before.

Arthur Doubleday and Phyllis Buckle had kept on seeing each other and Phyllis was with him when the King pinned the DFC on his coat, but Arthur did not want to 'make widows' so they did not marry until he finished his first tour. On 14 August 1943 they married at Beckenham in Kent. Bill Brill was best man. The Doubledays went to Haweswater for a six-day honeymoon in the Lake District, 'as far as you could get from the war and remain in England'. For a while Phyllis lived at the Goats Head Hotel in Lichfield, but even at the time of his marriage Arthur knew that he was going back to operations. The Doubledays had four months of marriage before Arthur flew to Berlin on the first operation of his second tour. After Arthur went to 61 Squadron in April 1944 he was instructed to go to London to do a course. He was then acting as master bomber and the BBC ran courses to teach the masters to speak clearly and concisely in the chaos over a target. With a day to spare at the end of the course, he arranged to meet Phyllis at the Regent Palace Hotel near Piccadilly Circus. At about 8 o'clock the next morning a V-1 blew a hole in the side of the Regent Palace and the blast knocked Arthur and Phyllis down a flight of stairs. Phyllis was then pregnant and the blast killed the twins that she was carrying.

Bob Murphy, Doubleday's navigator, married in England. Dave Shannon came back from the dams raid and asked Anne Fowler, a WAAF officer at Scampton, to marry him. Bruce Pitt claimed he got married because he could not find a pub with beer, so he went to a dance in Lincoln. There he met his future wife and took her home that night. On some mornings she would know that he was safely back from an operation because his Lancaster with its kangaroo insignia buzzed her house. They married at the end of his tour. Wade Rodgers, having severed his links with his Australian fiancee, avoided commitment while on operations but when he became a Lancaster test pilot he married Corporal Norah Dann from the Met office.

There was a lot of marrying going on – a result of the age of the men, the two years and more that most were in England, their frequent encounters with marriageable women, and perhaps their sense of their own impermanence. Early in 1945 the *Australian Women's Weekly* told its readers that 1,318 men of the RAAF had married in the United Kingdom. Soon that number passed 2,000. Compared with the rate of marriages of Australian women to American men it was a high rate of commitment of British women to men from across seas and cultures.

As Arthur Doubleday said, these were marriages in which a day, an hour and even minutes were precious. For some women the proximity of death was inescapable because their first boyfriend or husband was already dead. Molly Ellis was going out with David, and his letters were frequent and 'intense'. When the letters stopped she knew that he was 'missing'. John, David's closest friend, visited her, and ten months later Molly and John married. She was 19 years old and wore a dress made from parachute silk. One WAAF officer serving at Lichfield married a man who was sometimes impotent before operations, and that added depression to anxiety. On his return from operations he regained potency. When he was killed she married another Australian in Bomber Command. Pat Edwards' father, a regular RAF officer, had been killed when she was a small child, so Pat had lost both a father and a husband to the air force before she married Hughie, and she still had nearly three and a half years of war to endure. Harold Wright says that he and his close friend Johnny Jeffreys were 'both doing a line for the daughter of one of the local publicans'. When Jeffreys was shot down Wright said he 'just couldn't go back to that pub any more', and with one death the publican's daughter had lost two suitors.

On 21 November 1942 Mary Giddings received no phone call to tell her that Ron Middleton had returned from operations. The next day the senior doctor called her in and told her that Ron was missing. A few days later she was given details of his Stirling crashing into the Channel. Wanting either to go home or look for Ron who, she hoped, was still alive, Corporal Giddings was told to stay on duty at the hospital. After the funeral she arranged for a flower holder to be attached to Middleton's headstone at St John's Church, Beck Row. Later she married a RAF wireless operator from 622 Squadron.

Joe Ford's letters to Joane stopped suddenly after 7 May 1944, and hers were

They were lovely days and evenings – 1943 was a beautiful spring and summer, and at times the war seemed very far away until I looked at the wings on his tunic and my heart would lurch and I'd wonder how long, how long. He never talked of it, it was always the other crews who 'got the chop' or 'bought it'. Funny how most air crew grew a shell around themselves and accepted (outwardly at any rate) the empty chairs at the table after a raid. But we didn't waste time talking about it ... there were the usual dances and pictures – Vera Lynn singing 'Silver Wings in the Moonlight', 'Yours', 'You'll Never Know' – all the sentimental songs that made the heart ache when the leave was over and there were just the letters. Always the letters ... Every letter had a number in the corner, that meant so many ops done.

(Joyce Thomas, WAAF radio operator, married Norman Thomas, RAAF pilot 15 Squadron.)

'Returned on Advice of Air Ministry'. She did not know what had happened until August when Joe telephoned her. He had parachuted out over France, been picked up by the Resistance, only just evaded capture, and escaped to join the advancing Americans. Joe and Joane were married in December, honeymooned in Edinburgh and then both returned to duty – Joane to Whitehall and Joe, because of his recent experience, was attached to intelligence and sent to France.

These marriages of disruption, intensity and hazard were often marriages of the young – so young that some of the men had to write home and obtain parental consent. Veronica was 13 when the war started and by 1944 she was serving in the Women's Land Army. She met Stuart, a pilot in 158 Squadron, at a dance:

> He approached and started chatting. 'I'm committed to taking this girl, Amy, home,' he announced, 'But you could hang around and wait. I'll come back and take you home too.' What a nerve, I thought, and didn't wait.

They met the next day, Stuart proposed before the end of the war, and they married after it ended.

Joyce was a schoolgirl evacuated from London at the start of the war. In 1943, when she was 17, she went to the Bournemouth Pavilion tea dance where she met Stuart Edgerley, a 19-year-old Australian on his way to becoming a navigator with 467 Squadron. They continued to meet, but on his 28th operation he was shot down over France. Rescued by the Resistance, he reappeared after two months and they married in October 1945.

The young wives who married in the last years of the war and the early postwar were not women who changed behaviour during the war; they were so young in 1939 that all of the time in which they had been 'courting' and 'walking out' with young men – to use the disappearing language of the prewar – was wartime. They could not think back on a time when as women they knew the

[I flew one operation without Bluey as skipper.] The captain of my host crew shortly afterwards was married to a WAAF from the control tower. In accordance with the practices of the time, she was posted to another station not far away, to spare her the ordeal of waiting in the tower some night when the call sign of her husband's aircraft failed to emerge from the surrounding ether. She was already a Bomber Command widow, and her second marriage was not to last long as her new husband and his crew were all lost a few weeks later.

(Robert Hilliard, 35 Squadron, Graveley.)

rules and had the expectations of peace. In 1939 they had been thinking about their first years in secondary school.

If 2,000 Australians were marrying English women, then it was also inevitable that a lot of them were in other sorts of relationships with varying degrees of intimacy. When the weather at Lichfield stopped all flying, J. Boormann went out walking with Margaret: 'Canoodelled on a little stone bridge over the canal – lovely – peaceful – the mist slowly creeping across the fields – bird calls in the night'. A few months later when he was flying out of Waddington he went dancing and shopping with Doreen and he 'thought he was doing fairly well', but Doreen, he wrote in his diary, was having 'no funny business'.

When the 18-year-old WAAF Pip Beck arrived at Waddington she too was cautious. But she was also vulnerable. Seeing some sergeants, she 'knew from the brevets they wore that these were aircrew – the fabulous beings that I admired and hero-worshipped … they were young gods and all about me … and I blushed for the purple prose of my fancies'. One of the first women she met on the station, a parachute packer, told her, 'You can have a different boyfriend every night if you want to – it's wizzo!' At a dance in the sergeants' mess, the air thick with smoke and the smell of beer, she met a RAF gunner, and over the next weeks they fell in love. But he failed to return from one raid and soon it was clear he had not been diverted or taken prisoner. Beck cried and kept on working in the watchtower. Soon she was attracted to a Rhodesian pilot and took him home with her, but when Pattie, a fellow WAAF, saw Beck's enthusiasm for the pilot she told her that Marjorie, working in accounts, knew the pilot was married – she saw the allotment of pay to dependants. Beck then went out regularly with Mike, an Australian, took a New Zealander and an American to her home and corresponded with the wife of an older Australian. Those letters continued after the Australian had moved to another posting. She danced with a quiet Scot who was killed on his next flight.

Pip Beck worked with one woman who was always having quiet conversations with men then slipping outside for a while. One of the officers complained that she was turning the watchtower into a 'bloody knocking shop'.

Beck had not heard the expression before but knew enough not to ask what it meant. She reported Ina for noisily entertaining a New Zealander in the next bed in their shared room and Ina was confined to camp and lost a fortnight's pay. Looking back after more than 40 years, Beck said of those wartime days lived so intensely that a 'new world' had opened to her, and she 'would not have missed any of it'. Rosemary Hayes, WAAF driver, aged 14 in September 1939, said, 'Most of us lost boyfriends. In our hut there was always drama ... The agony of being young!'

Tom Simpson said that 'Blondie', an intelligence officer at Scampton, 'had a few small joy rides' in 'P' for Popsie. With a set of aircrew wings pinned to her battle dress and wearing slacks, she sat in the second dickey seat next to Mick Martin. It was not just part of Martin's flamboyance and indifference to rules or that Blondie was 'good-looking', many WAAFs flew with aircrew. Pip Beck hid her curls under a helmet, took the parachute scrounged for her, walked across to the Lancaster hidden within the group of airmen, and stood next to the navigator in a low-level formation exercise. Joyce Brotherton flew locally a few times, and then at the end of the war she was taken on an 'Exodus' flight to Europe when the bomber squadrons were called in to bring the newly released prisoners of war home. After he had left an operating station, Wade Rodgers took Norah Dann on several flights. Coming back from Scotland they flew into a German air raid and Rodgers thought Norah might have been the only WAAF to experience a raid while in the air. Perhaps she was, but WAAFs almost certainly flew on operations and some WAAFs disappeared, presumed casualties on a raid. Aircrew certainly took men from their ground crew – Halsall, Nielsen and Stooke, for example, all write about carrying ground crew as guests or stowaways.

Close to D-Day, when the squadrons were flying frequently, John Beede had his rear gunner operating from an airfield in Surrey:

> If flying was the order of the day, *l'amour* reigned by night. The wheat was ripening in the fields. This we soon found was an uncomfortable base for such recreation. The

The WAAFs on the station filled every capacity. They cook very well & make good maintenance hands on the aircraft. They have lost what morals they may have had. They play with the Poles and go the whole hog. They are recognized as the Poles' ground sheets. Rather crude, but true. A very grim show.

(*Ralph Wilson, on Blind Approach Training Course, Newton, Nottinghamshire, diary, 7 April 1942.*)

procedure was for the boys to take the femmes of their choice and a blanket each to the nearest field, trample an area flat, lay the blanket over the hay and they had an excellent couch for love-making.

For those who favoured this particular type of outdoor entertainment there was no lack of partners as the W.A.A.F. and land army girls were very generous.

Beede made it clear that the couples were not irresponsible: they did not trample a new site every night but returned to one flattened earlier.

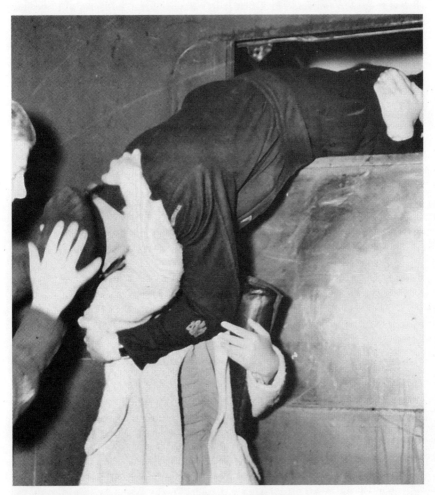

It was a war of many farewells. Here a RAAF Warrant Officer says goodbye to his English girlfriend on Brighton railway station. August 1945. *AWM UK3140.*

Beede's personal experience and knowledge transformed into a novel cannot always be taken as descriptions of remembered reality, but if he exaggerated the numbers of copulating couples and the damage to the 1944 harvest, there is other evidence of sex on and around airfields. After all, the airmen had the world's best chat-up line – they had come thousands of miles to fight, and probably die, for England. It was a line so obvious it did not have to be spoken. Eric Silbert said a common conclusion to conversations in the mess was that they should not die without knowing the joys of sex. Cathy, at OTU Little Horwood, found it easy to persuade Eric that it was unwise for a 'bull virgin' to go into battle, and in the Strand Palace in London on a 48-hour pass she made sure that Eric had thrills to remember (and look forward to) when he flew on operations from Mildenhall. Terry Charles, already successful at Brighton in getting women to go to bed with him, continued his winning ways at a succession of stations. The letters record his intimate relationships with Frankie, Margaret, Marion, Susie, Penny and Rosalie. Frankie wrote that she had a quiet Christmas; 'had to be the <u>dutiful</u> wife & mother, <u>he</u> was home for 7 days'. Margaret, too, went back to her husband whom the war had taken away for six years, but she did not want Terry to think she was 'devoid of all feeling' because she liked him a 'great deal'. Susie was also married, or had been married, and she and Terry often travelled together – even to distant Devon – when they had leave. Some of Terry's other girls were just companions at wild parties – the ones who liked 'fratting' (fraternising) with officers. As Frankie wrote to him in 1946: 'What memories!!'

The stories of parties that ended with the room awash with drink, broken glass, and WAAFs in various states of undress are countered by the diaries of men who escaped to quarters or went to the pictures for a quieter evening. And in the wildest, most uninhibited revelry, drunkenness and destructive male larrikinism dominated over lust. In the mess, men fired off Very signalling pistols, rode motorbikes, and played spontaneous games of bring-your-own-rules football. Wing Commander Thomas White, who flew some raids over Germany, was a member of the Australian Flying Corps in World War I, a minister in the Australian government between the wars, and commander of the reception centres at Bournemouth and Brighton in World War II. He wrote:

A rugger scrum developed in a corner
With all Dominions and the R.A.F. involved.
Wrestling too was available to enthusiasts
And a P/O dive bombing from the mantelshelf
Crashed realistically among the chairs.
Others played 'The Muffin Man', balancing pint pots
Upon their heads, singing and gyrating till they spilled.
While the F/O who offended with the saxophone
Was de-bagged and had his trousers hung on high …
The C.O. discreetly left at midnight …
Just as gymnasts began to swing among the rafters.

As at the Strand Palace in London, parties culminated in – or had as interim diversion – the stacking of furniture and men into a pyramid, and a light and agile man climbed for altitude. Held head down and with his blackened bare feet or bum on the ceiling, he left imprints to intrigue the sober. In the two-storey halls of old stations, the footprints were an achievement and a memorial.

There were always musicians among aircrew. On leave at Weston-super-Mare near Bristol, Cliff Halsall said:

The scene outside the Ring o' Bells Inn after closing time was a typical 'Merry England' scene with Butch playing the piano accordion and folks singing and dancing. A cop arrived and crabbed the show. He had a good laugh just the same.

The standard story is of someone in the mess asking, 'Does anyone here play the piano?' A diffident navigator says he's a bit rusty but will give it a try. He pushes stiff fingers on a few notes, and a cheerful gunner announces, 'The bloody goanna's thirsty'. He whips up the piano lid and splashes a pint over the wires. The navigator immediately gives a burst from Stravinsky's Firebird suite, drifts into a few frenetic snatches from 'The Gangs All Here', and then settles into 'They say there's a Lancaster leaving Berlin …', and the singing begins. The bawdiness increases, the WAAFs leave to 'Goodnight ladies' and the songs and the beer flow on.

Every six weeks the airmen took six days' leave. My friends and I would go to London, where we booked into the Strand Palace hotel for a binge of drinking and sex to block out what was behind – and ahead. I'd be almost incoherent for two days after a mission. On leave you'd find women first and then get on the piss.

(Geoffrey Williams, rear gunner, 90 and 514 Squadrons.)

Hughie Edwards, a strict station commander, would sing a solo, and others had their party trick. Sometimes at Binbrook or Waddington there was a cry, 'Clear the runway! Bill Brill will do the impossible!' Airmen shifted furniture and bodies to clear a strip, a sofa was set across the far end and beyond it a leather officer's chair was laid on its back. Brill in his socks ran flat out down the runway, grabbed the back of the sofa with his hands, somersaulted, landed in the chair, and his momentum turned the chair upright, leaving Squadron Leader Brill sitting at ease in an armchair. The act was a challenge to others, especially those misled by drink-induced confidence. Soon the end of the runway was littered with pranged airmen who had crash-dived into the sofa, chair, wall and floor. Other champions of eccentric physical fitness and drinking prowess demonstrated their skills.

Some men needed alcohol to survive and some believed it lubricated camaraderie and lifted morale, so they used it deliberately. In 1944 Doubleday was given the rare honour for an Empire Air Training Scheme graduate of being sent to command 61 Squadron, one of the older RAF squadrons. Given short warning of his posting, Doubleday and his crew arrived at Skellingthorpe to find that 61 Squadron had suffered high losses over Berlin and had just had three aircraft shot down on the Nuremberg raid and another two damaged in crashes. Bob Murphy, Doubleday's navigator, said that they walked into the mess, and 'you could hear a pin drop'. On their second night at Skellingthorpe, Doubleday's crew tried to lift morale:

> We decided to put on a party … Got the beer flowing, blackened a few bottoms and put the impressions on the ceiling of the mess – generally livened the place up and within a few weeks we had a tremendous spirit going in the squadron.

Murphy believed that the 'guys' that lived were the ones that:

> got out and relaxed, got a flight van if operations were scrubbed, put a few WAAFs into it, and went out and had a party. Those who stayed at home in the mess – read books, wrote letters every night – for some reason or other seemed to be the ones that got shot down early.

Doubleday, who brought a quieter, more deliberate style of leadership to the mess, saved his flamboyance for the air where he flew his aircraft to the extremes of its capacities. Later Doubleday said that his six months with 61 Squadron were the most satisfying of his air force career.

It is doubtful that wild escapism increased the chances of surviving on operations, but individuals certainly believed it helped them survive tension and the aftermath of crises. Rollo Kingsford-Smith said that in the dark days of early 1944 he 'was keeping going by drinking solidly' and the company in the bar was part of the 'therapy'. Harold Wright was just as explicit. Suffering from sinus trouble, he was sent to hospital, and while there his crew, skippered by Syd Cook, picked up a spare navigator and on 4 October 1944 their aircraft was shot down in a raid on Frankfurt:

> Pat Day, she was a section officer in intelligence ... rang me and we were both bawling over the phone. Well, I went and I got dressed and I went down to the local pub, and then every night for about seven days while I was in that hospital I'd just go down to the pub ... the nurses used to wait at a break in the hedge and get me back to bed and keep it hidden from the doctors ... I always maintain it was the old booze that kept me sane, because I was fortunate in this respect also that I always seemed to realise when the old nerves were being stretched a little too much ... I'd get the twitches in the hand and I'd get the tics in the face, and so I'd declare a week on the booze and every night we weren't flying I'd get a tummyful and I tended to relax.

Wright and Cook had flown over 50 operations together, and Wright continued to fly.

Of the 97 airmen heading for England on the *Umtali* in 1943, about half drank alcohol. The balance tipped slightly towards the drinkers during the voyage. Ted Desmond said that, as a Catholic, he had taken the pledge at his confirmation not to drink until he was 21, but he got an early start at Panama. And because of the age of aircrew, the fact that they were in groups of young men, and because of what they faced, the number of drinkers increased in England. Before he went to Initial Training School, Ralph Wilson was an 18-year-old prefect at school, and presumably not drinking much. By the time he was 20 and at flying schools he would sometimes start drinking steadily and then 'set to work'. After he left OTU (where he had flown his first operation) and his arrival at 83 Squadron there is a gap in his diary. He explained: 'We were drunk from Tuesday evening, until Thursday morning. I passed out on Thursday morning'. Yet there were still many aircrew on operations drinking little or no alcohol. Jack Currie said that the padre usually met them when they came off an operation and offered them a cup of coffee and a tot of rum. As Larry Myring, the Australian bomb-aimer, was the only drinker in their crew, he downed the seven rums quickly, and six tired, distressed airmen and one bomb-aimer in cheerful song wandered from debriefing.

Those men not seeking solace in booze and women were still repeatedly shifting between the violence of war and some sharp contrast. That life of oscillating extremes was inescapable. On 17 July 1944 Geoff Berglund, a rear gunner with 463 Squadron at Waddington, went to the home of the English bomb-aimer George Boyes who came from Scalby near Scarborough. The Boyes had a 'lovely home' and a garden rich in 'strawberries, gooseberries, raspberries etc'. Geoff and George had a 'wizard dinner', then went to a dance, had a swim and came home to strawberries and cream. The next morning Geoff did not get up until 10 o'clock, and he then had a long talk with Mrs Boyes. Before reporting back to Waddington in the evening, Berglund took the train back to Lincoln, had tea at the Savoy and saw 'quite a good picture'. On 19 July he learnt that another crew had gone missing while he was away, and he did a daylight raid over France. The bombers ran into 'very heavy flak over the target but George pranged it good'. They flew again on 20 July, a night raid with 'bags' of fighters and aircraft going down in flames. When operations were cancelled on 21 July, Geoff rang Joan who worked in Lincoln but she could not go out, so he just went into Lincoln for a meal. From encounters in town he learnt five more of his aircrew mates had died, and noted that soon there would be few of the 'old ones left'. Operations were scrubbed again on 22 and 23 July and he took Joan to a dance. Over St-Cyr, Paris, on 25 July, flak put a 'great hole' in his turret's perspex – an inch to the left and it would have gone through his head. In a raid on Stuttgart on 28 July he saw 'Combats everywhere and it wasn't a very pleasant sight to see kites go down in flames'. Again they got 'hell knocked' out of them with flak, and after more than eight hours in the air were interrogated, had breakfast and went to bed. That night he went out with Joan and 'had quite a nice night, despite it raining and my feeling tired'. On 1 August he left Waddington for nine days' leave in Edinburgh.

In that fortnight Berglund had been to an attractive English home, swum, danced, been to the pictures, had meals in Lincoln, recorded the deaths of fellow aircrew, flown four operations, narrowly missed death, seen aircraft go down in flames, had three operations scrubbed, been out twice with Joan, and gone on leave to Edinburgh. It was not an unusual fortnight for a member of aircrew in Bomber Command, but the shifts between peace and war could have been greater – he could have been to a bacchanalian party or shared a Land Army girl's cot. He could have gone further and faster if had owned a car or a motorcycle. The selection criteria that asked for a 'mechanical bent' and a 'leaning towards swift forms of locomotion' meant that many aircrew bought cars and drove them with scant regard for narrow roads and tight corners. Maurice Dalton bought a Ford eight-horsepower sedan, and his flight engineer had a three-wheeler Morgan and later an Austin 10. The crew was always mobile, although beating petrol rationing by using high-octane aviation fuel and breaking it down with petrol and kerosene meant a smoke trail and the chance of clogged carburettors and spark plugs. Syd Gooding 'stooged' around in his faded blue Ford Anglia. At Mildenhall, Eric Silbert's crew had three cars and a motorbike – and a flight engineer to do the maintenance. On short notice of a scrub, crews with their own transport could make a dash to scramble the Grimsby night fighters (women) or make a raid on York, six squashed inside a car and one sitting on the front mudguard to guide them through the fog. And Berglund, in that fortnight described, did not mention the fact that at Waddington he was living and working alongside WAAFS – they handed him his parachute, drove him, waved him off, talked him home and debriefed him. It was, as one pilot said, a great life, except that they were being killed.

In evening several of us went to the Tivoli in Grimsby to see a tawdry show. Wasn't worth sixpence. We will probably operate tomorrow.

(*Errol Crapp, pilot, 100 Squadron, killed on operations the next day, 4 March 1942.*)

The funeral of Flight Sergeant Cecil R. Frizzell of 467 Squadron at Waddington. Frizzell, aged 20, of South Brook, Queensland, was killed in a flying battle on 5 December, 1943. His body was later reburied in the Cambridge City Cemetery. *AWM SUK11650A.*

10

GOING FOR A BURTON

In World War II, an average of 2.3 per cent of aircraft were lost on each Bomber Command operation. That figure includes aircraft making flights to collect meteorological information or dropping leaflets and does not include aircraft that crashed in the United Kingdom when leaving or returning. A more accurate rate of loss on what were normally thought of as bombing operations is close to 3 per cent. For aircrew, that could seem to allow a reasonable chance of survival. Before a major battle most men at the start line – and the officers who did the planning and the medical staff waiting to receive the casualties – would have thought that a 97 per cent chance of surviving was acceptable odds. With a loss rate of 3 per cent Bomber Command could replace aircraft and men, and morale and efficiency could be maintained – it was a sustainable rate. But an airman with 30 operations to fly to complete a tour could make a simple calculation: 30 times three was 90. A 90 per cent chance of death was close enough, as they said at the time, to a dead certainty. In fact a 3 per cent loss rate gave a 40 per cent chance of survival because those lost on each raid were being replaced and some of the replacements were dying. It was not a case of taking three more from the original 100 on each additional raid. A 40 per cent chance of life was a lot better than 10 per cent but it was still less than an even break.

> Operational experience in this war ... indicates that a strategic bomber force would become relatively ineffective if it suffered operational losses in the region of 7% over a period of 3 months' intensive operations, and that its operational effectiveness may become unacceptably low if losses of 5% were sustained over this period.
>
> *(Director of Bomber Operations, 16 March 1944.)*

The variation in death rates on large raids was surprisingly slight. The Nuremberg raid of 30 March 1944 was the most disastrous: 795 aircraft left and 95 were lost. That was 11.9 per cent of the force. When those that crashed close to home were added, the cost rose to 13.5 per cent. Bill Brill said Nuremberg was the 'most frightening' of all his flights. Everything went wrong. There was a half moon, the forecast high protective cloud was not there, snow on the ground reflected and increased the light of the moon and the flares, the bombers left contrails, strong winds pushed aircraft off-course, there was cloud over the target, the flight plan included a long straight leg over Germany, and the German fighters were not deceived by the spoof raids. Seen against the cloud below them, the bombers were like black flies on a white tablecloth. The trip started badly for Doubleday. The air speed indicator failed, and when Bob Murphy asked what speed to use to calculate their position, Arthur said that he thought the 'Lanc' would be doing about 220 miles an hour on the power setting he was using. That seemed to work. But almost immediately they crossed the enemy coast they 'took a solid pounding' as the night fighters attacked.

The bombers then faced nearly 250 miles of continuous flying battle. Brill said cannon tracers in 'three nice colours, white, pale green and red' cut across the sky. The track over Europe, marked at briefing by red tape, was soon lit by burning wrecks. Bombers flew close by Brill 'flames from stem to stern', and he was puzzled by the number of aircraft that seemed to be hit without taking evasive action or returning fire. Bob Curtis said that he 'personally saw at least 25 of our aircraft shot down around us'. As the bomber stream had been pushed north, 'some bright spark' bombed Schweinfurt. Searchlights lit up that area and other aircrew then thought Schweinfurt was the target. Dispersed bombers were also attacking to the south and up to ten miles short of Nuremberg. 'When things get hectic', Brill conceded, 'it is certainly a great relief to unburden the bombs'. In clear sky with the cloud below him, Brill suddenly saw a violent explosion and a sheet of flame in front of him. He flew through a pall of smoke and something solid hit his aircraft. He flew on and bombed on a 'Wanganui', the coloured stars of a parachute flare dropped by the Pathfinders to mark targets hidden by cloud. As Brill slowly pulled away with the port outer engine stopped and the rear gun turret out of action he was attacked by a fighter, but he turned towards it and the cannon fire went wide. The fighter did not return for another try, which was just as well because the port inner engine suddenly stopped, and Brill told the crew to get ready to bale out – as he had over Berlin two months earlier. When one of the engines, its propeller windmilling uselessly, coughed and spluttered back to life, Brill set out for a slow flight home. He arrived one hour after the rest of the squadron; only his brother Vic was slower. Bill Brill learnt later that part of a belt of 303 ammunition had been found in the wing of his Lancaster, cutting the oil lines to the outer engine. He had flown through the debris of an exploded bomber. Air Vice-Marshal Ralph Cochrane, commander of 5 Group, was visiting Waddington on the morning the bombers returned from Nuremberg and he asked Doubleday how the trip went. Doubleday said, 'I believe the Jerries scored a century before lunch'.

Where smaller numbers of aircraft were involved percentages were sometimes higher, most notably in the dams raid, and in some of the early daylight raids. For example, on 12 May 1940, 42 Blenheims set out to bomb bridges to delay advancing German troops and 11 failed to return – a 26 per cent loss. But the general range of losses was apparent in three night raids on railway yards at Trappes, west of Paris. On 6 March 1944, 267 aircraft left on a raid and none was lost; 219 left on 31 May and four were lost; and 16 aircraft out of 128 failed to return on 2 June – a loss of 12.5 per cent.

It was nearly 13.3 per cent. Doug Bancroft of 158 Squadron said that 2 June was moonlit, 'perfect for the enemy night fighter pilots', his Halifax was badly shot up, and his own bomb load exploded and blew holes in the fuselage. One wounded crew member disappeared, perhaps falling through a hole in the floor, and in the confusion two baled out. Bancroft and the three remaining crew members beat out the fires, limped home and made a forced landing at Hurn near Bournemouth.

While the range of losses was between nil and 14 per cent, the variation on main raids was rarely more than 4 or 5 per cent. But that was significant; over 30 operations an average 2 per cent loss meant that 54.5 per cent survived, and at an average 5 per cent loss, just 21.5 per cent survived. Given that change in the odds, which raids aircrew flew was obviously critical. On his first tour Bill Brill flew minor operations for the first month, but from the time of the 8 April, 1942 Hamburg raid he usually flew on what were up to then Bomber Command's heaviest raids. The losses were 5 per cent or more on several such

---

Dear Mum and Dad

A few lines to let you know I have received my birthday cake. It was sent on the 4th Sept so has taken fifteen weeks to get here. Sealing the tin up kept the cake in perfect condition and it arrived lovely and moist.

(P-O Jack Bairstow, killed in flying accident, 30 August 1944, aged 25.)

raids, and on the highest – the 26 July raid to Hamburg – over 7 per cent of the 403 bombers were lost. Throughout Brill's first tour there was an average loss of just under 3 per cent – right on the Bomber Command norm. During those months of mid 1942, 460 Squadron normally had a maximum of 18 operating Wellingtons, and it often sent eight to ten to war on operating nights. The squadron lost 12 aircraft on operations in which Brill flew, and in the five months that it took Brill to complete his tour the squadron had lost 22 crews. In five months, then, Brill saw the squadron's fighting force replaced nearly one and half times. Doubleday, the first to complete a tour in 460 Squadron, and Brill, who finished one trip later, were lucky to survive – the odds pushed slightly in their favour because they had had some 'fresher' flights at the start of their tour.

When Brill and Doubleday returned for their second tours at the end of 1943, the Battle of Berlin had just begun. In Bomber slang Berlin was the 'Big City'. It was 'big' in the length of the flight, in the strength of its defences, in spectacle, in significance in the war, and in the imagination of those who learnt it was their target. After one flight as second dickey when the loss rate was 4.5 per cent, Brill flew to Berlin on 20 January 1944 when 4.6 per cent of aircraft were lost; to Berlin on 27 January, when 6.4 per cent were lost; to Berlin on 30 January, when 6.2 per cent were lost; and, after leave, to Leipzig on 19 February, where 9.5 per cent of aircraft were lost. These were appalling rates. Losses averaging close to 6 per cent were not sustainable. The impact on particular men and squadrons was obvious. Allan Brown from Cessnock had a standard training for a navigator. He had been to Air Observers' School at Cootamundra, Bombing and Air Gunnery at Sale, Air Navigation at Parkes, Advanced Flying Unit at Dumfries in Scotland, OTU at Church Broughton, Heavy Conversion at Lindholme and was posted to 460 Squadron in September 1943. His last four operations were successive flights to Berlin with losses of 2.4 per cent, 3.4 per cent, 6.2 per cent and 8.7 per cent. Brown, aged 22, went missing on his seventh operation, and his body was never identified. On 2 December 1943, the night that Brown failed to return, 460 Squadron lost five crews. During December 460 Squadron lost a total of 11 crews, all on operations against Berlin. In January and February another 14 crews were lost, six on Berlin raids. That was 25 aircraft destroyed. By then 460 Squadron was operating three flights, so the equivalent of the fighting force of the squadron had to be replaced in three months.

After aircrew left their line of pyres across Europe on the Nuremberg raid, both Brill and Doubleday flew their next operations to France. In the three raids that Doubleday flew in April, just one aircraft was destroyed by enemy fire. Because most operations in support of the D-Day landings were short and the demand for Bomber Command participation was high, men arriving at squadrons could finish a tour quickly. In those dreary months of December 1943 and January and February 1944, 460 Squadron operated on just 21 nights. But in August 1944 alone it operated 21 times. Men arrived, flew a tour and were screened inside three months. A few left inside two months. But because a squadron was flying often, its casualties in a month might still be high: 460 Squadron lost eight crews in May 1944, six in June and five in July. That was still two-thirds of the squadron being replaced in three months.

In the last six months of the war the average loss on raids had fallen to around 1 per cent – more at night, less in daylight operations. Yet even with this loss rate the chances of surviving 30 operations was still just 74 per cent. With one-quarter of the force becoming casualties, Australian aircrew in Bomber Command were, even at these best of times, still in greater danger of being killed in combat than men serving in any Australian army battalions in 1944 and 1945.

Scientists, technicians and tacticians were constantly trying to reduce losses in Bomber Command. The balance in the battle of the boffins was always shifting, with each advance by the Allies or the Germans giving a brief advantage until it was countered. That balance was critical for the odds determining life and death for individual aircrew. The reasoning behind the basic tactical device, the bomber stream, was simple. The German fighters, not knowing where the bombers would strike, had to be dispersed. And if the bombers were spread across a wide area and were over enemy land for a long time, then more fighters could be brought against them for a longer time. The aim was to concentrate the

On Australia Day [1944] all the Aussies in London on 'leave' attended the service at St Martin-in-the-Fields. After the service we each got a piece of gum tips (apparently the trees are growing down Sussex way where it is warmer). Mr Bruce, the High Commissioner, and some of the 'heads' were there.

(P-O Jack Bairstow from South Guildford, Western Australia.)

bomber stream so that close to 1,000 aircraft were confined to a cigar shape about 70 miles long and all could pass across the target in just 20 minutes. The bombers, pressed into a narrow corridor, could hope to avoid many of the fighters: the shorter the distance between the first and last bomber the less time that the fighters had to find them. And the faster they passed through the dangers of the target area the safer they were. But when the bombers were concentrated, it was all the more important that the enemy should not know the target until the last possible moment. As a result it became standard to have crews from OTUs, squadrons equipped with aging aircraft, and the versatile Mosquitoes fly spoof raids and drop window to further confuse the Germans about numbers and intent. The main bomber stream usually changed direction three or four times before making its final run towards the target. A few aircraft made brief raids on other targets, and Mosquitoes dropped route and target-marking flares at points where no other bombers would fly. The Germans, through intelligence reports, listening devices, radar and reconnaissance were constantly trying to learn about the track and target of the bomber stream. They, too, tried dropping marker flares to confuse the bombers and ignited fuel fires so that they looked like targets hit by the first wave of incendiaries. They marshalled their fighters around communication beacons so that they could respond quickly to the first authoritative location of the stream, and German aircraft tracked the bombers and dropped fighter flares that lit the sky so brightly the bomber crews complained they could sit in their cockpits and read newspapers.

When window first disrupted German radar, ground stations could no longer direct a fighter to a bomber. One response was for night fighters to freelance over the target, using the light of fires, flares and searchlights to find the bombers. Although the anti-aircraft gunners might keep to a known ceiling, the night fighters risked being hit by flak, falling bombs and exploding aircraft. These 'wild boar' fighters, introduced as the Battle of Berlin began, attacked the bombers when still loaded and committed to their bombing run. From early 1944, the 'tame boar' fighters, equipped with on-board radar sets, watching for vapour trails and exhaust flames and feeling the turbulence of the bombers, joined the bomber stream. The fighters came from below and behind and played their *schräge Musik* — their jazz (literally slanting) music. The *schräge Musik* were cannons mounted at an angle on a Messerschmitt 110 so that the pilot did not have to fly directly at his target. Not armed with luminous tracers, the *schräge Musik* fired into the fuel tank of a bomber still carrying up to five hours of fuel, and it exploded into flames. Brill and the other aircrew who watched bombers destroyed without sign of flak, tracer or return fire had seen early victims of *schräge Musik*. In the Battle of Berlin aircrew faced a long flight over enemy territory at a time when the tactics and the technical advantages were with the fighters, and that was the combination pushing losses towards 5 and 6 per cent per raid.

The boffins knew they had to help the navigators – to keep within the stream and on time, to find the target, and to return to the airfield they had left. Gee was introduced in 1942. From three transmitters sending pulses to a cathode-ray tube carried on board, the navigator could calculate his exact location. Although Gee was limited in range and was ineffective over Germany, it was a great aid to tired crews finding their way home. Oboe (its pulses emitted a musical sound), used from late 1942 and early 1943, enabled an aircraft to fly a set course and meet another pulse line, the junction marking the point over a target. While Oboe allowed the Pathfinders to drop marker flares on cloud immediately over a target, Oboe did not follow the curvature of the earth so that over the Ruhr only the high-flying Mosquitoes could use it. Further east was beyond the range of Oboe. H2S was one of the first radar sets that could be carried within an aircraft. On the cathode-ray tube the navigator could read an echo of the land below. Coastlines, lakes, rivers and cities could normally be distinguished, and it was possible for a bomber in cloud to 'see' a target or to find a distinguishing feature close to the target and make a timed run to a bombing point. Monica and Fishpond, introduced later, were also on-board radar devices that allowed the crew to detect aircraft close to them. But every technical advance could be diverted, jammed or exploited by the enemy.

Gee operated for five months before the Germans jammed it – a relatively long unfettered life – and while it was still used by the crews close to home, the Luftwaffe also learnt to tap it when they attacked targets in England. Gee then had to be encoded, making it more complicated. Oboe was also jammed, but improved versions of Oboe and the advance of the transmitting stations to the Continent after D-Day meant that Oboe remained effective and its range pushed east. The handicap with the radar sets carried on the bombers was that German fighters could fix on them. And the H2S sets helped the Germans identify which was the main force. But, in turn, Mosquitoes equipped with 'serratte' could home in on the German fighters' radar. In flight, aircrew tried to confuse Luftwaffe communications. Bill Pearce said he did his share of 'tinselling'. Monitors in England sent him the frequency being used by German fighters. With his Morse key and the signal from a microphone attached to one of the

Lancaster's engines, he sent intermittent blasts of engine noise over the frequency. In 101 Squadron Syd Gooding was carrying an eighth crew member and an 'airborne cigar' (secret electronic equipment). Fluent German speakers jammed the German communication system and cut into night fighter radio traffic to give false directions and commands. But again they had to operate in short bursts or otherwise they could be tracked by German operators. The techniques of jamming and counter-jamming were constantly refined.

Losses fell sharply in the raid on Hamburg on 24 July 1943 when aircrew first littered the air and ground with window. While window remained effective, and 'chaff tossing' a standard task, Bomber Command's casualties quickly returned to pre-window levels. On 23 August, one month after the Hamburg raid, Bomber Command lost 56 aircraft, its worst night to that date. *Schräge Musik* and then the wild and tame boar tactics were taking their toll. Aircrew were told before raids the likely German identification colours of the day, and a bomber crew facing the final burst from an attacking fighter could fire a Very pistol and hope it might cause a German pilot to hesitate. With the air turbulent from the slipstreams and engine noise of 2,000 aircraft, both sides using flares and counter flares, and electronic pulses being distorted and exploited, the night sky was an astonishing battleground of the visible and invisible.

From the Butt report of 1941, Bomber Command knew it had to be more accurate to be effective. Just getting more bombers carrying more bombs over a broad target was not enough. The destruction of a city required concentrated bombing at particular points and shifting the aiming point during a raid or in later raids. And the Allies needed Bomber Command to hit particular targets. These included factories and launching sites of the V-1 and V-2 rockets, radar stations and gun positions that threatened the success of the D-Day invasion, targets in occupied countries where the civilian population were to be spared, and selected factories, fuel production and storage sites, and communication

I was in contact with the various pyrotechnic experts ... and we got all sorts of fireworks under way ... Some high-powered candles were produced, which we named Target Indicators. These were my special requirements, and we used them extensively for the rest of the war. They were made in all colours and varieties, plain red, plain green, yellow, white, and each of those colours as a basic colour with ejecting stars of the same or different colours. Many combinations were, therefore, available for us to use as and when we chose ...

(Donald Bennett, Pathfinder.)

systems in Germany. The boffins made their contribution and aircrew had to develop the appropriate tactics and acquire new skills.

In mid 1942 Donald Bennett was appointed to establish the Pathfinder Force: he had to select and train crews and direct them to mark targets. Many of those invited to join Pathfinders were experienced crews, but some that had demonstrated efficiency in training went straight from OTUs. Eric Silbert had flown eight operations before transferring to Pathfinders, Hilliard 15 and Harold Wright 29. Kemble Wood had done none, but he had been in England for nearly a year and had logged much non-operational flying. Syd Johnson was asked to join Pathfinders while still at Brighton and 'didn't have a moment's doubt'. A Pathfinder crew often had two navigators: one a screen reader and the other working at his bench. Crews newly arrived at one of the Pathfinder squadrons flew as 'supporters' with a normal bomb load, and as they demonstrated competence on operations and in training flights they became 'illuminators' dropping the early flares, and then became responsible for placing ground and sky target markers. On the dams raid 617 Squadron used radio to enable an observing aircraft to guide the one attacking. By 1944 the use of radio communication over the target had become standard, with a master bomber or controller directing the bombers to particular flares and calling in the 'backers-up' to relocate the target when the bombers were confused or an area completely destroyed. As markers gained experience they dropped target indicators away from the actual target to allow for wind and the tendency of aircrew to 'creep back' (drop short).

For the crews in the main force, the flares increased in importance. Once they saw the flares they knew they had reached the right place in the sky, and to do their job they had to drop their bombs on them — flares challenged aircrew to defy flak and turmoil and press on. No wonder the code names of flares recur in their memoirs: 'Newhaven', a ground marker placed by an aircraft able to see the target; 'Parramatta', dropped by an aircraft using H2S; and 'Wanganui', a sky marker floating above cloud on a parachute. Bennett says the code names Wanganui and Newhaven were chosen from the home towns of a New Zealander and a WAAF, and he chose Parramatta to 'keep the balance'. A Pathfinder aircraft, carrying its full load of flares and bombs, hit by flak and exploding in the air, was an awesome sight.

Even with the technical and tactical advances, aircrew still did not hit all targets. On 14 July 1944 Cliff Halsall flew to Revigny to attack the railway yards. ('Nancy', Halsall noted in his diary, 'is a nearby well-known town'.) A week earlier the bombers had searched for Revigny, half had brought their bombs home, and those that had dropped them had done little damage to the railways. Now, Halsall said, this was to be an even 'shakier do'. The illuminating flares went down over the 'brilliantly lighted target', but no target indicators followed. The crews could hear the master bomber and his deputy talking, then a 'Jerry fighter' hit the master bomber's plane and the marker flares 'went down all right'. A few crews bombed the flares in 'the burning kite', but they were not in the railway yards. Fighter flares were dropped, air battles broke out and 'Lancasters appeared to be going down everywhere'. The deputy master bomber called to abandon the attack. Halsall said that they 'belted away' in 'J' for Joy, got back still with their bomb load after more than eight hours in the air, and the trains were 'still running through Revigny'.

Harris had opposed the formation of the Pathfinder Force, and group and station commanders did not like the setting up of an elite force. It took some of their best crews, and implied that they could not hit targets. Harris supported the Pathfinders once the decision was made, but other senior officers within Bomber Command were not convinced by Bennett's confident, strong arguments. In 5 Group, the squadrons continued to develop their own ways of increasing accuracy so that the master bombers, deputies, backers-up, various flares and low-level marking could all be used when no Pathfinder aircraft were on the raid.

The new marking tactics could also change the odds of survival. On 4 June 1944 Bob Curtis wrote on his route map for a raid on Cherbourg, 'Controller again — what a bastard'. As controller, Brill would arrive early and bomb late, and the longer in the target area the greater the risk. Curtis also knew what had happened on previous operations. In an attack on Brest, Brill as controller checked the winds and the location of the target indicator and by the time he came in to bomb, all the defences were angry and active. Having directed others to the target, he felt obliged to bomb accurately. Refusing to look beyond his

> ... we soon learnt all the jargon. Going on operations meant 'dicing with death' or 'juggling with Jesus'. Difficult targets were 'the arse-hole of death'. Crews that did not return had 'bought it', 'gone for a Burton (a beer)' or more commonly 'gone for a shit'. Much of the talk was about the number of operations a crew had done.... After a night of operations by Five Group a report was circulated on the Group's activities and posted on the squadron bulletin board. Missing crews were identified. There was full disclosure of casualties. No one was under any illusion ... [we knew] the odds of completing a tour of operations were poor.
>
> *(Peter Knox, 619 Squadron.)*

instruments, he held course until the bombs were away and the photograph taken, then dived and twisted until out of range. But they had been 'plastered'. One engine stopped soon after they left Brest, and the rear gunner said bits were falling off the starboard elevator. When they landed at Waddington they found 140 holes in the fuselage between the two gunners. They had a perfect aiming-point photograph, but Curtis, who often flew as a gunner, did not want a repeat.

While a tour was always around 30 operations, the way it was measured varied from time to time. Hours, points per raid, or simply the number of operations could be used. When Bomber Command began supporting the D-Day invasion, policy changed to reduce the value of the short trips. At first a raid on a target west of the Rhine was worth one-third of a trip to Berlin, but this undervalued shorter operations, and under a revised points system aircrew were given five points for a flight to Germany and three points for a raid over occupied western Europe. They then needed a total of 150 points to complete a tour. When Bob Hilliard did the 'double Duisburg' he earned ten points in 20 hours. To make full use of their expertise the Pathfinder crews were at first required to fly a tour of 60 operations, later reduced to 45 (225 points). As the change to reduce the value of the short trips included operations already completed, crews who thought they had just one or two trips to go found they had four and five, and what had looked probable was once again doubtful. Also, crews found it more difficult to know just how many trips they had to do. Ivan Pellas, beginning his tour in August 1944, flew on 37 operations. David Scholes, flying in the same months, flew 35. Operating earlier, Brill and Doubleday flew 31 times on their first tours and Don Charlwood 30. Even if the average loss rate was down to 2 per cent, seven extra raids made a significant difference to the equation of hope and despair.

Aircrew differ about when they became aware of the chances of survival, and the impact of this on them. Hilliard said that the 'crews were only too well aware of the mathematics of their situation'. When Bennett was at 77 Squadron early in 1942, the casualty rate was 'running at around 4 to 5 per cent per raid', and 'anybody with a reasonable mathematical knowledge', he said, 'could calculate the risk of survival'. The BBC lunch-time news often carried a report of the previous night's operations and said how many aircraft had 'failed to return'; the newspapers soon had their accounts cleared by censors; men heard about what was happening to those that had trained and travelled with them, every squadron knew about its own losses, and commanders at various levels circulated statements for all personnel setting out achievements and casualties. The statistics appear to have been inescapable. But Bennett also said some of the men with varied capacities in mathematics 'achieved all sorts of ideas as to what the possibilities might be'.

Faced with the evidence, a few men simply accepted death. Doubleday says he thought he would not survive, and Micky Martin, after his first few operations, decided it was inevitable that he would soon be dead. Martin had set aside hope, the enemy of morale. But as Charlwood asked, 'I wonder still how many men were really able to surrender hope'. And this did not mean that either Doubleday or Martin thought they were unable to reduce danger – both were meticulous in preparation, careful in their calculation of risk, and pushed their own and their aircrafts' strengths to the limit. When air battles broke out Doubleday would urge the crew to 'get your eyes on the sky. There's a quota tonight, and your job is to keep us out of the quota'. Yet some aircrew claim that at the time they did not know the odds. David Leicester said that it 'just didn't cross our minds at all that we were going into a dangerous occupation'. Dan Conway says that the 'last thing we were thinking of on ops was statistics'. And 50 years later, when he worked out the casualties per operation among other aircrew flying at the same time as he did, he was surprised that it was over 5 per cent. He says he 'had no idea they were running at this rate'. When Bob Curtis now reads some accounts of Bomber Command he finds the emphasis on death and the nearness of death misleading. These accounts do not evoke the exciting, careless times that he associates with operating squadrons. Both Leicester and Curtis were 18 years old when they began training, and perhaps older men were less likely to share that exuberant optimism. Ken Gray expressed the basic mental shield used by many: 'It was always ... going to happen to the other

BERLIN 'BLITZ'

The 'Evening News' aviation writer quotes Swedish reports that a large force of Allied bombers was over Sweden on Friday night. He says these suggest that our bombers followed a devious route and flew several hundred miles extra to outwit the German defences.

A communique on the raid says a strong force of Lancasters made the raid. Twenty-two bombers were lost in the attack and other operations.

(Sydney Morning Herald, 6 September 1943.)

fellow … you just felt deep down that it was you who was going to be all right. Now I suppose that was the same with all the fellows who did buy it'.

Aircrew were right to be afraid, or at least apprehensive, before their first operation. A survey of men killed in action on 460 Squadron showed over 11 per cent died on their first operation. The only flight more dangerous was the third one, with 12 per cent dying. Nearly half of all deaths took place on the first six operations, although by the sixth operation the death rate was already falling sharply. About 3 per cent of deaths were on the sixth operation. The third was often the most dangerous because novice crews were sometimes given less dangerous tasks on their first two operations – mining or bumphleteering – and pilots might make their initial flights with experienced crews. As a result, the third operation was often a crew's first operation against a tough target. The death rate fell sharply after the fifth operation and continued to fall slowly from then on. About 2 per cent of deaths occurred on the 20th operation.

Aircrew fear of death increased as they came close to completing a tour. From the 20th operation the odds that had once seemed so outrageously in favour of death had turned. It was again rational to plan a future – to hope. But that could mean a return of tension, and exhaustion was setting in. Aircrew believed that the accident rate went up as men neared the end of a tour. In fact the death rate in operations 20–25 was higher than in 25–30. Experience and determination to get home safely after having come so far offset increased mental and physical fatigue.

The statistics on the danger of operations over a tour have to take into account the simple fact that many more men flew their first operation than their tenth or 20th, and very few flew their 30th. But even when a 3 or 4 per cent decline in numbers with each operation is taken into account, the death rate on the first five operations was still exceptionally high. Those experienced airmen who allowed themselves to look at sprog crews self-consciously drawing flying gear to take a test flight or sitting at the back at their first briefing, saw chop crews – those who would make up so much of the percentage harvested by the

At this stage, with 20 up, we feel pretty sure we will get through. Here's hoping anyway. I will put in for my commission tomorrow.

(Cliff Halsall, 460 Squadron, diary, 8 August 1944.)

fighter, flak and accident reaper. Some experienced airmen avoided the new crews from a sense of guilt; it was as though there was a fixed quota on each raid, and the old crews survived because so much of the quota was filled by the new. Sprog crews slept in the beds of dead men, and there was a high chance that another sprog crew would soon sleep in theirs.

Aircrew and writers about aircrew have often assumed that when a crew began operations the alternatives were to complete a tour, be taken prisoner or die. For most men they were indeed the possibilities. But of 700 men beginning operations over the four years from 1942 to 1945, just over 40 per cent did not complete a tour but were not killed, imprisoned or interned. A small number, around 1 per cent, evaded capture, and some of them were forbidden to fly again over Europe. After Ted Coates parachuted from his burning Wellington and escaped across occupied France, he thought he would be sent back to operations. But as he had been reported dead by the Germans he was not allowed to fly over Europe again. If he were recaptured he could have enabled the Germans to correct their records and he might have been forced to incriminate those who had helped him on his long journey to the Spanish border. Ted Coates' operations finished with his 13th flight in 'Old Bill' ('W' for William) in 115 Squadron.

Fewer men were interned than evaded capture. From the 3,000 who flew with 460 Squadron, just ten were interned. Those briefly interned in Sweden might have gone back to operations. Francis Randall bombed Berlin on 3 September 1943, was caught in searchlights, attacked by fighters and his Lancaster was badly damaged. Expecting the engines to fail at any moment, he headed north, and he jumped a minute after the last of his crew. He and his English mid-upper gunner, H. Bell, were plucked from the waters of the narrow sound between Denmark and Sweden, and taken to Sweden. Three other members of the crew landed in Denmark: two (A. O'Brien from Australia and H. Ward from Canada) became prisoners and one, the flight engineer, (A. Johns)

> Sometimes the 'mood' in the mess, at the meal after an 'op', would be very gloomy. This would be on the occasion of an aircraft having 'failed to return' ... We accepted this, it happened regularly enough, and who was to be next?? I guess all we really did was mutter something like 'poor bloody Joe', or Jack or Fred or whoever, shrug our shoulders, eat our meal and go to bed. Then, at the earliest opportunity, we would sneak to their crew's quarters, and pinch what was left of their coal supply.
>
> *(Bill Pearce.)*

escaped capture, crossed to Sweden and he too was interned. Another crew member, the navigator N. Conway, died in the sea and the seventh, the bomb-aimer L. Greenaway, jumped or fell from the plane over Berlin and survived as a prisoner of war. Randall, carrying with him silk stockings and photographic film made in Berlin, was flown out of Stockholm on 30 September. He was so cramped in the civil aircraft that when he arrived at Leuchars, north of St. Andrews in Scotland, he had to be prised limb by limb from his seat. Back at Binbrook, he picked up a new crew and returned to operations. Bell and Johns, the other two internees, did not fly again with 460 Squadron.

Many did not complete a tour because they were sick or injured, or the war ended, or they transferred to other squadrons. If they went to Pathfinders they might complete, or try to complete, an even longer tour. From all Australians serving as aircrew in Bomber Command, 564 returned wounded from operations or were injured in ground accidents. That injury rate of about 6 per cent understated the frequency of wounding, as prisoners were often injured, either before or after leaving their aircraft, and some who were already injured died in later air crashes. But many of the 6 per cent returned to flying duties. Deterioration in hearing or eyesight, acute airsickness and various diseases could ground airmen, but in his official history of medical services Allan Walker says:

> There was little serious illness among aircrew. Nor did they often seek treatment for injuries sustained during operations. For the most part, they went missing or came back intact.

After accounting for those who were incapacitated, interned, evaded, ran out of war or who shifted to other squadrons in Bomber Command and kept flying, the number not completing a tour because they were posted elsewhere was still significant. Perhaps 10 per cent of airmen were free and physically healthy and did not complete a tour.

Tom Scotland went to Marston Moor to convert to Halifaxes, but just as he and his crew were ready to go to war they were invited to join Pathfinders. They agreed and were sent to 614 Squadron operating from Italy. After harrowing flights attacking oilfields and storages in eastern Europe, Scotland's English navigator told him that he had been to see the squadron doctor and had been grounded. The navigator retrained, was commissioned, and became an air traffic controller. After 25 operations his rear gunner, Bill Smith, said he too could take no more, and was given a doctor's certificate exempting him from flying. Smithy, Scotland said, disappeared from the squadron overnight, taking his 'courage and dedication' with him. On 20 March 1945 Scotland completed his tour, with four of his original crew still with him. Compassionate dispensation was more common than condemnation – by superior officers or by fellow aircrew.

Like Smithy, some ceased flying when close to completing a tour. But they were more likely to stop after just a few operations. Where the third operation was the most dangerous, the first was the most critical for those who left aircrew. Squadron lists contain several men who flew just one operation. Those who found that they were either physically or mentally incapable of being effective airmen made wise decisions, and those destined to be their fellow crewmen have reason to be grateful to them and to the officers who directed them elsewhere. The slight increase in those stopping flying late in their tours reflects the accumulating stress and fatigue the airmen were subject to – conditions which men thought increased the death rate but probably did not.

Those limited, stark options – death, imprisonment or a full tour – were closer to reality for pilots than for other members of aircrew. In 463 and 467 Squadrons, 432 pilots arrived at Bottesford or Waddington expecting to see their names listed for 'ops'. Nearly all of them became casualties (over 40 per cent), completed a tour (33 per cent), or were still flying when the war ended or had transferred to other bomber squadrons (about 25 per cent). Only a small minority of pilots – perhaps fewer than the average dying on one bad raid – did not press on. Dan Conway at 467 Squadron remembers a crew suddenly being stood down in February 1944 after 21 operations, and a few others that were 'pulled off' before the 'statutory 30'. He thinks that the squadron medical officer had noticed increased signs of stress and grounded them. Conway's memory is confirmed by the statistics: few pilots were taken off operations, and unlike other aircrew they were rarely shifted after just one or two raids.

One evening when the planes of 467 Squadron were taxiing in line to the take-off point, one stopped and all in the queue were forced to halt. Wing Commander Brill jumped in a vehicle, and dashed down to see what the trouble

… there was a case where I went around to a crew who had done twenty-seven or twenty-eight trips, and I think something like eight to Berlin in that, and the captain just couldn't go. He just shook and said he couldn't go. I said that's all right. Took him off and sent him on two weeks leave, one week medical leave, one week recreational leave, and he went to a farm in the country, and he came back, finished, no trouble at all.

(Arthur Doubleday.)

was. The pilot said he could not go on, in his condition he was going to kill the other six in the crew. Brill said he would bring them home. He went and got his flying gear and he flew the raid with the crew. He then arranged for the pilot to be given rest and counselling – he sent him to stay with Hugh Thompson, scientist and brain specialist, and Brill's navigator on his first tour.

When the compassion of officers and medical staff was inappropriate or absent, then, as Doubleday said, 'the next stage in this is LMF'. The finding, 'Lack of Moral Fibre', the stripping of rank, the rapid transfer to a menial task, and the marking of papers 'LMF' was rare. Doubleday said it was 'something that everybody knows about and smiles about but nobody talks about'. Some aircrew do not know of one case. Some heard of someone who suddenly disappeared from the squadron, and afterwards wondered what had happened to the person. Wade Rodgers said that at East Kirby just before take-off a 'poor lad' made the 'usual excuse' to step behind a hedge, and he disappeared completely. Three weeks later he was picked up trying to board a ship to Ireland. Harold Wright witnessed one public declaration of LMF: 'on 103 Squadron, a gunner, mid-upper gunner, refused to fly on an op and he was publicly stripped of his brevet and stripes in a hollow square of the assembled airmen'.

One of the hardest decisions for crews was when they had to tell one of their members that he was not capable of doing his job. When early in a tour a man froze at a critical moment and could not fire his guns, or the flight engineer sat white and still while the pilot shouted for an engine to be shut down, the decision was unavoidable. But later in the tour when the crew had shared intense experiences of war and peace, and had a sense of mutual dependence, it was extremely difficult to confront a fellow member of the crew and tell him that he could no longer do his job and was endangering the rest of the crew. That meant forcing a crewmate to cast himself on the uncertain sympathies of the squadron commander and doctor. A wireless operator on 460 Squadron said that they became worried about their bomb-aimer: he seemed to have lost the confidence to guide them over the target. They thought they saw his failing self-assurance in his behaviour when they were out of the aircraft, and their early and wide bombing was obvious on the photographs. In danger of being branded 'flak-shy', the crew thought they had better have a meeting without the bomb-aimer present and decide what to do. So as not to draw attention to themselves, they retired to a pub – probably the Marquis of Granby in Binbrook – and agreed that the bomb-aimer had one more chance. That night the bomb-aimer took them over the target with cold, deliberate instructions, 'left, left, steady, steady'.

Then still calm he said, 'Sorry Skip, take her round again'. They circled, crossing the flight paths of other aircraft, and again the bomb-aimer guided them relentlessly across the target, this time releasing at the last moment on the flaring target indicator. The sweating crew heard the calm 'bombs away' and felt the lift in the lightened aircraft. The question of the competence of the bomb-aimer was not raised again, and no one in the crew could bring themselves to ask him if he had heard of their doubts about him and whether their two runs across the target were just coincidence. That crew flew 22 operations with no changes in the crew, and the same bomb-aimer, navigator and pilot flew together through all 30 operations.

Pilots were more likely to die and less likely to be taken prisoner than the average member of an aircrew. Having to keep the plane steady for others to jump and being the last to leave had obvious dangers. While still training, Tom Scotland accepted the responsibilities of pilot and captain. In a fighter evasion exercise, an engine ripped from its moorings, tore the wing and took fire. Knowing the wing would soon break, Tom ordered the crew to bale out. But when he grabbed his own parachute and looked through the escape hatch he saw houses and factories. Returning to the controls, he headed for a patch of green, lifted over a road, smashed power lines, ripped across a stone fence, staggered over a creek and stopped in Devil's Glen, Leeds, just short of the houses. An urchin raced up and asked, 'Say mister, can I have the tail?' Scotland looked back and saw that he had left several tons of tail and rear turret down the valley.

A pilot's responsibilities and dangers increased over enemy land. After hitting trees when over the Dortmund-Ems Canal, Les Knight struggled to gain height. He ditched the 12,000 pound bomb, and the crew threw out excess ammunition and anything else disposable, but with the two port engines stopped the Lancaster could not climb much above 1,000 feet. Harry O'Brien, a Canadian gunner and 'a huge lumbering bear', lay in the front turret and held a broken rudder cable to keep the aircraft on a straight course. With the temperature rising dangerously in a remaining engine, Knight ordered the crew to bale out. As they carried an extra gunner for the front turret, eight had to leave from two hatches. Seven jumped, leaving Knight with his parachute hooked to his harness and the Lancaster dangerously low. Either because he could not, or because he thought he had more chance of surviving a crash-landing, Les Knight stayed in the Lancaster. The accountant, rechabite and Methodist from Melbourne died instantly when the aircraft hit an earth bank beside a ditch. All the other seven parachuted into Holland, five escaped to Spain and two became prisoners of war. On his third day back in London the other Australian in Knight's crew,

Dennis Adams, Australian war artist. *Down Through the Night*. 1945. *AWM ART22192*.

Bob Kellow, was asked if he wanted to keep flying, and if so where. In February 1944 Kellow left England for Australia and Transport Command. He had completed 27 operations with Bomber Command.

Rawdon Middleton, jackaroo, flew an old, inefficient Stirling to bomb the Fiat works in Turin. Hit by flak, Middleton, the co-pilot and the wireless operator were wounded and the aircraft damaged. Having reached the English coast with only a few minutes of fuel left, Middleton flew parallel to the shore so that the crew could bale out. Five came down on the land and survived. Two stayed with Middleton to the last moment and then landed in the Channel and drowned. Middleton, weak from loss of blood and with the automatic pilot destroyed, had no chance of reaching the escape hatch and rolling into the night. He flew out to sea and died in his ditched aircraft. He was, the citation for his Victoria Cross said, a 'gallant captain'.

Sam Weller was piloting a Lancaster over Munich when it was attacked by fighters. His navigator, Ash Taylor, gave him a course for Switzerland, but with flames enveloping the aircraft he ordered the crew to bale out. Three jumped and Sam was holding the burning Lancaster steady when it exploded. Sam, Ash and Fred Dunn, an English gunner, were thrown clear. As all three were unconscious on their descent, they do not know how or when their parachutes opened. Bill Edmonds, the rear gunner, was the only member of the crew killed. Sam Weller survived, but he did not have to leave the aircraft – it left him.

On his 17th operation, Geoff Coombes' Halifax lost an engine over the Baltic and as he came in over Berlin the sky was lit as bright as daylight by two rows of fighter flares. A German fighter made a series of attacks, wounded Coombes and the bomb-aimer, stopped two engines and took pieces out of the aircraft. Uncertain where the fighter was, Coombes called for the crew to bale out, just before the intercom went dead. All the forward crew and the mid-upper gunner went out the front hatch. Coombes assumed that the rear gunner had rolled out the back, and he was getting out of his seat when the emergency intercom light lit up. Only the rear gunner could have switched it on. Coombes went back into his seat, sent a series of 'Bs' for 'bale out' on the emergency communication system, and tried to hold the nose of the plane up as it spiralled down. Rapidly losing height and caught in cloud so he had no idea where he was going, he decided there was 'not much good bloody riding her down to the ground'. He jumped. Later the Germans told him that the rear gunner had died in the plane, but whether he was wounded or his turret jammed was unknown. Two other members of the crew who had baled out, and appeared to land safely, also died.

Had Coombes stayed in the Halifax he would almost certainly have died with the rear gunner. But it was still a tough decision for him to make and physically difficult for him to force his wounded body from the falling aircraft. And the survivors would never know whether the rear gunner lived through the descent and whether there was some act – unlikely and close to miraculous – that one of them could have taken to save him.

Where on average aircrew had an 8 per cent chance of being taken prisoner, pilots may have had just a 5 per cent chance. For pilots, the alternatives were pretty well to fly a tour, or a high number of raids, or die. That was almost an even break, but with the odds favouring disaster, slightly more pilots becoming casualties than completing a tour.

The number of men who did not complete a tour, as well as the casualties, have to be taken into account when looking at the low number of deaths by the time crews had flown 20 operations. There were simply not many who survived stress and disaster to fly more than 20 raids.

Freeman Dyson, a young civilian scientist in the Operational Research Section of Bomber Command, said later: 'Experienced and inexperienced crews were mown down as impartially as the boys who walked into the German machine gun nests at the battle of the Somme in 1916'. He said a skilful and experienced crew might be able to bring back a crippled aircraft that a new crew would have been forced to abandon, but such heroics were too few to change the random mass of statistics. Dyson was certain that by the Battle of Berlin, from mid November 1943 to the end of March 1944, enemy and error chose by chance the 1,117 aircraft that were destroyed. Although he overstated the case, by then two factors were increasing the importance of luck over skill. By determining the height, speed, route and time for each aircraft, Bomber Command was eliminating the options open to crews. German flak and the fighters equipped with radar and *schräge Musik* were often indiscriminate killers. Many crews died or baled out with their skill and courage apparently untested when their aircraft suddenly exploded. But if crews that had flown more than five operations were less likely to die, then experience and skill did matter.

The crews themselves believed that skill and experience mattered. Without the hope that their chances of survival would increase after the first few raids, and without the belief that they could influence their own fate, then morale would have plummeted. Men would have reduced themselves to tin ducks in a sideshow shooting gallery. (Ken Marks met one pilot who accepted he was a tin duck. Claiming all was determined by fate, he refused to weave or even do much to evade flak. He – and his crew – were shot down.) Experienced airmen knew that bad crews would not survive. Harold Wright flew as navigator for one crew that was a 'shocker' and on his return he said they would not last long – and they didn't. But the experienced also knew that the very best crews needed luck to survive. Sometimes they said it was 80 per cent luck and 20 per cent skill. That may have been about right, although the percentages varied over the course of the war. The importance of skill increased when the operations were most demanding of pilots and navigators and when they allowed or required crews to make decisions in flight.

Surviving crews certainly learnt on their first few operations. That was inevitable given the brief time they spent training in heavy bombers, and the impossibility of simulating the reality of Berlin or the Ruhr. Flight engineers and gunners often came to operations with little experience. Training had improved from the days when Tom Simpson first saw the guns and turret he would use in battle just a few hours before take-off, or when Joe Grose arrived at Breighton as a replacement gunner for Peter Isaacson's crew in August 1942 without having flown at night. Geoff Berglund, who began his flying training at Evans Head and ended it at Lancaster Finishing School, had completed over 60 hours of night flying when he arrived at Waddington in July 1944. But even in 1944 crews came raw to operations. Like most pilots, Syd Gooding had never taken off in a Lancaster fully loaded with fuel and bombs before his first mission. He asked senior pilots what it was like lifting 12,000 pounds of bombs and 2,000 gallons of fuel from the tarmac. They said it was 'a piece of piss'. He asked for more details, and they told him to wind the Lancaster up to 120 miles per hour and he would be right. On 26 September 1944 he took off for Karlsruhe with that basic advice, and it turned out to be sufficient. On his first mission Ivan Pellas found dense cloud over the V2 rocket stores in France and was told to bring his bombs back. Having so little experience landing a Halifax loaded or unloaded, his anxiety scarcely went up when he found he had to land with a heavy and dangerous load.

Nearly all crews were constantly trying to increase that small fraction of their chance of survival determined by their own decisions and skills. When Bill Brill returned for his second tour early in 1944 he flew a re-introduction flight as second dickey on a raid on Stettin. For the first time he saw the flares laid down to guide the bomber stream. Fearing they were as much help to the German fighters as they were to bomber navigators, Brill 'firmly decided never to cross a track marker'. On his way to Berlin a fortnight later he noted the green and yellow stars at point 'A' on his pilot's map, but being "'an old dog for a hard road" … we kept well away'. Ivan Pellas began drifting out of the stream a few minutes before a turn and later edged back in. But by the time he was flying operations in late 1944 and early 1945 he was avoiding collision rather than the fighters.

Some ground staff collaborated to ensure that their crew had slightly above the prescribed amount of fuel for an operation. It was better to start with the extra weight and have a reserve that might be used in evasive flying or lost when engines, tanks or fuel lines were damaged. Other pilots and navigators colluded to nurse the aircraft through the first hour, cutting corners and climbing gently to give themselves a reserve of fuel. 'It was an offence', Gus Belford said, 'but we intended to be survivors'. When Syd Gooding arrived at Ludford Magna, the bomb-aimer George McKean went around the experienced crews and asked for the 'gen'. He was told that they should work the one minute tolerance that was allowed: if in the first wave be one minute late, if last be a minute early, and never get more than two miles off course because enemy radar and fighters picked up, then picked off, isolated bombers. On his first raid with 218 Squadron, a conscientious Ken Marks stuck carefully to the briefing instructions and after bombing found himself at the back of the pack and under fighter attack. He learnt, but was not warned, to pick up speed by putting the nose down and getting out of the target area quickly.

The repeated advice of 'the higher the fewer' – fewer fighters, fewer flak bursts, fewer collisions and fewer bombs in descent – encouraged most crews to fly as high as instructions, conditions and aircraft performance allowed. It also meant that crews with height had more space in which to escape from searchlights and fighters, and by flying a long shallow dive they could pass at speed through danger areas. When Geoff Coombes lost an engine over the Baltic he decided to press on because he had the Halifax at 22,000 feet. By gradually losing height he thought he could keep up with the stream and bomb Berlin with the mob. He was wrong, and spent the rest of the war in Stalag Luft III. Laurie Field said that on the way back to Binbrook the pilot made sure that they had the height to exploit in a dash across the flak belt on the coast and escape at speed over the North Sea. But when Bill Brill was ten minutes from the Dutch coast after a raid on Bremen, he throttled back hoping a fast-flying Halifax would pass him and test the defences. When the Halifax also eased back Brill knew the Halifax pilot 'was not a newcomer to the game … so we had to lead him out'. Over strongly defended targets, pilots took advantage of another bomber being coned and drawing the fire of the anti-aircraft gunners to make their bombing run. Ken Gray also used other aircraft; whenever possible he flew with other bombers positioned on the most likely line of attack of the fighters.

Pilots disagreed on the safest tactics. Some flew an irregular weaving course to leave a less predictable trace on German radar, enable their gunners to see below from port and then starboard on the turns, and in the hope that German fighters might decide it was better to pick an easier target. Other pilots thought weaving used precious fuel, slowed the aircraft and increased the chance of collision. When 1 Group increased the bomb load in Lancasters, and so made the aircraft fly lower and be less manoeuvrable, crews responded by ditching bombs over the North Sea. Bennett claimed that the same thing happened in the Battle of Berlin. Instead of reducing the bomb load to offset the weight of increased fuel for the long flight, the total weight carried by the Lancasters was increased. Senior Pathfinder crews reported that on 'raid after raid' they saw 'scores of bombs being jettisoned'. The crews just would not accept a marginal reduction in their chances of survival.

Senior officers and the inboard camera made aircrew press on and press home the attack. The numbers of aircrew reporting sick, aircraft being found unserviceable, and crews returning before reaching the target were simple measures of the morale of squadrons – and of the quality of the senior officers. Squadron, station and group commanders pushed crews to fly and keep on flying. For officers who ensured high morale by personality and example there were few problems, but ambitious officers without that standing were seen to be forcing crews to take unnecessary risks. In his reminiscences, Don Charlwood said that the wing commander at 103 Squadron 'shamed' crews into flying when they should have turned back: 'No doubt it was better for the squadron's reputation to have aircraft lost than aircraft abort'. In his diary Charlwood was more explicit, claiming that the commander was forcing crews into the air 'for his own glorification … He is hated by all'. When close friends in another crew were killed Charlwood thought the 'rotten wingco' contributed: they had taken off last with an obviously faulty engine. The citation for Ivan Pellas's DFC says:

'When detailed to attack Soesterberg while still some distance from the target, one engine of his aircraft failed but Flying Officer Pellas pressed on and the mission was successfully completed'. Pellas had consulted the crew, and all thought they should keep going, but Pellas says that later in their tour, when they were more able to assess the risks and were confident of their right to make judgments, they would have turned back.

When the inboard camera was first introduced, crews thought of it as the 'official spy'. And it took several years of war before the camera was standard equipment. On the first 1,000 bomber raid on Cologne in May 1942, about one-quarter of the aircraft were fitted with cameras, but by the end of the year all were. The camera became the primary evidence of what was bombed and what damage was done, and it prolonged the time of greatest danger. Having dropped their bombs crews had to hold the aircraft steady for another 20 seconds or so until the photo-flash went (timed to coincide with the explosion of the bomb) and then they could go like the clappers. Within hours of the end of the flight the photograph revealed how accurate crews had been, and their time and height over the target. Photographs closest to the aiming point were displayed and aircrew who returned with the best photograph noted it in their logs. Crews on some squadrons contributed to a kitty and the crew with the best photograph took the pool. The skill and press-on spirit of a squadron could be assessed from its photographs. There was a sense in which crews flew for the photograph: no photograph, no evidence and maybe no operation. Without a photograph, they had to have a strong argument and other evidence before being given the benefit of the doubt.

Aircrew say it was the support of those around them, and the fear of letting others down and of failing in front of them, that enabled them to fly into enemy fire, to fly in the night not knowing when they were to be suddenly incinerated, and to keep doing it. When it was 'Night after night – Essen, Essen Essen', Don Charlwood wrote in his diary, 'I am damned sure I would hold no hope in my heart if I trusted solely in myself'. Charlwood was conscious of the rest of the crew, and of his distant family whose photographs he carried with him. 'My recollection', Bruce Pitt said, 'is that your major concern was not to let the rest of the crew down'. Those who were not the most skilful, and those who were frightened, tried to do the best they could 'for the crew – that's the sort of thing I remember most'. Men in army units often make the same comment on the importance of the presence and opinion of comrades, but the sense of being a unit in a bomber crew was intense because they were enclosed together and could rarely get help or even communicate with another aircraft. Each crew member had different tasks, and it was the total of their skills that made the crew.

The fact that so many crews could keep operating certainly needs explaining. What is much more difficult to explain is why many men kept flying when they had a reasonable excuse to be stood down, and why they chose to fly after the end of a tour. Pete Stevens flew 56 operations and, Harold Wright said, was sick on nearly every one:

> All he had to do was to go and see the MO if he wanted to, and he could have been grounded for the rest of the war because that was a legitimate excuse for not flying. But old Pete, he used to make a joke of it. He had a tin which was tied with a pink ribbon and he used to hold it out as he was walking to the plane, and that was his sick tin.

Others concealed their fragility throughout training and during operations. After several operations Jack Currie was surprised to find that his navigator, Jim Cassidy, carried brown paper bags among his maps and tools of trade. Cassidy admitted that he always vomited soon after take-off, and usually later in the flight. But as the wireless operator said, Cassidy was 'ever so neat about it', as he was in his work.

Without being harassed by thoughtless officers, crews took actions beyond any reasonable call of duty to join operations. Andy Andrews, an English flight engineer who flew with George Jarratt from Sydney, says that on take-off the bomb-aimer's hatch fell on the runway. Jarratt circled until all the Binbrook aircraft were in the air, then landed the Lancaster carrying full bomb and fuel load, found and fitted the hatch and took off. They survived the two extra

Peter Stevens joined the RAAF at eighteen and trained at Pearce, Mt Gambier, Nhill and Port Pirie. He logged 330 operational hours. The citation for the Bar to his DFC said: 'this officer has continued to display exceptional courage and coolness, skilfully overcoming intense opposition and guiding the attacks of his aircraft fearlessly and accurately. His outstanding efficiency as a navigator has been highly commendable'.

(AWM65)

hazards they had imposed on themselves – the chance of running short of fuel and of being behind the bomber stream. On 26 July 1942 Brill was listed for his 28th operation of his first tour. The aircraft that Brill normally used was being flown by another crew on a sea search, and when it was late returning the ground crew had just 45 minutes to prepare another Wellington. Brill arrived to find the Wellington already had its two engines running, but as he prepared for take-off he found an oil leak in the starboard engine. The crew thought that would be the end of war for the night, but when Brill reported the oil leak the squadron commander told him to take the aircraft of an inexperienced crew that had been stood down because of the threatening weather. By the time Brill found his crew they had taken off their harness, Mae Wests and outer flying gear and had eaten their flying rations. Although they were on those last nervous flights at the end of their tour, Brill and the crew took off for Hamburg. They survived, but two other 460 crews were lost that night.

So that a crew could finish a tour together, individual men chose to fly extra operations. Two of the gunners who flew with Middleton on his last flight had both completed their tours, and they volunteered to stay on operations until Middleton had finished. One of the gunners, John Mackie, delayed leaving Middleton until the last moment, and died when he parachuted into the sea. After Robert Hilliard completed his tour, the pilot Bluey Osmond agreed to fly three more raids to 'finish Jack off'. Having done that, Osmond flew another four operations so that two other members of the crew did not have to find a new pilot. Brill, like Doubleday and other squadron commanders conscious of their responsibilities, flew with inexperienced crews. After the pilot of a crew was killed flying as second dickey, Brill took the other six men on an attack against railway yards at Limoges, rather than sending them back to re-crew and retrain. As it was just after D-Day, they saw below them the opposing armies 'blazing away'. Brill said that the 'excitement and enthusiasm expressed by the crew members repaid my small effort'.

Those men agreeing to sign-on for a second tour went back to battle knowing exactly what they were doing and their chances of success. Don Charlwood wrote:

A few outstanding men recognized that the Command needed their leadership and expertise. Their presence on a squadron lifted morale enormously – provided they stayed alive ... Epitomizing such men at Lichfield were two former Riverina farmers, Arthur Doubleday and Bill Brill. They were squadron leaders, each commanding a Lichfield training flight.

It is a fine tribute, yet a senior officer wrote at Lichfield that Brill was just a 'good steady plodder' and gave him four out of ten for initiative. That judgment was in sharp contrast to those who knew Brill as 'charismatic' and a leader of 'outstanding personality'. Perhaps Brill manifested those qualities of leadership only when they were needed – on an operational squadron – but that seems unlikely. In volunteering for a second tour, Brill and Doubleday had committed themselves to another 20 raids.

Brill and Doubleday picked up most of their new crew members while still instructing. Ron Fuller says that they were having a beer in the mess at Lichfield when Brill said he was going back to operations, and he wanted Bob Curtis and Ted Freeman to fly with him. Ron said that he would go with them, but Brill thought there was no chance that Ron would be allowed to go as he had already done 50 operations, nearly all in North Africa. Fuller insisted he was going anyway so Brill asked for his release, and to everyone's surprise it was granted. When Doubleday arrived at the Conversion Unit he still did not have a navigator, but Bob Murphy, a navigation instructor there, was already a friend of Arthur's. Bob said that going on a second tour was 'normally a voluntary job, but they asked me and I couldn't knock 'em back'.

No men from Brill and Doubleday's first crews flew with them on their second tours, although at least one, Doubleday's first navigator Gordon Goodwin, flew a second tour with Pathfinders. Brill's crew was Ron 'Tubby' Fuller (mid-upper gunner) from Booleroo Centre in South Australia, Ted 'Bluey' Freeman (navigator) from Melbourne, Bill McMahon (bomb-aimer) from Taree in New South Wales, Bob Curtis (wireless operator and air gunner) from Sydney, Len Smith (flight engineer) from London, and Bill McDonald, an Australian rear gunner picked up at Waddington. Curtis had served a first tour in North Africa, Len Smith, Bill McDonald and Bill McMahon were new to battle, and only Brill and Freeman had previously flown a full tour in Bomber Command.

To transfer to Pathfinders could mean doing more than an extended tour. Given that the Pathfinders were most in demand on difficult raids, had an obligation to be accurate and were likely to pass over the target to mark and pass over again to bomb, aircrew were under no delusion that this was a longer, but softer, option. And although Pathfinder losses were close to average, early casualties were high. Yet crews volunteered for Pathfinders when the reward was little more than an increased chance of promotion and the prestige that went with a certificate and the right to wear the golden Pathfinder wings. At the end of his first tour Peter Isaacson tried to explain why he and his crew had decided to transfer to Pathfinders. If he came back to Bomber Command for a second tour after a break of six months or more he would have to fly with a different crew. Equipment and tactics would be unfamiliar and he thought that German defences might be getting stronger – not an unreasonable assumption early in 1943. Fifty years later he also conceded that his crew had an irrational sense of their 'invincibility'.

David Leicester had flown Halifaxes in 158 Squadron in 1943 when losses were high, but at the end of his tour he chose to fly with Pathfinders. Not one of his crew wanted to go, so he went alone and picked up a crew from other individual volunteers. Neither Isaacson nor Leicester wanted the alternative – instructing at OTU. For others the crew often made the decision. Dalton and his crew decided that they would go to Pathfinders if they all wanted to – it would be a unanimous not a majority decision. They stayed with 44 Squadron at Spilsby. Robert Hilliard said that he and others in Bluey Osmond's crew talked about applying to join Pathfinders, but 'responses lacked something in enthusiasm'. They were therefore taken by surprise when posted to Pathfinders. They suspected that the unconventional Bluey had 'volunteered' them, but they accepted the decision – and the new target of 45 operations.

Bomber aircrew who volunteered to fly a second tour or transfer to Pathfinders not only had a detailed knowledge of what they were going to have to do, but compared with others who have gone into battle they also had an exceptionally precise knowledge of the chances of survival. To fly 50 operations at a 2 per cent loss rate per operation gave a 36 per cent chance of survival. Three per cent (the most likely loss rate) meant 22 per cent survived, and 4 per cent meant just 13 per cent of aircrew survived. In the heat of battle exceptional men take actions when they know the chances of surviving are low, but these were large numbers of men (over 3,600 men of all nationalities died in Pathfinder squadrons) making free decisions, with knowledge and the chance to talk it over in the mess and the pub.

A Halifax over a flying bomb launch site on a moonlit night, 5 and 6 July, 1944. The Halifax survived. *AWM SUK12408*.

11

COUNTING THEM IN

By 1943 Berlin's air defences stretched across more than 40 miles of searchlights and anti-aircraft guns. At the height of a raid, aircrew said, the searchlights were like a forest of bamboo and the flak was so thick you could step out of a plane and walk on it. The guns on the flak towers hurled explosives over 40,000 feet into the air, and the hundreds and hundreds of light and heavy flak guns were not directed at a particular aircraft but patterned an area with streams of fire and shell bursts. On the margins of the city decoy fires were lit, incendiaries and high explosives fell on ten or more miles of the city and beyond, and photo flashes, marker flares, fighter flares, multi-coloured target indicators, tracer fire and exploding aircraft lit the sky and ground of battle.

The targets were such extraordinary sights that aircrew could not help but look in awe. Like many other pilots, Brill tried to describe what he had seen, and what he was drawn to look at again and again. After an attack on Emden in June 1942 he escaped out over the North Sea, but then he:

> turned the kite around to have a look at the show. It was an unforgettable sight. Must have been seventy or more flares hanging over the centre of the town, with the usual searchlight cones and more than the usual amount of coloured flak weaving its way up. Fires and gun flashes on the ground and flak bursts in the sky made the picture complete. And the whole issue was reflected in the water.

On his second tour Brill was deputy controller on a raid on an ammunition dump at Sable-sur-Sarthe. Having bombed early and seeing no sign of fighters he flew at 10,000 feet to watch aircraft streaming through, bombs going down, explosions at increasing tempo and the 'whole area a bubbling boiling mass'. The crew could even feel and hear sounds above the roar of the engines. The scene,

Brill said, was 'probably more vivid than the fireworks at the Calgary Stampede 3 years before'. No aircraft was lost and 'a good time was had by all'. For aircrew the spectacle was an immediate measure of the enormity of what they had to do and what they did: it was gratifying, seductive and terrifying.

With bombs gone and nearly half the fuel used, the bombers could climb higher and faster and respond more quickly to the controls. As they turned for home, crews believed that although the journey was half completed, more than half the risks were overcome. The German fighters, more limited in range, might even be landing to refuel. But because the bombers usually faced a headwind, the return flight could take longer than the loaded outward flight. Battling into a 50–80 miles per hour westerly could cut the ground speed to 130 miles per hour, and the crew could easily believe that they were suspended in the air, not moving further from the glow of the target and not getting closer to the Dutch coast.

A few of the longest raids were not out and back, but staged through other landing fields. After the Allies recaptured North Africa, commanders (by plan) and crews (in emergency) had new airfields to exploit. In June 1943, 467 Squadron left Bottesford and attacked the Zeppelin works at Friedrichshafen. The Lancasters crossed into Switzerland to attack Friedrichshafen from across Lake Constance. Bill Manifold said that after bombing they 'set course for what was the really exciting part of the trip: Algeria!' In one of the early 'shuttle' raids the aircraft flew south into daylight near the Italian coast and arrived at Blida near Algiers in clear light. Some aircraft, running short of fuel, were forced to

'It was five times larger than the biggest bushfires I have ever seen,' said Pilot Officer Doubleday describing his experience in staccato sentences. 'Earlier arrivals had set the place well alight. We had a perfect target and it was impossible to miss. We dropped ton after ton of bombs in the middle of the blazing factories. My cobbers said they were able to see the fires and smoke from the Dutch coastline approximately two hundred miles distant. The flak was murderous as usual till towards the end of the raid. The Hun gunners practically gave up the ghost. They must have got sick of shooting at us. The Hun night fighters were pretty active. My gunners squirted at a couple which quickly sheered off and did not molest us again.'

(Daily Mirror, *press cable on raid on Cologne of 29 May 1942.*)

> It is a wizard sight to look back when you get over the target and see the main force coming in. A hundred or so Lancs in a great gaggle getting closer and closer. They come in so close to each other that to bomb they almost have to jostle for space.
>
> *(Harold Wright, Pathfinder, quoted in press release, April 1944.)*

make emergency landings, one ploughing to a halt in a vineyard. The Australians were soon wandering about with their shirts off, looking at gum trees, visiting the swimming pool, going to the beach, and buying what was in short supply in England. In spite of the fact that they had another bombing raid to do on the way back, most aircraft were stacked with bunches of grapes, bottles of wine and other goods to be used for gifts or trade.

On 12 February, 617 Squadron returned to the south of France to attack the Antheor viaduct on the coastal railway being used by the Germans to support their troops in Italy. Knowing that they had to be accurate to be effective, Leonard Cheshire and Micky Martin made runs but were forced wide by accurate gunfire. Coming from inland, Martin dived out of a ravine on to the viaduct, and just before Bob Hay released the bombs a shell struck and exploded at the front of 'P' for Popsie. As Martin struggled to keep the Lancaster above the surface of the sea, the crew checked the damage. Bob Hay, bomb-aimer on the dam busters raid, was probably dead, Ivan Whittaker, flight engineer, was badly wounded in the leg, but was able to use his tie as a tourniquet to stop the bleeding. With power from only two engines, the electrical system out and other damage, the crew had to think about where to go – North Africa, Gibraltar, Sicily, Corsica or Sardinia. Martin chose Corsica, the closest, then on radio advice changed course to Sardinia where the Americans had the facilities to provide immediate aid to the wounded.

Martin's crew left Bob Hay DFC and Bar, civil servant of Gawler South Australia, in a grave in Sardinia, and flew on with a patched up Popsie and flight engineer to Blida. In three days in Algeria they bought up a 'good sized truck-load of liquor and fruit, etc' and flew it back across Spain. Even after donating grog to the mess and keeping a personal supply, the crew had a profit of £250 to split among themselves. It funded a great leave.

John Holden, wireless operator, flew inside the Arctic Circle three times in attempts to sink the German battleship *Tirpitz*. Sheltering in Kaa Fiord in the extreme north of Norway, the *Tirpitz* was a threat to Allied shipping supporting the Russians. Unable to reach the *Tirpitz* from airfields in Britain, the bombers landed on 'very primitive runways made out of logs' at Yagodnik near Archangel in Russia. After waiting for clear weather, on 15 September 1944, 28 Lancasters tried to make a surprise daylight attack on the *Tirpitz* in its narrow, steep-sided fiord. In a Lancaster equipped with two 35 millimetre cameras to film events, Holden's crew had to arrive early, stay longer and fly lower. Satisfied that they had a complete film record, they left for home, flying almost at sea level to get below the cloud. With all excess weight removed and extra fuel tanks fitted, they made the flight from Yagodnik to Kaa Fiord to Waddington in 14 hours and 33 minutes, the longest flight for a Lancaster on an operation. The Germans shifted the crippled *Tirpitz* further south to Tromso, and as Allied intelligence was uncertain whether the *Tirpitz* was still a threat Bomber Command continued its pursuit. Twice more Holden flew on the film unit aircraft. The *Tirpitz* was now within range of the most northern airfields and the planes took off from and returned to Lossiemouth and Kinloss in Scotland on the 2,250-mile trip. Flying over the Alps on the Sweden–Norway border with the snow and glaciers 'tinted by the Northern Lights' was 'something to be wondered about'. On the third trip Bruce Buckam, the pilot of the film unit Lancaster, circled low over the obviously damaged *Tirpitz*. He decided they had taken enough risks and used enough precious fuel so had set course for home when the rear gunner yelled, 'Turn around, Buck, she's tipped over'. He turned, and the crew saw the red paint on the battleship's keel. As they left, the *Tirpitz* was lying on her side in the shallow fiord. This time they flew straight home to 'our own base – good old Waddo'. It was another flight of over 14 hours.

When the crews were furthest from home, over enemy territory and with the North Sea to cross to reach uncertain weather over home airfields, they faced alone some of their toughest decisions.

On the night of 5 March 1945 Gus Belford was bringing a Lancaster in over the target, a synthetic oil plant near Leipzig, but the visual confusion was worse than normal as the marker flares were being swept along by wind and diffused by cloud. Unable to bomb on the first run, he turned away for a second try and anti-aircraft shells exploded in and around the Lancaster. Belford was hit in the right leg but did not know how badly, and the plane, holed in several places, spiralled down. He told the crew to prepare to bale out. Belford and the flight engineer Horry Burchett reduced the rate of fall and turn, and with the release of the bombs brought the aircraft onto level flight. When the crew assessed the damage, they found that Peter Shipperd, the mid-upper gunner, was unconscious, but they were able to stop the bleeding in his neck wound, lie him down, inject him with morphia, fix his parachute to him, and have him ready to be thrown out in an emergency. Percy Jobson, the rear gunner, although temporarily blinded by fragments, seemed to have superficial injuries and Belford's leg needed no immediate treatment. But the wounds to the Lancaster itself were near fatal. One empty petrol tank was blown out of a wing, holes gaped in the fuselage from the wings to the tail, the starboard aileron was almost blown off, and other controls and navigation equipment were damaged. The plane was skidding to the right, and slowed by drag, but the four engines were undamaged. Belford could still control direction and the Lancaster had some capacity to climb. They headed south towards Austria, still on the course set for bombers leaving the target.

Other bombers, travelling at more than 30 miles an hour faster, overtook them and disappeared into the night, but one, by dropping its wheels and flaps, was able to slow down and fly alongside. The pilot was Len Buckenara, a fellow Western Australian, and he recognised Belford's Lancaster. Buckenara crossed below then came over the top of the crippled Lancaster. Having finished his circle of inspection, he signalled with a torch: 'THAT IS SOME HOLE. WHERE ARE YOU TO'. On Belford's instructions, Alan Beer, flying his first trip as second dickey, flashed a reply saying that they were on their way to Switzerland and would see them in a week. Buckenara then left them.

Belford knew that he did not have enough fuel to reach the nearest airfield in England, and that there was a high chance of further deterioration in the structure, controls or engines. The crew now re-assessed its options. Belford found he could not safely force the Lancaster above 7,000 feet, so that meant they could not cross the mountains of Austria and the Swiss border: Switzerland was out. By flying east for 40 minutes, they could be over Russian-held territory where they could bale out. But none of the crew wanted to take their chances with the Russians. They could fly west for longer, into a headwind and through a weather front with the danger of ice weighing on their fragile aircraft, and either bale out over Allied territory or try to fly to Juvincourt, an airfield in northern France. Baling out at night was risky, and they had one injured man to cast into the night. With a line attached to jerk open his parachute, the injured man would float down, but could do nothing to save himself if he landed in water, and he might end up a long way from the rest of the crew and help. But to fly another two hours, find a distant airport, land with few controls and probably end up sliding the belly of the aircraft along the tarmac with the chance of fire was obviously taking a high risk. At the start of the war Gus Belford, the pilot, was 15 years old and Doug Wheeler, the navigator, was 14. The two men whose skills most influenced their chances were both 20 in March 1945. They went looking for an Allied airfield to their west.

They saw no fighters and little flak, but ice forced them down and dangerously close to unseen mountains. Aided by Gee, effective as they came closer to the sending stations, Wheeler brought them over Juvincourt, inside the Allied perimeter. At the first attempt to land in rain and low cloud they almost collided with the control tower, and sliced through its radio and radar antennae as they climbed for a second try. Again Belford gave crew members a chance to jump, but all chose to stick with the plane. On the second attempt one wing and

---

CRIPPLED BOMBER GETS HOME

London Dec 9 (Official Wireless). How two Australians helped to bring a badly damaged Lancaster safely home from the recent raid on Leipzig was told to-day by the Air Ministry's news service.

The Lancaster was first attacked by an ME110 not many miles from the target. The first burst of cannon fire killed the rear-gunner, and set fire to the main plane and petrol tank.

The mid-upper gunner, Flight-Sergeant M.N. Williams of Booleroo, South Australia, had a narrow escape. The turret windows were smashed, and his oxygen mask was smashed.

The captain of the plane, Flight-Lieutenant M.T. Foram of Gilgandra, New South Wales, gave the order to fix parachutes, but while the crew were doing this the flight engineer saw another ME110 which opened fire at 25 yards, causing more damage.

With the aircraft on fire, the captain knew he could not go to Leipzig, so despite a fierce barrage, he bombed his alternative target [Dessau].

On the way home the Lancaster was again attacked. Foram put his aircraft into a dive to throw the fighter off, and like a miracle to the crew, the dive put out the fire in the main plane and petrol tank.

When safely past the enemy coast, the Lancaster suddenly became extremely unstable, and it was decided to come down into the sea. But the crew found holes in the dinghy, and with a great struggle, Foram kept on his course, and landed safely, despite a tendency by the Lancaster to turn on its back.

(Sydney Morning Herald, *10 December 1943*.)

---

one wheel hit the runway together, the plane slewed to one side, one wheel was ripped off in a bomb crater, the other collapsed, and they slid to a stop. The most severely injured in the landing were two men in the control tower who had jumped when they thought they were about to be hit.

The Canadians at Juvincourt took the two injured men, Percy Jobson and Peter Shipperd, to hospital in Rheims, and the next day the rest of the crew went into Juvincourt where the French made it clear that they preferred the Germans. Later, the crew members who were fit hitched a ride back to Waddington. Belford found his personal possessions neatly stacked, ready to be parcelled and sent to his father. A telegram had already been sent saying that he was posted missing. Nineteen days later, with two replacement gunners, Belford and his crew again flew on a bombing raid.

Bill Manifold was taking a turn as officer in charge of night flying in the control tower at Bottesford. As the pilot on duty he dealt with flying problems outside the competence of the controllers. All aircraft except 'L' Lucy returned from Italy. After a long delay Lucy called in. The pilot was flying with no elevator, had only 15 minutes of fuel and wanted to land immediately. He explained that he had practised landing on cloud on the way home, and thought there was no other fault that would stop him using his limited control to land. By this time all options were effectively closed. He did not have enough fuel to reach an airfield with a longer 'crash' runway or to climb and let the men bale out. The pilot brought the plane in perfectly, but suddenly the complete tail plane broke off and the rest of the aircraft crashed and instantly burst into fire. The pilot of 'L' Lucy had made the wrong decision, but he had done all he could to get it right.

[The pilot of an all-Australian crew] on one of their early trips, decided that the state of the aircraft was so bad and the conditions prevailing so adverse that he would abandon the sortie. He asked the navigator to give him a course for home. The navigator, supported by the rest of the crew, refused to do so. To resolve this deadlock, one of the crew knocked the pilot out and he was then removed to the casualty bed and strapped down. Flying the aircraft as best they could, this crew proceeded to the target, bombed it and returned to base. They then released the pilot and ordered him to land the aircraft, which none of them could have done. They told the pilot that if he promised never to turn back again, unless they all agreed to that course, they would say nothing about the incident ... They flew a very successful tour of operations; the pilot was awarded the DFC and the rest of crew received no recognition.

(Noble Frankland, navigator, 50 Squadron and British official historian of Bomber Command.)

The crew was not a flying democracy – the pilot, as captain, had ultimate responsibility. A pilot's position was often enforced by rank and by the convention of calling crews by the name of the pilot. It was just the pilot's name that was chalked on the operations' board. It was the pilot who systematically checked that all his crew were awake and connected by a working intercom, and it was the pilot who was most likely to set the way the intercom was used for casual conversation – or singing. When Brill dropped low over Paris to get below the cloud and the flak came streaming up, his gunners screamed at him to get height. Brill 'had to bawl at them a bit'. But the crew were able to have their say. In November 1942 Ted Coates was flying a Wellington back from a raid on Stuttgart. Over an hour into the return flight the navigator asked if he could 'take an astro shot' to confirm their location. But that required holding the plane steady and in a straight line. Immediately the Canadian rear gunner, Curly Payie, had his say:

'Don't be silly Skip, it's going to be bloody dangerous up here in this bright moonlight. Let's hit the deck'. He conveyed his annoyance with a few more lurid remarks.

Ted Coates switched to automatic pilot so that the Wellington flew smoothly knowing he might be allowing German ground staff every chance to fix his height and direction. Curly Payie and the navigator were both killed when the Wellington was attacked by a fighter.

Over Hamburg, Brill had trouble finding the target and suggested that he stooge into the centre of the flak to find out what he could see from there: 'The suggestion was promptly greeted by "Drop the damn things, and go home" from every corner of the kite'. They dropped the bombs, Brill hoped they did not hit a hospital or school, and 'so home to interrogation and bacon and eggs'.

Pilots asked for advice. Caught ten minutes behind time and with a doubtful electrical system, Sam Weller 'checked with each one and it was unanimously agreed' to go to Munich. When the flight engineer confirmed that they would be short of fuel on the return journey, Weller again consulted all the crew. But when decisions had to be made and no particular man could claim authority because of his special skills, then leadership established on the ground (about whether they drank at the Saracen's Head or went to a dance, or joined Pathfinders) could play a part. A bomb-aimer or a gunner could, by steadiness or humour, hold a crew together. Infrequently crews overruled their captain, and there were stories of pilots being belted into pressing on or bombing short.

No one completed a tour on Bomber Command without narrow escapes. Most crews went close to death as a result of more than one of the major dangers: enemy fighters and flak, fellow airmen who could collide with them or bomb them, the weather, equipment failure, or human error. Many crews survived encounters with all of them. Brill met most before he was halfway through his first tour. On his second operation and the first time he was taking off in a fully loaded Wellington, Brill pushed the throttles forward but forgot that they eased back unless he kept pressure on them. His attempt at a half throttle take-off was almost his last. On his return from the same flight he found Breighton under fog and had to divert to another field. Attempting to reach Hamburg on his eighth operation he again had trouble with the weather. Arthur Doubleday was caught in the same electrical storm, and with his Wellington icing up was in much greater trouble. Ice was rightly feared by aircrew; when controls and aerodynamics were lost the aircraft could simply fall like a brick. By his

A Halifax crew of 466 Squadron returns from a raid on Berlin, 20 January, 1944. Of 769 aircraft, 4.6 per cent were lost. The crew from left to right: Pilot Officer A.F. Studders, Pilot Officer D.D. Graham, Pilot Officer M.F. Manning, Pilot Officer J.M. Cunningham, Pilot Officer C. Cobb, Sergeant J. Ellis, and Sergeant R.E. Catt. *AWM UK0955*.

15th operation Brill had been caught in searchlights, had his aircraft holed by flak at least twice, suffered an electrical fault that dropped incendiaries on the tarmac under his stationary Wellington, and continued an operation after the rear turret 'packed up' early in the flight. While he had found fighters 'troublesome' on his first tour, it was not until he returned to operations early in 1944 that he was involved in sustained air battles.

The closeness of disaster is obvious in the brief entries in nearly all logbooks. In less than four months at 12 Squadron, Kenneth Hesketh, navigator, recorded: 'port outer fired', 'diverted Elsham', 'rear turret holed by flak', 'coned six minutes', and 'iced up lost three engines'. 'G' for George was obviously a lucky Lancaster. It survived 90 operations and, unlike nearly all other Lancasters, survived the peace and is preserved in the Australian War Memorial. But on its first 30 operations it was holed by flak ten times. In the returning bomber stream, and trailing behind, there were always many damaged bombers.

For many airmen, awareness of having been close to disaster was complicated when others died in their place. That was one factor in the intense grief felt by Harold Wright when he was in hospital and the rest of Syd Cook's crew (and a replacement navigator) died over Frankfurt. But this was not the only time that Wright evaded death. Having completed an extended tour with Pathfinders, Wright was in London on leave where he met George Loder. George had finished his tour of 45 operations with 156 Squadron, but he was going to fly a few more trips so his crew could all complete their tour together. As his bomb-aimer had fallen off a bus and broken his wrist, Loder asked Wright to fly as a replacement. Wright agreed, but the commanding officer on the squadron blocked him. Loder was killed over Germany on 20 December 1943, on what would have been his second-last operation. After the commanding officer changed, Wright returned to flying occasional operations, but when Dicky Walbourn asked him to switch squadrons and join his crew as a permanent member he was not keen. Pestered by Walbourn, Wright tossed a coin, and its fall determined that he went with Walbourn to 582 Squadron, still in Pathfinders. The navigator who replaced him at 156 Squadron died on the first operation after Wright left.

> On our return flight [from Saarbrücken], the sky cleared over France and we were in brilliant moonlight. Suddenly our aircraft was raked with a fusillade of 20mm. shells. The noise could be likened to being in a 10,000 gallon watertank, with about 50 kids each wielding a stick battering the outside.
>
> *(Norm Wright, wireless operator.)*

Given that Wright flew 71 night operations and six day operations, from Düsseldorf in September 1942 to Stuttgart in July 1944, he certainly provided chance with a good many opportunities to play its part. But there were also aircrew who had flown just a few operations when they swapped from rear gunner to mid-upper for the flight and the rear gunner was killed. Or they had gone to do a course on Gee when the rest of the crew disappeared over the North Sea, or cut a hand on broken glass at the Horse and Jockey and missed Nuremberg. Good luck could simply be someone else's bad luck.

Finding the United Kingdom, even England, if not the right airfield, on the return flight should have been easy. But many pilots were given one wrong course direction during a tour, or misinterpreted one direction, and even when they were on the right heading an unpredicted wind could, in two or three hours of flying, push an aircraft more than 100 miles off course. The cheerful, elderly gunner, Cliff O'Riordan (he was officially 33 and thought by his young colleagues to be over 40) wrote about turning for home at the end of a raid on La Spezia in Italy. After flying in cloud for an hour or so, the crew realised that no one had seen the Alps. Later they crossed lighted towns that quickly switched off their lights, then came out over the sea and 'kept stooging along'. After eight hours in the air they admitted they were hopelessly lost, and the radio operator broke silence and was given a course. Surprised to find themselves again over land they came down to find out where they were, and were blasted by flak — they were over France. Having refuelled in southern England, they got home to Breighton late in the afternoon. They had flown 'bang across Spain', out over the Bay of Biscay, then turned north when given the correct course, but they were still south of Brittany and so they cut across France before reaching the south coast of England. O'Riordan celebrated his survival by catching the train to London and doing a 'pub crawl'. He was killed three months later over Hamburg.

Ken Gray also 'got lost on the way back'. He missed a wind change, and as they were running short of fuel the crew tossed everything possible overboard, including the guns. They crossed what they thought was the English coast and 'screaming "mayday"' came over a lighted airfield only to find it was a Luftwaffe station on the Cherbourg Peninsula. When they finally landed at Exeter they had been in the air for over 11 hours, and only two engines still had fuel to shift their aircraft off the runway. Returning on the last trip of his first tour, Bob Murphy, who was soon to be an instructing navigator, noted the coastline, announced they were right on track, saw the colours of the day fired in case some myopic British gunner opened up, and sat back and had a cigarette, although this was against regulations and imprudent when oxygen and fuel fumes might be lingering. Suddenly all the flak of the port of Brest opened up on them. They were holed, and the pilot dived so low the aircraft picked up a tree branch before they escaped out to sea. Murphy also called for a radio fix, and they limped back to England. If experienced crews and leading navigators could have such difficulty, then it must be assumed that many of the crews listed as missing flew west in cloud over the Bay of Biscay or the North Sea and never found land before fuel and hope were exhausted.

Those who knew they were over England, and were within yards of their runway, were still not safe. German fighters followed the bombers home looking for an easy target as a tired crew, lit by the increasing light in the east, came in to land. And there was also always the chance of being defeated by that other enemy – the weather. Low cloud settled quickly across the low Norfolk fens and the Lincoln and Yorkshire wolds, rain squalls that were supposed to be passing did not move, and unannounced lows swept in from the sea. Francis Randall, who had been plucked from the sea and interned briefly in Sweden before rejoining 460 Squadron, flew to Berlin on 16 December 1943. On his return he could not find Binbrook in the thick fog. He circled, radioed that he had come down so low he had brushed a tree, and 40 minutes later reported the crew were firing Very cartridges in the hope that the Binbrook watch tower might see them. He crashed ten miles south at Market Stainton, detonated an ammunition dump and killed all on board. Randall had lived long enough to learn that he had been awarded a DFC, but not long enough to collect it. His father received the decoration for him at Government House in Sydney in November 1944. Randall, a science student from the University of Sydney, was 21 years old when he died.

On that night of 16 December 1943 the weather was the most lethal enemy. Of the 483 Lancasters setting out just after 4 o'clock in the winter evening, 25 were lost in the attack on Berlin (over 5 per cent) and 29 crashed on landing or after their crews had baled out. Randall's aircraft was one of four 460

Squadron Lancaster that crashed near Binbrook. In the three other crashes only one airman was killed, a lucky result in a disastrous night.

On 4 July Brill told his crew that this was the last trip for those on their second tour. They took off in the night with the moon 'about three axe-handles high'. Setting course for an attack on an underground store of flying bombs at St. Leu d'Esserent, they passed close to London where searchlights were following the flight of incoming V-1s and every available gun was firing. The crew 'had a box seat' well above the flying bombs. After bombing they were attacked by two night fighters. One was content with just a single burst, but the other was tenacious, making seven or eight attacks. Brill was forced into sustained evasion; it was a torrid end to the tour for Bob Curtis, Tubby Fuller and Blue Freeman. Brill, as squadron commander, chose to keep flying. And the other two regular members of the crew, Bill McMahon and Len Smith (English flight engineer) who were on their first tour had to keep flying. Both survived. McMahon was lucky. On a flight with another crew, he baled out, landed on the roof of a German farmhouse, and was taken prisoner.

Crews finishing a tour were often given the right to land first. On 2 February 1945 Syd Gooding flew one of over 500 aircraft to Wiesbaden on his 30th operation. It was, he says, an unsatisfactory raid: they were in cloud from the Channel, and they bombed through cloud. As they came out of the target area at maximum continuous power, the bomb-aimer said, 'Keep her going skip'. Syd thought, why the hell not, and they rattled back across Europe and the North Sea. When he came over Ludford Magna he was so early the DREM (landing system) was not on, and the tower assumed that he must have turned short of

[They stood again] on oil-rainbowed English tarmac ... Crew transport driven by WAAFs would arrive then and there would be much yawning and stretching as the men picked up helmets, Mae Wests, gloves, parachute harnesses and packs, navigation satchels, charts, logs, coffee flasks, computers, dropped pencils and clip-boards of classified signals and navigation information. There was, at this point, a tendency to move and walk in a slowed down, slightly disorientated kind of way like mourners after a burial.

(Geoff Taylor 1979, p.116.)

the target and 'boomeranged'. The rest of the squadron came in and orbited, thinking they were giving Syd the privilege to call up first. By then Syd was already in the crew room.

Cliff Halsall's last raid was on the Dutch island of Walcheren, which the Germans had exploited as a gun platform. Wave after wave of Lancasters came in to hit the dykes, and as the crews looked down on what they had done they thought they saw a sinking island. Halsall's crew had taken Jack Watson, the sergeant of the ground crew, along to share the occasion and they came back low across the Wash and 'shot-up' a few farms before they landed at Binbrook. Like many of those who seached for a way to describe their feelings before an operation, Halsall chose a sporting analogy to say what it was like at the end: 'It was a great feeling to have got through a tour – something akin to being a member of a football premiership team'.

On his last operation Don Charlwood went again to Happy Valley, and the flak over the Ruhr was as thick as ever. With a wind of 110 miles an hour pushing the stream off course, and heavy cloud, Charlwood was one of the few navigators to bring his aircraft across the target indicators. Charlwood wrote in his diary:

> What joy there was in the plane as we crossed the Channel to Dungeness! We raced up England at 230 indicated [air speed] & were first to reach base. For the last time we heard a <u>delightful feminine voice</u> call that best of all words, 'Pancake! Pancake! [Go in and land] ... WAAFs have thrown their arms round our necks; all ranks have shaken our hands & slapped our backs.

On his last trip George Jarratt would have been first back to Binbrook, but he and the crew went a few extra miles to the west to pay their 'last flying respects to Lincoln Cathedral'.

On his way home for the last time, Geoff Berglund's aircraft was hit by lightning: 'I thought the kite was blown to bits. Sparks everywhere'. Back at Waddington news came through confirming that he had completed his tour: 'We can't believe it and yet it is true. Yippee, Hurray, Whacko. We're that mad that Lord only knows what we'll do tonight'. But Hilliard at the end of his extended Pathfinder tour wrote: 'I felt no urge to kiss the Mother Earth or celebrate riotously; all one could do was wonder why some could beat the odds and others not'.

Finishing a tour was a relief, but it also meant an end to that life of intense oscillating excitement, and not all men were ready to give that life away. It also meant an end to a crew. The men themselves were aware that those casually formed teams that had subsequently shared so much, and learnt so much about each other, would break up. Halsall wrote: 'one thing in the back of our minds … was that now we would be split up as a crew'. Hilliard wrote with more feeling of the end of the crew than of the tour: 'The break-up of our crew was something we now had to face. Five of us had been together since Lichfield days sixteen months earlier and all seven for over a year'. The men from the United Kingdom had homes to go to, and they and the men who had married in England had another base and other relationships. Differences in nationality also took men into different administrative systems and these re-assigned them with no thought for the crews that had once been so close. Differences in rank and muster again became important. Two Australians from a crew might be sent to Lichfield as instructors and so stay together, but many crews celebrated, went on leave and dispersed.

On leave at the end of his tour, Jack Currie wrote of his crew: 'Sometimes I thought about the others: Lanham was kicking up his heels in Scotland, waiting for a ship to take him home; Cassidy was staying with relatives in Ireland; Protheroe was in Pembrokeshire, Walker in the Wirral, Fairbairn in Northumberland, Myring only he knew where … We were … no more a part of one another's fate'. Of the three Australians in the crew, Charlie Lanham was on his way home, Jim Cassidy was posted to a conversion unit and Larry Myring went to 27 OTU Lichfield.

12

KRIEGIES

At the end of an operation, those airmen going to breakfast had one final statistic to consider: what was the chance of survival for a crew that now had 'missing' chalked beside its pilot's name on the operation board? Were all, or even one, of that crew likely to wander in after a few days and say that they ditched at Dijon, rode a bike into Vichy France, caught a train, walked to Spain and got flown out of Gibraltar – 'piece of cake'. How many of the names of the 'missing' would reappear in the lists of prisoners of war?

About 125,000 men of all nationalities served as aircrew in training and operating squadrons in Bomber Command. Of them, 55,500 were killed in battle and accidents (44 per cent), 9,838 were taken prisoner (8 per cent), 8,500 were wounded (7 per cent), about 1,500 evaded capture after crash-landing or baling out over enemy territory and 100 escaped from German prison camps (1.3 per cent). The chance of becoming a casualty (being killed, wounded or captured) was 60 per cent. The balance of killed on operations (47,000) against the total of prisoners, evaders and escapers (11,500) meant that the odds of the 'failed to return' surviving were about one in four. The odds of them turning up in the mess with tales of foot slogging across the Continent were about one in 30. Conscientious crews practised the drills for ditching, for inflating and climbing into a dinghy, and for baling out, and noted when they had cut a few seconds off their best. But after a short time on an operating squadron, they knew that they were just giving themselves a slight advantage in circumstances where only one-quarter of them were going to survive. Like much else in Bomber Command, baling out, evading and escaping were high risk, and prudent men exploited the little within their control to help themselves – and did not dwell on the numbers.

Just after the end of the war, Ivan Pellas got on the London tube and sat opposite Joe Herman from Hughenden in north Queensland. Both had flown on 466 Squadron. Herman was unable or reluctant to say much about what had happened to him since he had been a senior pilot in the same wing as Pellas. Both were lucky to be where they were. Herman was astonishingly lucky.

On 4 November 1944 Joe Herman took off from Driffield for a raid on Bochum in the Ruhr. As darkness fell over the North Sea his Halifax became one of 700 bombers in the stream. Coned twice over the target, Herman was relieved when the bombs were gone and the photograph taken, but just as they were 'on course for home' something thudded into the Halifax. The gunners saw no fighters, and the crew guessed they had been hit by flak. In his windscreen Herman could see the reflection of the flames behind him, and the engineer, Harry Knott, went back to try and put them out. Suddenly the Halifax was hit twice more. With more fires breaking out in the wings, Herman called, 'Bale out! Bale Out!'. Herman heard the rear gunner leave before the intercom went dead and guessed that the bomb-aimer and navigator had gone through the open front hatch. He saw the mid-upper gunner, another Australian, John ('Irish') Vivash, dragging his wounded leg as he crawled along the fuselage towards the hatch. Herman decided it was time to leave his seat, grab his parachute and clip it to his harness. Just then the plane rolled, spun and exploded. Herman found himself in the air with objects around him, and in the dim light of the moon and searchlights he thought he was stationary in the air. Then he realised that he and bits of aircraft were all falling earthwards together. He even thought that among the debris he might be able to find his parachute pack. After a long time falling – he may have fallen two miles – he crashed into something. In his dazed state he heard Irish Vivash say, 'Is there anybody around?' Joe then realised that he had his arms around one of Irish's legs. Irish, with one leg badly gashed from flak, and with the distractions of parachuting through the night sky, had not been quick to realise that he had the skipper clinging to him. It seems that Irish had not opened his parachute until late, otherwise Herman, falling faster, would have been below him. In one of Irish's pendulum swings below his canopy, Herman had collided with his legs and grabbed one.

Irish suggested that as they got close to earth, Joe might 'drop off', but Joe was non-committal. 'Maybe', he said. The ground rushed at them, they brushed a tree, Joe hit the ground, Irish landed on Joe's chest, and cracked a couple of Joe's ribs. Battered from flak, explosion and the heavy landing, Herman and Vivash stumbled west towards Holland for five nights until hunger and cold forced them to ask for help at a farmhouse. The German police picked them up the next day, and the two Australians were on their way to prison camp. In Stalag Luft III Herman wrote a paragraph saying what had happened to him. He began: 'This story is no <u>line shoot</u>'. He also told another Australian prisoner, F/Lt Paul Brickhill, how he survived. Brickhill, a Sydney journalist shot down in North Africa, published Herman's story in *Escape to Danger* in 1946. Herman's was one of the stories that helped convince Brickhill that he might be a writer of the air war.

While Joe Herman was the extreme case, all men who combated wind and gravitational forces in a spinning, burning aircraft in the dark had extraordinary stories to suppress or tell. Reg Bain was the navigator with Peter Fontaine's crew in 460 Squadron over Tubingen in October 1944. After leaving the target, they found they had a 'hang-up' – one bomb had not released. Reg wanted the pilot to put the nose down, get out of the area and drop the bomb in the Channel, but the pilot decided to fly straight while the bomb was released manually. They were hit, went into a spin and the pilot called, 'Bale out'. Reg found it almost impossible to move, but when he finally reached and opened a hatch, he did not have to jump, he 'swooshed out', even leaving his flying boots behind. When he went to pull the D-ring on his rip cord, it was not there. His parachute was still firmly attached to him but it had been sucked over his head and was trailing above him. He pulled it down, found the rip cord and floated in rain and darkness. Having landed in a ploughed field, he got the wind on his right cheek, knew he was facing in the right direction, and set off walking. Reg was the only one of the crew to survive.

When Bill Pearce's aircraft was hit by *schräge Musik*, the rear gunner was killed, an engine exploded and fire broke out. Bill 'didn't have to be told twice'

I was just ... about to unclip the chute when there was what seemed to be a heavy dull explosion behind me and someone saying 'bloody hell'. The next thing I knew I was in mid-air, floating down on one strap of my harness! The explosion, a stray flak which scored a direct hit on ['P' for] Peter, blew me straight out through the nose and just blew the kite to hell ... it took a long time to come down and it was a fantastic experience – I could see the last of the raid, all the flak and searchlights at the target, the fires in the city, PFF [Pathfinder Force] flares burning out and strings of bombs bursting – looked like a fairyland somehow, everything seemed so unreal. At first I mistook the cloud for the ground and made several 'perfect book landings' only to find I went right through the 'ground' ... Finally I came to earth ... I was sprawled out in a wheat field.

(Keith Campbell, wireless operator, 466 Squadron, who baled out over Stuttgart.)

and immediately discarded his helmet and mask. The lack of oxygen soon had its effect, slowing him down, but also taking away a 'lot of the terror' from baling out. The mid-upper gunner picked up his parachute by the D-ring, it released and he jumped holding armfuls of silk. The wind caught the parachute, wrapped it on the tail, and the gunner was probably killed as he hit the aircraft. Pearce remembers crouching on the door ledge, then fell or was sucked out. He floated down, crashed in a heap on the ground, hurt his shoulder, but remembered his instructions about releasing the parachute, gathering and burying it. Three other members of the crew were still alive.

When the rear gunner of a crew that needed one operation to complete a tour went sick, Charles Ellis of 467 Squadron nominated himself to fly. It would have been the last operation of his second tour. At the briefing for a raid on Siegen he said, 'We are a moral to get the "chop" tonight'. After they were hit, he turned his turret and escaped into the fuselage. There he met Ray Browne, the mid-upper gunner, who said, 'You bastard Ellis. You "mozzed" us!' After he jumped, he could still hear Ray, somewhere below him, shouting into the night, 'You bastard Ellis!' The next day he was re-united with Ray: they were both then prisoners of war. All except the pilot, J. Keith Livingstone, survived.

All aircrew had heard stories of the Luftwaffe giving men no chance of jumping from crippled aircraft, of men being shot on the way down, and of civilians on the ground taking revenge on the 'terror flyers'. Lloyd Trotter was on a mission with 138 Squadron to drop supplies to the Polish resistance when he was attacked over the Baltic. As he struggled with the controls of the Halifax, which obviously had just a few moments of life left, the German fighter flew alongside, making sure that they could not escape, but giving them every chance to bale out or control their descent into the Baltic. Harold Wright says that when incendiaries from above hit his aircraft, a fighter came within 50 yards of them, saw that they had an engine in flames and did not fire. Wright had seen fighters show the same restraint a 'couple of times' before, and he had no doubt they were being given a chance to jump. In spite of the fact that they had no hydraulics or electrical system, the three engines of the Lancaster pulled them through an evasive dive and turn, and home from Hanover.

Caterpillar Club. The Irvin Chute Company of Hertfordshire provided a card and a gold caterpillar pin for those men saved by an Irvin parachute. An officer at the relevant station usually supplied the number of the parachute, but some of the numbers arrived from prisoner of war camps. The caterpillar was the silkworm – these were the men saved by silk. Leslie Irvin was the honorary secretary of the club. The G.Q. Parachute Company of Woking also gave a badge for those in the G.Q Club.

Goldfish Club. With the support of the Messrs P.B. Chow and Company, makers of air-sea rescue equipment, a badge showing a winged goldfish flying over two waves was given to those whose lives were saved by Mae Wests and rubber dinghies. A few men in quick succession qualified for both the Caterpillar and Goldfish Clubs.

Once on the ground, airmen faced an equally varied response. After Geoff Coombes baled out over Berlin, he was picked up in a searchlight beam and landed just 30 or so yards from the light. The youths from the searchlight came over, saw that Coombes had been shot through the knee, carried him into their barracks, gave him ersatz coffee, and called a doctor, 'a great guy', who treated him competently and gave him a bottle of beer. Locked in a cell, he was dozing when 'this guy like a bloody gorilla' came in, picked him up and threw him across the room into the wall, then left. Two of the men who baled out before Coombes, the navigator and the mid-upper gunner, were healthy when they left the aircraft and Coombes believes they might have been killed after they reached the ground. Peter Balderston, the wireless operator on Coombes' crew, parachuted over the centre of Berlin:

> As I neared the ground, the hot air from the fires must have kept me up just enough to clear them; my trousers were charred and fell to pieces from the thighs to the top of my boots. I just had time to see an unbroken roof approaching and, making sure that I kept my feet together, I swung for it, going clean through and landing in the attic of a three-storeyed house … On the way to the Tempelhof [airport] I saw an English airman who had been strung up to a street lamp standard, and another had been thrown or had fallen into a burning building as all I saw was his flying boots.

Many men being escorted through cities, especially after 1943, were left in no doubt what the German people thought of them. Bill Pearce said that in Cologne they wanted him 'hanging by the neck'. Dan London said that at Hamburg railway station the crowd surged forward, spat and threw rubbish at them — it was just the determination of the armed guards that kept the crowd at bay. While being escorted across Frankfurt, Carl Larkin was grateful to the guards who gave him and four other airmen German jackets to protect them from the anger of civilians. Downed aircrew were more objects of curiosity in the country, with children coming to look shyly at them. Some airmen were well fed, but they were also robbed and jostled. Ash Taylor was stared at, fed, abused, had his watch stolen and was given a jug of beer. In postwar trials Germans were convicted of killing captured airmen.

In the early months of the war, Allied airmen baling out in western Europe could hope to evade capture because the German administration was not yet established across occupied countries, and until Dunkirk they could reach safety without making the difficult crossing to neutral countries. But by the time most Australians were flying in Bomber Command the escape route was long and hazardous. It was not until the last nine months of the war that the Allies again held a wide front in the west, and by then those in occupied Europe ready to take a risk to help aircrew were growing in numbers and confidence.

On 16 September 1943 Bob Kellow of 617 Squadron became one of many casualties of the attempts to destroy the Dortmund-Ems canal when he landed on wet grass in north Holland. Cutting some strips from his parachute in case he needed bandages, he hid the remains with his Mae West. He took all insignia from his jacket, checked that he had his silk maps, compass, concentrated rations and Dutch, Belgian and French currency, and started walking south. Before dawn he saw a man milking a cow. Kellow indicated that he was thirsty and the man handed him the bucket to have a drink. After a few nights of walking and sleeping in the day he met an old couple, and when he mimed that he was hungry they looked around, saw no one and invited him in. They found a Dutchman who spoke some English and he drilled Bob on how to ask for a train ticket in Dutch and where he would have to change trains. After more walking he caught the

Quite a crowd of locals came in and there was plenty of animated talk amongst them. One old lady came up and fingered my woollen pullover and said 'Eenglish Goot' meaning it was good quality, not like their ersatz ones. So far the attitude of the crowd seemed to be more of curiosity than anything else ... I knew I would be thoroughly searched, so if anyone was going to get my maps, various currency notes, compass etc. I would rather the civilians got them ... When I offered the few remaining chocolates to the children, they were reluctant to eat them. I had to eat one to reassure them.

(Ralph Parsons, 466 Squadron, shot down in a raid on Frankfurt, December 1943.)

train, but missed a connecting train and had to ask a Dutch railway official for directions. He was told, in English, what he had to do. Standing at the end of a crowded carriage, he suddenly felt something being pressed into his hands he held behind him. It was a Dutch magazine, so he took it and pretended to read. Someone had realised who he was and wanted him to look less obvious. Bob never knew which person made the gesture. Two Dutchmen who may have been border police – or simply smugglers – took him across the frontier to Belgium and told him to contact the Abbey Postel in the next village.

From Belgium Kellow was in the hands of the organised underground. By questioning him and having the answers confirmed by radio, the Resistance knew that Bob was who he said he was. At one stage he spent 15 days living with a Belgian family. From north Belgium he travelled in civilian clothes and with guides. Normally he and a few other Allied airmen would travel within sight of, but not with, a guide – often a woman. He was equipped with two sets of identity papers, including photographs; one for Belgium and one for France. Having found their way through Paris on the Metro, the evaders switched to bicycles close to the Spanish border. Their progress was made difficult because one of the Americans could not ride a bike, and the women guides were far fitter than the airmen. Two guides, also making a living as smugglers, took Bob and three other airmen on a tough night walk across the Pyrenees. Travel across Spain required careful negotiation with the Spanish police, but eventually they crossed no-man's-land and were met by a British Bobby at the entrance to Gibraltar. After a ten-hour flight Kellow was back in London. It was over 11 weeks since he had taken off from Coningsby. Many people in three nations had taken great risks to get him home.

On the way home from Stuttgart, Ted Coates baled out in northern France, not far from where other Australians had been to war a generation earlier. Wounded in the leg, he limped away, travelling south by night. But soon he realised he had to risk asking for help. He knocked on a succession of doors or

[Lloyd Trotter was rescued from his ditched Halifax and brought ashore in Denmark.] The German guards ... indicated by a shove in the back that we were to walk across the cobbled area to a house in which lights were now burning. I stopped and indicated that I had lost my shoes and could not walk on the cobbles. A further shove in the back with the rifle and I stumbled forward. At this point, an old man came forward and took off his clogs and put them on my feet. These brave people had not been subdued.

(Lloyd Trotter, 138 Squadron, POW.)

> We had been briefed that, if shot down, we were to make for Paris, where we would receive sympathetic treatment in the brothels. With that in mind, the Mid Upper Gunner and myself set out Westwards.
>
> *(Norm Wright, wireless operator; shot down in September 1942 and captured by Germans.)*

spoke to people he met, often choosing poor people. After he announced who he was in his limited schoolboy French, he was nearly always treated generously. White-haired, sabot-wearing women called him 'pauvre homme' and gave him food and a warm bed. And he shared a lot of red wine with the men. When he dried the dishes in one house, he was told he was not acting like a Frenchman. As he travelled by foot, bicycle and train, he constantly expected to be picked up by the underground, but through luck and the spontaneous gestures of the unorganised he got into Spain in 55 days. He then took a ship from Gibraltar to England.

A fortnight after D-Day, Peter Knox buried his parachute under pine needles, checked his escape kit, removed the top of his flying boots so that they would not instantly give him away, and began walking. Having failed to reach Cologne in the air, he was uncertain what country he was in, but it was Belgian farmers who found and hid him. After a few weeks in a tent in the woods, or bricked into a small shelter and taking a break in corn fields and behind hedges, a priest guided him and another airman into Turnhout, and from there they were escorted to Brussels on a train. After two weeks in Brussels, he saw the confusion and celebration of the liberation on 4 September. With the Allied forces was Geoff Hutton from the Melbourne *Argus*, the paper managed by Knox's father. Hutton filed a story on Peter's survival and so Peter's father learnt that his son was alive and free.

Evasion was always difficult, and failure was likely close to the Spanish border. Dick Malins, a wireless operator, was shot down on 14 September 1943. Equipped with a beret, a loaf of bread and a bottle of wine (half consumed), he walked confidently through railway stations, but when he went to meet the guides to take him through the Pyrenees they were Germans. Gordon Stooke was at first helped by generous Belgians, then came under the care of what appeared to be the Belgian resistance. In fact a Belgian group in the pay of the Germans collected a group of evaders and handed them over to the Germans in Paris. Stooke's one month of freedom ended in sudden arrest, tough interrogation and a spell in Fresnes gaol in Paris.

In July 1944 Stan Hawken was one of three to escape alive from a 630

Squadron Lancaster in a raid on the Revigny railway yard. He landed among trees and was knocked unconscious. Regaining his senses, he freed himself from his parachute and walked clear of the area. A British pilot from another aircraft was not so fortunate. He baled out too late, his parachute did not open fully and he was skewered and killed on a tree. The 'hostile French population took off his clothes and left him in pants only'. In his six months living with the French, Hawken learnt quickly of the complexities of French reactions to him and the war. Those with relatives and houses damaged in raids thought the British fought the Boche at their expense and they wanted quick revenge against aircrew. A few, such as Jean Vidal, the local school teacher at the village of Saint Vrain, and his wife Margot, hid and fed him, knowing that others in the village would write to the Germans to denounce them. (They were saved by the postman who intercepted the letter.)

The local maquis were divided. Groups made up of young men who were avoiding being conscripted into German labour camps were well-armed, concerned about surviving until the Germans left, did not want to engage in effective sabotage, and exploited their licence to take food and whatever else they liked from the French people. The communists and other politically organised groups in the maquis wanted to be in a position of strength at liberation, and they competed as much with each other as they did with the Germans. When the maquis blew up a bridge or pulled up railway track the Germans were likely to murder people in the nearest village, as Hawken saw. Whatever sympathy the ordinary French had for the maquis, they did not want them attacking Germans close to them. As the Allied forces came closer, French who had been neutral or pro-German were eager to join the winners, and the maquis, with increasing strength and confidence, were in a position to punish those they labelled collaborators. Having been present at what he called a 'kangaroo court', Hawken heard the gunfire that meant the sentence of execution had been carried out. In the six weeks from when he baled out until he met the Americans and celebrated in Paris, Hawken, the grade eight leaver from Culfearn State School in northern Victoria, had gathered memories that

> We remember our Helpers, those people, from every walk of life who rose up in the middle of oppression and tyranny, and exhibited enormous compassion and fellow feeling for us, the lost and stranded ... How fortunate we were to have been able to so enrich our understanding of human values in time of danger.
>
> *(Royal Air Force Escaping Society toast to helpers in occupied countries.)*

delighted and appalled him. But it was his own burning plane that returned in nightmares.

Just how many Australians in Bomber Command evaded capture in German-controlled Europe is uncertain. Perhaps a total of 150 men reached safety. Nearly all came home through Spain, a few through Switzerland and Scandinavia, and after the Allies' advance in 1944 around 50 reached friendly ground troops, most in the west and a few in the east.

Once in the hands of the Germans and transferred to Germany, escape was difficult and staying free almost impossible. Before the turmoil of the last days of the war, just two men from the RAAF serving in Bomber Command escaped from German prison camps and got back to England: W.G. Reed of 460 Squadron and A.F. McSweyn of 115 Squadron. Persistence, perhaps obsession, and knowledge from hard-won experience were essential.

Bill Reed, aged 22, had been a clerk in a Sydney car firm and was recently married to an English woman. At the time of his capture in 1942 he was a sergeant rear gunner. A fellow crew member and prisoner at Lamsdorf described Reed as 'a rank individualist in every way with an air of complete self-sufficiency and aloofness'. His first attempt to escape by cutting the wire ended when the guards saw what was going on and opened fire. Reed scrambled back before the guards were able to identify him. On his second attempt he changed identity so that he could join a working party outside the camp, teamed up with a German speaker and reached Stettin where he was recaptured on a Swedish boat. On his third attempt he was partnered by a German speaker, a Jewish labourer, and again he changed identity with another prisoner to get outside the camp on a work party. This time he and his companion were arrested near the docks at Stettin. He then changed his appearance by removing his false teeth and shaving his head, swapped identities with Private Elykim Wald and persuaded another German speaker to join him on a fourth attempt. Having reached Stettin by train, the two escapers were helped by a Swedish seaman and passed through the last German check. He sent a letter with a Swedish postmark to his crewmate, Dave Radke, who was still in Lamsdorf. Reed took just over two years of persistent, calculated risk to gain freedom.

Of the three men who survived from Max Johnston's crew, Max Wyllie was killed attempting to escape, Reed escaped and Radke was released by the English troops on 30 March 1945. Later, when he filled out a form stating what had happened to him, Reed said that from July 1942 he had been

> I continued cycling and by-passed Bremen. Here I passed a fighter station of M.E.110s. I spent the day hiding and watching the aircraft and noticed one isolated plane on the boundary of the aerodrome. While it was dark I crawled into the field and ran up to the plane. I got into it and tried, unsuccessfully, to get it up. The ground crew, who must have heard the engine ticking over, came up and took me prisoner.
>
> *(Allan McSweyn, on his first attempt to get back to England.)*

a prisoner 'on and off'. Reed was the first member of the RAAF to be awarded a DCM.

Allan McSweyn was an accountant in Sydney before the war. When he was shot down near Bremen he was a 22-year-old flight lieutenant and Wellington pilot. McSweyn made even more attempts to escape than Reed; he tried stealing a German fighter, scaling walls with rope, cutting wire, digging tunnels, and hiding in the laundry cart. By mid 1943 he knew what was needed for a successful escape. Having taken the identity of a private soldier, he was transferred to a work camp where the first steps in the escape were simpler. With a New Zealander (Driver F.D. Williamson) who spoke German, and with papers claiming that he was a French worker being sent home to Marseilles, he crossed into France. Helped by an escape organisation he reached Gibraltar in December 1943.

Because the Germans knew the value of trained aircrew and what damage they could do, the barriers to escape from the camps holding aircrew were greater, and the reprisals for those caught escaping could be more savage. That was the case in the reaction to the famous tunnelling exploits from Stalag Luft III at Sagan in March 1944. Of the 200 ready to make their escape, just 80 had left the tunnel when the break-out was discovered. Under the 'Sagan order' Hitler said that half of the men were to be shot, and in fact 50 were killed – executed. They were said to have been shot while trying to escape. Four Australians were among them: J. Catanach, A.H. Hake, R.V. Kierath, and J.E.A. Williams.

Nearly half of the 600 Australian prisoners of war from Bomber Command were captured in late 1943 and early 1944, the time when many Australians were arriving at operating squadrons and when Bomber Command was making its long and costly raids against Berlin and other German cities. As less than 20 Australians were taken prisoner in the first two years of the war, few had to endure four or five years of confinement. Many had 18 months to two years in the stalags, and well over 100 had less than nine months. A large number of prisoners went through the same sequence of camps and questioning; it was so consistent that some aircrew experienced exactly what intelligence briefings had told them to expect. Taken to the interrogation centre, the Dulag Luft, at Oberursel on the edge of Frankfurt, they were left alone in a small cell. After waiting in intense cold or heat they were escorted to various meetings; the German pretending to be a Red Cross officer from Geneva asked for details so that the prisoners' parents could be told what had happened to their son; the smooth German officer with the impeccable English offered cigarettes and suggested that a regrettable error had sent the prisoner to solitary confinement and he would soon sort things out once they had had a chat; and other German officers raged and threatened. In spite of warnings, prisoners were surprised by the Germans' detailed knowledge of who they were and what they had been doing. Pulling out a file marked 466 Squadron, a German officer told Peter Balderston things about the squadron that he did not know himself. Bill Pearce heard an apparently casual German tell him the names of the other members of his crew, his squadron number, his station, the runway the squadron had used and the target on their last flight. And for the first time Bill learnt that three fellow members of his crew were dead. Ash Taylor had the even more surprising experience of having a German officer go through his personal file details – his education, where he had trained, the troop ships he travelled on and the English stations where he had served. The officer then read from what seemed to be the 460 Squadron form setting out all the crews operating on the night he was shot down. Aircrew also encountered men who were probably Germans pretending to be fellow airmen, and guessed that when put in contact with other airmen their conversations were being picked up by microphones.

After a week or a fortnight, when the Germans decided that they were not going to get more than name, rank and number, and when a group of prisoners had accumulated at Dulag Luft, the prisoners were moved to permanent camps. As they gathered at railway stations and travelled on trains, men who were captured in the first four years of the war were often disappointed at the small amount of damage they saw in towns – all that effort, all those casualties for little obvious result. But in the last year of the war aircrew looked on devastation.

At times the Germans deliberately took them through areas where houses, apartments, shops, schools and hospitals had been destroyed. Ash Taylor, who was captured after a raid on Munich, was taken back across Germany and with other Munich survivors driven on a tour of the damaged museum, opera house and rows of flattened buildings. 'But', Taylor wrote, 'it was no different to the bomb damage caused to London and many other English cities in the early stages of the war, and we felt no remorse at what we were shown'.

Most of the camps were in eastern Germany or beyond the German border among peoples who at other times belonged to other nations. They stretched from the Baltic in the north to Yugoslavia. The camps best known to the Australians were Stalag Luft III at Sagan; Stalag IV at Mühlberg; Stalag VIIIB (later 344) at Lamsdorf; Stalag VIIA at Moosburg; Stalag 357 at Thorn; Stalag XVIIID at Marburg; Stalag Luft VI at Heydekrug; Stalag Luft IV at Gross Tychow; and Oflag IVC at Colditz. In November 1944 there were 261 Australians among 10,091 Allied prisoners at Sagan, but Australians, separated from the main aircrew camps, were spread widely. By June 1943 the Australian Red Cross thought that there were Australian servicemen in at least 30 German camps. In crowded huts and wired compounds under surveillance boxes, aircrew turned 'kriegies' fought the old enemy, the weather, and battled boredom, hunger and the trauma of their recent experiences. Under the Geneva Convention, aircrew – as either officers or senior non-commissioned officers – could not be compelled to work, and because of their status as 'special category' prisoners they were more confined and more watched than the men from the Australian army captured in North Africa, Greece and Crete.

Most of the physical wounds that young men brought with them into prison camps healed quickly, but the memories stayed with them; memories of air battles, near misses, baling out into the night, seeing their aircraft plunge and explode with some of the crew still on board, and of falling, landing and learning who was still alive. The English pilot, Robert Kee, wrote:

> Every prisoner suffered from cycles of depression, more frequent but almost as regular as the changing seasons. With some people the effect was just numbing: the man would lie on his bed all day like a piece of dead wood. With others it brought a violent distress of spirit often visible on faces for days on end.

For many, depression was a result of the delayed shock of escape from and through horror, and of survivor guilt, that strange affliction that burdens the living. It was intensely felt by lone survivors from crews bound in close

Kriegie (abbreviation of *Kriegsgefangenen*, literally 'war-prisoner')
Oflag (abbreviation of *Offizierlager*, officers' *lager* or camp)
Stalag (abbreviation of *Mannschaft-Stammlager*, men's camp)
Stalag Luft (camp for aircrew)

mateship. Ash Taylor says that at night the hut was often disturbed by men with nightmares. One young Englishman relived his escape from a burning aircraft, and while still asleep struggled from his bunk and 'baled out'. In spite of being cut and bruised in the morning he refused to swap his top bunk for one that would give him less altitude at the time he launched himself towards the brick floor.

The hunger of the men was obvious. The Red Cross representative wrote of prisoners in Stalag Luft III at Sagan: 'General loss of weight noted'. And the men displayed their obsession with the food they lacked. Prisoners who in civilian life took no interest in cooking wrote detailed recipes in their diaries (even how to make cinnamon toast — 'toast bread and spread evenly with butter ...'), carefully recorded the contents of food parcels, and wrote about what they would eat on their release. They were saved by Red Cross parcels — one a week in the good times, and less often during the final months of the war and at the camps furthest from Switzerland. Red Cross did its best when the German railways were dislocated by those Allied airmen still with tours to complete. Over 1,000 commandeered cars, each displaying a large red cross, carried the parcels to the camps and were used to chase the prisoners forced to move ahead of battle.

To combat boredom and 'barbed wire fever', men gave talks, organised debates, put on plays and musical evenings, joined the 40-voice RAF choir at Lamsdorf, and studied. London University coordinated many of the examinations, reporting in August 1944 that in the previous 12 months 5,718 Allied prisoner of war candidates sat for examinations in everything from

Christmas parcels for prisoners in Europe contain 1 tin chocolate, 1 tin cheese, 1 block chocolate, 1 tin plum pudding, 1 tin jam, 1 tin butter, 1 tin steak and spaghetti, 1 tin steak and tomato, 1 tin condensed milk, 1 tablet soap, 3 bars sugar, 1 packet tea, 1 tin Christmas cake, 1 tin sweets.

(Australian Red Cross Society, Notes on Activities, November 1942. National Red Cross parcels were pooled in Geneva so Australian prisoners were more likely to receive the more numerous British or American parcels than one from Australia with its familiar labels.)

accountancy to beekeeping, brewing, spectacle making, and stable management sponsored by the Institute of the Horse and Pony Club. Prisoners played sport when space allowed them to, including cricket test matches in Sagan and Lamsdorf. Dave Radke, a test selector, said that one of his great memories was of 'Nick Wallace's trundling and match winning 48 runs in about 3 overs to defeat the Poms' on a matting wicket at Lamsdorf. The Australian Rules players at Heydekrug, the most north-eastern camp on the Baltic, staged a match on Anzac Day 1944. Geoff Blacket recorded the scores: Lager A, 5-2, defeated Lager K, 2-7.

Escaping, although so rarely successful, was important to the morale of the men: it occupied time and combated their own sense of impotence in the war. But some plans worked on at length were never really intended to be put into action, and some men conceded relief when their plans were thwarted. In spite of the postwar books and films on escapers, and the justified praise of their perseverance and daring, escapers were not always popular in the camps because they increased danger, provoked harsh reaction and reminded others of their duty to try and escape.

Men fought the cold whatever way they could. They wore all their clothes in bed and they fed their stoves with everything that was disposable and combustible. Any spare wood in the frame of the hut and slats from beds were burnt, putting huts in danger of collapsing and men in top bunks of crashing on those below. The weather was closest to victory in the bitter winter of 1944–45. Having lost weight and energy, the men were ill-equipped when rumours began to circulate in the eastern camps that they would be on the move. To escape battle and the advancing Russians, the Germans were shifting the camps west. At Lamsdorf the long, relentless trudge began on the evening of 22 January 1945. Soon men began discarding items from their packs. Dave Radke dropped a two-volume edition of Goethe's Faust into an icy river – he could do without a literary pact with the devil. Usually moving along side roads, the long columns of prisoners were travelling with German families who had the advantage of horse-drawn wagons; with a few displaced Germans and conscripted labourers no better off than the prisoners; with Russian, Polish and other prisoners who were worse off; and with German military units that demanded priority and forced them off the road. Their guards, sometimes aggressive at the start, were often reduced to the very old and very young at the end, and they suffered almost equally from deprivation. And where the prisoners walked in hope, the guards were increasingly apprehensive. Often

All sorts of valuables are being exchanged today for bread with the civvies. There are dozens of school children with bread trying to get watches. The guards are not doing much to stop the exchanging as they are trying to get some bargains themselves.

(Joint diary kept by Reg Cantillon, Gordon Castle and Jack Kean on march from Lamsdorf, 8 March 1945.)

the confused columns were halted for hours in the snow with no one seeming to know why they had stopped. Then they were forced to march for hours through 'eerie and nightmarish' nights.

Geoff Blacket left Gross Tychow on 6 February, averaging over 20 kilometres a day on the first five days. On 12 February he wrote:

Cold, damp & misty, rough through forest, received 1 cup of barley soup from the field kitchen, the first since leaving, they may just as well have left the kitchen and boilers behind. Stop at Bastychow sleep in pig pen, the others over & with some sheep.

Like other groups straggling west, Blacket and his group often slept at farms, the lucky ones finding space in barns where hay and the crush of bodies provided some warmth. Much of the time they were foraging and bartering for food, with those at the front leaving little for those following. The prisoners' advantage was that they still had the remnants of Red Cross parcels, and sometimes the Red Cross found the travelling columns. That meant that they had cigarettes and soap to trade, they had a little cash and a few had a reserve of energy. On 13 February Blacket walked in snow, then rain and 'mud ankle deep'. At the end of the day, the prisoners bought a sheep from a farmer for 50 marks and used it to make a 'watery soup' for 600 men. The 16th day was tough – they covered 33 kilometres. On 12 March Blacket cut wood and the farmer paid him in sandwiches and a loaf of bread and on 18 March he 'slipped into civvy house & sold my very old pullover for $^1/_2$ loaf, 6 eggs & some wurst. A good bargain'.

The first prisoners liberated north of the Rhine were presented with Welcome Back parcels in a marquee situated in German forest country. On a pole in the centre of the marquee the [Welcome Back] poster was hanging. It is difficult to explain the pleasure with which the Australian ex-prisoners of war spotted the picture of the Australian girl holding the bunch of wattle. Some said: 'You beaut!'. Others drew the attention of their British, Canadian, South African and New Zealand colleagues and said: 'That's the kind of girl we have in Australia.'

(Australian Red Cross Society, Notes on Activities, December 1945, p.14.)

At times the men heard artillery in the distance and saw aerial battles overhead. Bill Pearce was 'bloody scared', the most frightened he had been in the war, when an American fighter strafed the column, killing some men at the front. All the time men were wondering whether they should leave the march, hide and wait for the Russians. But as they were uncertain how they could persuade the Russians who they were, and there were rumours of German troops shooting those who tried to escape, most decided to stay with mob. In March, after walking nearly 800 kilometres, Dave Radke met tanks marked with the Allies' white stars. He was back in England before the war ended. Geoff Blacket had been hearing rumours of approaching troops for weeks before he saw the tanks of the 6th Airborne Division. Their white bread 'tasted like cake'. When the Allied troops were close, the Germans gave the prisoners at Mühlburg a choice about whether they stayed or shifted. With chaos about them they chose to stay. In the early hours of 23 April, Ash Taylor heard the 'horrific' noise of battle, and by daylight the sounds had passed beyond the camp and the guards were gone. Then:

> To our amazement and disbelief, out of the cloud of dust appeared four Russian Cossacks, crouched menacingly over the heads of their shaggy, long haired horses. The Cossacks were wild looking horsemen, dressed in heavy greatcoats with bandoliers packed tight with ammunition across their chests, and bristling with vicious looking automatic weapons and pistols.

With Russian troops, liberated Russian prisoners, many now armed, and various others who had been treated appallingly roaming the countryside ready to root, shoot and loot, 'many of the inoffensive and defenceless German civilians lost their lives in terrible and indescribable ways'. Bill Pearce said that in Moosburg German women who were left without any fit men in their households asked British and American prisoners to come and live with them, in the hope that this would give them some protection.

When I eventually stood on the bridge [over the Seine] and gazed at the famous Place de la Concorde, I was overawed. I was free at last – and in the centre of a city that I had dreamed about so many times during my school days, and later. I was in no hurry to move on – I wanted to make those moments last. When I revisited Paris, many years after the war, to re-live those emotional few moments, I again took the same walk, alone.

(Stanley Hawken, evader, who met the advancing Americans and hitched a ride to Paris.)

Gathered at airfields in Belgium, France and Germany, some having driven themselves in style in commandeered cars, the ex-prisoners were flown out in operation 'exodus'. Bill Pearce was delighted to see the Lancasters lined up at Juvincourt, but the captain told the eager ex-kriegies to shed some of their souvenirs or he could never lift them off the ground. Pearce made his contribution by dumping a German 'coal scuttle' helmet. The rescuing crew gave them all a turn to look out of the astro-dome to see the English coast coming up. In a 'lovely Lancaster' Ash Taylor sat beside a fellow navigator, and they sidetracked to look at the devastation caused by the bombers before they saw the white cliffs of Dover. Later that day Taylor had fish and chips at Brighton, then retired to the Metropole Hotel: many of the ex-prisoners were back at their starting point for the war in Europe. Their meeting place at the Australian Red Cross Centre in Brighton became known as 'Kriegies' Corner'; the vocabulary carried references to experiences unthought of by newly arriving dominion men.

From about 1,000 RAAF prisoners of war in Europe, 23 had died as prisoners. The death rate of 2 per cent was low; as many men had been wounded in air battles or injured on landing. It could easily have been higher. Without the flow of Red Cross parcels the men would have been much weaker and more vulnerable. As it was, men who were already below their normal weight lost another two stone on the march west, and a few were still suffering from beri-beri and vitamin deficiency when they arrived in England. They were compensated by being issued with an expectant mother's ration card. Aerial and land battles, particularly when the men were on the move, took place over and around them, but the Australians avoided high casualties. When prisoner of war statistics are restricted just to the RAAF in Bomber Command, then only five men died out of just under 600 who became prisoners of war. That was less than 1 per cent. It was safer to be a prisoner of war than to fly just one operation. But the problem was that if an aircraft was hit, the crew were four times more likely to die than be taken prisoner.

> Some knelt and kissed the ground; some danced and sang; some were quiet and bewildered; some buttonholed one of the welcoming committee and talked of their POW experiences; some quietly wept ... But, as a member of the welcoming party my brief was to hasten our guests into the delousing cubicle in a hangar.
>
> *(Stanley Harrison, RAF Bomber Command pilot, who met ex-prisoners flown to Wescott.)*

Australian aircrew imprisoned before the middle of 1944 had rarely flown west over continental Europe in daylight. And many of those who had seen the English coast in the dawn, often with folds and wisps of fog across it, and above it heavy clouds glowing pink as though they had a coal fire within, had done so with greater relief than normal because they were dangerously late home. On 8 May 1942 Bill Brill and nearly 200 other aircraft were briefed to bomb the Heinkel aircraft factory in the Baltic port of Warnemünde. It was an eight-hour return flight in the Wellington, a long flight to make in the rapidly contracting nights of early May. Unable to dodge the searchlights on the way in, Brill could not see the target clearly and, like most crews, bombed somewhere over the town. By the time he had escaped over the sea and turned west the 'glow of the ... sun in the northeast was frightening'. He began losing height to escape the sky growing lighter above and behind him. But the sun was faster than the Wellington. By the time he crossed the west coast of Denmark he was down to 400 feet. The sun chased him across the North Sea and the East Riding of Yorkshire to Breighton. Ten per cent of the bombers were lost on the Warnemünde raid.

For many kriegies the flight east was their last flight in a bomber. Some of the crews who took them home thought the 'exodus' flights, in skies with light and without threat, and with a restless, joyful cargo, were the best of the war.

The wedding of Squadron Leader Arthur Doubleday, DFC, to Miss Phyllis Buckle at Beckenham, Kent on 14 August, 1943. Others left to right: Mrs Isabel Buckle (mother of the bride), Miss Joy Turner, Mrs Sylvia Blackman (bride's sister) and Squadron Leader Bill Brill, DFC. *AWM UK0384*.

13

BAGS OF SWANK AND THE GOOD GEN

Bill Brill arrived back in Australia in January 1945. It was three years and ten months since Ilma Kitto had gone to Sydney too late to see him before he sailed for Canada. On 29 January 1945 Bill and Ilma were married in the Ganmain Methodist church, just five miles east of the Brill family home at Clearview. Wing Commander Brill was 28 years old. For a while he was stationed at Tocumwal on the Murray, a three-hour drive south across familiar Riverina country.

Arthur Doubleday was on his way via the United States to join the Pacific war when it ended. With that same uninhibited generosity that Americans had shown the Australians on their way east, a man thrust a bottle of Scotch into Doubleday's hand and told him to keep it. Doubleday asked why, continued the conversation with the stranger, and ended up staying the night as his guest in San Diego. Doubleday was 'delighted' the war was over and delighted he was 'going to be alive tomorrow', but all that had determined his life had suddenly 'gone'. Now Wing Commander Doubleday, aged 33, had to get his English wife to Australia, and decide what he would do in an Australia that he had not seen for four and a half years.

> With the end of the war in Europe ... there was dancing in the market square of the town and inevitably someone was to hoist a pair of WAAF 'blackouts' (knickers) on the mayor's flagpole. And finally someone was to reach the town clock to stop the hands at 2230 hours – the official timing of the end of hostilities in Europe. The person responsible was easily identifiable: he was, of course, an Ozzie wearing the navy blue uniform of the RAAF – 'good on you cobber'.
>
> *(Group Captain T.G. Mahaddie, RAF.)*

Like Brill and Doubleday, many men from Bomber Command were on their way back to Australia before the end of the war. Peter Isaacson's crew came home in a new Lancaster 'Q' for Queenie, landing at Amberley, Queensland on 3 June 1943. In tours to show Australians and New Zealanders their first Lancaster and to encourage young men to recruit and all citizens to put their savings into war bonds, Isaacson landed at major towns and at many of the strips the men had known in training, such as Mallala, Mt Gambier, Nhill, Benalla, Deniliquin, Parkes and Sale. Crowds in tens of thousands turned out, and Isaacson responded with equal exuberance with steep turns and low flying, culminating in a flight under Sydney Harbour Bridge that surprised the rest of the crew and worried officials. By September 1943, Clarrie Herbert had completed his operational flying, accepted an invitation to Buckingham Palace, collected his DFC, and been sent back to Markham to be an instructor. He complained: 'Forty million Englishmen in this country & they can't release me. Went to R.A.A.F. headquarters on the way back, but couldn't get any change out of them. Ended up abusing them ...'. After a few days instructing, he wrote: 'You have to watch the pupils like hawks or they'll kill you as sure as eggs are apples'. Herbert relieved the tension by 'beating' up a nearby American squadron before the air force decided it would rather have him back in Australia. Early in 1944, after completing his travels by ship and train around the globe, he was back in Fremantle – where he had left his dad's image reflected in the water next to the wharf in March 1941.

In the last six months of the war in Europe the RAAF processed some 3,000 men at Brighton and found space for them on ships. David Scholes wrote in his diary on 3 April 1945, 'Just two years since I finished up at Deniliquin'. He was then halfway across the Pacific on his way home. But by May 1945 there were still more than 13,000 Australian airmen in Britain, and with over half the Australian aircrew still dispersed through RAF squadrons, securing their release and gathering them together was not simple. With released army and air force prisoners already back across the Channel, there were many Australians in England to celebrate Germany's surrender on 7 May and V-E Day on 8 May 1945. Terry Charles said that the Australians at Driffield, knowing that peace was coming, motored to the Castle, a favourite pub in York, took the train to London and booked into the Strand Palace. Having heard the Prime Minister's speech in the crowded foyer ('& this is some pub', he reminded his mother), he went up to the Australians' fifth floor room to watch the 'madcap acts', the jostling crowd, and the 'flags, streamers, rattles, whistles ...'. Later Charles 'braved the storms' of the crowds and saw for the first time The Strand, Fleet Street and Trafalgar Square with the blackout lifted. Some buildings were floodlit, 'St Pauls being amazingly beautiful'. Searchlights weaved their shafts across the sky, American bombers flew overhead firing off Very lights, and the bonfires in Hyde Park attracted crowds with no intention of going home. The 'City', Terry said, 'was practically drunk dry'.

Aircrew who were prepared to join the final bombing assault on Japan volunteered for Tiger Force. But the Americans were not eager for help, the war in the Pacific ended quickly, and the Lancasters did not add their tons of bombs to the destruction that science and the B-29s were delivering to Japan. From May, the numbers of airmen leaving England increased from over 1,000 in June to over 2,000 in both September and October. But there were incentives for some to stay. Australian airmen were allowed to take jobs where the experience added to their professional knowledge, and they were admitted to vocational and academic courses. Some courses were specially created to meet the needs of the ex-servicemen. For example, the University of London put on a four-week course in Modern Educational Developments. The many aircrew who had once been clerks, teachers and university students were well placed to exploit the opportunities, and others with just two and three years of post-primary education saw the chance to continue a transformation of their lives. Over 2,000 signed up for courses.

The waiting airmen continued to travel and play sport. From 1944 they had time for more public and representative contests. On 3 September 1944 the RAAF staged what was claimed to be the 'first Surfing Carnival held in Britain'. The RAAF cricket team, with five Sheffield Shield representatives, played matches at Lords against the RAF, the British army and, with MCC permission, as 'Australia' against England. On his second day back in England from Stalag IVB, Ash Taylor obtained a ticket to the unofficial 'victory test' between the Australian combined services team playing as 'Australia' and England. On 21 May 1945 he saw 'Mosquito pilot' Keith Miller hit a 'bright and entertaining 105'. The RAAF tennis team played the United States Army Air Force, the RAF,

Twelve RAAF officers returning across the Pacific on the British ship *HMS Empire Battleaxe* were given the instruction '2359 WILL BE THE 21ST SEPT. 0001 WILL BE 23RD SEPTEMBER'. But the 22 September was Bob Curtis's birthday. Wireless operator/air gunner Curtis, 66 operations, had his 22nd birthday stolen by the International Dateline.

South Africa and Norway, and the RAAF rugby team competed against club and representative sides in Great Britain and France.

From September 1945 some of the ships taking aircrew home contained the largest concentrations of airmen that many of the Australians had encountered in their service careers. There were over 2,000 on the *Aquitania* in October. But they left behind their English wives, fiancees and girlfriends. Barbara Gowan, who met Bill in Grimsby in 1943, was one of the few to get away early; she left England with just three others on the *Trojan Star* in April 1945. As it was before the end of the war, she went without farewells and with warnings that 'a slip of the lip may sink a ship'. The many waiting brides, after frustrating post-ponements and watching the publicity given to the many GI brides travelling across the Atlantic, gathered in London and staged a self-conscious 'demo' carrying banners demanding 'Ships for Aussie Brides'. The press gave the 'bush brides' enthusiastic support and from early 1946 the bride ships, *Stirling Castle*, *Athlone Castle*, *Highland Princess*, *Rangitata* and others, were on their way through the heat of the tropics to Australia. Some ships carried troops and women, but others, such as the *Atlantis*, had every cabin and bunk filled with 400 brides and their children. The priorities were wives with children first, then lone wives and finally fiancees, who were only given passage if the fiancé paid a bond and the couple were married within 30 days of arrival in Australia. Someone lost money on Corinne who could not force herself off the *Ormonde*, and took the round trip back to England. In the Suez Canal the bride ships passed crowded transports bringing the British troops back from the Far East. The men shouted out to the women that they were going the wrong way, and by then a few women were having doubts. Many of the women spoke with the accents of Lincolnshire and Yorkshire, the counties of the bomber airfields. Thelma Robson travelled

French Rugby Tour 1945

At Chambery the Australians viewed one of the most impressive beginnings of a Rugby game that has ever been arranged. Both teams were introduced to the public by tannoy [public address system] and then took up their respective positions on the football field. Both National Anthems were played and as the chords of the Marseillaise faded away a plane glided over the field with marvellous timing dropping the ball as if the Aussies had kicked off and the game commenced. The French explained later that this method of commencement was staged by the French Air Force. in appreciation of the R.A.A.F. during the war ... the R.A.A.F. again triumphed winning 19 to 5.

(Percy Cochrane, RAAF, Welfare officer.)

with two other girls from the same Lincolnshire village, but most women were young, alone, unlikely to see their families for many years and committing themselves to live in unknown places among unknown communities. On an Australian wharf or railway station some couples saw each other for the first time wearing civilian clothes. Joane Ford, who followed her husband Joe after a delay of four months, said that it was a 'most tremendous adventure', and she thought her English girlfriends considered her lucky. She did not regret her decision.

How many women refused to leave England and how many Australian men abandoned English women are unknown. But recently one Australian family was intrigued to meet a middle-aged Englishman who arrived in Australia looking for his father. He was the son of an Australian who had served in Bomber Command, returned home, married and given no hint of a previous intimate and fruitful relationship. The English visitor's Australian father had died, but he met many half-relatives.

Ash Taylor and Bill Pearce, both ex-kriegies, came back on the *Orion*. The war against Japan ended when they were in the Atlantic Ocean and so, Bill said, they 'missed the second lot of victory celebrations', but the officer who made the announcement on the ship's public address was 'well and truly "plastered"'. As the troop transports came close to the Australian coast the decks were crowded and men climbed into the rigging for the first sight of Australia and the best view as they came through the Heads and into the Harbour. Bands, relatives and friends competed for attention as ships drew alongside the wharf. Many men still had to reverse that long train journey they had made when leaving Australia. Gus Belford, a West Australian, followed the New South Welshmen ashore at Circular Quay, Sydney but received no welcome. He spent a couple of nights at Bradfield Park, a couple more on a bench at No 1 Personnel Depot (the Melbourne Cricket Ground) and then continued by train to Perth Central Station. Geoff Berglund had a shorter journey. He came ashore in Sydney and caught the train to Cowra, the 'Good old Cowra Mail'. Like others who survived he ended his diary when he reached home. He had not, he said, put everything in his diary, but what he had put in was true: 'I prefer', he wrote, 'to forget the horror of war'. But there was one duty that many performed that made forgetting more difficult: they went to see girlfriends, wives and parents of friends and crew mates who had not come back.

> **Tues June 19 1945**
> Throughout the day the boys were looking out for land – good old Aussie but at dusk it had not shown up. At 13 past 6 the skipper tannoyed the light at South Head had been seen. Practically everyone was down below and a wild cheer echoed around the old Rangitata.
>
> The lights commenced to show up brighter – red and green – no blackout. We passed through the heads at 8 and after entering the booms anchored for the night. The Captain Cook, pilot boat, had met us. Saw the ferries brightly lit up.
>
> Chaps in the boom boat yelled 'No grog, No beer'.
>
> The most popular comment made by the boys when they saw the most beautiful, or second most beautiful, harbour in the world – 'I never thought I would see that again.' Others said, others would not.
>
> **Wed June 20**
> Up at 6 a.m. to see dawn break over Sydney Harbour.
>
> *(Cliff Halsall, last entries in diary.)*

Families with missing sons and husbands, anxious for news, welcomed visits from returned aircrew, but the meetings were difficult when the returned men thought they saw questions behind the distress they witnessed. They felt that the families were wondering why it was that this man, and not theirs, had survived. And many families of aircrew lost on operations had not been given irrefutable evidence of death. Like Paddy Rowling's father, they had first been told that 'although your son has been reported missing, he is not necessarily killed or wounded'. Six months later the Rowlings were advised that 'all hope' of finding Paddy alive 'must be abandoned', and in another month they were informed that 'for official purposes' it was now 'presumed … Flying Officer Percy William Rowling lost his life'. Families looking for the slightest evidence to retain hope clung to words such as 'presumed'. But the very presence of those who had indeed survived, and the advice they gave, helped destroy the remote chance that a familiar voice might one day telephone, or a familiar figure might walk in the door.

The task of finalising the files of the Australians in Bomber Command who would not be coming home was difficult, and it has not ended. In 1944 nearly 3,000 Australian aircrew, most of whom were from Bomber Command, were still posted as 'missing'. Air force teams followed the Allied advance checking crash sites and graves, and interviewing witnesses; but ten years after the war half of the 3,000 were still 'missing'. The number of missing, still over 1,300, continues to decline. In 2001, on land previously closed to searchers by East Germany, the wing of an aircraft was unearthed and identified as belonging to a 467 Squadron Lancaster last flown by Flight Lieutenant Ivan (Joe) Durston of Brisbane. Durston had completed his tour, but agreed to fly one more mission so that the five Australians in the crew could finish together. Taking off from Waddington in January 1944, Durston's Lancaster was shot down on his approach to Berlin. Three metres below ground level the Germans found the remains of three or four airmen. One was Joe Durston and the others may yet be identified.

In 1945 the known graves of dead Australian aircrew were scattered across the lands where they had trained and operated. In the British Isles, Australian airmen were buried in cemeteries through Ireland and Cornwall to the Shetlands. Some of the dead were gathered into central cemeteries: 252 are in the Cambridge cemetery on the east of the town and 97 at Harrogate. Between the Pathfinder airfields on the west and 3 Group on the north and east, Cambridge was well known to many of the Australians who could later say in a line-shoot that they 'went through Cambridge', pause, and then add, 'one Sunday on a forty-eight hour pass'. The Harrogate cemetery, west of the Halifax fields of Driffield and Leconfield and the early 460 Squadron home at Breighton, is on the edge of the town and beyond the cemetery's hedge are rich north Yorkshire farm fields. Twenty Australians are buried at Chester and 16 close to the thatched roofs of postcard Cottesmore. But most of the graves of Australian airmen are in churchyards and public cemeteries close to where the men died. At the end of the war the parishes were asked if they wanted the graves of the dominion men shifted. They also had to answer a tougher question: did they want the bodies of German airmen to stay in their churchyards? Nearly all communities said that all the airmen could remain where they were. So at St John the Baptist, Scampton, within sight of the spires of Lincoln Cathedral, ally, enemy and local lie in the same churchyard, just a hurdle fence separating them from farmlands. The neat rows of the airmen's white headstones stand out against the dark and varied headstones of the parish departed.

There are over 630 graves of Australian airmen in France, 360 in Holland and

200 in Belgium. The most Australian airmen dead in any one place in France are 38 at the Commonwealth War Graves cemetery at Choloy near Toul in the 'heart of Lorraine'. At the French National Cemetery at La Doua in Lyon there is just one Australian, Flying Officer Archie Swan, who is buried with the rest of the crew of his Stirling. Among the hectares of graves of French men ('*Mort pour La France*') at La Doua, there is a wall where a German firing squad executed groups of resistance fighters. Swan was trying to drop supplies to the maquis when he was killed on 8 May 1944. There are smaller numbers of Australian graves in various countries, including those neutral lands whose lighted towns beckoned aircrew: nine in Sweden (four in the Overlulea New Churchyard in the far north) and seven in Switzerland. All the Australians in Switzerland are buried alongside 42 other Allied servicemen from World War II in St Martin's churchyard at Vevey. Visitors to St Martins follow a steep walkway under hanging wisteria, and in the cemetery with its conifers and roses they can look at vineyards clinging to steep hillsides or back across the tiles and shutters of Vevey to Lake Geneva and to distant Alps where snow and clouds merge.

The 1,380 graves of Australian airmen in Germany have been concentrated into nine cemeteries. Two of the largest are in the north-west at Reichswald Forest (327 graves) and Rheinberg (238 graves), both close to the Ruhr. The other main cemeteries are Durnbach (261 graves), south of Munich, Berlin (215 graves) and Hanover (142 graves). Here, as elsewhere, graves are located by crews and by date of death rather than nationality, and so the Australians are dispersed among the headstones of thousands of aircrew who flew in and with the RAF — just under 10,000 at cemeteries of the Ruhr and Berlin. Where

> The skies over the target were indeed in turmoil, but the target area itself was in even greater turmoil as 4,000 lb bombs – 'cookies' – smashed amid the built-up area and thousands of incendiaries cascaded down and took a hold among the blocks of buildings ... From the time we sighted [the target-indicators], about ten miles out, until we passed beyond them was the most exciting ten minutes through which I have lived. The two central figures in that brief period were [Squadron-Leader William] Forbes and the bomb-aimer, Pilot-Officer William Grime, of Ealing, London – two 'Bills' who co-operated directly and instructed each other over the intercom phones. I stood behind the imperturbable Forbes and watched the fascinating and fantastic scene over his shoulder.
>
> (*A.W.V. King*, Sydney Morning Herald, *4 December 1943. King had taken a great risk to get his story. Two other correspondents who flew over Berlin on that night of 2 December died, including Norman Stockton of the* Sydney Sun. *Stockton is buried with aircrew in Berlin. Forbes, 463 and 467 Squadrons, from Bundaberg, was killed in action in February 1945.*)

individual bodies of aircrew could not be distinguished one from another, the headstones were joined together. The young men with accents of Quebec, Auckland, Albury, Edinburgh and Bristol, who fought and died together, are publicly remembered together. In Berlin the aircrew are buried on the edge of the Grünewald – the entrance is a cathedral of trees. Their graves are immaculately preserved within the city they tried so hard to destroy.

At Runnymede on the Thames, overlooking the site where King John signed Magna Carta, there is a memorial for the British Empire and Commonwealth airmen who flew from the United Kingdom and north-west Europe and have no known graves. Within its cloisters are the names of over 20,000 men: 1,400 of them served in the Royal Australian Air Force. In Lincoln Cathedral, among many reminders of war, there is a stained glass window dedicated to Bomber Command, an airmen's chapel with one bench commemorating Australians ('In loving memory of our noble boys'), and three books, one on display in a glass cabinet. A plaque says: 'These memorial books contain the names of 25,611 men who flew from Royal Air Force stations in or near Lincolnshire during the Second World War and never returned'. Included are the names of 1,140 Australians. The pages of the book on display are turned regularly, revealing another set of names of men never to look again on the spires of the cathedral.

The Australians who served as aircrew in Bomber Command had an extraordinary experience of war. It was new and it will not be repeated. No bombers carrying a seven-man crew flew before the war. Since the end of World War II similar bombers have not flown against strongly defended targets – the 'flak cities'.

All the Australians in Bomber Command were volunteers, some volunteering several times – for the armed services, for aircrew, and even for Bomber Command, and then for a second tour or Pathfinders. By the time the men were on their way to an operating squadron they had been through more than a year of intense and expensive training, faced numerous tests where others were 'scrubbed', reached at least the rank of sergeant and moved among young men who were above average in motor skills and education. Those few men who had little formal education and were still selected for aircrew training were most conscious of the standing of their peers, and of their own achievement. Stan Hawken said: 'Now, for the first time in my life, in the Air Force, I was being treated as an equal by those who had enjoyed the advantages of a good education and had come from families which were financially secure'. At the end of training they were flying the most technically advanced aircraft in the world, they were about to join those few Allied servicemen who, through much of the war, were on the offensive and taking battle to the enemy's homeland, and they had some idea of the danger and enormity of that task. They could reasonably think that they were a select group, and that their nation was conscious of its heavy investment in them and its high expectations of them. They could march with 'bags of swank'.

Aircrew were from that generation whose parents had been through the Great War and the Depression. Those experiences ensured pressure on sons to take secure jobs in banks, the public service, teaching and the largest firms, and to continue with further education – and pressure too, to keep away from trenches in the next war. They were from those Australians who had relatives in the British Isles and they had a strong sense of being British. They did not think there was any contradiction in being both consciously British and Australian, even aggressively Australian and sensitive to any suggestions that English people and ways were superior. As with most other Australians of the time, they believed that the great events of the world were determined in Europe. Except for the months when Australia was under immediate threat of invasion from the Japanese, most wanted to fight in Europe. In World War II Australian airmen went early to England, were in greater numbers than other Australian servicemen, and stayed longest.

Their travels within Australia to various courses and then across oceans and continents to war strengthened their sense of separation from the person they had been in civilian life. The starting of diaries as they left Australia was in part a recognition that this was the beginning of significant experiences that they would need to set down so that they might understand them. The frequent changes in the group with which they trained and travelled was just one of the ways in which war for aircrew was different from that of most soldiers. Many infantrymen joined a battalion that had a strong local basis. Men trained, travelled, fought, went on leave and returned and fought again in the same battalion. In the air force, at the end of Initial Training School (or later) they divided into pilots, navigators, wireless operators/air gunners, and gunners.

After gaining their wings they were sent to different theatres and to different commands. In 1941, 82 men trained at Parkes in 10 Course as wireless operators/air gunners – they were the 10 Course WAGS. The 23 of them who were killed in the war died in Australia, New Guinea, South-East Asia, Crete, India, Africa and the seas between. Even those men who went to the same theatre and command were unlikely to serve in the same squadron. Of the seven 10 Course WAGS who reached Bomber Command squadrons, only two ended up in the same squadron. An airman in Bomber Command who survived one tour might spend just three to six months of his four-year air force career on an operating squadron. After he was 'screened' he separated from his crew and his unit and became an instructor or changed commands and theatres. Many aircrew met and learnt of the experiences of other members of their squadron postwar, often after they retired from work and had the time to go to reunions and wanted to recover more of a life they had known.

Aircrew retained a sense of belonging to many of the groups that they joined briefly. They hold reunions and have written about those who trained together, travelled together to war on the same ship, served in the same squadron, were posted to the same station and those who were in the same command. The squadron (or squadrons – Doubleday flew operations with three squadrons, Brill with two) was of course important because it was in a squadron that they went to war. But in an operating squadron the men were divided by rank, and aircrew were constantly coming and going. While musterings met so that navigators knew other navigators, and men gathered informally in the mess and went together to pubs, pictures and dances, or the Strand Palace, most close relationships on operating stations were within crews.

Most men in crews did not know one another as civilians, they did not share induction into the air force, they did not go to the same training schools and they did not even share nationality. They formed out of brief and casual meetings, changed personnel during operations (although often a core of five or six remained constant) and only the successful and lucky were together for more than three months. But mutual dependence, the high physical and mental demands and the intensity of the experience welded most crews together. Only other members of the same crew saw and heard how each other behaved in battle. It was crews more than flights or squadrons that went to war, especially in night bombing. Arthur Hope, one of two survivors of Pilot Officer John Heckendorf's crew, wrote to John's mother in Lockhart on 20 August 1945 telling her of their 'smashing' crew, and their hope that 'if anything was coming, it would come to all of us, <u>as a crew</u>, which speaks a lot for the unity and feeling which existed among us'. Even given that Hope, recently released from a prisoner of war camp, was writing to comfort a mother, it is a strong statement about a crew that 'wanted to go, if we had to, as a crew'. Yet the core of that crew did not fly together until May 1943; it collected its flight engineer in July, and carried a replacement bomb-aimer on its last operation against Frankfurt on 20 December 1943. As well, Arthur Hope was an Englishman writing to the mother of his Australian pilot.

Compared with most other servicemen, bomber crews often made decisions about whether they aborted a mission, about whether they bombed and where they bombed, and whether they baled out or stuck with a crippled plane. They were making decisions in extreme situations involving injured men and complex machinery, decisions determining their lives and the lives of others, often made without any chance of consulting anyone outside their aircraft. Those making the decisions were younger than those in an infantry battalion, and each member was essential to the security of the crew and could speak with authority from particular expertise.

Bomber crews were called on to perform a variety of duties. They dropped mines and pamphlets; bombed in support of armies; made precision low level attacks on canals, flying bomb launch-sites, and factories in occupied countries; they flew in support of the Resistance; and they bombed German and Italian cities. But going into battle in Bomber Command was a more predictable experience than it was for most soldiers. An Australian in the 6th Division might have fought in North Africa, Greece, Crete and New Guinea. In contrasting terrain and circumstances, soldiers went on patrols, fought skirmishes and joined battles, all of which were could vary greatly in terms of time, extent and casualties. Aircrew knew what route and height they had to fly, the time they had to be at turning points, where they were most likely to be confronted by flak and searchlights, where they would be within range of German guns, and where they were most vulnerable to fighters. After three or four operations they had a good idea what they would see, and how they and other members of the crew would react. If they got back they knew what they would have for breakfast and

> The closest bondings in my life have been with the people I flew with in aircrews. Nothing else approaches that for bonding.
>
> *(Arthur Hoyle, navigator, 460 Squadron.)*

where they would sleep. Once the target was announced they could make a reasonable guess about the number of casualties. If it was Berlin in the winter of 1943–1944 and there was little cloud cover and a wind to disperse the bomber stream, then the 'reaper would be out' and 5 to 7 per cent of the aircraft would be lost. If the target was Turin or army support in Normandy then 1 to 3 per cent would not return. What they did not know, of course, was whether flak, fighters, technical failure, a crew mistake, or accident would put them in the percentage of missing. The extent to which events were both broadly predictable and, for particular crews, a matter of chance, were both exceptional.

Servicemen signed on 'for the duration', but the task for aircrew was finite. They flew a tour, and while many were told they would be required to fly a second tour, in practice nearly all of those who flew more than one tour volunteered – again. Their opponents in the Luftwaffe night fighters did not fly tours – the German pilots flew until they were incapacitated, dead, transferred or the war ended. Bomber Command aircrew were in a system that offered hope. While operations, battles and the war would go on, for each crew there was a known finishing point. The requirement to repeat a dangerous act for a set number of times encouraged crews to take every opportunity to increase their skills and their cooperation, work all tactics to increase their own safety, ensure all risks with faulty equipment and weather were assessed rationally, carry lucky charms, make appeals to God, and stick to successful routines. But crews also wanted to do their job properly – that was what they had trained for and their sense of duty and self-respect required it. Each man was performing in front of the rest of the crew, the crew was being measured against others in the squadron, and their officers could check some of what they had done,

> Immediately after bombing a violent explosion ... sent the aircraft several hundred feet up from where it dropped like a stone. Inside the aircraft things were chaotic with bodies and things thrown around everywhere. One of the 'things' was our auxiliary urinal – a cut down kerosene tin generously supplied by our ground crew for use by the cabin crew on long trips to avoid the long trip down the back to the Elsan ... The tin, usually stowed behind the pilot's seat, was at one stage floating around his head before it eventually tipped up over the blackout curtain separating him from the navigator. The contents flowed over the H2S set which 'sparked up' a bit and then went u/s for some reason. The deluge continued over the navigation table and charts. Fortunately the pilot regained control of the aircraft ... but I plotted on those charts for the next five and a half hours and looked forward with some evil joy to handing them over to the navigation leader for his perusal on our return.
>
> (John Harrod, on raid to Königsberg, 29 August 1944.)

particularly by examining photographs taken of the target. A crew might decide that it would never do a dummy run across Berlin, but most crews did not put safety above the order to bomb at a particular time and place. Crews also learnt that while they could quickly and easily kill themselves by making an error, they could not ensure their own survival. A tour offered hope but completing it was dependent on luck, and for some men that sense of impotence in the face of danger was an added burden.

Australian prisoners of war in Europe encountered Polish women prisoners of war, Russian women soldiers and women who fought in the war in Europe as partisans and as formally trained soldiers. But for Australian airmen the presence of so many women on Bomber airfields, and the roles that they took, were unexpected. In their diaries, the meetings with women, ranging from quiet conversations to joking and close intimate relationships, were important. Leaving the WAAF drivers who dropped them at their aircraft and later returning to the WAAF voices that called them from the control tower, were part of the crews' sudden shifts between peace and war. A navigator could be lying with a young WAAF on the grass at Tealby, just where Tennyson's brook burbles out of the wolds, and a few hours later he could be over the flak belts of the Ruhr. The next night he could be rotten drunk in 'Skeggy' or leaving the Strand Palace for the ballet. The pattern of emotions that went with operations and the chance of death encouraged the men to intensify the contrasts. They had to pack everything in because it might well be their last chance, and the pressure before operations, the emotional extreme of being over the target, and the troubled, lethargic aftermath of operations set up a sequence of emotional swings. When an operation was scrubbed and when on leave, some men continued the pattern with frenetic activity and drinking followed by exhaustion and hangovers.

J. Glenn Gray was a young American officer with the troops fighting their way across Europe. Fifteen years later, in his reflections on men in battle, he pointed out the importance of spectacle and destruction, and sex and death. Soldiers, he said, saw scenes of havoc and magnificence. Gun teams unleashing a barrage that shook the earth took a 'delight in destruction'. Close to battlegrounds women made themselves available for sex after brief encounters and in unlikely places, and men took crude, physical pleasure or enjoyed brief, intense romances. There seemed to be, Gray thought, a relationship between the proximity of death and the sexual encounters, and it influenced the women as well as the men. Compared with most soldiers, aircrew saw more that was astonishing, beguiling and terrifying; they often witnessed and even came away with an exaggerated impression of the destructive power of their bombs; and for the months that they were closest to death they were always within a few hours of many women.

An airman might perform with skill and composure on several operations, but there was a cumulative cost that came from anticipation, the long dangerous flight, and the climactic bombing run. No crews got through a tour without sharp reminders of the proximity of death. They were hit by flak, caught by searchlights, and saw other aircraft explode or go down in flames with only two or three parachutes opening. The accumulating stress and the trauma of near misses was increased by the knowledge that there was another operation in one or two days, then another and another. A few men could not keep 'dicing with death'. For some, that point was reached after one or two operations. For others it was ten or 20 operations, or even into a second tour. Men who were decorated for bravery reached the point where they could not continue. Noble Frankland says that the great distortion in the film of the Dam Busters was the portrayal of Guy Gibson. Played by Richard Todd, Gibson is seen as a dashing 'clean-cut natural leader'. In fact, by 1943 the handsome 25-year-old Gibson was at the end of a third tour and was, Frankland says, 'exhausted by responsibility and hazard, had developed a carbuncle on his face, was afflicted with arthritic feet, and on the morning of the dams raid, was declared by the medical officer to be unfit to fly'. Of course he flew, and performed superbly, but he was not immune to the incremental cost.

The explanations given at the time for the impact of operations on individuals may be contrasted and simplified as, 'every man had his breaking point', and those men who failed in operations were revealing 'weakness under pressure'. In the first explanation, it did not matter how well trained or led, or how brave and determined a man might be, eventually he would show signs of stress, and have to be taken off operations. Men varied in the length of time that they could endure operations, not simply in their capacity to endure. In the second explanation some deficiency in personality or upbringing showed under

Threatened by death, everyone lived for the moment. Once, a friend and I were picked up by two well-to-do women who'd come to London from the Home Counties in search of distraction while their husbands were fighting in the Middle East. The four of us spent five days in the Strand Palace, leaving the bedrooms only to eat and drink. Especially drink.

(Flying Officer Geoffrey Williams, rear gunner.)

stress. It followed that those who were well adjusted, those with strong personalities, could cope with the pressure of operations and could do so indefinitely. They might suffer from tiredness, the same as any civilian working long and hard, but tiredness was cured by rest. Officers and doctors who favoured the second explanation also thought that fear was an important reason influencing those men displaying the symptoms that apparently made them unfit to fly. And fear had to be countered with strong measures on the squadron. If it could not be countered with harsh words, shame and penalties, then the fearful had to be removed quickly because fear was a contagion that spread. Among senior officers and service psychiatrists the second explanation of 'weakness under pressure' and of fear was favoured, although doctors and officers on squadrons often acted with compassion. Long-term squadron medical officer at Leconfield, John Coto, said that he saw only two 'moral fibre cases' during his time with Bomber Command.

By 1939 the understanding of 'shell shock' that had emerged after World War I had been pushed aside by explanations that blamed individuals (and their parents) for the failure of young men exposed to repeated danger, and that was to the detriment of the men in Bomber Command. As Wade Rodgers said, courage and guts frittered away when tested again and again, and he directed his anger at those who would not accept that some of his colleagues were 'legitimately ill'. The dominant explanation also meant that there was little understanding after the war for those who took the symptoms of stress into civilian life. Now it is generally recognised that combat stress has nothing to do with pre-existing weakness. It is a normal condition that occurs in ordinary men operating in sustained, dangerous conditions. Those suffering from combat stress display a variety of reactions: muscle cramps, tremors and tics, sweating, bowel and urinary tract reactions, rapid heart beat, quick breathing, increased blood

We did my thirteenth trip to Antwerp at a mere 7,100 feet ... On the run over the city we were met with a stack of searchlights and the heaviest concentration of flak I ever saw. At this height everything could have a go at us and it did. Light machine guns, Bofors, 20 mm cannon, 'flaming onions' (yellow strings of blobs of tracer) – and of course, the heavy 88 mm barrage ... I flew straight and level for the run up and the bombing and the eternal camera run, a full thirty seconds; went through the whole gamut without a scratch ... But I had nightmares about this and a couple of other events for all of forty years – the same thing over and over again ... [They recur] at odd intervals right up to the present. This was one of the prices a lot of us have to pay after it was all over.

(Wade Rodgers, 630 Squadron.)

pressure, inability to sleep, panic, sensitivity to irritation, apathy, and extreme post-combat responses of euphoria or depression. From 1980 those symptoms were accepted as similar to those used for the diagnosis of Post Traumatic Stress Disorder.

What is difficult to explain is not why a few men could not complete a tour, but why so many could. The fact that it was the sort of action that quickly impairs ordinary men – repeated exposure to unseen and seen dangers, to near misses, to death and disfigurement of others who were known and close – makes it all the more inexplicable. Even more difficult to explain is why men who knew exactly what to expect volunteered for more. Part of the reason was that they still felt the sense of duty that had motivated them when they first agreed to fight. And since their arrival in England their belief that they were in a just war and that the bombers were making a significant contribution had been strengthened. Some thought that there would be increasing pressure on them in the future to return to operations, and it was better to go back at a time of their own choosing rather than later when equipment, tactics and defences would have changed and they would have to re-enter the war as sprogs. After operations, screened aircrew often found instructing unrewarding, sometimes dangerous, and the training squadrons lacking in spirit and camaraderie. Also, some experienced aircrew were worried about instructing men to do what they could do better and with a greater chance of surviving.

A consequence of the very danger that they had already survived may also have drawn aircrew back to operations. In the aftermath of operations men sometimes suffered depression, and one way of lifting that depression was to

Born in 1920, C.W.J. ('Bill') Falkinder of Lindisfarne went to Hobart High and at 19 began initial training at Somers. Scrubbed for low flying at Narromine, he went to schools at Cootamundra, Evans Head and Parkes and qualified as an observer. In England he was posted to 405 (RCAF) Squadron, and then 419 (another Canadian squadron). After instructing at 11 OTU, Falkinder retrained for Mosquitoes and joined 105 then 109, Pathfinder Squadrons. Falkinder, DSO, DFC and Bar, flew 114 operations, ten to Essen alone. Asked to name 'an outstanding sortie or incident', he said that this was a question 'conducive to "lines"', but he put an asterisk beside one on the night of the 5/6 June 1944 when he had navigated the Mosquito that dropped the first target marker to begin the D-Day assault. In 1944 he married Dulcie, then serving in the WAAFs, and returned to Australia early in 1945. Elected in 1946 at age 25 as the Member for Franklin, the softly spoken Falkinder was in the Australian parliament for 20 years. He died in 1993. The most decorated navigator in the RAAF in Europe, Falkinder flew 365 hours on operations.

return to the cycle of the briefing, the anticipation, the intensity of the raid, and post-operation exhaustion. Adrenaline, Kingsford-Smith said, 'was God's gift to aircrew'. Adrenaline gave aircrew the capacity to respond rapidly, but it pushed the oscillations between peace and war to greater extremes and it could come at the cost of dependence. Testosterone, stimulated and required at times of aggression, also ebbed and flowed, so that the young men were responding to what their bodies released and what they poured into them. Men went back to operating squadrons for high-minded and selfless reasons, and operating squadrons lured them because of the intensity, sense of purpose, spontaneity and mateship that men found there. And for a few men the only apparent escape from the troubled depression that descended on them after operations, and the only way to recapture the euphoria of operations, was to return to them.

The number of Australians in Bomber Command who died, including those killed in air accidents from the time they joined Operational Training Units in England, stands at 4,050. In all the fighting that the Australian army did against Italy and Germany – in North Africa (including Tobruk and El Alamein), Greece, Crete and Syria – it suffered 3,552 dead. The navy suffered 903 dead in the war in Europe and its seas, and the most losses suffered by the air force in any other command was 408 in Coastal Command. Compared with the three divisions of the AIF, Australians in Bomber Command were few, but they carried a dis-proportion of Australia's cost in the war in Europe.

The 4,050 deaths in Bomber Command are also significant when compared with losses in the war against Japan. For Australia the most costly battles were Singapore (1,789 dead), and Papua (over 2,000 in the separate battles of Kokoda, Milne Bay and Buna-Gona). The total deaths in action from all services in the war against Japan (9,500) was almost the same as the losses in the war against Germany and Italy (9,370). In the lists of Australian casualties of World War II, two figures stand out: the number who died in Bomber Command and the 8,000 Australian servicemen and women who died as prisoners of war of the Japanese – those who went to war in the air and those who died after they had formally ceased to be at war.

A few men arriving home early from Bomber Command were astounded to be met at Melbourne or Sydney with the charge of being a 'Jap dodger'. Arthur Doubleday says that before they left England 'there were boys on 467 Squadron who got white feathers from people at home'. Strangely, that was at a time when the Australians in the air war against Japan felt they had been side-lined, were threatening a 'jack-up', and suffering casualties much lower than those in Bomber Command. The misdirected insults were a sign of the alarm felt by Australians in 1942, and of the shift in Australians' concern from events in Europe to those in their north; they were not a measure of Australian knowledge and assessment of the men who had served in Bomber Command. Generally, both the men returning from the air war in Europe and from the Japanese prison camps were high in public recognition and regard. Where the Bomber Command men came back in large groups they were met by bands and taken in cavalcades through city streets. Bill Pearce said that in Brisbane they were picked up in a convoy of private cars, shops were shut and 'Queen Street was crowded'. The high public opinion of aircrew was apparent to the political parties. On his way back, Doubleday was cabled in America asking him if he would stand for election for the conservatives, and when he got home he had another offer of a seat and the party said it would pay a manager to look after his farm. Isaacson stood for the Victorian parliament in 1945 but was defeated by a handful of votes. Bill Falkinder won the seat of Franklin, defeating the Minister for Repatriation, and became the youngest man then to enter the House of Representatives. In the House, he sat next to his old Group Captain, Thomas White. Roberts Dunstan, the one-legged gunner, was not elected to the Victorian parliament until 1956, but at 33 years he was still the youngest member of the Legislative Assembly.

The public response to Guy Gibson's posthumous *Enemy Coast Ahead* (1946) and Paul Brickhill's *The Dam Busters* (1951) confirmed the status of Bomber Command aircrew. The *Dam Busters*, claimed to be 'Britain's biggest selling war book', and the 1954 film with its stirring 'Dam Busters March' helped retain interest through the postwar decade. The accounts of evaders, escapers and prisoners, such as *The Great Escape* (book) and *The Wooden Horse* (film) 1950 which told the story of the escape from Stalag Luft III, also kept the kriegies in public notice. In fact, in the United Kingdom, the prisoners who had returned from the stalags may have been better known than the prisoners from the Far East. But for Australians, the experiences of the prisoners of war of the Japanese soon overshadowed and then dominated public consciousness of prisoners. The war against Japan was relatively more important to Australians than it was to the

United Kingdom and the prisoners of war of the Japanese more numerous and atrocities immeasurably greater. The recovery and return of 14,000 prisoners from Rabaul and Ambon to Hokkaido went on for months. Many were so obviously emaciated in newspaper and newsreel photographs, and many had horrific stories to tell. Australians wrote books about being prisoners of war of the Japanese, but rarely about being prisoners of the Germans. Rohan Rivett's *Behind Bamboo* (1946), Russell Braddon's *The Naked Island* (1951), and Betty Jeffrey's *White Coolies* (1954), sold in large numbers, publishers of *The Naked Island* claiming 'more than one million copies sold'. Trials of Japanese war criminals, with further revelations of the brutal treatment of prisoners, continued in Australian New Guinea until 1951.

Australians began forgetting Bomber Command aircrew and the prisoners of war of the Japanese in the 1960s and that continued in the 1970s. The decline in public consciousness of the ex-prisoners was less, partly because of the periodic reminders by books and films, such as *King Rat* (book, 1962, film, 1965) and Ray Parkin's trilogy that began with *Out of the Smoke* (book, 1960). Renewed interest in the ex-prisoners began in the early 1980s. It was more than a revival of public awareness of what had happened, it made the experiences of the ex-prisoners one of the defining incidents in Australian history. At his death in 1993, Sir Edward 'Weary' Dunlop was one of the most famous Australians, but 20 and 30 years closer to the events in which he had excelled he was scarcely known to the general public. From the 1980s 'Changi' became one of the most evocative words in Australian folk history – perhaps below Gallipoli and Anzac, but alongside Eureka and Kokoda. Prime Ministers visited the memorial at Hellfire Pass on the Burma–Thailand Railway, they laid wreaths at the prisoner of war cemeteries in South-East Asia, and Australians began visiting the sites where the prisoners had suffered.

There was no parallel revival in interest in the Australians who had fought in Bomber Command. The Australian dam busters, (such as Mick Martin and Dave Shannon), Middleton VC, and the Riverina twins, Brill and Doubleday, were lost to public recognition. More importantly, most Australians do not know that over 4,000 of their countrymen died in Bomber Command. The significance of that number is immediately apparent when it is compared with the 339 Australians from all services who died in Korea and the 519 who died in Vietnam. Most Australians do not know that the names of 1,400 men are commemorated at the Air Forces Memorial, Runnymede, and 1,140 at Lincoln Cathedral. No Australian Prime Minister visits those sites, locates the deaths of the men of

Bomber Command in Australian history and says that it is from them that 'we have chosen to draw our inspiration'. In 2001 the Australian government granted $25,000 to ex-prisoners of war of the Japanese and their widows, but the ex-prisoners of the Germans were not compensated and (more significantly) scarcely mentioned.

The ignorance of young Australians and the neglect by old Australians of the men who served in Bomber Command is all the more surprising because aircrew were an elite by selection, training, the task they were asked to do and the losses that they suffered. And they have been articulate about their own experiences. But of the ex-members of Bomber Command who have written about who they were and what they did, only Don Charlwood (*No Moon Tonight*, 1956, and *Journeys into Night*, 1991) and John Beede (*They Hosed Them Out*, 1965) have reached a wider audience. The British in scholarly and popular history have not neglected Bomber Command: Lincoln is still the Bomber County, and shops along Steep Hill and High Street in Lincoln sell books of careful re-evaluation, memorabilia, postcards and Bomber Command tea towels.

Some reasons why Australians have failed to keep the men who flew the bombers in their history are clear. Firstly, there is no obvious site for private and public remembering. The battles were scattered across skies from the United Kingdom to Italy and central Europe. Many of the dead are buried close to where they died, singly, in twos and threes and sometimes all seven of a crew together. Only three Commonwealth War Graves cemeteries have more than 250 Australian graves (Reichswald Forest, Durnbach and Cambridge) and in all three the Australian graves are dispersed and are a minority of all aircrew graves in those cemeteries. The old airfields are associated with particular squadrons, and in any case Waddington is still a working station so public access is often denied. Breighton is being taken over by industry, Binbrook by housing and Driffield by army cadets and grain storages. Runnymede Memorial and Lincoln Cathedral, both potential sites for public or private ceremonies, are strangely unknown.

Secondly, the dispersal of so many Australians through crews from the counties, colonies and dominions, and the fact that in the nominally Australian squadrons most of the ground staff and many aircrew were not Australians, has made it difficult for historians to write about an Australian experience. The problem was acute for the official historian, John Herington, in his two volume history of the Australians in the air war over Europe. It is as though he had to write about Australian soldiers serving in units in which at the platoon and section level many men, often most men, belonged to another nationality; where equipment, food and accommodation were supplied by another nation; where much of the final training was controlled by another nation; and where planning, strategy and tactics were decided by another nation. But the decision of Australian governments to scatter 10,000 aircrew, and make group biography difficult, is not an adequate excuse to forget them.

Thirdly, Australians now see a relevance in battles of the Coral Sea, Kokoda and Singapore, but not in combat in skies over Berlin, Essen, Düsseldorf, Stuttgart or Hamburg. The Australians fighting in the north were obviously fighting in defence of their homeland. They can be seen as the first mass engagement of Australians with the region, and when Australian Prime Ministers speak at the cemeteries in Kranji or Kanchanaburi they are evoking a long-term commitment of Australians to Asia. There has been also a deliberate policy by some Australians to bring the symbols of nationalism closer to home. The claim for the elevation of the battles to the north over all others was made most strongly by Paul Keating:

> The Australians who served ... in Papua New Guinea fought and died not in defence of the old world, but the new world. Their world. They died in defence of Australia, and the civilization and values which had grown up there. That is why it might be said that, for Australians, the battles in Papua New Guinea were the most important ever fought.

The Australian government was right to worry about the capacity of the British to reinforce the base in Singapore, right to bring the troops back from the Middle East, and it obviously had a primary obligation to defend Australia. But it was also true that Australia was in a world war in which Germany was the main enemy, and when the Australians were fighting on the Kokoda Trail, the course of the war was being decided in Russia, North Africa, the seas of the Atlantic, the air in Europe and the factories of the United States. The Australians who fought in the air war in Europe (or at El Alamein) were in the determining battles. In any case, the elevation of the significance of Kokoda does not require that those who fought in Europe should be neglected. National history can be comprehensive.

Fourthly, it is difficult to remember the men in Bomber Command for what they did without questioning the policy that they executed; to praise those who flew again and again through flak without also asking what each Lancaster's six tons of bombs did after they left the aircraft. As Australian aircrew in Bomber

Command had no influence on the selection of targets, bomb loads, or tactics, they can reasonably hope to be remembered for, and judged on, how they did their job and not on what was beyond their control – the policy outlined in the Directives to the Air Officer Commanding-in-Chief, Bomber Command, and its implementation by senior officers of the RAF. The distinction between actors and the consequence of acts is important, but the questions about the effectiveness and morality of what the crews did should not be avoided. The senior RAAF officers and the Australian government that committed Australians to another air force retained some responsibility for their appropriate use.

Some men were certainly worried about what they had to do. Before going on his first raid in September 1942 Don Charlwood wrote in his diary:

> Tonight our orders are, 'Bomb the centre of Bremen; make it uninhabitable for the workers.' England! Cricket! Huh! Justifiable? I do not know. I only know that I shall kill women and children soon.

A fortnight later he admitted it was necessary to preserve the 'democratic way of life', but, he added, 'I cannot imagine Christ bidding men bomb little children. What things we mice have to answer for!' Geoff Maddern, Charlwood's pilot, asked Don to keep his thoughts to himself for the sake of the morale of the crew. But Maddern had his own doubts about raids that were, he wrote in his diary, close to the 'one thing we are supposed to be fighting against – barbarism'.

In battle some riflemen cannot bring themselves to fire, and sometimes a soldier will make a conscious decision that unless it is close fighting in which he and his comrades depend on each other to survive he will always fire wide. The justification is that one soldier does not decide a battle, but he can kill. Whether any aircrew had reached a similar conclusion is unknown. But a few of the bombs seen falling in the sea may not have been a result only of crews wanting an aircraft able to fly higher and respond more quickly in air battles. For a few of those who bombed wide and shy, self-preservation and morality may have come together.

Charlwood said that 'most prefer to fight on unthinkingly'. Perhaps this was so, but questions about the effectiveness and morality of bombing were raised in the British parliament and German propaganda about *Terrorflieger* reached England. And comments from neutral countries' press with correspondents in German cities were sometimes carried in British newspapers. As a result, most aircrew thought about what they were doing and decided that, on balance, bombing was justified. Doubleday said:

I left home with the quite clear determination that the heart of the problem that I was involved in lay in Berlin and any other place where the sinews of war could be developed and that included the fellow on the lathe who was doing it and anyone else ... we weren't going to win by any half measure and if we didn't win, there was nothing left to have ... The whole future of civilisation was at stake. So I had no qualms about it at all. I know a lot of people did, but I didn't.

Reacting to a V-2 bomb that fell in a residential area and killed civilians, David Scholes made the consciously exaggerated statement: 'All I hope is that my bombs didn't kill outright those they fell upon, but caused suffering, pain and shock, before death!'

Most aircrew then or later had few doubts about what they did. They believed that they fought evil, the enemy had deliberately and frequently killed civilians, and through much of the war they knew that bombing was the only effective weapon that the Allies had. On operations, aircrew were consumed by doing their job and surviving. When not anticipating or recovering from operations, they were young men with much living to pack into what might well be brief lives. It was also clear that when raids inflicted obvious and extensive damage on targets, morale went up – 'good prang' they noted in logs. It was not that aircrew were unconscious of the criticisms of Bomber Command, but they had little time for doubts; to dwell on such doubts was not likely to help them survive, and to believe in them was to diminish what they went through and the deaths of other crews.

In the strongest postwar criticism of Bomber Command it was said that bombing was ineffective, neither destroying German morale nor impeding German industry's capacity to support war. If bombing was a misdirection of effort then the killing of civilians was certainly unjustified: the claimed ineffectiveness simplified the moral argument. But in fact bombing was indeed significant. The bombers were important in deterring German invasion of Britain

The vapour trails are lit up like white train lines running in a curve straight over the middle of Dresden ... Jock (navigator), you've never seen a target ... come and have a look at this one, you won't see this again ...

Jock is standing with tears running down his face – Christ you poor bastards, you poor bastards. I never want to see that again skipper, don't ever show me again, what poor bastards.

(Flying Officer Eric Barton, 186 Squadron, Bevis 1988.)

and in laying mines in German waters. They lifted morale and they shifted the war to Germany. They induced Germany to change its aircraft production and deployment from offence to defence and direct vast resources into the defence of cities. They prepared the way for the American bombers who effectively drew the German fighters into battle where the Allies destroyed them and won dominance in the air. They disrupted German industry and late in the war had a critical impact on transport and oil. Without the bombing campaign the Russians would have been under greater pressure and the invasion of Europe in June 1944 would have been more dangerous, requiring more troops, and the battles across France and into Germany more protracted and costly. The bombers played a part in the Battle of the Atlantic, the reduction of the threat from flying bombs and in supporting resistance movements. And once the bombers had demonstrated that they were formidable then Germany was less likely to use gas or biological weapons. In his summary, Noble Frankland says that the 'strategic air offensive ... made a decisive and indispensable contribution to victory'.

Bomber Command made mistakes. Area bombing was continued for too long. It was continued after bombing directed at specific targets was possible and more effective. The bombing of Dresden in February 1945 by successive British and American raids was morally and militarily unjustified. The same judgment could probably be made on the raids on Worms, a week after Dresden, and on Pforzheim, another two days later. Pforzheim had the third highest number of deaths in a raid (after Hamburg and Dresden). Worms, Pforzheim and other towns attacked in 1945 for the first time were clearly not of critical importance, and destroying them at that late stage was not going to have much impact on war production. The Battle of Berlin late in 1943 and ending in 1944 was not a victory. And had it continued it was likely to have led to the destruction of Bomber Command before Berlin. Harris did not begin area bombing nor was he primarily responsible for the bombing of Dresden, but he and other senior officers promised too much – the destruction of distant fortified cities was more difficult than they proclaimed, and they were unable to bring about the collapse of German morale.

In the prewar conferences several proposals to limit bombing were put forward. Firstly, it was suggested that unfortified cities should not be bombed. During the war most German cities were defended tenaciously. Secondly, those about to launch a bombing raid were asked to warn civilians of their intent. Generally Bomber Command dropped leaflets warning of the terrible destruction to come. Marie Vassiltchikov wrote in her diary on 1 August 1943:

The fate of Hamburg arouses great anxiety here for last night Allied planes dropped leaflets that called upon all women and children in Berlin to leave at once, as they did before the raids on Hamburg. This sounds ominous. Berlin may be next.

As a result, many people on their own initiative and on government orders left the city before the Battle of Berlin began. Thirdly, it was argued that only those cities close to ground combat should be bombed. This would have restricted bombing to those targets about to be hit by artillery. But this turned out to be an absurd idea as it gave advantage to the aggressor. It would have allowed Hitler to make his rapid advance on Warsaw or Rotterdam, and strike those cities with dive-bombers, while knowing that German cities were immune from attack. In so far as these superficial constraints meant anything, Bomber Command made some compliance.

One terrible and striking characteristic of World War II was the number of civilian deaths. In the countries that suffered the greatest casualties (Russia, China and Poland) many more civilians than service personnel were killed: a total of close to 30,000,000 civilians. Most of those were killed by means other than aerial bombing. In Germany about 500,000 civilians died as a result of bombing. Many of the 500,000 (but less than half) were killed by the United States Army Air Force. In the German siege of Leningrad – the tactic used for thousands of years to conquer cities – a million civilians died. In the two-week battle for Manila in 1945 nearly 100,000 Filipino civilians were killed and the city destroyed. The total number of civilians killed in Manila was probably close to the total killed in the firestorms of both Hamburg and Dresden, and more than the total killed by all German air raids on Britain. In World War II civilians died in millions because governments killed their own or captured citizens, or countries broke down into civil war, or civilians were trapped in battles or sieges. Bombing was a minor cause of civilian deaths in both Europe and the Pacific. It is important to get the relative importance of bombing established, and it is equally important not to use comparisons to diminish and disguise wrongs. The deaths of 50,000 in Dresden remain, whether or not many more died in Leningrad, Manila and Auschwitz.

An argument against bombing is that it led to the acceptance of an incremental increase in atrocities. In this argument, the bombing of civilians in colonies is seen to lead to Guernica, Warsaw, Coventry, Hamburg, Dresden and Hiroshima. It is an argument to be taken seriously, but it is considering selected events in chronological order. It omits events out of sequence. (Most of what was attempted by bombing in World War II was attempted in World War I.) What was technically possible looks as relevant to the sequence as incremental neglect for humanity. Had they possessed the machines and the bombs, the belligerents in World War I would have done much more bombing of civilians. And had Hitler possessed an atomic bomb, would he have used it? The sequence is not a chain (to break one link has no impact on others), and there is no necessary cause and effect connecting successive events. In any case, for Australians in Bomber Command, the argument about increasing tolerance of civilian deaths ends with Dresden and Pforzheim. And had there been no Dresden then it is unlikely that the questioning of the morality of the policies of Bomber Command would have reached the consciousness of a wider public.

There is another sequence important to any evaluation of the history of bombing. The high casualties and the inaccuracy of Allied bombing, such as in the Bomber Command raid on Nuremberg and the even more costly American raids on Schweinfurt in August and October 1943, led to methods that were more accurate and less dangerous to those who had to deliver the bombs. In the bombing over Europe the historian has to evaluate the efficiency and morality of a policy that often sent men on operations that killed more of the bombers than the bombed, that killed more of those in the area of a target, than at the target. By Iraq and Kosovo the risk to the bombers was almost removed, and the questions of morality and effect were concentrated on the impact on the bombed.

Through six years of war Bomber Command used and misused a potent weapon, and any moral judgment of policies involves complex issues – few would condemn all that it did and a different few would approve all. In those circumstances there was an increased obligation on Australian senior officers and politicians to hold Australians in units, keep them under Australian control and monitor what they were being asked to do. The problems that went with the dispersal of Australian forces and placing them at the disposal of officers in other national forces went beyond the questions of promotion, leave, medical care, rations and length of combat service. They went to the fundamental issues of policy effectiveness and morality.

Australia committed itself generously to the air defences of Britain. It selected and trained aircrew efficiently, lost effective control of them and saw them perform superbly and suffer higher casualties in action than any other major group of Australian servicemen in World War II. It remembered and honoured them briefly, and then – in a country so concerned about its performance in wars overseas – forgot them.

Although the number of Australians in Bomber Command varied, they were always a small minority. There were more than twice as many Australians in Bomber Command in January 1945 (1,500) as there were in April 1944 (650). The most accurate quantitative measure of Australia's contribution to Bomber Command is that 7.3 per cent of aircrew deaths were of men serving in the RAAF. Relative to population, both Canada (with 17.8 per cent of deaths) and New Zealand (3 per cent) made a greater contribution to Bomber Command. But from December 1941 Australia (compared with New Zealand and Canada) was committing more of its air force to the war against Japan. Bomber Command cost the three white dominions 15,648 men.

Casualties in Bomber Command

Royal Air Force	38,462	(69.2%)
Royal Canadian Air Force	9,919	(17.8%)
Royal Australian Air Force	4,050	(7.3%)
Royal New Zealand Air Force	1,697	(3.0%)
Polish Air Force	929	(1.7%)
Other Allied Air Forces	473	(0.9%)
South African and other	61	(0.1%)

For Australians, the equation in which deaths in Bomber Command secured fewer deaths on the ground was not of immediate national interest. That was not the case for the New Zealanders, with ground troops fighting their way north in Italy, and it was critical for the Canadians. In the 11 months after D-Day, the Canadians lost over 11,000 dead in north-west Europe, more than their total deaths in Bomber Command. Without Bomber Command the casualties on the ground would have been greater, but would they have been two or three or four times greater? Would the numbers of casualties of civilians caught in battles have been significantly greater?

While a comparison of the performances of different nationalities in Bomber

Command is obviously difficult, there is some readily available evidence. In 1943–1944 Bomber Command tested the skills of arriving aircrew and Australians and New Zealanders scored well. On operations the Australians were generally thought to have high competence. Other qualities, at least as important, are more difficult to assess objectively, but Martin Middlebrook, who has written both prolifically and carefully on Bomber Command, says that during the high losses in the Battle of Berlin:

> The Pathfinders, feeling themselves a selected elite, held well. The small number of Australian squadrons – three out of the four were flying Lancasters – were also steady. The Canadians of 6 Group had been expanded too rapidly, sometimes suffered from poor leadership and were mostly flying the Halifax, which nearly always suffered heavier casualties than the Lancaster when committed to action. Their morale and that of most of 4 Group was not so high, although it varied from squadron to squadron. The picture in the Main Force Lancaster squadrons which bore the brunt of the Battle of Berlin was more one of enormous strain, mostly faced and endured, morale being sustained by the crews' faith in the aircraft they flew.

Given the weather, the length of the flights, the strength of the defences, the frequency of operations and the accumulating losses, the judgment, 'were also steady', is an exceptional tribute. The statistics of the Australian squadrons are also evidence of their sustained morale, efficiency and frequent exposure to danger.

460 SQUADRON:
Sent more aircraft on operations than any other squadron in 1 Group.
Had the highest percentage of losses of all Wellington squadrons.
Sent more Lancasters on operations than any other squadron in Bomber Command.
Lost more Lancasters than any other squadron in 1 Group.
Probably dropped a greater tonnage of bombs than any other squadron in Bomber Command.
Lost on operations 169 aircraft and 1,018 aircrew.

When Stan Hawken was discharged he still had few skills of immediate use in civilian life. He took the government's ten quid grant, bought tools, and went back to digging drains for plumbers. He says he will never forget when he went from the life in the officers' mess to his first full day in a trench. But soon he bought a bike, then a truck, started tendering for larger jobs, employed over 50 men, and moved into other businesses. He went into local politics, became a Melbourne suburban mayor and was appointed to state institutions. That change also took him away from the woman he had married before he joined the air force, and to divorce and remarriage. It was, he said, selection for aircrew and the succession of schools and experience in the air war that had changed his ideas about his own capacities and what he might do in life.

All civilians who go into the services and combat have disrupted lives. But the men who went to war in Bomber Command were likely to have their lives transformed as well as disrupted. The many courses and selection tests, the journeys and the experiences in the air and on the ground in Europe were likely to lead to changed careers and identities.

Bill Brill and Arthur Doubleday had already been back to study and passed their first aircrew tests when they met on the train on Armistice Day 1940. Their lives then kept a remarkable parallel. The fact that their names started with 'B' and 'D' meant that their service numbers were close, and in the military's arbitrary way they were often drafted together. But still the close similarities in their careers defied chance and personal differences. The two farmers had both been to Yanco Agricultural High, both went to the same air training schools, were selected for pilot training, were shipped to Canada, won their wings and were commissioned as pilot officers in Calgary. Both men crossed the Atlantic on the same ship, trained together on Wellingtons at Lichfield, were appointed among the first crews to 460 Squadron, flew on the first 460 Squadron raid, completed their tours within days of each other and returned to Lichfield as instructors. Both then came back for a second tour to Waddington (Brill with 463 Squadron and Doubleday with 467 Squadron) and both were appointed to command squadrons (Bill taking over 467 and Arthur shifting a few miles to Skellingthorpe to command 61 Squadron). And both ended their operational careers as Wing Commander, DSO, DFC. Brill had a Bar to his DFC, and he had completed 58 operations and Doubleday 54.

Their careers diverged at the end of their second tours. After coming home and marrying Ilma, Brill stayed in the RAAF. He commanded several Australian stations, served as director of personnel services and in 1960 was promoted to group captain. Before taking up an appointment as commander of the RAAF station at Townsville, Brill took extended sick leave, but died of a heart attack on 12 October 1964, aged 48. Perhaps the officers who had assessed him in 1940 as a 'rather slow ... quiet country chap' were at his funeral. Ilma stayed on in Canberra, caring for her three children, her memories of Bill and her beautiful garden.

Arthur Doubleday's English bride Phyllis joined him on the farm at Coolamon. But the droughts of the early 1940s were still having their impact, and storms, picking up dust from further west, swept through the area leaving all surfaces covered in grit. Arthur had rejected politics and farming did not look promising. He said everything 'seemed to be an anti-climax' and he had a 'pretty rough year'. He was invited to apply for jobs in civil aviation and was offered the position of District Superintendent of Queensland. He accepted, and later transferred to New South Wales as Regional Director of Civil Aviation, and following departmental amalgamations was Director of Transport, New South Wales until he retired in 1977. Active and always learning, Doubleday lived in retirement in Sydney. Phyllis died in 1982 and he remarried in 1987. Arthur Doubleday, aged 89, died in August 2001.

Howard Griffiths interviewed Arthur Doubleday for his television documentary *Wings of the Storm*, completed in 1987. In notes on the interview, Griffiths wrote 'a profoundly decent man'.

Bob Curtis, who had been with Brill at Lichfield and then flew with him on his second tour, said that at Waddington a pilot of another crew was clearly under stress. As the pilot had lost a lot of weight, he was known as 'Bones'. Brill thought it would help Bones if – against procedure – he called him up during a raid. The name 'Bones' provoked Brill to use a stage Black American accent. As they came close to the target, Brill switched on his RT and called, 'Is you out there, Bones?' There was an immediate, clear response, 'Yes, Boss, I'm here. Where's you?' As Bones sounded close, Brill said, 'I'll switch on my navigation lights so you can see me'. This was met by a storm of protest from Brill's crew, but he flashed his lights and Bones called, 'Ah sees you, Boss'. That exchange in the night, twice defying good sense and instructions, Curtis says, reduced the tension in two crews.

Both Brill and Doubleday had the presence of leaders. Brill was more irreverent, Doubleday quieter, but still a persuasive public speaker. As Doubleday said, he could 'yap'.

For Brill and Doubleday, a familiarity with trucks and tractors, listening to the note of the engine during long hours of working the fallow, a knowledge of fuel mix, revolutions, engine power and the limits of machinery may have eased their way into the cockpit of a Wellington. But the qualities that made them outstanding pilots and leaders came from broader values, and from themselves.

Two of the identifying characteristics that they had carried into the war, Riverina and farmer, were both displaced by the war.

Of course Brill and Doubleday were lucky. About 40 per cent of the Australians who served in Bomber Command were killed and over half were casualties (killed, wounded or imprisoned). They were lucky, too, that in all the hammerings that they took over targets, the failures of equipment and the dicing with weather, they never suffered one of the horrific flights – one in which a member of the crew was burnt and blinded, or shredded with flak and died in agony in a four-hour flight back to base. Such incidents scarred crews, reduced their capacity to perform, and stayed with them.

Australians may have forgotten those who served in Bomber Command, but surviving aircrew came back with memories that were dense and varied – from the exhilaration and horror of flying, to weeks of boredom in reception centres, nights at the Strand Palace, and seeing the flesh at the Windmill. Speaking at a squadron reunion in Melbourne in 1998, Peter Isaacson asked his audience:

> Can you see the briefing room with the map on the wall, the strands of coloured wool stretching across England, across the Channel or North Sea, across Europe to a place on the map deep in enemy territory …

> Do you recall the murmur of the debriefing, the savoury smell and taste of cigarettes, the sight of anguish on the faces of the men as they read the names on the operation board which did not have a landed time against their names?

They all could.

Endnotes

Chapter 1

Information on Arthur Doubleday comes from a transcript of an interview recorded for the Keith Murdoch Sound Archives of Australia in the War of 1939–45, Australian War Memorial [AWM], in 1989; interviews in 2000; and from files – RAAF Service Dossier A9300/1, and A705/15, 163/28/129, National Archives of Australia [NAA], and RAAF biographical file, AWM65. Quotes from Doubleday are from the transcript unless stated otherwise. The 'sunlit plains extended' is from A.B. Paterson, 'Clancy of the Overflow'. Gammage 1986 described McCaughey's homestead. Bill Brill's Service Dossier includes the form completed by the interviewing panel. There should be a service dossier for all RAAF who served in Bomber Command, and an AWM RAAF biographical file for some. Fay Jones (nee Brill), Ilma Brill, Vic Brill, Bill Gammage and Joyce Dennis provided information on the area and on the Brill and Doubleday families.

The figures on recruitment are from Gillison (1962 p. 69). Sources on Belford, Piper, Manifold, Whishaw, Bain, O'Connor, Rodgers and other airmen are listed in the bibliography. The endnotes to subsequent chapters will refer only to sources on individual airmen where the source is unclear. Keith Miller's biographical file is in the AWM. The story of George Hawes is told by Rope (1984). Charlwood (1991, p. VII), referred to 'children of empire' and Charlwood (1990, p.196), wrote the 'air raids are simply awful …'. Simpson (1995) describes Martin. Pratt (1946), in his valuable thesis, reprints guides for selection panels for aircrew.

Whitrod (2001) (Coastal Command) is excellent on the influence of Sunday School, young men's church associations and the influence of English comics and stories. England 'then was an extension of Australia' (p. 21). He also notes the influence of scouting on his values and his readiness to go to England to fight (p. 56).

B.E. Finucane (died 1942) was Irish, and K.W. Truscott (died 1943) was

Australian. Mobbs (1947) says that in 1939 15 per cent of Commonwealth Bank clerical staff were women, and in 1944, 46 per cent. Mobbs gives RAAF enlistments. Esther Davies, a teacher at Canberra High, organised students to research the names on the honour roll. The results are preserved at the school. McCalman (1993) notes that in her survey of the Scotch College entry class of 1934, 16 died in the air force, 11 in the army and one in the navy. Long (1952, p. 58, footnote) gives the ages of the 6th Division. The ages of the 8th Division were calculated by taking one man in ten from the 2/21st, 2/22nd and 2/40th Battalions. Aircrew ages are based on Ilbery (1999, pp. 125–59). Dyson (1979, p. 29), also picks up 'children's crusade' and applies it to Bomber Command. The specification, 'of pure European descent', was on the 1939 form 'Application for Air Crew'. Hall (1989, p. 62) has written on Leonard Waters.

Chapter 2

Firkins (1964, p. 75) refers to Oakeshott, and Herington (1954, p. 554) gives the size tests for aircrew. Pratt (1946, Appendix D) sets out the criteria for wireless operators and gunners. Bruce Pitt, transcript, tells the story of the recruit ready to go home until the RAAF was ready. There are several histories of airfields used by training schools, for example, Ilbery (1999), Maslin (1990), Telford (1997), and Wordley and Madigan (1982). Some town histories include sections on local airfields; for example, Bushby (1980) on Deniliquin and Synan (1994) on Sale. Unit diaries of the training schools are held in the AWM. In the RAAF Historical Section series, Canberra (1995), vol. 8 is on training units. The quotes from Terry Charles are from letters he wrote to his mother, particularly on 4 and 17 June 1943. The Wirraway was used in battle, most notably and disastrously at Rabaul in January 1942. Ilbery (1999) and McCarthy (1988) both provide course failure rates. The 10 Course WAGS wrote their own stories and these were edited by Owen (1986). Worley's private papers are in the AWM, and his experiences were turned into a play: Simon Hopkinson, *Just a bloke from Murwillumbah*. The quote about the 'tooting of cars' is from Owen (1986). Hawes's statement about officers is from Rope (1984). McCarthy (1988) also has a section on commissioning of officers (pp. 44–51). Lang (1997) provides the information on Rowling.

Aircrew were, of course, being posted to the Pacific and Southeast Asia before December 1941, but not then to war. Honan (1987) tells the story of Smith, the pilot and gunner. When enemy submarines were operating off the Australian coast some trainees were on flights where contact with the enemy was possible, and there is a slight chance one aircraft out of Mt Gambier was hit by a Japanese submarine (Telford 1997, p. 70). The material on Roberts Dunstan is from Dunstan and Graham (1945); biographical file, 1133, AWM65 which includes newspaper reports; and obituary, *Age*, 12 October 1989.

Chapter 3

John Robertson and John McCarthy (1985) published many of the relevant documents on the formation of the Empire Air Training Scheme (pp. 44–72). The Canadian instructor made his comment on Brill in Brill's logbook, held by Ilma Brill. Others who have looked at the statistics on the movements of aircrew have said that the different figures are hard to reconcile (eg Robertson 1981, p. 54), and here most are rounded. Rolfe (1995) refers to 'Pluto' Wilson. Two boxes of relevant material put together postwar, are in files 81/4/56–9, AWM54. Winter (1982) gathered the stories of those who trained in Rhodesia, and McManus (1998) those who sailed on the *Umtali*. Both provide valuable accounts of cohorts. Pearson (1995) told the story of 'Dorrigo'. Leach (1999) wrote of Lees. Herington (1950) commented on the zest of Fuller. Betty Mills compiled notes on Reg Bain, and I am indebted to her for a copy.

Chapter 4

The statement by Loder is from Charlwood (1991) and Charlwood made his own comment on the same page (52). Betty Mills compiled the story of John Ansell (Reg Bain is in the same folder) and gave me a copy. English units had also cut their badges into the chalk – just as other peoples had cut the outlines of horses into the hillsides further north. Herington (1954, pp. 539–41 and 1963, p. 287) records numbers waiting at reception depots.

Edwin Charles souvenired a program of a Bournemouth Pavilion concert, and other airmen kept theatre tickets and programs in albums. Harper records the story of Kingsmill and Cathcart. Dalton printed a copy of Lady Ryder's advice (p. 38). Lang (1997) reprints Rowling's letters and diaries, and he disposes of his property in file 163/55/253, A750, NAA. Scotland (1991) was indicating where his mother's ancestors had come from, not where she came from. In the remodelled Strand Palace the ceiling has, alas, been lowered.

Chapter 5

Mick Martin's entry into Bomber Command is recounted by Simpson (1995). Knox's essay on his experiences is included in Telford (1997). Herington (1954) notes that it was British policy to disperse dominion men in training units (p. 458) and comments on Australians at Lichfield (pp. 302 and 547), and there is further detail in Herington (1963, p. 282). In contrast to the British system, the Americans were more likely to be assigned to crews, and the division in rank between pilots and navigators (as officers) and gunners (NCOs) was more marked.

Bruce Otton's account of crewing-up is from Pearson (1995), and Morrison told his story in Blundell (1975). Brill wrote manuscript accounts of both tours, each operation being dealt with separately. He commented on his first crew at the start of the first manuscript. Don Wall described his crew 'led by a 6'2" redheaded English bank clerk' in Holliday (1992). Herington (1963) gives concentrations of Australians in squadrons. The letter by Johnson, the Canadian gunner, is with Kemble Wood's papers in the AWM. Webster and Frankland (1961, vol. 2, p. 92, footnote) comment on the changing aircraft.

Middlebrook and Everitt (1996), in addition to listing all operations, provide much other information. In an addenda, Middlebrook considers survival rates from downed aircraft, and elsewhere provides statistics on the loss rates of various aircraft. Garbett and Goulding (1991) suggest that two Lancasters may have flown 130 operations. The fact that the Lancaster could fly further and carry a heavier bomb load made it more attractive to planners and commanders, not necessarily to those who flew it. The quote that the switch to Lancasters was 'very popular' is from Herington (1954). Harris 1998 made his judgment on the Lancaster. Rope (1984) quotes Hawes, and Charlwood (1991) quotes Maddern. Wade Rodgers described his first sight of the Lancaster in Rodgers (1988). Nielsen (1984) and Warner (2000) provide information on Delaney.

Chapter 6

The official histories are essential reading on the policy within which the crews operated. Webster and Frankland (1961, vol. 4) reprint many of the basic documents going back to 1923 and include the directives to the Air Officer Commanding-in-Chief, Bomber Command, some correspondence between Harris and Churchill, and German documents. The statements by Trenchard are from Webster and Frankland (1961, vol. 4). Frankland (1998) wrote of his part in the official history and its reception. The most relevant three Australian volumes are: Gillison (1962), and Herington (1954, 1963). In the Canadian official history (Wise 1980) the volumes by Douglas and Greenhous and in the New Zealand history the volumes by Thompson (1953, 1956) are most useful.

What the Australians called the Empire Air Training Scheme, the Canadians called the British Commonwealth Air Training Plan.

Steer's report on Guernica is reprinted in Coster (1997). Charlton in Charlton, Garratt and Fletcher (1938) wrote of 'monster aircraft', and Garratt asked about the effect of gas. Harris (1998) described his early experiences. Webster and Frankland (1962, vol. 1) give a prediction of British casualties in a bomber assault. Lindquist (2001) provides an unusual history of bombing. Gibson (1946) wrote of his own entry to war. The note on Mulligan and Ross is from their biographical files, AWM65.

Gibson (1946) and Cheshire (1943) gave their own accounts of their pleasant and privileged early lives. Braddon (1972) deliberately played on the qualities of the languid flannelled Oxford undergraduate. Loveless's background is included in Brotherton's manuscript. Edwards's early career is covered by Hoyle (1996). The suggestion that the pamphlets might cause panic is from Webster and Franklin (1961, vol. 1, p. 100, footnote). The pamphlets may have had some influence in occupied countries, and where they warned of impending raids probably saved lives. The new light bombers – Venturas, Mosquitoes and Bostons – later flew on daylight raids.

The Butt report – which brought a reality to British bombing – was based on 6,104 aircraft that took off, and of these 4,065 claimed to have reached the target. Harris's statement about a 'speedy and complete' victory is from Webster and Franklin (1961, vol. 1, p. 340). Harriman (1975) wrote of the meeting between Churchill and Stalin.

Chapter 7

Herington (1954, p .9) gives the figures for the numbers of Australians in the RAF at the start of the war. Harper wrote of Moore and other Australians who joined the RAF on the eve of war. Honan (1989) was then an unsuccessful applicant. Nielsen (1984) provided information on Grose. Dannecker (no date) described the accidents at Cootamundra and Honan the escape at Mallala. Jay (1996) told of Mitchell's determination to get to war. Charlwood (1991) quoted Bryant. Hilliard recorded the fate of Fettell's crew. Doubleday's story of his narrow escape is in his transcript, and there is another account in Rowe (1999).

The casualties are from Herington (1963). A 'casualty' had to be of sufficient severity for the next of kin to be notified. In the army a 'casualty' was more likely to be wounded than killed. In Bomber Command more than ten were killed to each wounded. Bill (1991) described Middleton's funeral. Some of the Lichfield dead were buried in Chester so the number of Fradley graves understates the total deaths from the OTU. Seven Lichfield aircraft were lost on operations, some flown by instructors. Lichfield operations are noted in RAAF Narrative of Flying Training in the UK, vol. 2, Section C, Part 4, p. 566, 8/1/B, AWM173. The information from the Wright transcript is supplemented with RAAF biographical file, AWM65. Coventry told his story in Rolland (1999).

While the Canadians were more successful in forming Canadian squadrons, Canadian historians have pointed out that more Canadians flew in the RAF than in the RCAF; to the detriment of a Canadian national force, much Canadian effort was diverted to training men from other nations; the Canadians gained no influence over strategy; and the Canadians were not able to coordinate their ground troops in Europe with their air force.

Hawes' comments are in Rope (1984); Maddern's in Charlwood (1991); Knox's in Telford (1997); and Rowling's in Lang (1997). A common modification made by rear gunners was to cut away the perspex. That gave a clearer view, but at the cost of greater discomfort. The White Swan's visitors' book is held in the AWM (3DRL/7563).

Chapter 8

Taylor (1956) used 'the magic word "Ops"', and Charlwood (1991) 'we're on again tonight'. Winfield (1976) wrote of being a doctor on a squadron. Several ex-Bomber Command aircrew have written excellent accounts of preparations for raids, for example, Belford (1995) and Conway (1995). The term 'gut-gripping theatre' is from Conway (1995). Rowling's file, A705/15, 163/55/253, NAA, adds to information from Lang (1997). The description of clothing by London is from *We Flew We Fell* (1990). Goulevitch is described in Firkins (1985), Nelmes and Jenkins (2000), and on the 460 Squadron Web site.

As previously, the information on Rowling is taken from Lang (1997) and on Loveless from Brotherton's manuscript. Firkins (1985), Hoyle (1999) and Nelmes and Jenkins (2000) wrote about the exploding bombs at Binbrook. Taylor (1956) noted that other squadrons were acting in the same way. Lawton's tour is from 460 Squadron decorations and awards 401/1/P1, A11270, NAA – and this file lists the tours of others recommended for awards. Brill's manuscript of his second tour details each operation, and Doubleday's second tour is taken from his biographical file, AWM65. The *Daily Express* report on the Le Creusot raid was republished by Lang (1997). Gibson (1946) also writes on the Le

Creusot operation. Pearson (1995) recorded Stutter's account of the Königsberg raid, and Rolland (1999) recorded Coventry.

Webster and Frankland (1961, vol. 2) list all crews on the dambuster raid. Gibson (1946) reported the conversation over the dams (pp. 295–6). Herington (1954) called the dambusters 'Homeric'. Scholes's description of his raid is from his published diary (1997, p. 82) – one of several excellent Bomber Command diaries. Coates (1995) said his squadron had a 'few crews' who were flak-shy. Middlebrook (1980) noted the extent of the creep-back and the *Report of the British Bombing Survey* gives losses from flak. Brill's narrow escape over Berlin is based on his manuscript on his second tour, Owen (1986) (includes Curtis's letter), Herington (1954), and conversations with Curtis and Fuller. Brill's statement about always getting into tight spots is from a press release on his biographical file, AWM65. Blundell (1975) recorded Doubleday's response. Firkins (1985) reported the pre-landing radio communication between Brill and Doubleday.

Chapter 9

Hilling (1997), a history of Downham Market airfield, describes a working station and its personnel. Other histories of airfields are Hancock (1996), and Otter (1996, 1998). Pearce (2000) wrote of the women crying, and Drummond-Hay (1994) of 'blackouts' and 'twilights'. Fitch (2001) says that after an operation with heavy losses 'there was a saying "there will be weeping in the Waafery tonight"' (p. 23). Peggy Mills recorded her observations for Silverstone and Parker (1992). Rosemary Hayes wrote for Drummond-Hay (1994) of driving to Sleap, the 'glamour job' and joining the WAAFs at 17. Beck (1989) and Brotherton's manuscripts are rare, extensive WAAF memoirs. Chorley (1981) gave a brief account of the death of Dorothy Robson. Bill (1991) described the Giddings-Middleton romance. Joane Ford wrote of her memories in a letter to the author. The account of Edwards' marriage is based on Hoyle (1999). Doubleday's file, A9300/1, NAA, is used to add to his transcript report of his marriage. Joyce Thomas's typescript reminiscence is with Howard Griffith's papers, AWM.

In *Overseas War Brides* (2001) Molly Ellis, Veronica, Joyce Edgerly and others wrote of their marriages. Hastings (1981) says that there is evidence that the Germans found a WAAF in a crashed Stirling (p. 81). The quoted lines by White are from *Sky Saga*, his 89-page poem, Part 5, 'Bomber Command'. Brill's 'impossible' was described by Conway (1995) and in Curtis' interview. Sir Ralph

Cochrane confirmed that he sent Doubleday to a squadron 'in trouble' and he 'quickly restored morale' (Blundell 1975, p. IX). McManus (1998) collected the stories of the men on the *Umtali*.

Chapter 10

Basic statistics are taken from Webster and Frankland (1961, vol. 4); Herington (1963); and Middlebrook and Everitt (1996). All students of Bomber Command are indebted to Middlebrook and Everitt's careful comments on each raid and the accumulated statistics. Doubleday's remark to Cochrane on the German's pre-lunch century is recorded in Blundell (1975). Bancroft's hazardous flight home is from Halpenny (1984) and Herington (1963). Brown's tour is from Navigator sorties, 460 Squadron, 3DRL/4029 AWM. The statistics of 460 Squadron are from RAAF unit history sheets 460 Squadron, 147 A9186/7 NAA; Operations Record Book 460 Squadron, 1/293 AWM64; Firkins (1985); and the 460 Web site (prepared by John Watson). Webster and Frankland (1961, vol. 4, annexes,) provide an introduction to the technical changes and the war of the boffins.

During the war 'Pathfinder Force' was 'Path Finder Force'. The plaque on Castle Hill House, Huntingdon, says it was the wartime headquarters of 'Path Finder Force'. But 'Pathfinder', as one word, has become common. Both Bennett (1998) and Harris (1998) comment on the beginning of Pathfinder Force.

Curtis's comment on being controller is with Brill's papers, held by Mrs Ilma Brill. The quotation from Knox is published in Telford (1997). The British news reports usually did not give the total number of aircraft involved and exaggerated the amount of damage done, but were generally accurate in giving the number of aircraft lost over Germany and occupied Europe. The reports did not say how many aircraft crashed on or near England; that is, they did not reveal more than the enemy already knew. The chances of death on first and subsequent operations is based on a survey of 727 men killed in action in 460 Squadron. Brickhill (1954) made the comment on Martin's acceptance of death. The information on Randall is from his biographical file AWM65 and Presentation Government House, Sydney, 15 Nov. 1944, AWM88.

Webster and Frankland (1961, vol. 4), say that more RAAF were 'wounded' in non-operational accidents than on operations (p. 442). The quote from the official medical history is from Walker (1961, p. 232). Blundell (1985) provided the statistics on 463 and 467 Squadrons. The story of the crew that had doubts about its bomb-aimer was told to me by a wireless operator, now deceased. The shorter odds on pilots surviving are based on 463 and 467 Squadron figures from Blundell (1985). Freeman Dyson (1979) says that 'the number transferred out of squadrons before the end of their tour was roughly equal to the number completing the full tour'. His number of transfers seems higher than that in Australian squadrons – perhaps because he was particularly concerned with the time of the Battle of Berlin. The number of aircraft destroyed in the Battle of Berlin is from Middlebrook and Everitt (1996, p. 488). Another 113 aircraft on, or attempting to be on, operations crashed in England.

Nelmes and Jenkins (2000) note that refuellers might add an extra 100 gallons (p. 23). (A Lancaster carried 2,000 gallons on a long flight.) The citation for Pellas's DFC is from his biographical file, AWM 65. Webster and Frankland (1961, vol. 1), used the term 'official spy' for the camera (p. 426). The story of Jarratt returning for a hatch is from Halpenny (1984). Firkins (1985) has another case of a 460 Squadron pilot returning to replace a hatch. Charlwood (1991) commented on Brill and Doubleday. The assessment of Brill as a 'plodder' is on his file A9300, NAA. Conway 1995 called Brill 'charismatic'. Isaacson's sense of 'invincibility' is from Warner (2000).

Chapter 11

The *Daily Mirror* press cutting is on Doubleday's biographical file AWM65. Brill wrote about turning around to look at the target in his manuscript account of his first tour, and his comment on the fireworks at Calgary is from his account of his second tour. The press release in which Wright expressed his delight in the 'wizard sight' is on his biographical file AWM65. Martin's flight to Corsica was reported by Brickhill (1954) and Simpson (1995). The *Turpitz* raid is from Holden transcript, Blundell (1975), Herington (1963), and Middlebook and Everitt (1985). Herington gives Belford's birth date as 2 April 1924, and Wheeler's as 23 September 1924.

Frankland's account of the crew that used force on their pilot is in his reminiscences (Frankland 1998). Weller was Ash Taylor's pilot (Taylor 2000). Hesketh recorded his narrow escapes in his logbook, PR 87/083 AWM. The frequency of the battering of 'G' George was calculated from Nelmes and Jenkins (2000). O'Riordan's dairy is reproduced in Herington (1963). Firkins (1985) commented on O'Riordan's age. Randall's tragic flight was described by Chorley (1992–98, vol. 4); Firkins (1985); Otter (1999); and biographical file AWM65. Jarratt's end of tour is from Halpenny (1984).

Chapter 12

Again, basic statistics are from the official histories and Middlebrook and Everitt (1996). The numbers of RAAF prisoners of war of the Germans is confusing in the official histories. Herington (1963, p. 473) says: 'Of the 1,476 Australians who were captured ...'. But in Appendix 3, the total RAAF captured in Europe is said to be 795. If those captured in the Middle East are included then the total goes up to 996. So Herington varies between 1,476 in the text to 996 in the tables in the appendix, the difference seeming to be too great to be accounted for by the distinction between 'Australian' and 'RAAF'. Gavin Long (1963, Appendix 7), in the consolidated statistics, says that 1,043 members of the RAAF became prisoners of the Germans. Webster and Frankland (1961, vol. 4, Appendix 41) claim that 595 RAAF in Bomber Command were imprisoned. This omits those Australians who had joined the RAF. From these figures it would seem that about 1,000 Australians in the RAAF were imprisoned by the Germans (including those captured in the Middle East and at some time imprisoned by the Italians) and that around 600 of these were from Bomber Command.

Herington (1963, p. 473) says: 'of every 12 R.A.A.F. men lost over enemy territory, 8 would be killed, one would evade capture and 3 would become prisoners of war'. (On p. 468 he says one evaded to every seven who became prisoners.) In Bomber Command as a whole, for each man that evaded or escaped, six became prisoners of war. It is very difficult to calculate just how many were killed over enemy territory as opposed to those who were killed elsewhere. But if 'killed' is taken to be all those who died on operations, and accidents etc are omitted, then it can be said that in Bomber Command as a whole out of 35 men lost over enemy territory six would become prisoners and one would evade or escape. The Australian ratio of prisoners in Bomber Command (c600) to killed on operations (c3,400) was close to that of Bomber Command as a whole. It is uncertain how many Australians evaded, but if the figures given by Herington for all RAAF are correct (over 200) then Australians were more successful at evading than men from other nationalities. Given the variation in the statistics, this cannot be assumed to be true.

Herman gave a brief version of his escape in Gould (1994), and a longer account in Silverstone and Parker (1992). Campbell told his story to Silvertone and Parker (1992). Ellis's manuscript of 'My Last Raid' is held in the Imperial War Museum. Trotter wrote for *We Flew We Fell*, (1990), and Parsons for Silverstone and Parker (1992). Norm Wright recorded his advice about heading for brothels in Holliday (1992). The problem with going to Paris brothels for help was that German officers and soldiers were likely to be patrons of the better establishments, and escaping airmen were told to visit the cheapest and dirtiest. The crew member who remembered Reed was Radke, Holliday (1992). Other information on Reed is from his biographical file AWM65, Herington (1963), and Firkins (1985). The account of McSweyn is based on his biographical file AWM65, 779/10/12 AWM54 (which includes the quote about stealing an aircraft), and Herington (1963). The Australians who survived the 'Sagan order' are listed in Herington (1963). Balderston wrote of his interrogation for Silverstone and Parker (1992).

The distribution of Australians in the camps is from Herington (1963), the Australian Red Cross archives, Melbourne, and the Australian Red Cross Society, *Notes on Activities*, June 1943. Kee (1982) wrote of the cycles of depression. Radke's memories and the joint diary of Cantillon, Castle and Kean are in Holliday (1992). Mackenzie (1995) has a graphic account of the confusion at the end of his days as a prisoner. In addition to operation 'exodus' Bomber crews flew on operation 'manna', the dropping of food to the starving population of Holland, another task the crews enjoyed. The figures on the death rate of prisoners are from Long (1963) and Webster and Frankland (1961, vol. 4).

Chapter 13

Mahaddie made his comment on Australian behaviour at the end of the war in Hilling (1997). Isaacson's early return to Australia is recorded in Nielsen (1984), Nelmes and Jenkins (2000), and Warner (2000). Herington (1963) provided the numbers of Australians in Britain at the end of the war. Terry Charles wrote of the victory celebrations in letters to his family on 22 May 1945. Curtis regretted the loss of his birthday in his reminiscence. Cochrane noted the sport played (3DRL/4128 AWM). The brides recorded their journeys in *Overseas War Brides*. Joane Ford wrote to the author.

The notification of Rowling's death is in his file, 163/55/253, A705 NAA. The *Sunday Age*, 5 August 2001, reported the finding of Durston's Lancaster. The Australian graves in Europe can be located from the various volumes of *The War Dead of the British Commonwealth and Empire*, published by the Imperial War Graves Commission. Cleworth (1999) provides a guide to those graves west of the German border. The comments are a result of visits to the main Australian cemeteries and memorials.

Owen (1986) collected the memories of the 10 Course WAGS. The papers of John Heckendorf are held by Warwick Heckendorf. Harrod wrote of his flight to Konigsberg for Blundell (1975). Frankland (1998) wrote of Gibson. Walker (1961) quoted Coto on 'moral fibre cases'. Conde (1997) and Takla, Koffman and Bailey (1994) survey research on stress in combat. Falkinder said a question was 'conducive to "lines"' in his biographical file AWM65 and there is additional information on Falkinder in B170 AWM76. Coulthard-Clark (1996) noted the disproportionate number of ex-RAAF who held ministries.

The era of films of prisoners in Germany culminated in *The Great Escape* (1962). H.E. Bates' novel, *Fair Stood the Wind for France* (1944), was one of the first books on evaders and the resistance. The statement about those from whom Australians have drawn 'our inspiration' was by Paul Keating at Kanchanaburi in Thailand in 1994; and he spoke of the importance of the battles in Papua New Guinea in Port Moresby in 1995. Frankland (1970) made the judgment that Bomber Command was decisive. The table of casualties is from Webster and Frankland (1961, vol. 4). The tests on arriving aircrew were reported in RAAF Narrative of Flying Training in the UK, vol. 2 Section C, 8/2A and 8/2B AWM173. Middlebrook made his assessment of the crews in *The Berlin Raids*, pp. 314–5. Howard Griffith's papers are in the AWM. Isaacson's speech at the Melbourne reunion is in Warner (2000).

Bibliography

A fully footnoted manuscript is in the Australian War Memorial.

Accounts by Aircrew

Biographies, autobiographies, other books in which aircrew speak for themselves, interviews, and unpublished papers by aircrew:

Bain, Reg interviewed by H. Nelson [interview].

Bairstow, John ('Jack') diary, AWM.

Bashford, T. G., logbook, Imperial War Museum.

Beede, John 1976, *Rear Gunner*, Tandem, London.

Belford, A. C. 1995, *Born to Fly*, privately published.

Bennett, Donald 1998, *Pathfinder: A War Autobiography*, Goodall, Manchester, (first published 1958).

Berglund, Geoff, diary and logbook, AWM.

Bevis, Lewis (ed) 1988, *Odd Bods at War 1939–1945*, privately published.

Bill, Stuart 1991, *Middleton VC*, privately published.

Blacket, Geoff, diary, AWM.

Brill, Bill, two manuscript accounts of his first and second tours, logbooks, and papers, held by Ilma Brill.

Blundell, H. M. 1975, *They Flew from Waddington! 463–467 Lancaster Squadrons, Royal Air Force*, privately published.

Brotherton, Joyce, Press On Regardless, manuscript, Imperial War Museum.

Bryant, Frank 1991, *There's Always Bloody Something!*, Samaria Concepts, Benalla.

Boorman, J., diaries and logbook, Imperial War Museum.

Charles, Terence & Edwin, letters to Mrs Beryl Charles (mother) and other papers, held by A. Fewster.

Charlwood, Don, transcript of interview, Keith Murdoch Sound Archive of Australia in the War of 1939–45, AWM.

Charlwood, Don, diary, State Library of Victoria.

—— 1987, *No Moon Tonight*, Penguin, Ringwood.

—— 1991, *Journeys into Night*, Hudson, Hawthorn.

Cheshire, Leonard 1954?, *Bomber Pilot*, Hutchinson, London (first published 1943).

Coates, Ted 1995, *Lone Evader: The Escape from France of RAAF Sergeant Pilot Ted Coates 1942–1943*, Australian Military History Publications, Loftus.

Cockrane, Percy, papers of RAAF welfare officer, AWM.

Collumbell, Don, transcript, AWM.

Conway, Dan 1995, *The Trenches in the Sky*, Hesperian Press, Perth.

Coombes, Geoffrey, transcript, AWM.

Crapp, Errol, diary, letters and logbook, AWM.

Currie, Jack 1986, *Lancaster Target: The story of a crew who flew from Wickenby*, Goodall Publications, Manchester (first published 1977).

Curtis, Bob, interview.

—— *What Did You Do in the War Grandpa? The Wartime Experiences of Bob Curtis RAAF 1941–1945*, privately published.

Dalton, Maurice (n. d.) *An Adventure of a Lifetime: My Service with the R.A.A.F. 1942–1946*, privately published.

Dunstan, Roberts & Graham, Burton 1945, *The Sand and the Sky*, Robertson and Mullens, Melbourne.

Dixon, Frank, transcript, AWM.

Doubleday, Arthur, transcript, AWM.

—— interview.

Ellis, Charles, My Last Raid, manuscript, Imperial War Museum.

Easton, Arnold 1997, *We Flew Old Fred – The Fox, Lancaster PO-F (DV372)*, Hudson, Hawthorn.

—— letters, Imperial War Museum.

Field, Laurie, research papers, AWM.

Fitch, Ron 2001, *Recollections: A Lancaster Bomber Crew 55 Years On*, Desert Pea Press, Sydney.

Fitzgerald, Tom, transcript, AWM.

Ford, Joe & Joane, memoir and letters, copies held by H. Nelson.

Frankland, Noble 1998, *History at War: The Campaigns of an Historian*, Giles de la Mare Publishers, London.

Fry, Eric 1993, *An Airman Far Away: The Story of an Australian Dambuster*, Kangaroo Press, Sydney.

Fuller, Ron, interview.

George, Karen 1999, *A Place of Their Own: The Men and Women of War Service Land*

Settlement at Loxton after the Second World War [includes Howard Hendrick, 460 Squadron], Wakefield Press, Adelaide.

Gibbes, Bobby 1994, *You Live But Once*, privately published.

Gibson, Guy 1946, *Enemy Coast Ahead*, Michael Joseph, London.

Gray, Ken, transcript, AWM.

Gooding, Sydney, interview.

Gould, Alex and 115 co-authors 1994, *Tales from the Sagan Woods*, privately published.

Griffiths, Howard, papers related to his television documentary, *Wings of the Storm*, AWM.

Halsall, Cliff, diaries, logbook and manuscript, AWM.

Halpeny, Bruce Barrymore 1984, *To Shatter the Sky: Bomber Airfield at War*, Patrick Stephens, Cambridge.

Harris, Arthur 1998, *Bomber Offensive*, Greenhill Books, London (first published 1947).

Harrison, Stanley 2001, *A Bomber Command Survivor: the wartime reminiscences of a Bomber Command pilot,* privately published.

Hawkin, Stanley 1989, *Missing Presumed Dead*, Hill of Content, Melbourne.

Heckendorf, John, logbook and papers, Warwick Heckendorf.

Herbert, H. C. ('Clarrie'), diary, State Library of Victoria.

Hesketh, Kenneth, logbook and papers, AWM.

Hewitt, Clement 1987, *Swifter Than Eagles*, privately published.

Hillary, Richard 1950, *The Last Enemy*, Macmillan, London.

Hilliard, Robert, Nothing on the Clock, manuscript, AWM.

Hogan, Harl 1991, *My Battle: An R.A.A.F. pilot's experiences during the air war 1939–1945*, privately published.

Holden, John, transcript, AWM.

Holliday, J. E. 1992, *Stories of the RAAF POWS of Lamsdorf including chronicles of their 500 Mile Trek*, privately published.

Honan, Robert 1989, *That's That: Memoirs of Wartime Service 1939–1945*, privately published.

Hooper, William, diary, AWM.

Hopkinson, Simon, Just a Bloke from Murwillumbah, typescript of play based on John Worley, AWM.

Hoyle, Arthur 1989, *Into the Darkness: A Personal Memoir*, privately published.

—— 1999, *Sir Hughie Edwards VC DSO DFC: The Fortunate Airman*, privately published.

—— transcript, AWM.

Johnson, Syd H. 1994, *It's Never Dark above the Clouds*, privately published.

Kee, Robert 1982, *A Crowd is Not Company*, Jonathon Cape, London.

Kellow, Bob 1992, *Paths to Freedom*, privately published.

Kingsford-Smith, Rollo 1999, *I Wouldn't Have Missed it for Quids*, privately published, Exeter.

Lang, Noella 1997, *The Rest of My Life with 50 Squadron: From the diaries and letters of F/O P.W. Rowling*, Access Press, Northbridge.

Leach, Joe 1999, *RAAF Flying Boats at War*, Australian Military History Publications, Loftus.

Lewis, Bruce 2000, *Aircrew: The Story of the Men who Flew the Bombers*, Cassell Military Paperbacks, London.

Leicester, David, transcript, AWM.

Mackenzie, Ron 1995, *An Ordinary War*, Shoestring Press, Wangaratta.

McManus, John 1998, *A Discourse Pertaining to the Royal Australian Air Force Overseas Draft aboard the S.S.* Umtali*, in Mid-1943*, privately published.

Manifold, Bill 1986, *Never a Dull!*, privately published.

Marks, Kenneth Henry (n. d.), *Get Your Hair Cut*, privately published.

Marshall, J. S. A., extracts from logbook, Imperial War Museum.

Maxton, William, interview.

Members of the Royal Air Forces Ex Prisoner of War Association (Western Australian branch) 1990, *We Flew We Fell We Survived: Stories of Survival*, vol. 1, 1991 *In the Bag* vol. 2.

Millett, John 1982, 'Tail Arse Charlie', *Poetry Australia*, Nov 82.

Mulvaney, John, interview.

Murphy, Bob, transcript, AWM.

Nelson, Earle 1989, *If Winter Comes*, privately published.

Nielsen, Robert 1984, *With the Stars Above*, privately published.

Norton, Charles, logbook, papers, AWM.

O'Connor, Peter, transcript, AWM.

Owen, Sep 1986, *10-Course WAGS: Stories of the Wireless Air Gunners*, privately published.

Payne, Stephen 1995, *If love were all ... the story of a second world war bomber crew*, privately published, Canberra.

Pearce, William George 2000, *A Real Life Adventure with the RAAF: The Wing is Clipped,* Slipstream Archives, Brisbane.

Pearson, Ross A. 1995, *Australians at War in the Air 1939–1945*, vol. 1, Kangaroo Press, Kenthurst.

Pellas, Ivan, interview.

Pitt, Bruce, transcript, AWM.

Rodgers, C. Wade. 1988, *There's No Future In It*, privately published.

Rolland, Derrick 1999, *Airmen I Have Met: Their Stories*, privately published.

Rope, Denise 1984, *For the Duration ...*, privately published.

Scholes, David 1997, *Air War Diary*, Kangaroo Press, Sydney.

——— interview.

Scotland, Tom 1991, *Voice from the Stars: A Pathfinder's Story*, privately published.

Silbert, Eric 1981, *Dinkum Mishpochah*, Artlook Publications, Perth.

Silverstone, Alby & Parker, Stan 1992, *Brave and True: A History of 466 RAAF Halifax Squadron whilst based in Yorkshire England as part of Four Group, Royal Air Force, Including a Short History of 462 RAAF Halifax Squadron from August 1944*, (ed.) Ross Pearson, 466–462 Squadron Association, Sydney.

Simpson, Tom 1995, *Lower than Low*, Libra Books, Sandy Bay.

Taylor, Assheton 2000, *One Way Flight to Munich*, Australian Military History Publications, Loftus.

Taylor, Geoff 1956, *Piece of Cake*, Peter Davies, London.

——— 1972, *Return Ticket*, Peter Davies, London.

Telford, Ron J. 1997, *A' OSIS Airfield: The History of No 2 Air Observers School Royal Australian Air Force 1940–1947* [includes essay by Peter Knox], privately published.

Thomas, Joyce, typescript reminiscence, Griffiths papers, AWM.

Warner, Denis 2000, *Pathfinder: In the Air — On the Ground The Peter Isaacson Story*, Information Australia, Melbourne.

Webb, Evan, letters, AWM.

Wheeler, Doug, interview.

White, T. W. 1943, *Sky Saga: A Story of Empire Airmen*, Hutchinson, Melbourne.

Whitrod, Ray 2001, *Before I Sleep: Memoirs of a Modern Police Commissioner*, University of Queensland Press, Brisbane.

Williams, C. R., letters, Imperial War Museum.

Williams, Geoffrey 2001, *Flying Backwards: Memoirs of a Rear Gunner*, privately published.

Williams, Keith (ed), 1990, *Letters to Mother: From a WWII RAAF Pilot*, privately published.

Winters, Vincent 1982, *Noble Six Hundred: The Story of the Empire Air Training Scheme with particular reference to 674 Australians who trained in Southern Rhodesia*, privately published.

Wilson, Ralph, diary (transcribed), AWM.

Wishaw, David 1997, *That Airman! Last of the Seven*, Libra Books, Sandy Bay.

Wood, Kemble, diary and logbook, AWM.

Worley, John, letters and logbook, AWM.

Wright, Harold 1983, *Pathfinders — 'Light the Way'*, McCann, Brisbane.

—— transcript, AWM.

Selected other publications

Australiana RAAF Official Christmas Magazine 1943, No 11 Personnel Despatch and Reception Centre.

Bates, H. E. 1944, *Fair Stood the Wind for France*, Michael Joseph and The Book Society, London.

Beck, Pip 1989, *A WAAF in Bomber Command*, Goodall Publications, London.

Bennett, Donald 1941, *The Complete Air Navigator*, Pitman, London (first published 1936).

Blundell, H. M. 1985, comp, *463 Squadron RAAF Operations from RAF Waddington*, privately published.

—— 1985, comp, *467 Squadron RAAF Operations from RAF Bottesford RAF Waddington*, privately published.

Braddon, Russell 1973, *Cheshire V.C.: A Story of War and Peace*, Arrow Books, London (first published 1954).

Brickhill, Paul & Norton, Conrad 1946, *Escape to Danger*, Faber, London.

Brickhill, Paul 1950, *The Great Escape*, Norton, New York.

——1951, *The Dam Busters*, Evans Bros, London.

——1952, *Escape or Die*, Evans Bros, London.

Bushby, John E. P. 1980, *Saltbush Country: History of the Deniliquin District*, privately published.

Charlton, L. E. O., Garratt, G. T. & Fletcher, R. 1938, *The Air Defence of Britain*, Penguin Books, Harmondsworth.

Chorley, W. R. 1981, *To See the Dawn Breaking: 76 Squadron Operations*, privately published.

——1992–1998 *Royal Air Force Bomber Command Losses of the Second World War*, vol. 1 1939–40, vol. 6 1945, Midland Counties Publication, Leicester.

Cleworth, Robert 1999, *A Guide to Australian Graves: Western Europe 1939–1945*, privately published.

Conde, Anne-Marie 1997, 'The Ordeal of Adjustment: Australian Psychiatric Casualties of the Second World War', *War & Society*, vol. 15, no. 2, October, pp. 61–74.

Coulthard-Clark, Chris 1996, *Soldiers in Politics: The Impact of the Military on Australian Political Life and Institutions*, Allen & Unwin, Sydney.

Dannecker, Ben, *Cootamundra Aerodrome*, privately published.

Dyer, S. W. 1997, *A Thirty Course War: Airmen of the RAAF at War 1941–1945*, privately published.

Dyson, Freeman 1979, *Disturbing the Universe*, Harper & Row, New York.

Drummond-Hay, Peggy 1994, *The Driving Force: Memoirs of Wartime WAAF Drivers 1665 HCU and 81 OTU*, The Book Guild, Lewes.

Falconer, Jonathan 1996, *RAF Bomber Command in Fact, Film and Fiction*, Sutton Publishing, Stroud.

Firkins, Peter 1985, *Strike and Return: The story of the exploits of No. 460 R.A.A.F. Heavy Bomber Squadron ...*, Westward Ho Publishing, Perth.

Frankland, Noble 1970, *Bomber Offensive: The Devastation of Europe*, Purnell's History of the Second World War, Macdonald, London.

Gammage, Bill 1986, *Narrandera Shire*, Narrandera Shire Council, Narrandera.

Garbett, M. & Goulding, B. 1991, *The Lancaster at War*, PRC Publishing, London.

Gillison, Douglas 1962, *Royal Australian Air Force 1939–1942*, Australian War Memorial, Canberra.

Harriman, Averell W. & Abel, Elie 1975, *Special Envoy to Churchill and Stalin, 1941–1946*, Random House, New York.

Harris, Arthur 1995, *Despatch on War Operations: 23rd February, 1942, to 8th May, 1945*, Frank Cass, London.

Harper, Helen, *22 Temporary Gentlemen*, privately published.

Hastings, Max 1981, *Bomber Command*, Pan Books, London (first published 1979).

Herington, John 1954, *Air War Against Germany and Italy 1939–1943*, Australian War Memorial, Canberra.

—— *1963, Air Power over Europe 1944–1945*, Australian War Memorial, Canberra.

Hilling, John 1997, *Strike Hard: A bomber airfield at war RAF Downham Market and its squadrons 1942–46*, Sutton Publishing, Stroud.

Johnson, Frank 1946, *R.A.A.F. Over Europe*, Eyre and Spottiswoode, London.

Lindquist, Sven 2001, *A History of Bombing*, Granta Books, London.

Long, Gavin 1952, *To Benghazi: Australians in the War of 1939–1945*, Australian War Memorial, Canberra.

—— *1963, The Final Campaigns,* Australian War Memorial, Canberra.

McCalman, Janet 1993, *Journeyings: The biography of a middle-class generation 1920–1990*, Melbourne University Press, Melbourne.

McCarthy, John 1988, *A Last Call of Empire: Australian aircrew, Britain and the Empire Air Training Scheme*, Australian War Memorial, Canberra.

MacKenzie, S. P. 1997, 'On Target: The Air Ministry, RAF Bomber Command and Feature Film Propaganda, 1941–1942', *War & Society*, vol. 15, no. 2, October, pp. 43–59.

Maslin, Ron 1990, *Wings over Temora: The story of No. 10 E.F.T.S.*, privately published, Temora.

Middlebrook, Martin 1998, *The Berlin Raids: RAF Bomber Command Winter 1943–44*, Cassell, London (first published 1988).

Middlebrook, Martin & Everitt, Chris 1996, *The Bomber Command War Diaries: An Operational Reference Book 1939–1945*, Midland Publishing, Leicester.

Neillands, Robin 2001, *The Bomber War: Arthur Harris and the Allied Bomber Offensive 1939–1945*, John Murray, London.

Nelmes, Michael & Jenkins, Ian 2000, *G-for-George: A memorial to RAAF bomber crews 1939–45*, Banner Books, Maryborough.

Otter, Patrick 1999, *Lincolnshire Airfields in the Second World War*, Countryside Books, Newbury.

—— 1998, *Yorkshire Airfields in the Second World War*, Countryside Books, Newbury.

Overseas War Brides 2001, Simon & Schuster, Sydney.

Richards, Denis 1994, *The Hardest Victory: RAF Bomber Command in the Second World War*, Hodder & Stoughton, London.

Robertson, John 1981, *Australia at War*, William Heinemann, Melbourne.

Robertson, John & McCarthy, John 1985, *Australian War Strategy 1939–1945: A Documentary History*, University of Queensland, Brisbane.

Rolfe, Mel 2000, *Looking Into Hell: Experiences of the Bomber Command War*, Cassell, London.

Rowe, Mark 1999, *The Day the Dump Went Up and the Flying Kangaroos*, privately published.

RAAF Historical Section 1995, *Units of the Royal Australian Air Force: A Concise History*, vol. 3, Bomber Units, vol. 8, Training Units, vol. 10, Chiefs of the Air Staff, Aircraft, Bibliography, Australian Government Publishing Service, Canberra.

Royal Australian Air Force Manual for Air Crew Reservists 1940, Commonwealth Government Printer, Canberra.

Royal Australian Air Force No. 11 Elementary Flying Training School Benalla World War II Unveiling of Plaque and Dedication of Memorial 1995, pamphlet.

Royal Australian Air Force Standard Notebook for Initial Training Schools, bound folder.

Saville-Sneath, R.A. 1944, *British Aircraft*, vols 1 & 2, Penguin Books, London.

The Strategic Air War Against Germany 1939–1945: Report of the British Bombing Survey Unit 1998, Frank Cass, London.

Stephens, Alan 1995, *Going Solo: The Royal Australian Air Force, 1946–1971*, Australian Government Publishing Service, Canberra.

—— 2001, *The Australian Centenary History of Defence*, vol. II, *The Royal Australian Air Force*, Oxford University Press, Melbourne.

Synan, Peter 1994, *Gippsland's Lucky City: A History of Sale*, privately published, Sale.

Takla, N. K., Koffman, R. & Bailey, D. A. 1994, 'Combat Stress, Combat Fatigue, and Psychiatric Disability in Aircrew', *Aviation, Space, and Environmental Medicine*, September, pp. 858–65.

Taylor, Geoff 1979, *The Nuremberg Massacre*, Hutchinson, Melbourne.

Tee Emm, 1 April 1941–5 March 1946, reprinted in 2 vols, facsimile edition.

Thompson, H. L. 1953, *New Zealanders with the Royal Air Force: vol. 1, European Theatre, September 1939 – December 1942*, War History Branch, Department of Internal Affairs, Wellington.

—— 1956, *New Zealanders with the Royal Air Force: vol. II, European Theatre, January 1943 – May 1945*, War History Branch, Department of Internal Affairs, Wellington.

Vassiltchikov, Marie 'Missie' 1999, *The Berlin Diaries 1840–1945*, Pimlico, London.

Vonnegut, Kurt 1969, *Slaughterhouse-Five or The Children's Crusade, A Duty-Dance with Death*, Delacorte, New York.

Walker, Allan 1961, *Medical Services of the R.A.N. and R.A.A.F.*, Australian War Memorial, Canberra.

Webster, Charles & Frankland, Noble 1961, *The Strategic Air Offensive Against Germany 1939–1945*, 4 vols, Her Majesty's Stationery Office, London.

Wise, S., Douglas, W. & Greenhouse, B. 1980–94, *The Official History of the Royal Canadian Air Force*, 3 vols, University of Toronto in Co-operation with the Department of National Defence, Toronto.

Wordley, Dick & Madigan, Ken 1982, *Port Pirie Remembers*, Port Pirie Council, Port Pirie.

Archives

Further information can be obtained from the National Archives of Australia web-site (naa.gov.au) and the Australian War Memorial site (awm.gov.au). It is possible to look up individual files such as RAAF service dossiers held by the Department of Defence through the NAA. They are in the series A9300 (officers), A9301 (NCOs) and A703 for officers who remained in the RAAF after 1959. There are also casualty files in the series A705/15. Another NAA file of interest is No 460 Squadron – Decorations and Awards – Recommendations 401/1/P1 Part 3, A11270. AWM files include RAAF biographical files for some men at AWM65; information on individuals – Governor General's Office, honours and awards file, AWM88; Role of Honour Circulars, 1939–1945 War, AWM10; and prisoners of war statements in the 1010/-/-files, AWM54. Other NAA and AWM files are noted in the endnotes.

Information on prisoners of war was also obtained from the archives of the International Red Cross, Geneva; and the Australian Red Cross, National Resource Centre, Melbourne.

Index

Page numbers in *italics* refer to illustrations